TEACHERS OF HISTORY

IN THE UNIVERSITIES
OF THE UNITED KINGDOM AND THE
REPUBLIC OF IRELAND

FEBRUARY 2014

Compiled by
Emma Bohan, Valerie Hall, Zoe Holman,
Maureen McTaggart and Jane Winters

Institute of Historical Research
School of Advanced Study
University of London

ISBN 978 1 905165 99 5

EXPLANATORY NOTES

This publication is a list of teachers of historical subjects on courses leading to university degrees. Not all of them are members of a School of History, and the principal departments represented are listed in the heading to each institution.

Teachers of history in universities in the Republic of Ireland are also included. We are very grateful to the Royal Irish Academy, and in particular to Professor Peter Gray, for their support in obtaining this information.

Information has been supplied by the universities and colleges represented, and warm thanks are expressed to heads of department and departmental administrators who unfailingly find time each year to send details of Teachers of History. Where no information was forthcoming, last year's entries have been repeated. Institutions which have not responded since before 2007 have been excluded. If your institution is missing from this year's publication, or if the details are incorrect, we would be delighted to receive updated information.

Names are listed alphabetically, and heads of departments, where known, are marked with an asterisk. Staff who have taken early retirement but are still teaching part-time may be indicated in various ways by different institutions. Abbreviated descriptions of teaching areas are appended within round brackets and current research interests are within square brackets. Email addresses are also supplied. An Index of Persons is at the end of the book.

A digital version of *Teachers of History* may be consulted as part of History Online on the IHR website (www.history.ac.uk). Here will be found detailed menus giving access to information concerning all the Teachers involved in each type of history, geographical area and period, or any combination of these. The 2014 information will be online in early spring.

Additions or corrections are always welcomed and should be sent to the Head of Publications, Institute of Historical Research, University of London, Senate House, London, WC1E 7HU. Tel: 020 7862 8780. Fax: 020 7862 8754. Email: ihrpub@sas.ac.uk.

ABBREVIATIONS

Admin. administration, administrative	Imp. imperial, imperialism
Afric. Africa, African	Ind. industrial, industry
Amer. America, American	Inst. institute
Anc. ancient	Int. international
Anthr. anthropology	Int. Rel. international relations
Archaeol. archaeological, archaeology	Lect. lecturer
Assoc. associate	Med. medieval
Brit. Britain, British	Mid. E. Middle East, Middle Eastern
Byz. Byzantine, Byzantium	Milit. military
c. century	Mod. modern
Constit. constitutional	Phil. philosophy
Cont. Educ. continuing education	Pol. political, politics
Contemp. contemporary	Prehist. prehistoric, prehistory
C'wealth Commonwealth	Princ. principal
Dept. department	Prof. professor
Div. divinity	p/t part-time
Eccles. ecclesiastical	Relig. religion, religious
Econ. economic, economics	Res. research
Educ. education, educational	Sc. science, scientific
Eng. English	Sch. school
esp. especially	Scot. Scottish
Eur. Europe, European	Sen. senior
Fac. faculty	Soc. social, sociology
Geog. geography	Stud. studies
Govt. government	Tech. technology
Hist. historical, history	Temp. temporary
Hon. honorary	Theol. theology, theological

UNIVERSITY OF **ABERDEEN**

Aberdeen, AB24 3FX. 01224 272000. Fax 01224 487048
www.abdn.ac.uk
School of Divinity, History & Philosophy
Department of History 01224 272199. Fax 01224 273750
www.abdn.ac.uk/history/
Department of History of Art 01224 273733. Fax 01224 273750
www.abdn.ac.uk/hoart/
Department of Divinity & Religious Studies 01224 272380. Fax 01224 273750
www.abdn.ac.uk/divinity/
School of Social Science
Department of Politics & International Relations
www.abdn.ac.uk/pir/

Jackson Armstrong, B.A. (Queen's, Ont.), M.Phil., Ph.D. (Cantab.), Lect. in Hist. (Med. & Early Mod.), j.armstrong@abdn.ac.uk

Colin Barr, B.A., M.Phil., Ph.D. (Cantab.), Sen. Lect. [Modern British, Irish & British imperial history], c.barr@abdn.ac.uk

Thomas Bartlett, B.A., Ph.D. (Belf.), Chair in Irish Hist. [U.S. history, 1800–70], t.bartlett@abdn.ac.uk

Andrew Blaikie, M.A. (Cantab.), Ph.D. (Lond.), Chair in Hist. Soc. [Modern & contemporary Scotland], a.blaikie@abdn.ac.uk

Stefan Brink, Fil.dr. (Uppsala), Sixth-c. Prof. of Scandinavian Stud., Director, Centre for Scandinavian Stud., s.brink@abdn.ac.uk

Michael Brown, B.A., Ph.D. (Dublin), Sen. Lect. in Hist. (Irish & Scot.), m.brown@abdn.ac.uk

Amy Bryzgel, B.A. (Boston), M.A. (S. Carolina), Ph.D. (Rutgers), Lect. in Hist. of Art (Mod. Contemp.) [Modern & contemporary Russian & eastern European art; performance art], a.bryzgel@abdn.ac.uk

Lisa Collinson, Ph.D. (Cantab.), Postdoctoral Res. Fellow [Scandinavian studies], l.a.collinson@abdn.ac.uk

Christoph Dartmann, B.A. (Lond.), Ph.D. (E.U.I.), Lect. in Hist. (Eur. & Mod. German, Soc. Welfare) [Welfare states in Europe 19th–20th c.; World War I], c.dartmann@abdn.ac.uk

Peter Davidson, B.A. (Cantab.), M.A. (Cantab. & York), Ph.D. (Cantab.), Prof. of Renaissance Stud., Scholar-Keeper of the University's Collections [Baroque arts; exile; recusancy; symbols & emblems], peter.davidson@abdn.ac.uk

Andrew Dilley, B.A., M.St., D.Phil. (Oxon.), Sen. Lect. in Hist. [British imperial history; Australian & Canadian history; history of the City of London], a.dilley@abdn.ac.uk

David N. Dumville, M.A., (Cantab.), Ph.D. (Edin.), Prof. of Hist. & Palaeography (Med.) [Medieval British & Irish history; palaeography; transmission of texts], d.n.dumville@abdn.ac.uk

Marie-Luise Ehrenschwendtner, M.A., Ph.D. (Eberhard-Karls Universitat, Tübingen), Lect. in Church Hist. (Med. & Early Mod.), m.ehrenschwendtner@abdn.ac.uk

*Karin Friedrich, M.A. (Munich), Ph.D. (Georgetown), Prof. in Early Mod. Eur. Hist. (Early Mod., Mod.) [Prussia & Poland; European Enlightenment; national identity; urban history], k.friedrich@abdn.ac.uk

Robert I. Frost, M.A. (St. And.), Ph.D. (Lond.), Burnett Fletcher Chair in Hist. (Early Mod.) [Polish history; war, state & society in the Baltic 1558–1721; Sweden; the Thirty Years' War], robert.frost@abdn.ac.uk

John M. Gash, B.A. (Oxon.), M.A. (Lond.), Sen. Lect. in Hist. of Art (Early Mod.) [Caravaggio & his followers], j.gash@abdn.ac.uk

Jane Geddes, B.A. (Cantab.), M.A., Ph.D. (Lond.), Prof. of Hist. of Art (Med.) [Medieval decorative ironwork; Scottish architecture; medieval manuscripts], j.geddes@abdn.ac.uk

Michael H. Gelting, Mag. art. (Aarhus), Fil.dr.h.c. (Gothenburg), Chair in Scandinavian Stud. [Medieval law in Denmark & the Nordic countries; Danish medieval society in a comparative perspective, 12th–14th c.; history of the Danish church, 10th–13th c.; Black Death], m.h.gelting@abdn.ac.uk

Marjory-Ann D. Harper, M.A., Ph.D. (Aberd.), Prof. of Hist. (Mod. Scot.) [Scottish emigration, 18th–20th c.], m.harper@abdn.ac.uk

Anthony Heywood, B.A. (Brist.), M.A. (Essex), Ph.D. (Leeds), Prof. of Hist. (Russia), t.heywood@abdn.ac.uk

Isabella Jackson, B.A., M.Phil. (Oxon.), Ph.D. (Brist.), Helen Bruce Lect. in Asian Hist. [Modern China; global history; urban history], i.jackson@abdn.ac.uk

Alistair J. Macdonald, M.A., Ph.D. (Aberd.), Mackie Lect. in Hist. (Med.) [Anglo-Scottish relations], a.j.macdonald@abdn.ac.uk

Kirsteen Mackenzie, M.A., Ph.D. (Aberd.), Teaching Fellow in Hist. (Early Mod.) [Early modern Scotland; print culture in Britain & Ireland], kirsteen.mackenzie@abdn.ac.uk

Andrew Mackillop, M.A., Ph.D. (Glas.), Sen. Lect. in Hist. (Scot. Hist.) [Scotland & the eastern British empire, 18th–19th c.], a.mackillop@abdn.ac.uk

Elizabeth Macknight, B.A. (Tasmania), Ph.D. (Melb.), D.E.A. (Versailles), Lect. in Hist. (Eur. Hist.) [Nobility; nobiliary law; politics & gender in modern France], e.macknight@abdn.ac.uk

Ben Marsden, M.A. (Cantab.), Ph.D. (Kent), Sen. Lect. in Hist. (Hist. of Sc. & Tech.) [Cultures of science & technology in 19th c. Britain], b.marsden@abdn.ac.uk

John C. Morrison, M.A., Ph.D. (St. And.), Prof. in Hist. of Art (Mod.) [Scottish cultural identity; Scottish painting; Scottish cultural institutions], j.c.morrison@abdn.ac.uk

William G. Naphy, B.A. (William & Mary), M.Div. (Southwestern Baptist), Ph.D. (St. And.), Prof. of Hist. [Medicine; the Reformation; France], w.g.naphy@abdn.ac.uk

Ralph O'Connor, B.A., M.Phil., Ph.D. (Cantab.), Prof. of Irish & Scot. Stud., r.oconnor@abdn.ac.uk

Frederik J.G. Pedersen, M.A. (York & Toronto), Ph.D. (Copenhagen & Toronto), Sen. Lect. in Hist. (Med.) [Law & reception of law; Hanseatic & Scandinavian history], f.pedersen@abdn.ac.uk

Helen Pierce, B.A., M.A., Ph.D. (York), Lect. in Hist. of Art (Early Mod. Brit., Art & Pol., Graphic Satire), h.pierce@abdn.ac.uk

Mary Pryor, M.A., Ph.D. (Aberd.), Sen. Teaching Fellow in Hist. of Art (Early Mod., Mod.) [Scottish art in cultural context], m.pryor@abdn.ac.uk

Karen Salt, B.A., M.A., Ph.D. (Purdue), Res. Fellow in Afric. Diaspora Stud. [Caribbean, American & Atlantic history], k.salt@abdn.ac.uk

Jane B. Stevenson, B.A., Ph.D. (Cantab.), Regius Chair of Humanity, Prof. of Latin (Med.) [Early medieval Britain & Europe], janebstevenson@yahoo.com

Thomas Weber, M.St., D.Phil. (Oxon.), Prof. of Mod. Eur., Int. & Global Hist., t.weber@abdn.ac.uk

Tarrin Wills, B.A., Ph.D. (Sydney), Sen. Lect. in Early Scandinavian Stud., t.wills@abdn.ac.uk

ABERYSTWYTH UNIVERSITY

Old College, King Street, Aberystwyth, SY23 2AX. 01970 623111
www.aber.ac.uk
Department of History & Welsh History
Hugh Owen Building, Aberystwyth, SY23 3DY. 01970 622662. Fax 01970 622676
www.aber.ac.uk/history/
Department of International Politics
International Politics Building, Penglais, Aberystwyth, SY23 3FE. 01970 622702.
Fax 01970 622709
www.aber.ac.uk/Interpol/

Martin S. Alexander, M.A., D.Phil. (Oxon.), Prof. of Int. Rel. [History of strategy; France since 1870; Vietnam War], saa@aber.ac.uk

Arddun Arwyn, B.A., M.A., Ph.D. (Wales), Lect. in Hist. (20th c. Brit & Eur.) [German expellees; oral history], aha08@aber.ac.uk

Huw Bennett, B.Sc., M.Sc., Ph.D. (Wales), Lect. in Int. Pol. & Intelligence Stud. [British military strategy, intelligence & operations since 1945], hab1@aber.ac.uk

Peter Borsay, B.A., Ph.D. (Lancaster), Prof. of Hist. (17th c. Brit., Urban Hist. 16th–19th c.) [British urban & cultural history 1660–1949; history of Bath 1700–2000; history of leisure in Britain since 1500; history of spas & seaside resorts; history of heritage], nnb@aber.ac.uk

Ian Clark, M.A. (Glas.), Ph.D. (A.N.U.), F.B.A., E.H. Carr Prof. of Int. Pol. [International history; international theory; nuclear strategy], iic@aber.ac.uk

Richard C. Coopey, B.A., M.A., Ph.D. (Warwick), Sen. Lect. in Soc. & Econ. Hist. (18th–20th c.) [I.T. policy & strategic trade resources; regional industry; banks & industry in Britain; history of water], rcc@aber.ac.uk

Campbell Craig, B.A. (Carleton), M.A. (Chicago), Ph.D. (Ohio), Prof. of Int. Pol. [U.S. foreign policy; the Cold War; the nuclear revolution; historical sociology], hoc@aber.ac.uk

Rhun Emlyn, B.A. (Aberystwyth), Lect. in Hist. (Late Med.) [Medieval universities; medieval Wales; migration], rre@aber.ac.uk

Patrick Finney, B.A., Ph.D. (Leeds), Sen. Lect. in Int. Hist. (19th–20th Eur. & Int.) [Origins of World War II; collective memory; Greece & Balkans; Holocaust; theory], pbf@aber.ac.uk

Jessica F. Gibbs, M.A., M.Phil., Ph.D. (Cantab.), Lect. in Hist. [19th–20th c. U.S. & Latin American history; migration history], jessica.gibbs@aber.ac.uk

Claudia Hillebrand, M.A. (Leipzig), Ph.D. (Aberystwyth), Lect. in Intelligence & Counter-Terrorism [Intelligence & counter-terrorism; intelligence & democratic accountability], ckh1@aber.ac.uk

R. Gerald Hughes, B.A. (Stirling), M.Sc.(Econ.), Ph.D. (Wales), Lect. in Hist. (20th c. Brit. Foreign Policy, Diplomatic Hist., Milit. Hist., Strategic Stud., Irish Hist.), rbh@aber.ac.uk

David Ceri Jones, B.A., Ph.D. (Wales), Lect. in Welsh Hist. (17th–18th c.) [Enlightenment & romanticism in Wales; popular evangelicalism in Wales & beyond], dmj@aber.ac.uk

Alastair Kocho-Williams, B.A., M.A., Ph.D. (Manc.), Sen. Lect. in Hist. (Russia & Soviet Union) [20th Century Russian & Soviet foreign policy; Russian & Soviet diplomacy; international Communism; Soviet anti-imperialism], amk6@aber.ac.uk

Peter A. Lambert, B.A. (Cantab.), D.Phil. (Sussex), Lect. in Hist. (19th–20th c. Eur., Historiography), pal@aber.ac.uk

John McEwan, B.A. (W. Ont.), M.A., Ph.D. (Lond.), Lect. in Hist. [Urban history; 13th c. England]

Colin McInnes, B.Sc.(Econ.), Ph.D. (Wales), Prof. of Int. Pol. & U.N.E.S.C.O. Prof. of H.I.V. & A.I.D.S., Educ. & Security in Afric. (20th c. Int. Hist.) [War in the 20th c.; British army]

*Jennifer G. Mathers, B.A. (Mt. Holyoke Coll., Mass.), M.Phil., D.Phil. (Oxon.), Sen. Lect. in Int. Pol. [20th c. Russia; women & war], zzk@aber.ac.uk

Iwan R. Morus, B.A., M.Phil., Ph.D. (Cantab.), Prof. of Hist. (19th c.) [History & philosophy of science], irm@aber.ac.uk

Elizabeth A. New, B.A. (Exeter), M.A. (York), Ph.D. (Lond.), Lect. in Hist. (Later Med. England & Wales) [Representation & identity (personal & communal); seals & sealing practices; material & visual culture; voluntary religious practices]

Siân H. Nicholas, B.A. (Cantab.), M.A. (N. Carolina), D.Phil. (Oxon.), Sen. Lect. in Hist., p/t (20th c. Brit., Media Hist.) [Mass media; national identity; Britain & the two world wars], shn@aber.ac.uk

Paul B. O'Leary, B.A., Ph.D. (Wales), Sen. Lect. in Welsh Hist. (19th–20th c.) [Irish migration to Wales 1790–1922; politics & national identity], ppo@aber.ac.uk

Matthew Phillips, B.A., M.A., Ph.D. (Lond.), Lect. in Hist. (Mod. Thailand) [Southeast Asia in the Cold War; consumer culture in Thailand], map67@aber.ac.uk

*Martyn J. Powell, B.A., Ph.D. (Wales), Sen. Lect. in Hist. (18th c. Brit., Irish & Imp. Hist.) [Politics & consumption in Ireland; caricature], mpp@aber.ac.uk

Michael F. Roberts, M.A., D.Phil. (Oxon.), Lect. in Hist. (16th–17th c. Brit. & Eur., Historiography) [Work; wages; women; early modern Wales], mfr@aber.ac.uk

Phillipp Schofield, B.A. (Lond.), D.Phil. (Oxon.), Prof. of Med. Hist. (Late Med. Soc. & Econ. Hist.) [Peasantry in medieval England], prs@aber.ac.uk

Len Scott, B.A. (Nott.), M.A. (Lond.), D.Phil. (Oxon.), Prof. of Int. Pol. (20th c.) [International history from 1945; intelligence; nuclear history; British & European security], lvs@aber.ac.uk

Steven Thompson, B.A., Ph.D. (Wales), Lect. in Hist. (19th–20th c. Brit.) [History of medicine], sdt@aber.ac.uk

James Vaughan, B.A., M.A., Ph.D. (Lond.), Lect. [Anglo-American relations; propaganda & the Cold War; history of the Middle East 1940s–50s], jrv@aber.ac.uk

Björn K.U. Weiler, M.A., Ph.D. (St. And.), Reader in Hist. (Brit. & Eur. 10th–13th c.) [Medieval kingship; 13th c. Anglo-German relations], bkw@aber.ac.uk

Eryn Mant White, B.A., Ph.D. (Wales), Sen. Lect. in Welsh Hist. (16th–18th c.), erw@aber.ac.uk

ANGLIA RUSKIN UNIVERSITY

Department of History
East Road, Cambridge, CB1 1PT. 01223 363271
www.anglia.ac.uk

Clarissa Campbell Orr, M.A. (Cantab. & York), Reader in Enlightenment, Gender & Court Stud. (18th c. Eur.) [19th c. women historians & biographers; queenship in Britain & Europe; 18th c. cultural history in France & England], clarissa.campbellorr@anglia.ac.uk

Jonathan Davis, B.A., Ph.D. (De Montfort), Lect. [Domestic & international socialism; British Labour party & the Soviet Union; British socialist history & Soviet Union, 1920–30], jonathan.davis@anglia.ac.uk

Seán Lang, M.A. (Oxon.), Ph.D. (Anglia Ruskin), Sen. Lect. (Imp. & C'wealth Hist.) [18th c. Britain; British empire; film & history; decolonisation; 19th c. Europe; history in the school curriculum], sean.lang@anglia.ac.uk

*Rohan A. McWilliam, B.A., M.A., D.Phil. (Sussex), Prof. of Mod. Brit. Hist. (19th & 20th c. Brit. & U.S.A.) [Popular politics & popular culture in 19th c. Britain; history of the West End of London], rohan.mcwilliam@anglia.ac.uk

ASTON UNIVERSITY

Aston Triangle, Birmingham, B4 7ET. 0121 359 3611. Fax 0121 359 7358
www.aston.ac.uk
School of Languages & Social Sciences
Politics & International Relations Academic Subject Group
0121 204 3760. Fax 0121 204 3766

*Nathaniel Copsey, B.A. (Oxon.), M.A. (College of Europe), D.Phil. (Sussex), Head of Pol. & Int. Rel. (Mod. Eur. Hist.) [European Union], n.copsey@aston.ac.uk
Lucian Leustean, B.A., M.A., Ph.D. (Lond.), Lect. in Pol. & Int. Rel. [Religion & politics in postwar Europe; history of the European Union; nationalism; Romania], l.leustean@aston.ac.uk
Daniel Schwartz, B.A. (Jerusalem), D.Phil. (Oxon.), Hon. Visiting Fellow [Aquinas; neoscholasticism; republicanism; nationalism in Latin America], d.schwartz@aston.ac.uk
Michael Sutton, B.A. (N.U.I.), M.Sc.(Econ.) (Lond.), Ph.D. (Lond.), Emeritus Prof. of Mod. Hist. & Int. Rel. (Intellectual Hist., Hist. of Ideas, Diplomatic Hist.) [French political & religious thought; French contemporary history; history of European integration], m.j.sutton@aston.ac.uk

BANGOR UNIVERSITY

Bangor, Gwynedd, LL57 2DG
www.bangor.ac.uk
School of History, Welsh History & Archaeology 01248 382144. Fax 01248 382759
www.bangor.ac.uk/history/

Kristján Ahronson, B.A. (Toronto), Ph.D. (Edin.), Lect. in Archaeol. (Prehistoric & Med. Archaeol.) [Human-environmental interactions; later prehistoric & early historic N.W. Europe & N.E. North America], k.ahronson@bangor.ac.uk
Anthony M. Claydon, B.A. (Oxon.), Ph.D. (Lond.), Prof. of Early Mod. Hist. (16th–17th c. Brit. & Eur.) [Religion, politics & national identity in 17th c. England, Ireland & America], t.claydon@bangor.ac.uk
Andrew C. Edwards, B.A., M.A., Ph.D. (Wales), Sen. Lect. in Hist. (20th c. Brit & Wales) [Modern & contemporary politics; political culture; oral history], a.c.edwards@bangor.ac.uk
Nancy Edwards, B.A. (Liv.), Ph.D. (Dunelm.), Prof. of Med. Archaeol. (Med. Archaeol. of Brit. & Ireland) [4th–12th c. archaeology, esp. Wales & Ireland; history of archaeology], n.edwards@bangor.ac.uk
Dinah Evans, B.A., M.A., Ph.D. (Wales), Lect. in Mod. Hist., p/t (20th c. Brit. & Wales) [Modern & contemporary social history; gender studies; urban history], his801@bangor.ac.uk

Mark Hagger, M.A., M.Litt., Ph.D. (St. And.), Lect. in Med. Hist. (Med. Hist.) [Government of Anglo-Norman England & Normandy, 10th–12th c.; Anglo-Norman aristocracy], m.hagger@bangor.ac.uk

Susan M. Johns, B.A., M.A., Ph.D. (Cardiff), Lect. in Hist. (Med. Hist.) [Norman history; gender studies], s.m.johns@bangor.ac.uk

Raimund Karl, Mag.dr.phil., P.D. (Vienna), Prof. of Archaeol. & Heritage (Later Prehist. Archaeol. of Brit. & Eur.) [Later prehistory; social archaeology; archaeological theory & practice; heritage legislation & management; archaeology labour market], r.karl@bangor.ac.uk

Christian Koller, Lic.phil., Dr.phil., P.D. (Zurich), Sen. Lect. in Hist. (Mod. Hist.) [19th & 20th c. European history; military history; history of racism & nationalism; history of football; labour history], c.koller@bangor.ac.uk

Katharine K. Olson, B.A. (Chicago), M.A., Ph.D. (Harv.), Lect. in Hist. (Med. & Early Mod. Hist.) [Religion, identity, culture & society in medieval/early modern Wales, Britain & Ireland], k.olson@bangor.ac.uk

Karen Pollock, B.A., Ph.D. (Wales), Lect. in Archaeol. & Heritage (Roman Brit.) [Roman Britain], his204@bangor.ac.uk

Nia M.W. Powell, B.A. (Wales), M.A. (Cantab.), Lect. in Welsh Hist. (Early Mod. Hist.) [Social, economic & cultural history; urban history], n.m.w.powell@bangor.ac.uk

Huw Pryce, M.A., D.Phil. (Oxon.), Prof. of Welsh Hist. (Med. & Mod. Hist.) [Medieval Wales; Welsh historiography], a.h.pryce@bangor.ac.uk

Lowri A. Rees, B.A., M.A. (Wales), Ph.D. (Aberystwyth), Lect. in Hist. (Mod. Hist.) [19th c. Britain & Wales; social history], hisc01@bangor.ac.uk

Euryn R. Roberts, B.A., M.A. (Wales), Welsh Medium Postgraduate Scholar (Med. Hist.) [Regional & national identity in medieval Wales], hip605@bangor.ac.uk

Gary Robinson, B.A., M.A., Ph.D. (Lond.), Lect. in Archaeol. (Prehist. Archaeol. of Brit. & Ireland) [Later prehistory; landscape archaeology; archaeological theory & practice; material culture studies; gender archaeology], g.robinson@bangor.ac.uk

Alexander Sedlmaier, M.A., Dr.phil. (Berlin), Sen. Lect. in Hist. (Mod. Hist.) [19th–20th c. European & American history; history of consumerism], a.sedlmaier@bangor.ac.uk

*Peter Shapely, B.A., Ph.D. (Manc. Met.), Sen. Lect. in Hist. (Mod. Hist.) [Urban governance, poverty & policy], p.shapely@bangor.ac.uk

Kate Waddington, B.A., M.A., Ph.D. (Cardiff), Lect. in Archaeol. (Prehist. Archaeol. of Brit. & Ireland) [Later prehistory; archaeological theory & practice; landscape & experimental archaeology; material culture studies], k.waddington@bangor.ac.uk

Mari William, B.A., M.A., Ph.D. (Wales), Lect. in Hist. (Mod. Hist.) [Modern Welsh history], hisa05@bangor.ac.uk

UNIVERSITY OF BATH

Claverton Down, Bath, Avon, BA2 7AY. 01225 384728. Fax 01225 386381
www.bath.ac.uk
History of Technology Research Unit

*R. Angus Buchanan, O.B.E., M.A., Ph.D. (Cantab.), D.Sc. (Chalmers Univ., Göteborg), Emeritus Prof. of Hist. of Tech., Hon. Director, Hist. of Tech Res. Unit, hssraab@bath.ac.uk

BATH SPA UNIVERSITY

Newton Park, Bath, Avon, BA2 9BN. 01225 875875. Fax 01225 875503
www.bathspa.ac.uk
School of Humanities & Cultural Industries: Department of History

Bobby Anderson, B.A. (C.N.A.A.), M.A. (Read.), Ph.D. (W. of Eng.), Lect. (Hist. Stud.)
[Early modern social & religious history; medieval history; James VI & I; diplomacy],
r.anderson@bathspa.ac.uk
Elaine Chalus, M.A. (Alberta), D.Phil. (Oxon.), Prof. (Hist. Stud.) [18th c. political culture;
women & politics; spa culture; gender & identity; diaries], e.chalus@bathspa.ac.uk
Kristin G. Doern, B.A. (Loughborough), M.A., Ph.D. (Sussex), Lect. (Hist. Stud.) [Anglo-North
American heritage policy & heritage management], k.doern@bathspa.ac.uk
Brian Griffin, B.A., M.A. (N.U.I.), Ph.D. (Loyola Univ., Chicago), Lect. (Hist. Stud.) [Irish
sports history; police & crime in Ireland, 19th–20th c.; 19th c. cycling; *Punch* & Ireland],
b.griffin@bathspa.ac.uk
Sarah Hackett, B.A., M.A., Ph.D. (Dunelm.), Lect. (Hist. Stud.) [European immigration; Islam
in Europe], a.hackett@bathspa.ac.uk
Alison Hems, B.A., Ph.D. (Liv.), Lect. (Hist. Stud.) [Heritage policy; heritage management,
learning & interpretation], a.hems@bathspa.ac.uk
Iftikhar H. Malik, B.A., M.A. (Punjab), M.A. (Oxon.), Ph.D. (Michigan State), Prof. (Hist. Stud.)
[Kashmir dispute & Indo-Pakistan relations; British Indian Punjab; Muslim history; U.S.
history], i.malik@bathspa.ac.uk
*Alan Marshall, B.A. (C.N.A.A.), M.A., Ph.D. (Lancaster), Lect. (Hist. Stud.) [Cromwellian &
Restoration Britain; military & espionage history, 1600–1899], a.marshall@bathspa.ac.uk
John Newsinger, B.A. (Hull), M.A. (Leicester), Prof. (Hist. Stud.) [Orwell's politics; British
foreign policy; counter insurgency; the British empire; American labour history],
j.newsinger@bathspa.ac.uk
Olivette Otele, BA., M.A., Ph.D. (Paris), Lect. (Hist. Stud.) [Slavery; abolition; collective
memory; empire; Atlantic world; race & ethnicity], o.otele@bathspa.ac.uk
Clifford Williamson, B.A., Ph.D. (Strathclyde), Lect. (Hist. Stud.) [U.S. & British cultural history;
politics & religion in the 20th c.; contemporary health policy], c.williamson@bathspa.ac.uk

THE QUEEN'S UNIVERSITY, BELFAST

The Queen's University, Belfast, BT7 1NN. 028 9024 5101. Fax 028 9024 5133
www.qub.ac.uk
School of History & Anthropology Fax 028 9031 3440

Stuart Aveyard, B.A. (York), M.A., Ph.D. (Belf.), Lect. in Hist. (Mod. Brit.) [Labour government
1974–9, esp. N. Ireland policy; politics of consumer credit], s.aveyard@qub.ac.uk
J. Brian Campbell, B.A. (Belf.), D.Phil. (Oxon.), Prof. of Roman Hist. [Land survey in the
ancient world; Roman army; warfare & society], brian.campbell@qub.ac.uk
Catherine Clinton, A.B. (Harv.), M.A. (Sussex), D.Phil. (Princeton), Prof. of Amer. Hist.
[Women's history; southern U.S. history; African-American history; the American Civil War],
c.clinton@qub.ac.uk
Marie Coleman, B.A., Ph.D. (N.U.I.), Lect. in Hist. (Mod. Ireland) [The Irish revolution; Irish
hospitals' sweepstake lottery], m.coleman@qub.ac.uk

Sean J. Connolly, B.A. (N.U.I.), D.Phil. (Ulster), Prof. of Irish Hist. [Popular culture, protest & social relations in Ireland c.1680–1850; civic culture of Belfast; Irish diaspora], s.connolly@qub.ac.uk

Paul Corthorn, B.A. (Cantab.), M.A. (Dunelm.), Ph.D. (Cantab.), Lect. in Hist. (Mod. Brit.) [The Left in Britain in the 1930s; the Labour party & the Soviet Union 1917–91; the cold war & Britain], p.corthorn@qub.ac.uk

John R. Curran, B.A., D.Phil. (Oxon.), Sen. Lect. in Anc. Hist. (Late Roman Empire, Roman Near East) [Late Roman Empire; Roman near east; Romano-Jewish relations], john.curran@qub.ac.uk

James Davis, B.A. (Dunelm.), M.Phil., Ph.D. (Cantab.), Lect. in Hist. (Med.) [English towns, markets & trade], james.davis@qub.ac.uk

Scott Dixon, M.A. (St. And.), Ph.D. (Cantab.), Sen. Lect. in Hist. (Early Mod. Eur.) [Reformation in Germany; historiography of Protestantism], s.dixon@qub.ac.uk

*Peter H. Gray, B.A., Ph.D. (Cantab.), Prof. of Mod. Irish Hist. [British-Irish relations c.1800–1870; the Great Famine of 1845–50; politics of poverty & land; the state in 19th c. Ireland], p.h.gray@qub.ac.uk

Crawford Gribben, M.A. (Dublin), Ph.D. (Strathclyde), Prof. of Early Mod. Brit. Hist (Mod. Brit.) [Early modern apocalyptic & millennial thought; print cultures of Puritanism & evangelicalism; contemporary American evangelicalism], c.gribben@qub.ac.uk

David W. Hayton, B.A. (Manc.), D.Phil. (Oxon.), Prof. of Early Mod. Irish & Brit. Hist. [Irish legislation 1690–1800; L.B. Namier & the history of parliament], d.hayton@qub.ac.uk

Andrew R. Holmes, B.A. (Belf.), M.Litt. (St. And.), Ph.D. (Belf.), Lect. in Hist. (Mod. Ireland) [Religion in Ireland c.1660 to the present, esp. Presbyterianism & evangelicalism], a.holmes@qub.ac.uk

Keith Jeffery, M.A., Ph.D. (Cantab.), Prof. of Brit. Hist. [Ireland & World War I; British empire; Secret Intelligence Service (M.I.6)], k.jeffery@qub.ac.uk

Rei Kanemura, M.A. (Manc.), Ph.D. (Cantab.), Lect. in Hist. (Early Mod. Brit.) [Theories of kingship & royalism in early Stuart period; Renaissance humanist political thought & education], r.kanemura@qub.ac.uk

Brian Kelly, B.A. (New Hampshire), M.A., Ph.D. (Brandeis), Reader in Hist. (U.S.) [American labour; southern history; African-American history], b.kelly@qub.ac.uk

Daniel Kowalsky, B.A. (Oregon), M.A. (New Mexico State), Ph.D. (Wis.), Lect. in Hist. (Mod. Eur.) [20th c. Spain; Spanish Civil War; fringe cinema], d.kowalsky@qub.ac.uk

Fearghal P. McGarry, B.A. (N.U.I.), Ph.D. (Dublin), Sen. Lect. in Hist. (Mod. Ireland) [Political history; radicalism in 20th c. Ireland; the Easter Rising; film & history], f.mcgarry@qub.ac.uk

Christopher W. Marsh, B.A., Ph.D. (Cantab.), Prof. of Early Mod. Cultural. Hist. [16th–17th c. English popular religion & culture, esp. music], c.marsh@qub.ac.uk

Eric Morier-Genoud, M.Sc. (Lond.), M.A., Ph.D. (New York State), Lect. in Hist. (Afric. & Imp.) [Southern Africa; the Portuguese-speaking world; Christian missions], e.morier-genoud@qub.ac.uk

Sean O'Connell, B.A. (Northumbria), Ph.D. (Warwick), Sen. Lect. in Hist. (Mod. Brit.) [Social & business history of mail order catalogues; working-class experiences of consumer credit & debt; 'joyriding'], s.oconnell@qub.ac.uk

Mary O'Dowd, B.A., Ph.D. (N.U.I.), Prof. of Gender Hist. [Gender & women's history; family history; early modern Ireland; historiography], m.odowd@qub.ac.uk

Sinead O'Sullivan, B.A., M.A. (N.U.I.), D.Phil. (Oxon.), Sen. Lect. in Hist. (Med. Eur.) [Glossing traditions of the early middle ages; Martianus Capella], s.osullivan@qub.ac.uk

Olwen Purdue, B.A., M.A., Ph.D. (Belf.), Lect. in Hist. (Mod. Ireland) [Poverty & welfare in 19th–20th c. Ireland; landed society in Ulster], o.purdue@qub.ac.uk

Emma Reisz, B.A., M.Phil., Ph.D. (Cantab.), Lect. in Hist. (Asia & Imp.) [Southeast Asia; south Asia; global history; transnational connections; British empire], emma.reisz@qub.ac.uk

Dion Smythe, M.A., Ph.D. (St. And.), Lect. in Hist. (Med.) [Byzantine history in the 11th & 12th c.; social outsiders; prosopography], d.smythe@qub.ac.uk

Anthony Stanonis, B.A. (Loyola), M.A., Ph.D. (Vanderbilt), Lect. in Hist. (U.S.) [Cultural rise of the American South, esp. urban history, foodways, tourism], a.stanonis@qub.ac.uk

Alexander Titov, B.A., M.A., Ph.D. (Lond.), Lect. in Hist. (Mod. Eur.) [Political thought & nationalism in 20th c. Russia; Nikita Khrushchev; Russian foreign policy], a.titov@qub.ac.uk

Katy Turton, M.A. (Aberd.), Ph.D. (Glas.), Lect. in Hist. (Mod. Eur.) [Women & family networks in the Russian revolutionary movement], k.turton@qub.ac.uk

Immo Warntjes, M.A. (Göttingen), Ph.D. (N.U.I.), Lect. in Hist. (Med.) [Medieval scientific thought, esp. computus; early medieval Ireland, esp. kingship & succession; medieval burial practices], i.warntjes@qub.ac.uk

Todd H. Weir, B.A. (Brown), M.A. (Humboldt), Ph.D. (Columbia), Lect. in Hist. (Mod. Eur.) [Religion & society in 20th c. Germany; secularism], t.weir@qub.ac.uk

David Whitehead, M.A., Ph.D. (Cantab.), Prof. of Anc. Hist. [Classical Greece, esp. Athens: society, politics, warfare], d.whitehead@qub.ac.uk

UNIVERSITY OF BIRMINGHAM

Edgbaston, Birmingham, B15 2TT. 0121 414 3344. Fax 0121 414 3971
www.bham.ac.uk
College of Arts & Law
School of History & Cultures
Department of History 0121 414 5497. Fax 0121 414 3595
Department of African Studies & Anthropology 0121 414 5128. Fax 0121 414 3595
Department of Classics, Ancient History & Archaeology 0121 414 5497
Ironbridge International Institute for Cultural Heritage 0121 414 5497
School of English, Drama & American & Canadian Studies
American & Canadian Studies 0121 414 5740. Fax 0121 414 6866
School of Modern Languages, Cultures, Art History & Music
Art History 0121 414 2218. Fax 0121 414 2727
School of Philosophy, Theology & Religion
Theology & Religion 0121 414 5666. Fax 0121 414 4381
Birmingham Law School 0121 414 3637. Fax 0121 414 3585
College of Medical & Dental Sciences: History of Medicine Unit 0121 415 8122

Dimiter Angelov, B.A. (Wabash), M.A., Ph.D. (Harv.), Prof. of Byz. Hist. (Byz. Hist.) [Intellectual, political & institutional history of the Byzantine Empire, esp. 13th, 14th & 15th c.], D.Angelov@bham.ac.uk

Eunice Apio, M.A. (Makerere), Marie Curie Fellow, E.O.Apio@bham.ac.uk

J. David Armstrong, B.Sc.(Econ.), M.Sc.(Econ.) (Lond.), Ph.D. (A.N.U.), Reader in Int. Stud.

Arezou Azad, B.A., B.S. (Boston), M.I.A., M.P.H. (Columbia), Ph.D. (Oxon.), Lect. in Med. Stud. (Med.), A.Azad@bham.ac.uk

Steven R. Bassett, B.A., Ph.D. (Birm.), Sen. Lect. in Med. Hist. [Early medieval history & archaeology; Anglo-Saxon England], S.R.Bassett@bham.ac.uk

Andrew Bayliss, B.A. (Hons), Dip.Ed., Ph.D, Lect. in Greek Hist. (Greek Hist.), A.Bayliss@bham.ac.uk

Laura Beers, A.B. (Princeton), Ph.D. (Harv.), Birmingham Fellow in Mod. Brit. Hist., L.Beers.1@bham.ac.uk

Francesca Berry, B.A., M.A., Ph.D. (Lond.), Lect. in the Hist. of Art (19th–20th c. France)
[Artistic & visual culture of the domestic interior], F.Berry@bham.ac.uk

Jonathan Boff, B.A. (Oxon.), M.A., Ph.D. (Lond.), Lect. in Mod. Hist., J.F.Boff@bham.ac.uk

Martin Bommas, M.A., Ph.D. (Heid.), Sen. Lect. in Egyptology (Egyptology) [Egyptology;
language, religion & rituals; archaeology; diffusion of Egyptian gods in the ancient world],
M.Bommas@bham.ac.uk

Megan B. Brickley, B.A. (Birm.), M.Sc., Ph.D. (Lond.), Reader in Biological Anthr.
[Human osteology & palaeopathology; environmental archaeology; human origins],
M.B.Brickley@bham.ac.uk

Nicholas P. Brooks, M.A., D.Phil. (Oxon.), F.B.A., Emeritus Prof. of Med. Hist. [Anglo-Saxon &
central medieval history & archaeology], N.P.Brooks@bham.ac.uk

Leslie Brubaker, B.A., M.A. (Penn.), Ph.D. (Johns Hopkins), Prof. of Byz. Art Hist. (Byz.
Material Culture), L.Brubaker@bham.ac.uk

Caterina Bruschi, Laurea, Ph.D., Lect. in Med. Hist. [Religious history; heresy & Inquisition,
esp. in Italy & France], C.Bruschi@bham.ac.uk

Jabal Buaben, B.A., Dip.Ed. (Cape Coast, Ghana), M.A., Ph.D. (Birm.), Lect. in Islam,
J.M.Buaben@bham.ac.uk

Philip Burton, B.A., Ph.D. (Cantab.), Reader in Biblical Language & New Testament Stud.
[Biblical language; New Testament studies], P.H.Burton@bham.ac.uk

Christopher P. Callow, B.A., Ph.D. (Birm.), Lect. in Med. Hist. [Medieval Iceland; early
medieval history & archaeology], C.P.Callow@bham.ac.uk

John Carman, M.Phil., Ph.D. (Cantab.), Sen. Lect. in Heritage Valuation (Archaeol. &
Heritage) [Heritage valuation], J.Carman@bham.ac.uk

Henry Chapman, B.A. (Exeter), Ph.D. (Hull), Sen. Lect. in Archaeol. & Visualisation
(Archaeol.) [Archaeology & visualisation; later prehistoric period; human activity &
environmental change within past landscapes; digital technologies within heritage],
H.Chapman@bham.ac.uk

Carl S.A. Chinn, M.B.E., B.A., Ph.D. (Birm.), Prof. of Birmingham Community Hist. [Urban
working-class history; manufacturing history; ethnic minorities; towns & cities; Birmingham
& Black Country history], carl@brummagem.fsnet.co.uk

*A. Simon Esmonde Cleary, B.A. (Lond.), D.Phil. (Oxon.), Reader, Head of Classics, Anc.
Hist. & Archaeol. [Roman provincial archaeology; late antiquity; urban archaeology],
A.S.Esmonde_Cleary@bham.ac.uk

Matthew Cole, B.A., M.A., P.G.C.E., Ph.D., Teaching Fellow (Mod. Hist.) [Constitutional &
party politics; local history], M.R.Cole@bham.ac.uk

Sir Neil Cossons, O.B.E., M.A., D.Litt., D.Soc.Sc. (Liv.), D.Univ. (Open), D.Litt. (Bradford),
Hon. Prof. [History of technology; museum management & curatorship]

*Nicholas J. Crowson, B.A., Ph.D. (Southampton), Reader in Mod. Hist., Head of Hist.
[20th c. Conservative party; appeasement; Britain & Europe; N.G.O.s; social activism],
N.J.Crowson@bham.ac.uk

Richard P. Cust, B.A., Ph.D. (Lond.), Prof. of Early Mod. Hist. [Political culture of the gentry
late 16th–early 17th c.; the politics of Charles I's reign], R.P.Cust@bham.ac.uk

Malcolm M. Dick, B.A., Ph.D. (Leicester), Director, Centre for W. Midlands Hist. [History of the
West Midlands region after 1700; environmental history; histories of minority communitites],
M.M.Dick@bham.ac.uk

Ken Dowden, M.A. (Oxon.), Prof. of Classics (Classics) [Religion, mythology & the ancient
novel], K.Dowden@bham.ac.uk

Archie Dunn, B.A. (Read.), M.A., Ph.D. (Birm.), Res. Fellow in Byz. [Byzantine archaeology;
Byzantine Greece & Cyprus], A.W.Dunn@bham.ac.uk

Christopher Farrell, B.A. (Brandeis), M.A., Ph.D. (Lond.), Teaching Fellow (Anc. Hist.)
[History of ideas in classical antiquity, esp. ancient political & religious thought],
C.A.Farrell@bham.ac.uk

Douglas Ford, Lect. in War Stud., D.Ford@bham.ac.uk

Matthew Francis, B.A. (Brist.), M.A. (Lond.), Ph.D. (Nott.), Teaching Fellowship in 20th c. Brit.
Hist., M.J.Francis@bham.ac.uk

Elaine Fulton, M.A., M.Litt., Ph.D. (St. And.), Sen. Lect. in Mod. Hist. [Religious, social,
political & environmental history of the German speaking lands of early modern Europe],
E.K.Fulton@bham.ac.uk

David Gange, Ph.D. (Cantab.), Lect. in Brit. Hist., D.J.Gange@bham.ac.uk

Paul J. Garwood, B.A., M.Sc. (Lond.), Lect. in Prehist. [European & British prehistory],
P.J.Garwood@bham.ac.uk

Eurydice Georganteli, M.A., Ph.D, Lect. in Numismatics (Numismatics) [Political ideology
& coinage; coins & routes in the Mediterranean & the Balkans; cityscapes on ancient &
medieval coins], E.Georganteli@bham.ac.uk

Peter Gray, B.Sc. (Dundee), LL.B. (Lond.), M.Phil (Cantab.), Ph.D. (Birm.), Sen. Res. Fellow
(Air Power Stud.) [Aspects of contemporary & historical air power], P.W.Gray@bham.ac.uk

Julian Greaves, B.A., Ph.D. (Birm.), Lect. in Mod. Hist. [19th & 20th c. British economic
history, with special reference to industrial & transport policy], J.I.Greaves@bham.ac.uk

Armin Grünbacher, M.A. (Tübingen), Ph.D. (Birm.), Lect. in Mod. Hist. [Post-war German
reconstruction & the Cold War; post-1945 German social & economic history],
A.Gruenbacher@bham.ac.uk

Jonathan Gumz, B.A., M.A. (Wis.), Ph.D. (Chicago), Lect. in Mod. Hist.,
J.E.Gumz@bham.ac.uk

Tara J. Hamling, B.A., M.Phil., D.Phil. (Sussex), R.C.U.K. Res. Fellow in Mod. Hist.
[Early modern cultural history in Britain; post-Reformation visual & material culture],
T.J.Hamling@bham.ac.uk

Matthew Harpster, B.A., M.Phil, Ph.D., Marie Curie Fellow (Classics & Anc. Hist.) [Maritime
archaeology; history of maritime archaeology in the Mediterranean region; promoting
an alternative approach to the interpretation & modelling of maritime communities in the
ancient Mediterranean], M.Harpster@bham.ac.uk

Victoria Harris, B.A. (Brown), M.Phil., Ph.D. (Cantab.), Birmingham Fellow in Mod. Eur. Hist.,
V.Harris.1@bham.ac.uk

Alfred G. Hatton, B.A. (Dunelm.), Lect. in Econ. & Soc. Hist.

Vanessa Heggie, B.Sc., M.Sc., Ph.D. (Manc.), Birmingham Res. Fellow [History of medicine;
history of life sciences; history of sport & exploration], V.Heggie@bham.ac.uk

*David E. Hemsoll, B.A. (East Anglia), B.Sc., M.A. (Lond.), Sen. Lect. in Hist. of Art
[Architecture of Sanmicheli; Renaissance architecture & theory; Renaissance art],
D.E.Hemsoll@bham.ac.uk

Steve Hewitt, B.A., M.A., Ph.D. (Saskatchewan), Lect. [20th c. Canadian history & politics;
Canadian studies; Canada-U.S. relations; North American regionalism; policing &
intelligence services; terrorism & counter-terrorism]

Christopher Hill, M.A., M.Litt. (St. And.), Teaching Fellow in 20th c. Brit. Hist.,
C.Hill.4@bham.ac.uk

Matthew J. Hilton, B.A., M.A., Ph.D. (Lancaster), Prof. of Soc. Hist. [British popular culture
& social history; history of consumer society & material culture; social movements],
M.J.Hilton@bham.ac.uk

Haifaa Jawad, B.A., M.A. (Baghdad), Ph.D. (Exeter), Sen. Lect. in Islamic & Mid. E. Stud.,
H.A.Jawad@bham.ac.uk

Peter M. Jones, B.A. (Leeds), D.Phil. (Oxon.), Prof. of French Hist. [French Revolution; French rural history; cultural history of science in the West Midlands, 1760–1820], P.M.Jones@bham.ac.uk

Martin L.B. Kolinsky, B.A. (Saskatchewan), Ph.D. (Lond.), Sen. Lect. in Pol. Sc. [British policy towards the Middle East 1936–45]

Simone H. Laqua-O'Donnell, B.A. (Cantab.), M.St., D.Phil. (Oxon.), Lect. in Early Mod. Hist. [Religious, social & cultural history of the Holy Roman Empire & Italy], S.Laquaodonnell@bham.ac.uk

Helen J. Laville, B.A. (Birm.), Ph.D. (Nott.), Sen. Lect. in Amer. & Canadian Stud. [20th c. American history; women's history; civil rights], H.Laville@bham.ac.uk

M. Anthony Leahy, M.A., Ph.D. (Cantab.), Sen. Lect. in Egyptology [Egyptology: language, history, religion & archaeology; Egypt in 1st millennium B.C.], M.A.Leahy@bham.ac.uk

Sabine Lee, Staatsexamen (Düsseldorf), M.Phil., Ph.D. (Cantab.), Prof. of Mod. Hist. (Mod. Hist.) [Studies of children born of war; history of 20th c. science, esp. physics], S.Lee@bham.ac.uk

Robert M. Lewis, M.A. (Oxon. & Illinois), M.A., Ph.D. (Johns Hopkins), Lect. in Amer. Hist. (19th c. Cultural Hist.) [Louisiana; race; recreation; leisure], R.M.Lewis@bham.ac.uk

Su Lin Lewis, B.A. (King's College, Halifax & Dalhousie), M.A. (Lond.), Ph.D. (Cantab.), Lect. in Asian Hist. (Asian Hist.) [Southeast Asia, esp. transnational connections & cross-cultural exchange], S.Lewis@bham.ac.uk

*Alasdair Livingstone, M.A. (Cantab.), Ph.D. (Birm.), Dr.habil. (Heid.), Reader in Assyriology [Western Asia; the history, languages & archaeology of Sumerian, Babylonian, Assyrian & Hittite civilisations; cuneiform inscriptions; pre-Islamic Arabia], A.Livingstone@bham.ac.uk

Niall Livingstone, M.A., D.Phil., Sen. Lect. in Classics (Classics) [Ancient Greek literature & thought], N.Livingstone@bham.ac.uk

Scott Lucas, B.A. (Vanderbilt), Ph.D. (Lond.), Prof. of Amer. Stud. [U.S. & British foreign policy after 1945; propaganda & media; culture, ideology & history; intelligence services], W.S.Lucas@bham.ac.uk

Jerzy T. Lukowski, M.A., Ph.D. (Cantab.), Prof. of Polish Hist. [18th c. Poland: nobility, esp. the nobility & the Enlightenment], J.T.Lukowski@bham.ac.uk

D. Hugh McLeod, B.A., Ph.D. (Cantab.), Emeritus Prof. of Church Hist. [Secularisation in 19th & 20th c. Europe; religion in the 1960s; religion & sport in modern Britain], D.H.Mcleod@bham.ac.uk

Ruth J. Macrides, B.A. (Columbia), Ph.D. (Lond.), Sen. Lect. in Byz. Stud. [Byzantine social, legal & literary history; ceremonial; historical writing], R.J.Macrides@bham.ac.uk

Christopher Moores, B.A., M.A., Ph.D. (Birm.), Birmingham Fellow in Mod. Brit. Hist. (Mod. Brit. Hist.), C.I.Moores@bham.ac.uk

Steve Morewood, B.A., Ph.D. (Brist.), Lect. in Int. Hist. [Conflict in the modern Middle East; British military projection in the E. Mediterranean; origins of World War II], S.Morewood@bham.ac.uk

Miriam Müller, B.A. (Sussex), M.Phil. (Cantab.), Ph.D. (Birm.), Lect. in Med. Hist. [Later medieval English social & economic history, esp. in relation to peasant societies], M.Muller@bham.ac.uk

Rhoads Murphey, M.A., Ph.D. (Chicago), Reader in Ottoman Stud., R.Murphey@bham.ac.uk

Gideon Nisbet, M.A., D.Phil. (Oxon.), Reader in Classics (Classics) [Greek & Latin literature, esp. epigram & Greek writers in the Roman Empire; ancient books on papyrus; the reception of classical antiquity in modern culture], G.Nisbet@bham.ac.uk

Maureen P. Perrie, M.A. (Edin. & Birm.), Prof. of Russian Hist., Centre for Russian & E. Eur. Stud. [Soviet cultural policy in 1930s–40s, esp. in relation to Russian history], M.P.Perrie@bham.ac.uk

Amanda Philips, B.A. (Chicago), M.A. (Mass.), D.Phil. (Oxon.), Marie Curie Fellow of the Gerda Henkel Stiftung (Byz., Ottoman & Mod. Greek Stud.) [Luxury & semi-luxury goods in the Ottoman Empire 1600–1800], A.Phillips@bham.ac.uk

Steffen Prauser, M.A. (Frankfurt), Ph.D. (E.U.I., Florence), Lect. in Mod. Hist. [France, Germany, Italy 1934–45; World War II in Europe], S.Prauser@bham.ac.uk

William J. Purkis, B.A., M.A., Ph.D. (Cantab.), Lect. in Med. Hist. [Crusading, pilgrimage & monasticism; cross-cultural encounters in Iberia & the Latin East], W.J.Purkis@bham.ac.uk

Pierre Purseigle, B.A. (Sciences Po, Lyon), D.E.A., Eur.Doct. (Toulouse), Hon. Fellow in Mod. Hist., Director, Centre for First World War Stud. [World War I Europe, incl. Britain; 20th c. France; comparative history]

Katrien Pype, Ph.D. (Louvain), Birmingham Fellow (Soc. & Cultural Anthr.) [Technology, religion & sociality; politics, visual media & memory], K.Pype@bham.ac.uk

Sadiah Qureshi, B.A., M.Phil., Ph.D. (Cantab.), Lect. in Mod. Hist., S.Qureshi.1@bham.ac.uk

Adrian J. Randall, B.A. (Birm.), M.A. (Sheff.), Ph.D. (Birm.), Emeritus Prof. of Eng. Soc. Hist. [British social & labour history, 1700–1950], A.J.Randall@bham.ac.uk

E. Arfon Rees, Reader in Soviet & Russian Hist., Centre for Russian & E. Eur. Stud., E.A.Rees@bham.ac.uk

Jonathan B. Reinarz, B.A. (Brit. Col.), M.A., Ph.D. (Warwick), Reader in Medical Hist., Hist. of Medicine Unit (Medical Hist.) [Modern medical history; history of occupational health & medicine; history of medical specialisation & medical education; hospitals & the senses], J.Reinarz@bham.ac.uk

Klaus Richter, Staatsexamen (Cologne), Ph.D. (Berlin), Lect. in War Stud. (War Stud.) [Modern history of East-Central Europe & the Baltics; history of nationalism & anti-Semitism; theories & methods of conceptual & praxeological history], K.Richter@bham.ac.uk

*Mike Robinson, B.A., P.G.C.E. (Northumbria), Ph.D. (East Anglia), Prof. of Cultural Heritage, Director of Ironbridge Int. Institute for Cultural Heritage (Cultural Heritage) [Categories of heritage within changing cultural & cross-cultural contexts], M.D.Robinson@bham.ac.uk

Jens U. Röhrkasten, M.A., P.D. (Freibourg), Dr.phil. (Freie Univ., Berlin), Lect. in Med. Hist. [Mendicant orders; medieval criminal law], J.Roehrkasten@bham.ac.uk

*Corey D. Ross, B.A. (E.M.C.), M.A. (Maryland), Ph.D. (Lond.), Head of Sch. of Hist. & Cultures, Prof. of Mod. Hist. [Empire & environment; 20th c. Germany, esp. popular culture & media; 20th c. Europe], C.D.Ross@bham.ac.uk

Gavin Schaffer, B.A., M.Phil. (Birm.), Ph.D. (Southampton), Prof. of Brit. Hist., G.Schaffer@bham.ac.uk

Gareth M. Sears, B.A., Ph.D. (Birm.), Sen. Lect. in Roman Hist. [North Africa in antiquity; later Roman history & archaeology; early Christian history & archaeology], G.M.Sears@bham.ac.uk

Berny Sèbe, D.Phil. (Oxon.), Lect. in Colonial & Post-Colonial Stud., B.C.Sebe@bham.ac.uk

Manu Sehgal, B.A., M.A., M.Phil. (Delhi), Ph.D. (Exeter), Hon. Res. Fellow, M.Sehgal@bham.ac.uk

*Keith Shear, B.A. Hons. (Witwatersrand), M.A. (Lond.), Ph.D. (Northwestern), Lect. in Afric. Pol., Head of Afric. Stud. & Anthr. [South African history; colonial history; contemporary African politics], K.S.Shear@bham.ac.uk

Ian Shields, Ph.D., Sen. Teaching Fellow [Military history, esp. World War II], I.E.Shields@bham.ac.uk

Alexander Skinner, M.A. (Oxon.), Ph.D. (Lond.), Lect. in Roman Hist. (Roman Hist.) [Social & political history of the later Roman Empire], A.G.Skinner@bham.ac.uk

Kate Skinner, B.A. (Oxon.), M.A. (Paris), Ph.D. (Birm.), Lect. in the Soc. Hist. of Afric. in the 20th c. [Social history of Africa in the 20th c.], K.A.Skinner.1@bham.ac.uk

Margaret A. Small, B.A., M.A., D.Phil. (Oxon.), Lect. in Early Mod. Hist. [European exploration & expansion; history of the classical tradition; history of geography], M.Small@bham.ac.uk

David Smith, M.A. (Cantab.), M.A., Ph.D. (Sheff.), Sen. Lect. in Environmental Archaeol. (Environmental Archaeol.) [Interpretation of insect remains from the archaeological record], D.N.Smith@bham.ac.uk

H. Camilla Smith, B.A., M.Phil., Ph.D. (Birm.), Lect. in the Hist. of Art. [18th c. Swiss & British visual culture], H.C.Smith@bham.ac.uk

Leonard D. Smith, B.Sc.(Econ.), M.A. (Lond.), Ph.D. (Birm.), Hon. Sen. Res. Fellow, Hist. of Medicine Unit [History of psychiatry & mental health institutions in England, 1750–2000; history of West Indies mental health institutions, 1820–1920], L.D.Smith@bham.ac.uk

Michael F. Snape, B.A., Ph.D. (Birm.), Sen. Lect. in Mod. Hist. [Religious & military history of Britain; 18th c. Church], M.F.Snape@bham.ac.uk

Diana Spencer, B.A. (Dublin), M.A. (Lond.), Ph.D. (Cantab.), Reader in Roman Intellectual Culture (Roman Hist.) [Roman intellectual culture], D.J.Spencer@bham.ac.uk

Paul S. Spencer-Longhurst, M.A. (Oxon. & Lond.), Ph.D. (Birm.), Lect. in Hist. of Art & Sen. Curator, Barber Inst. [French & British art c.1750–1870; history of collecting], P.S.Spencer-Longhurst@bham.ac.uk

Naomi Standen, B.A. (Lond.), Ph.D. (Dunelm.), Prof. of Med. Hist., N.Standen@bham.ac.uk

Robert N. Swanson, M.A., Ph.D. (Cantab.), Prof. of Med. Hist. [Church history 13th c.– c.1540], R.N.Swanson@bham.ac.uk

Elena Theodorakopoulos, Ph.D. (Brist.), Lect. in Classics (Classics) [Roman poetry of the Republic & Principate; the reception of classical culture & literature in contemporary film & literature], E.M.Theodorakopoulos@bham.ac.uk

David Thomas, M.A. (Oxon. & Cantab.), Ph.D. (Lancaster), Prof. of Christianity & Islam [Medieval Christians; Muslim dialogue & polemic], D.R.Thomas.1@bham.ac.uk

Dimitris Tziovas, Ph.D., Prof. of Mod. Greek Stud. (Mod. Greek) [Greek Modernism; the reception of Greek antiquity & Byzantium; Greek fiction, diaspora & travel writing; nationalism & Greek culture], D.P.Tziovas@bham.ac.uk

Frank Uekoetter, Habil., Ph.D. (Bielefeld), Birmingham Fellow in Environmental Humanities (Environmental Humanities) [The past & present of environmentalism; environmental resources], F.Uekoetter@bham.ac.uk

Jelle van Lottum, M.A. (V.U. University), Ph.D. (Utrecht), Birmingham Fellow [Economic history of labour migration], J.Vanlottum@bham.ac.uk

Jutta Vinzent, M.A. (Munich), Dr.phil. (Cologne), Ph.D. (Cantab.), Lect. in Mod. & Contemp. Art & Visual Culture [Migration studies], J.Vinzent@bham.ac.uk

Markus Vinzent, Dip.theol. (Eichstatt), Dr.theol. (Munich), Dr.theol.habil. (Heid.), H.G. Wood Prof. of Theol. [History of Christianity, esp. early Christianity; theologians in exile 1933–45; philosophy & theology; business & religions], M.Vinzent@bham.ac.uk

Eric Gruber von Arni, Ph.D. (Portsmouth), Hon. Sen. Res. Fellow, Hist. of Medicine Unit [History of military healthcare in the 17th & 18th c.], eegva@aol.com

Kenneth A. Wardle, M.A. (Cantab.), Ph.D. (Lond.), Sen. Lect. in Anc. Hist. & Archaeol. [Classical archaeology; Greek prehistory; prehistoric Macedonia], K.A.Wardle@bham.ac.uk

Ben White, M.A. (Edin.), M.St., D.Phil. (Oxon.), Lect. in Mod. Mid. E. Hist., B.T.White@bham.ac.uk

Roger White, B.A., Ph.D. (Liv.), Sen. Lect. in Cultural Heritage (Cultural Heritage) [Roman archaeology; heritage management; industrial archaeology], R.H.White@bham.ac.uk

Daniel Whittingham, B.A. (Oxon.), M.A., Ph.D. (Lond.), Lect. in War Stud. (War Stud.) [The conduct of war, with a particular focus on British military history, military thought & strategy], D.Whittingham@bham.ac.uk

Andrew N. Williams, B.A., B.M., B.Ch. (Oxon.), M.Sc. (Warwick), Hon. Sen. Res. Fellow, Hist. of Medicine Unit [History of paediatric neurology; life of Thomas Willis], history.med@bham.ac.uk

Jonathan Willis, B.A., M.A., Ph.D. (Warwick), Lect. in Early Mod. Hist., J.P.Willis@bham.ac.uk
Isabel Wollaston, B.A., Ph.D. (Dunelm.), Sen. Lect., I.L.Wollaston@bham.ac.uk
Anna Woodham, B.A., M.A. (Lond.), Ph.D. (Leicester), Teaching Fellow in Cultural Heritage
 (Cultural Heritage) [Museum audiences; social impacts of museum visiting; museum
 geographies], A.Woodham@bham.ac.uk
Simon S. Yarrow, B.A., M.A. (Newcastle), D.Phil. (Oxon.), Sen. Lect. in Med. Hist.
 [Hagiography; the cult of the saints & the interaction between popular & elite culture;
 Anglo-Saxon & Anglo-Norman narrative sources & constructions of identity & gender],
 S.S.Yarrow@bham.ac.uk
Shirley Ye, B.A. (Calif. at Berkeley), M.A. (N.Y.), Ph.D. (Harv.), Lect. in Asian Hist. (Asian
 Hist.) [Globalisation; cities; environmental history; history of science & technology; frontier
 & international history; international organisations; postcolonial & development studies;
 Chinese & global historiography; cultural studies & gender], S.Ye@bham.ac.uk

BIRMINGHAM CITY UNIVERSITY

City North Campus, Birmingham, B42 2SU. 0121 331 5000
www.bcu.ac.uk
Faculty of Education, Law & Social Sciences

Edward J. Johnson, B.A., M.A. (Lancaster), Ph.D. (Lond.), Reader in Pol. (Contemp.
 Hist. & Int. Rel.) [Contemporary history; British foreign policy & the United Nations],
 edward.johnson@bcu.ac.uk
John Warren, B.A. (Lancaster), M.Sc. (Oxon.), M.Ed., Ph.D. (Hull), Sen. Lect. in
 Hist. [Victorian cultural history; Harriet Martineau & the ideal of community],
 john.warren@bcu.ac.uk

UNIVERSITY OF BOLTON

Department of Health & Social Studies
Chadwick Street, Bolton, BL2 1JW. 01204 28851. Fax 01204 399074
www.bolton.ac.uk/hss/

Gerry Bryant, Lect. in Int. Rel. (Milit. Hist., India)
Janet Ellis, B.A. (C.N.A.A.), M.A. (Lond.), Lect. (Amer. Hist., 17th c. Brit.)
Bill Luckin, B.A. (Oxon.), M.Sc. (Lond.), Prof. in Urban & Cultural Stud. (Mod. Brit. Soc. &
 Econ. Hist.)
Ged Seacombe, B.A. (Lond.), M.A. (Salford), Lect. (Soc. & Urban Hist.) [Economic &
 industrial history; sociology]
David Sheen, Lect. in Soc. & Pol. Hist.
*David J. Wrench, B.A., Ph.D. (Wales), Princ. Lect., Head of Hist. (Mod. Brit. Pol., Ireland),
 djw1@bolton.ac.uk

UNIVERSITY OF **BRADFORD**

Bradford, West Yorkshire, BD7 1DP. 01274 733466. Fax 01274 305340
www.bradford.ac.uk
Department of Languages & European Studies

Gábor Bátonyi, M.A., D.Phil. (Oxon.), Lect. in Mod. Hist. (Central Eur.) [Britain & central
Europe; Hungary], G.Batonyi@bradford.ac.uk
James Gregory, B.A. (Oxon.), M.Phil. (Cantab.), Ph.D. (Southampton), Lect. in Mod. Hist.
[British political & cultural history, c.1760–1914], J.Gregory2@bradford.ac.uk
V. Martyn Housden, B.A. (Oxon.), M.A. (Sheff.), Ph.D. (Bradford), Reader in Mod. Hist.
(Germany, Phil. of Hist.), V.M.Housden@bradford.ac.uk
Munro Price, M.A., Ph.D. (Cantab.), Prof. of Mod. Eur. Hist. (Brit., France) [French political
history 1750–1848; French Revolution], M.Price2@bradford.ac.uk

UNIVERSITY OF **BRIGHTON**

Mithras House, Lewes Road, Brighton, BN2 4AT. 01273 600900
www.brighton.ac.uk
School of Historical & Critical Studies
10–11 Pavilion Parade, Brighton, East Sussex, BN2 1RA. 01273 643301

Cathy Bergin, B.A. (Dublin), M.A., D.Phil. (Sussex), Lect. (Literary Hist.) [African-American
cultural formations & communist politics during the Depression], c.j.bergin@brighton.ac.uk
Graham Dawson, B.A., Ph.D. (Birm.), Reader (19th–20th c.) [Cultural history & memory]
Frank Gray, B.A. (Sussex), Ph.D. (Brighton), [Cinema & media history]
Peter Jackson, B.A., B.Ed. (Melb.), Ph.D. (Exeter), Sen. Lect. (16th–18th c.)
*Patrick J. (Paddy) Maguire, B.A. (York), D.Phil. (Sussex), Head of Sch. (20th c.) [British
industrial politics post-1945], p.j.maguire@brighton.ac.uk
Lucy Noakes, B.A., D.Phil. (Sussex), [20th c. cultural history]
Anita Rupprecht, D.Phil. (Sussex), [History of slavery]
Gillian A. Scott, B.A., M.A., D.Phil. (Sussex), Sen. Lect. (19th–20th c.)
Jon Watson, B.A., P.G.C.E., M.A., D.Phil. (Sussex), Lect. (Amer. Hist.) [American history;
history of the civil rights movement]

UNIVERSITY OF **BRISTOL**

Senate House, Tyndall Avenue, Bristol, BS8 1TH. 0117 928 9000. Fax 0117 929 2396
www.bristol.ac.uk
Department of Historical Studies 13–15 Woodland Road, Bristol, BS8 1TB.
0117 928 7934/36. Fax 0117 331 7933
www.bristol.ac.uk/history/
Department of Archaeology 11 Woodland Road, Bristol, BS8 1TB. 0117 928 8877
www.bristol.ac.uk/archanth/
Department of Classics & Ancient History 11 Woodland Road, Bristol, BS8 1TB.
0117 928 7764. Fax 0117 928 8678
Department of History of Art 36 Tyndall's Park Road, Bristol, BS8 1PL. 0117 928 8591
www.bristol.ac.uk/arthistory/

Kenneth Austin, M.A., Ph.D. (St. And.), Sen. Lect. in Hist. (Continental Reformation) [Calvinism]

Victoria Bates, B.A. (Nott.), M.A., Ph.D. (Exeter), Lect. in Mod. Hist. (Mod. Hist.) [Histories of sexuality, childhood, forensic medicine & medical humanities], Victoria.Bates@bristol.ac.uk

Robert A. Bickers, B.A., Ph.D. (Lond.), Prof. of Hist. (Mod. China, Imp.) [Shanghai; imperial policing; colonial cultures], Robert.Bickers@bristol.ac.uk

Fernando Cervantes, M.A. (Oxon.), Ph.D. (Cantab.), Reader in Hist. [Early modern Europe; Spain & Spanish America; religious, cultural & intellectual history], F.Cervantes@bristol.ac.uk

Peter A. Coates, M.A. (St. And.), Ph.D. (Cantab.), Prof. of Amer. & Environmental Hist. (U.S.A., Environment) [Attitudes to natural world; history of environmental change], P.A.Coates@bristol.ac.uk

*Tim Cole, M.A., Ph.D. (Cantab.), Prof. of Soc. Hist. (Mod. Eur. Soc. & Cultural Hist.) [Holocaust ghettoisation in Hungary; representations of the Holocaust post-1945], Tim.Cole@bristol.ac.uk

Lucy Donkin, B.A. (Oxon.), M.A., Ph.D. (Lond.), (Med.) [Visual culture & concepts of place history in medieval Italy], Lucy.Donkin@bristol.ac.uk

Juliane Furst, M.A., D.Phil. (Oxon.), Sen. Lect. in Hist. [Soviet Russian history], Juliane.Furst@bristol.ac.uk

Anke Holdenreid, B.A. (Lond.), M.Phil. (Cantab.), Ph.D. (Lond.), Sen. Lect. in Hist. [The apocalypse in the middle ages; manuscript studies], A.Holdenreid@bristol.ac.uk

Mark C. Horton, M.A., Ph.D. (Cantab.), Prof. of Archaeol. [Medieval archaeology; trade; E. Africa; Swahili culture; landscape archaeology]

Ronald E. Hutton, M.A. (Cantab.), D.Phil. (Oxon.), Prof. of Hist. (16th & 17th c. Brit.) [Images of paganism & witchcraft in Britain 1800–2000], R.Hutton@bristol.ac.uk

Evan Jones, M.A. (York), M.A., Ph.D. (Edin.), Sen. Lect. in Econ. & Soc. Hist. (Early Mod. Soc. & Econ. Hist.) Evan.Jones@bristol.ac.uk

Josie McLellan, B.A. (Sussex), M.St. (Oxon.), Reader in Mod. Eur. Hist. [Post-war Europe; East German cultural history; memory], Josie.McLellan@bristol.ac.uk

Joanna Michlic, B.A. (Lodz), M.A., Ph.D. (Lond.), Lect. in Contemp. Hist [Jewish childhood; Holocaust; memory of war; Jewish history; genocide; nationalism], Joanna.B.Michlic@bristol.ac.uk

Roger Middleton, B.A. (Manc.), Ph.D. (Cantab.), Prof. of the Hist. of Pol. Econ. (20th c. Brit. & Eur., Computing in Hist.) [British economic policy & performance], Roger.Middleton@bristol.ac.uk

Neville D.G. Morley, M.A., Ph.D. (Cantab.), Prof. of Anc. Hist. [Ancient economy; city of Rome; historiography], N.D.G.Morley@bristol.ac.uk

Hugh Pemberton, B.A. (Open), M.A., Ph.D. (Brist.), Reader in Mod. Brit. Hist.
[Contemporary British history; British politics; political economy; pensions policy],
H.Pemberton@bristol.ac.uk
Simon Potter, B.A., Ph.D., Reader in Mod. Brit. Hist. (Imp. & C'wealth),
Simon.Potter@bristol.ac.uk
Kate A. Robson-Brown, M.A., Ph.D. (Cantab.), Prof. of Archaeol. [Human origins]
Jonathan Saha, B.A. (Sheff.), M.A., Ph.D. (Lond.), Lect. in Mod. Hist. (Mod. Hist.) [Corruption,
crime, madness & medicine in colonial Burma], J.Saha@bristol.ac.uk
Richard D. Sheldon, B.A. (C.N.A.A.), M.A. (Lond.), Ph.D. (Birm.), Lect. in Soc. & Econ. Hist.
(Mod. Eur.) [Food markets; protest movements; economic & social thought, 18th & 19th c.],
R.Sheldon@bristol.ac.uk
Robert Skinner, B.A., Ph.D. (Sussex), Teaching Fellow in Mod. Hist. (Mod. Brit. & Afric.),
Robert.Skinner@bristol.ac.uk
Brendan Smith, B.A., Ph.D. (Dublin), Reader in Hist. (Med. Brit. & Ireland) [English colony in
medieval Ireland], Brendan.Smith@bristol.ac.uk
James Thompson, B.A. (Oxon.), M.A. (Columbia), Ph.D. (Cantab.), Sen. Lect. in Mod. Brit.
Hist. [Political & intellectual history; popular political economy; visual political culture;
sexualities], James.Thompson@bristol.ac.uk
Ian P. Wei, B.A. (Manc.), Ph.D. (Brist.), Sen. Lect. in Hist. (Med. Eur.) [Intellectuals in
medieval society; university of Paris in 13th c.], Ian.P.Wei@bristol.ac.uk

BRUNEL UNIVERSITY

Uxbridge, Middlesex, UB8 3PH. 01895 274000
www.brunel.ac.uk/sss/politics/
School of Social Sciences: Politics & History
01895 266309. Fax 01895 269786

Alison Carrol, B.A., M.A., Ph.D. (Exeter), Lect. in Eur. Hist. (19th–20th c. Eur.) [Borders &
borderlands; Alsace; politics & identity in France], alison.carrol@brunel.ac.uk
Ingeborg Dornan, B.A. (Warwick), Ph.D. (Cantab.), Lect. in Hist. [18th c. America; women;
families], inge.dornan@brunel.ac.uk
Martin H. Folly, M.A. (Cantab.), Ph.D. (Lond.), Sen. Lect. (Int. Hist.) [International history of
the Cold War; Grand Alliance diplomacy in World War II; Anglo-American relations & the
foundation of N.A.T.O.], martin.folly@brunel.ac.uk
Matthew Hughes, B.A., M.Sc.(Econ.), Ph.D. (Lond.), Prof. (War Stud.) [Modern
military & international history & politics; First World War; Palestine; British Army],
matthew.hughes@brunel.ac.uk
Thomas P. Linehan, B.A. (York), Ph.D. (Lond.), Lect. (20th c. Brit. & Amer.) [British fascism &
British communism], thomas.linehan@brunel.ac.uk
Kenneth Morgan, B.A. (Leicester), D.Phil. (Oxon.), Prof. of Hist. (18th–19th c. Brit., Amer.,
Australia) [British overseas trade & expansion 1650–1850; slavery in the British Caribbean;
early American & Australian history], kenneth.morgan@brunel.ac.uk
Tamson Pietsch, B.A. (Adelaide), M.St., D.Phil. (Oxon.), Lect. (Imp. & Colonial) [Britain & its
empire, 1850–1950; history of universities; history of ideas; global & transnational history],
tamson.pietsch@brunel.ac.uk

Matthew S. Seligmann, M.A. (Edin.), D.Phil. (Sussex), Reader in Hist. [Anglo-German
   relations; the naval race; the origins of World War I], matthew.seligmann@brunel.ac.uk
Astrid Swenson, B.A. (Dijon), M.Phil., Ph.D. (Cantab.), Lect. in Eur. Hist.
   [18th–20th c. heritage & memory, politics & art; European & imperial networks],
   astrid.swenson@brunel.ac.uk
Hannah Whittaker, B.A. (Lond.), M.A. (Dunelm.), Ph.D. (Lond.), Lect. in Hist. [Africa; Kenya &
   Somalia; insurgency & counterinsurgency; banditry], hannah.whittaker@brunel.ac.uk

UNIVERSITY OF **BUCKINGHAM**

Buckingham, MK18 1EG. 01280 814080. Fax 01280 822245
www.buckingham.ac.uk
Department of History

Geoffrey Alderman, M.A., D.Litt., D.Phil. (Oxon.), Michael Gross Prof. of Pol. & Contemp. Hist.
   (19th & 20th c. Brit. & Eur.) [History of British Jewry], geoffrey.alderman@buckingham.ac.uk
*John C. Clarke, M.A., D.Phil. (Oxon.), Prof. of Hist. (18th–19th c. Brit. & Eur.) [S. Northants.
   in 19th c.; causation in history], john.clarke@buckingham.ac.uk
Jane Ridley, M.A., D.Phil. (Oxon.), Reader in Hist. (19th c. Brit. & Eur.) [Disraeli; King Edward
   VII; biography], jane.ridley@buckingham.ac.uk

UNIVERSITY OF **CAMBRIDGE**

01223 337733
Faculty of History West Road, Cambridge, CB3 9EF. 01223 335340. Fax 01223 335968
www.hist.cam.ac.uk
Department of History & Philosophy of Science Free School Lane, Cambridge, CB2 3RH.
01223 334540. Fax 01223 334554
Faculty of Economics Austin Robinson Building, Sidgwick Avenue, Cambridge, CB3 9DD.
01223 335200. Fax 01223 335475
www.econ.cam.ac.uk
History of Population & Social Structure Sir William Hardy Building, Downing Site,
Downing Place, Cambridge, CB2 3EN.
01223 333181. Fax 01223 333183
Faculty of Law 10 West Road, Cambridge, CB3 9DZ.
01223 330033. Fax 01223 330055

Professors
David S.H. Abulafia, M.A., Litt.D. (Cantab.), F.B.A., Gonville & Caius College, Prof.
   of Mediterranean Hist. (Med. & Renaissance Mediterranean) [Economic, social
   & political history of the Mediterranean lands in the middle ages & Renaissance],
   dsa1000@cam.ac.uk
Anthony J. Badger, M.A. (Cantab.), Ph.D. (Hull), Clare College, Paul Mellon Prof. of Amer.
   Hist. & Institutions [American history since 1930], ajb1001@cam.ac.uk

John H. Baker, M.A. (Cantab.), LL.D., Ph.D. (Lond.), F.B.A., St. Catharine's College, Downing Prof. of the Laws of England. [English legal history, esp. in the early modern period; early history of the inns of court; legal manuscripts], jhb16@cam.ac.uk

Alison Bashford, B.A., Ph.D. (Sydney), Jesus College, Vere Harmsworth Prof. of Imp. & Naval Hist.

W. Mary Beard, M.A., Ph.D. (Cantab.), F.B.A., Newnham College, Fac. of Classics, Prof. in Classics (Roman Hist.), mb127@cam.ac.uk

Eugenio F. Biagini, M.A., Ph.D. (S.N.S., Pisa), Sidney Sussex College, Prof. of Mod. & Contemp. Hist. (19th–20th c. Brit. & Eur.) [Britain & Ireland since the 1860s; Italy in the age of the Risorgimento], efb21@cam.ac.uk

M. Christine Carpenter, M.A., Ph.D. (Cantab.), Prof. of Eng. Med. Hist. (Anc. & Med. Hist., Econ., Soc. & Cultural Hist.) [Political, constitutional & social history of England 1200–1500], mcc1000@cam.ac.uk

Christopher M. Clark, B.A. (Sydney), Ph.D. (Cantab.), F.B.A., St. Catharine's College, Prof. of Mod. Eur. Hist. (Mod. Eur.) [Modern Germany, 19th & 20th c.], cmc11@cam.ac.uk

Martin J. Daunton, B.A. (Nott.), M.A., Litt.D. (Cantab.), Ph.D. (Kent), F.B.A., Trinity Hall, Prof. of Econ. Hist. (Mod. Brit. Hist., Econ., Soc. & Cultural Hist.) [Economic & social policy in Britain & its empire & in the U.S. in the 19th–20th c.], mjd42@cam.ac.uk

Eamon Duffy, B.A. (Hull), Ph.D., D.D. (Cantab.), F.B.A., Magdalene College, Prof. of the Hist. of Christianity (Relig. Hist., 15th–17th c. Brit.), ed10000@cam.ac.uk

Richard J. Evans, M.A., D.Phil. (Oxon.), Litt.D. (East Anglia), F.B.A., Wolfson College, Regius Prof. of Hist. [Modern German & European history, esp. social & cultural history, since the mid 19th c.], rje36@cam.ac.uk

John Forrester, M.Phil., Ph.D. (Cantab.), Dept. of Hist. & Phil. of Sc., Prof. of the Hist. & Phil. of Sc. [History & philosophy of psychoanalysis & human sciences]

Nicholas Jardine, M.A., Ph.D. (Cantab.), Darwin College, Prof. of Hist. & Phil. of Sc., Dept. of Hist. & Phil. of Sc. (Hist. & Phil. of Sc., Hist. of Cosmology) [Philosophy of history; history of cosmology; history of natural history], nj103@cam.ac.uk

Rosamond D. McKitterick, B.A. (W. Aust.), Ph.D., Litt.D. (Cantab.), Sidney Sussex College, Prof. of Med. Hist. (Early Med. Eur.) [Transmission of ideas in early middle ages], rdm21@cam.ac.uk

Peter Mandler, B.A. (Oxon.), M.A., Ph.D. (Harv.), Gonville & Caius College, Prof. of Mod. Hist. (Mod. Hist.) [British history since c.1800, esp. cultural, intellectual & social history], pm297@cam.ac.uk

David J.P. Maxwell, B.A. (Manc.), D.Phil. (Oxon.), Emmanuel College, Dixie Prof. of Eccles. Hist. (World Hist.) [Ecclesiastical history; 19th & 20th c. missionary movement; religious movements & politics; history of colonial science], djm223@cam.ac.uk

Michael O'Brien, M.A., Ph.D. (Cantab.), Jesus College, Prof. of Amer. Intellectual Hist. (Amer. Hist.) [19th & 20th c. intellectual culture of the American South; history of American intellectual life since the 17th c.], mo10003@cam.ac.uk

Sheilagh C. Ogilvie, M.A. (St. And. & Chicago), Ph.D. (Cantab.), F.B.A., Fac. of Econ., Prof. of Econ. Hist. (German & Brit. Econ. Hist., 18th–21st c.) [Economic history; historical demography; women's history; serfdom; history of central & eastern Europe], sco2@econ.cam.ac.uk

Jonathan P. Parry, M.A., Ph.D. (Cantab.), Pembroke College, Prof. of Mod. Brit. Hist. (Mod. Brit. Pol. Hist.) [19th c. British politics; Britain & Europe; Britain & the Middle East], jpp3@cam.ac.uk

*David J. Reynolds, M.A., Ph.D. (Cantab.), Christ's College, Prof. of Int. Hist., Fac. Chairman (Int. Rel., Mod. U.S.) [World War II; Cold War], djr17@cam.ac.uk

John C. Robertson, M.A., D.Phil. (Oxon.), Clare College, Prof. of Hist. of Pol. Thought [Political, social & historical thought across the 17th & 18th c.], jcr57@cam.ac.uk

Ulinka C. Rublack, M.A. (Hamburg), Ph.D. (Cantab.), St. John's College, Prof. in Early Mod. Eur. Hist. (Early Mod. Eur. Hist.) [Social, cultural & religious history of Europe in the 16th & 17th c.], ucr10@cam.ac.uk

Jim A. Secord, B.A., Ph.D., Dept. of Hist. & Phil. of Sc., Prof. of Hist. & Phil. of Sc. [Social history of science since 1750; life & earth sciences]

Richard M. Smith, B.A. (Lond.), M.A. (Oxon.), Ph.D. (Cantab.), F.B.A., Downing College, Cambridge Group for the Hist. of Population & Soc. Structure, Prof. of Hist. Geog. & Demography (Hist. of Medicine, Hist. of Demography) [Determinants of longevity & the demographic correlates of welfare systems], rms20@cam.ac.uk

Simon R.S. Szreter, M.A., Ph.D. (Cantab.), St. John's College, Prof. of Hist. & Public Policy (Early Mod. & Mod. Brit. Soc. & Econ. Hist.) [History of demographic, social & economic change in Britain since c.1750; history of international thought in the empirical social sciences & demography], srss@hermes.cam.ac.uk

Robert P. Tombs, M.A., Ph.D. (Cantab.), St. John's College, Prof. of French Hist. (Mod. Eur.) [Modern France; history of Franco-British relations], rpt1000@hermes.cam.ac.uk

Megan A. Vaughan, B.A. (Kent), Ph.D. (Lond.), King's College, Smuts Prof. of C'wealth Hist. [Mauritius in the 18th c.: creation of colonial society & history of slavery; Malawi & Zambia recent history], mav26@cam.ac.uk

Alexandra Walsham, B.A., M.A. (Melb.), Ph.D. (Cantab.), F.B.A., Trinity College, Prof. of Mod. Hist. [Religious & cultural history of the Reformation], amw23@cam.ac.uk

Readers
There are fuller details for some staff under college lists:

Annabel S. Brett, Gonville & Caius College, Reader in the Hist. of Pol. Thought
Joya Chatterji, Trinity College, Reader in S. Asian Hist.
Mark A. Goldie, Churchill College, Reader in Brit. Intellectual Hist.
Tim Harper, Magdalene College, Reader in S.E. Asian & Int. Hist.
Mary R. Laven, Jesus College, Reader
Jon Lawrence, Emmanuel College, Reader
J. Craig Muldrew, Queens' College, Reader in Early Mod. Brit. Soc. & Econ. Hist.
Solomos Solomou, B.Sc., M.Sc. (Lond.), Ph.D. (Cantab.), Fac. of Econ., Reader
Liba Taub, Newnham College, Dept. of Hist. & Phil. of Sc., Reader in Hist. & Phil. of Sc.

University Senior Lecturers and Lecturers
There are fuller details for some staff under college lists:

Andrew Arsan, St. John's College
Julie Barrau, Emmanuel College
Felicitas Becker, Peterhouse
Nora Berend, St. Catharine's College
Christopher Briggs, Selwyn College
Paul R. Cavill, Pembroke College
Leigh Denault, Churchill College
Amy Erickson, Robinson College
Zoe Groves, Peterhouse
Henning Grunwald, Pembroke College
Nick D. Hopwood, Dept. of Hist. & Phil. of Sc.
Sara Horrell, Fac. of Econ., sh111@cam.ac.uk
Joel Isaac, Christ's College
Hubertus F. Jahn, Clare College

Leslie James, Ph.D. (Lond.), Centre of Afric. Stud., Temp. Lect. in World Hist. [Political & intellectual history of Africa & the African diaspora], lej34@cam.ac.uk
Shruti Kapila, Corpus Christi College
Lauren Kassell, Pembroke College, Dept. of Hist. of Phil. & Sc.
Lawrence E. Klein, Emmanuel College
Patrick Lantschner, Gonville & Caius College
Simon Layton, St. Catharine's College
Rachel Leow, Murray Edwards College
*Christopher Meckstroth, Lect. in the Hist. of Pol. Thought, cm753@cam.ac.uk
Natalia Mora-Sitja, Downing College
Renaud Morieux, Jesus College
William O'Reilly, Trinity Hall
Sarah M.S. Pearsall, Robinson College
Sunil Purushotham, Centre of S. Asian Stud., Temp. Lect. in C'wealth Hist., sp536@cam.ac.uk
Andrew Preston, Clare College
Gabriela P. Ramos, Newnham College
Pedro Ramos Pinto, Trinity Hall
Magnus Ryan, Peterhouse
Peter A.V. Sarris, Trinity College
Michael J. Sewell, Selwyn College
Leigh Shaw-Taylor, Dept. of Geog. (Hist. of Population & Soc. Structure) [Social & economic developments in England between the mid 16th & late 19th c., esp. the development of agrarian capitalism & the Industrial Revolution], lmws2@cam.ac.uk
Sujit P. Sivasundaram, Gonville & Caius College
Emma Spary, Corpus Christi College
Geraint Thomas, Emmanuel College
Hester Vaizey, Clare College
Carl S. Watkins, Magdalene College
Ruth I. Watson, Clare College
M. Teresa J. Webber, Trinity College

Christ's College CB2 3BU. 01223 334900. Fax 01223 334967
Sarah Howard, M.A., M.Phil., Ph.D. (Cantab.), Fellow & College Lect., Director of Stud. in Hist. [Social & cultural history of post-World War II France & the Algerian war], sfh22@cam.ac.uk
Joel Isaac, B.A., M.A. (Lond.), Ph.D. (Cantab.), Lect. (Hist. of Mod. Pol. Thought) [American history; political thought & intellectual history; cultural history of the Cold War], jti20@cam.ac.uk

Churchill College CB3 0DS. 01223 336000. Fax 01223 336180
Piers Brendon, M.A. (Cantab.), Ph.D. (Kent), Fellow (Mod. Brit.), pb204@cam.ac.uk
Leigh T. Denault, B.A. (Mt. Holyoke Coll., Mass.), Ph.D. (Cantab.), Fellow & Director of Stud., Hist. (Mod. S. Asia, Digital Humanities in/re India) [History of education & the family], ltd22@cam.ac.uk
Mark A. Goldie, M.A., Ph.D. (Cantab.), Fellow (Pol. Thought, Early Mod. Brit.) [Restoration political thought; John Locke], mag1010@cam.ac.uk
Allen G. Packwood, B.A. (Nott.), M.Phil. (Cantab.), Fellow & Director, Churchill Archives Centre (20th c. Brit.), agp20@cam.ac.uk
Richard J. Partington, M.A. (Cantab.), Fellow & Sen. Tutor (Med. Eng.) [Late medieval English politics, esp. Edward III; war & the maintenance of order], rjp1001@cam.ac.uk

Alice Reid, B.A. (Oxon.), M.Sc. (Lond.), Ph.D.. (Cantab.), Fellow & Director of Stud. in Geog. (Hist. Demography) [Child health & mortality in 19th & 20th c. Britain], amr1001@cam.ac.uk

Clare College CB2 1TL. 01223 333200. Fax 01223 333219
Hubertus F. Jahn, M.A. (Munich), Ph.D. (Georgetown), Dr.phil.habil. (Erlangen), Sen. Lect. (Russian Hist.) [Russian social & cultural history], hfj21@cam.ac.uk
Andrew Preston, Sen. Lect. in Amer. Hist. (Amer. Hist.) [History of American foreign relations], amp33@cam.ac.uk
Hester Vaizey, Director of Stud. & Fellow (Mod. German Hist.), hlv20@cam.ac.uk
Ruth I. Watson, B.A. (Melb.), D.Phil. (Oxon.), Lect. [Social & cultural history of colonial West Africa, esp. 19th–20th c. Nigeria], riw21@cam.ac.uk

Corpus Christi College CB2 1RH. 01223 338000. Fax 01223 338061
Shruti Kapila (Pol. Thought & Intellectual Hist., World Hist.) [Political thought & intellectual history; world history], sk555@cam.ac.uk
Emma Spary, B.A., M.A., Ph.D. (Cantab.), (Hist. of 18th c. Medicine) [Health; nutrition; medical chemistry; the Parisian corporations; the French food & drugs trade]

Downing College CB2 1DQ. 01223 334800. Fax 01223 467934
Paul C. Millett, M.A., Ph.D. (Cantab.), Fellow & Director of Stud. in Classics (Econ. & Soc. Hist.) [Ancient Greece], pcm1000@cam.ac.uk
Natalia Mora-Sitja, B.Sc., M.A. (Barcelona), M.Sc. (Oxon.), Fellow (Econ. Hist.) [Economic growth & labour markets], nm371@cam.ac.uk
David R. Pratt, M.A., Ph.D. (Cantab.), Fellow & Director of Stud. in Hist. [Political thought & court culture of the early middle ages], drp14@cam.ac.uk

Emmanuel College CB2 3AP. 01223 334200. Fax 01223 334426
Julie Barrau, Ph.D. (Paris), Fellow [British Medieval political history], jb534@cam.ac.uk
Lawrence E. Klein, B.A. (Rochester), M.A., Ph.D. (Johns Hopkins), Fellow [18th c. British cultural history], lek26@cam.ac.uk
Jon Lawrence, M.A., Ph.D. (Cantab.), Fellow (19th–20th c. Brit.) [Popular politics & role of party in U.K.; social class in U.K.], jml55@cam.ac.uk
Geraint Thomas, Ph.D. (Camb.), Fellow [British modern political history], glt22@cam.ac.uk
Elisabeth M.C. van Houts, M.A., Litt.D. (Cantab.), Ph.D. (Groningen), Fellow, Reader & Hon. Prof. (Med. Eur.) [Medieval historiography 800–1200; Anglo-Norman history; history of gender], emcv2@cam.ac.uk

Fitzwilliam College CB3 0DG. 01223 332000. Fax 01223 464162
Sir James Holt, M.A., D.Phil. (Oxon.), D.Litt. (Nott.), Litt.D. (Read.), F.B.A., Hon. Fellow & Emeritus Prof. (Med. Eng.)
Rosemary E. Horrox, M.A., Ph.D. (Cantab.), Fellow & Director of Stud. (Med. Eng.) [Medieval royal court; relationship of central & local government], reh37@cam.ac.uk
David M. Thompson, M.A., Ph.D., B.D. (Cantab.), Emeritus Prof. of Mod. Church Hist., Fac. of Div. (Mod. Brit., esp. Eccles. Hist.) [Church, state & society in Britain, Europe & N. America since 1800], dmt3@cam.ac.uk

Girton College CB3 0JG. 01223 338999. Fax 01223 338896
Benjamin J. Griffin, M.A., M.Phil., Ph.D. (Cantab.), Fellow & Lect. (19th–20th c. Brit. Hist.) [Political history; masculinity; feminism], bjg22@cam.ac.uk

Alastair J. Reid, M.A., Ph.D. (Cantab.), Fellow & Lect. (Mod. Brit.) [Trade unions; popular radicalism & counter-cultures], ajr49@cam.ac.uk

Samantha Williams, B.A. (Lancaster), M.Sc., Ph.D., Fellow & Lect. (18th & 19th c. Brit. Hist.) [Poverty; gender; social history], skw30@cam.ac.uk

Gonville & Caius College CB2 1TA. 01223 332400. Fax 01223 332456

Andrew G. Bell, M.St., M.A., D.Phil. (Oxon.), Fellow, Admissions Tutor & Director of Stud. in Anglo-Saxon, Norse & Celtic (Anc. & Med. Hist.) [Ancient & medieval history], agb38@cam.ac.uk

Annabel S. Brett, M.A., Ph.D. (Cantab.), Fellow (Hist. of Pol. Thought) [Medieval & early modern political thought, esp. 16th c. Spain & natural law tradition], asb21@cam.ac.uk

*Melissa T. Calaresu, B.A. (Huron Coll., W. Ont.), M.A. (Queen's, Ont.), Ph.D. (Cantab.), Fellow & Director of Stud. (Part I) (18th c. Eur. Intellectual & Cultural Hist.) [Italy, esp. Naples; Enlightenment; Grand Tour], mtc12@cam.ac.uk

Emma Hunter, M.A., M.Phil., Ph.D. (Cantab.), Fellow & Director of Stud. (Part II) (World Hist.) [Modern African history & global history, esp. political & intellectual history of East Africa], elh35@cam.ac.uk

Patrick Lantschner, Bye-Fellow (Med. Eur. Hist.), pl394@cam.ac.uk

Ruth G. Scurr, M.A. (Oxon.), Ph.D. (Cantab.), Fellow, Assistant Director of Stud., Graduate Tutor [18th c. political thought; French Revolution], re10032@cam.ac.uk

Sujit P. Sivasundaram, M.A., M.Phil., Ph.D. (Cantab.), Fellow & Tutor (World & Imp. Hist., esp. 18th & 19th c.) [History of Pacific, S. & S.E. Asia; global history of science, medicine, archaeology, culture, Buddhism & Christianity], sps20@cam.ac.uk

Joachim Whaley, M.A., Ph.D. (Cantab.), Fellow [German history, thought & culture from 1500 to the present day], jw10005@cam.ac.uk

Homerton College CB2 2PH. 01223 507111. Fax 01223 507120

David I. Black, B.Mus., M.A., Ph.D. (Harv.), Junior Res. Fellow [J.S. Bach; Mozart; sources; compositional process]

Peter J. Cunningham, M.A. (Cantab. & East Anglia), Ph.D. (Leeds), Sen. Res. Fellow (Hist. of Educ.) [Oral history of teachers; teacher training; professional identity], pjc36@cam.ac.uk

William H. Foster, B.A. (Penn.), M.A. (Smith), M.A., Ph.D. (Cornell), Fellow, Director of Stud. for Hist. & College Lect. (American Hist.) [American history, esp. slavery, gender, early modern frontiers], whf21@cam.ac.uk

Katharine B. Pretty, M.A., Ph.D. (Cantab.), Principal [Archaeology & history of N.W. Europe, esp. early Christian; Vikings], kp10002@cam.ac.uk

Peter M. Warner, Ph.D. (Leicester), Dean (Archaeol. & Med. Hist., 17th c. East Anglia) [Landscape archaeology; origins of the shire; Suffolk], pmw21@cam.ac.uk

Hughes Hall CB1 2EW. 01223 334898. Fax 01223 311179

Michael J. Franklin, M.A., Ph.D. (Cantab.), Fellow & Director of Stud. in Hist. & in Anglo-Saxon, Norse & Celtic [Medieval ecclesiastical history], mjf3@cam.ac.uk

Jesus College CB5 8BL. 01223 339339. Fax 01223 324910

Mary R. Laven, B.A., Ph.D. (Leicester), Reader in Hist. (Early Mod. Hist.) [Social & cultural history of early modern Italy & Europe esp. religion, gender, sociability & material culture], mrl25@cam.ac.uk

Renaud Morieux, Ph.D. (Lille), Lect. (Brit. Hist.) [18th c. British & French history: migrations; borders; maritime spaces; war captivity; trade; interest groups], rm656@cam.ac.uk

King's College CB2 1ST. 01223 331100. Fax 01223 331315
Michael Sonenscher, B.A., Ph.D. (Warwick), Fellow & Director of Stud. (Mod. Eur.) [French
History c.1650–1848; history of political thought, particularly in France; origins of political
economy, social science, anthropology], ms138@cam.ac.uk

Lucy Cavendish College CB3 0BU. 01223 332190. Fax 01223 332178
Anna B. Sapir Abulafia, M.A., Ph.D. (Amsterdam), College Lect. in Hist. & Director of Stud.
(Anc. & Med. Hist. & Hist. of Pol. Thought) [12th & 13th c. intellectual history; medieval
Jewish-Christian relations], asa1001@cam.ac.uk
Helen Roche, M.Phil., Ph.D. (Cantab.), Res. Fellow (Mod. Eur. Hist.) [Impact of philhellenism
on politics & diplomacy during the Third Reich], hber2@cam.ac.uk

Magdalene College CB3 0AG. 01223 332100. Fax 01223 363637
Gareth Atkins, M.A., Ph.D. (Cantab.), Fellow (Mod. Brit. Hist.) [18th & 19th c. British history;
religion, politics & political networks; religious culture; representations of the Navy & naval
heroes], ga240@cam.ac.uk
Tim Harper, M.A., Ph.D. (Cantab.), Fellow (World Hist.) [World history; Mod. S.E. Asian hist.],
tnh1000@cam.ac.uk
Ronald Hyam, M.A., Ph.D., Litt.D. (Cantab.), Emeritus Fellow [British empire; decolonisation]
Carl S. Watkins, M.A., Ph.D. (Cantab.), Fellow (Med. Hist.) [Medieval religious history, esp.
popular religion in England], csw14@cam.ac.uk

Murray Edwards College CB3 0DF. 01223 351721. Fax 01223 352941
Kate Peters, M.A., Ph.D. (Cantab.), Fellow & Director of Stud. in Hist. [Early modern British
history; print culture & Quakers in the 1650s], mkp30@cam.ac.uk

Newnham College CB3 9DF. 01223 335700. Fax 01223 359155/357898
*D'Maris Coffman, B.Sc., M.A. (Penn.), M.A. (Cantab.), Ph.D. (Penn.), Res. Fellow & Director
of the Centre for Financial Hist. (Early Mod. Hist., Econ., Soc. & Cultural Hist.) [Early
modern public finance; state formation; economic history], ddc22@cam.ac.uk
Kate Fleet, B.A., Ph.D. (Lond.), Fellow & Director of Skilliter Centre in Ottoman Hist. (Turkish
Hist.) [Ottoman & early Turkish Republican social & economic history], khf11@cam.ac.uk
Bianca Gardenz, M.A. (Florence), M.Phil., Ph.D. (Cantab.), Res. Fellow (Mod. Eur.)
[Comparative fascisms; Italy; Germany; women], bg265@cam.ac.uk
Gabriela P. Ramos, B.A. (Lima), M.A. (Columbia), Ph.D. (Penn.), Fellow & College Lect. in
Hist. (Latin Amer. Hist.) ['Colonial', religious & political history], gr266@cam.ac.uk
Joyce M. Reynolds, M.A. (Oxon. & Cantab.), D.Litt. (Newcastle), F.B.A., Hon. Fellow (Roman
Hist.) [Epigraphy of Hellenistic & Roman periods in N. Africa & Turkey], jmr38@cam.ac.uk
Gillian R. Sutherland, M.A. (Oxon. & Cantab.), D.Phil. (Oxon.), Ph.D. (Cantab.), Fellow
Emerita (Mod. Brit.) [Higher education of women; constructions of childhood literacy],
gs10012@cam.ac.uk
Liba Taub, B.A. (Tulane), M.A. (Chicago), Ph.D. (Oklahoma), Director of Stud. in Hist. & Phil.
of Sc. [History of scientific instruments; early science & astronomy], lct1001@cam.ac.uk

Pembroke College CB2 1RF. 01223 338100. Fax 01223 338163
Caroline Burt, M.A., M.Phil., Ph.D. (Cantab.), College Lect. in Hist. (High & Late Med. Pol. &
Soc. Hist.) [Edward I & II; English governance; political ideas], cb237@cam.ac.uk
Paul R. Cavill, M.A., M.St., D.Phil. (Oxon.), University Lect. in Hist. (Early Mod. Brit. Hist.)
[Early & mid Tudor political history], pc504@cam.ac.uk
Henning Grunwald, M.A., Ph.D. (Cantab.), Fellow (Mod. Eur. Hist.) [Memory studies; Weimar
Germany; political theatre history], eheg2@cam.ac.uk

Lauren Kassell, B.A., D.Phil. (Oxon.), Fellow in Hist. of Sc. [Alchemy & medicine in early modern England]

Siân Pooley, M.A., M.Phil., Ph.D. (Cantab.), Fellow (19th–20th c. Brit. Soc., Cultural & Econ. Hist.) [Family; childhood; welfare; identity], skp30@cam.ac.uk

Katharina Rietzler, Diplom-Kulturwirt (Passau), M.A., Ph.D. (Lond.), Bye-Fellow (Amer. Hist.) [20th c. international history; transnational history; philanthropy; conceptions of world order], ker34@cam.ac.uk

Peterhouse CB2 1RD. 01223 338200. Fax 01223 337578

John S.A. Adamson, B.A. (Melb.), Ph.D. (Cantab.), Fellow (16th–17th c. Eng. & Eur.) [Political & cultural history of early modern Britain & Europe], ja29@cam.ac.uk

Felicitas Becker, M.A. (Lond.), Ph.D. (Cantab.), Fellow (Mod. Afric.) [Islam in E. Africa; colonial & post-colonial politics]

Martin S. Golding, M.A. (Cantab.), Fellow (Mod. Intellectual Hist.) [Recollection of childhood & art in England 19th–20th c.], msg1004@cam.ac.uk

Scott H. Mandelbrote, M.A. (Oxon.), Fellow (17th–18th c.) [Early modern British & European intellectual history, esp. the history of scholarship & the history of science], shm24@cam.ac.uk

Zoe Groves, B.A., M.Res., Ph.D. (Keele), Sen. Res. Assoc. (Afric.)

Magnus Ryan, M.A., Ph.D. (Cantab.), Fellow (Anc. & Med. Hist., Pol. Thought, Int. Hist.) [History of medieval political ideas; legal history; medieval politics], mjr28@cam.ac.uk

Brendan P. Simms, B.A. (Dublin), Ph.D. (Cantab.), Fellow (18th–20th c. Eur.) [British foreign policy 1690–1815; neo-conservatism; Prussian geopolitics, 1701–1871; European geopolitics, 1453–2009], bps11@cam.ac.uk

Queens' College CB3 9ET. 01223 335511. Fax 01223 335566

Rebekah Clements, B.A. (A.N.U.), M.A. (Waseda), Ph.D. (Cantab.), Res. Fellow [East Asian history; early modern Japan], rec55@cam.ac.uk

J. Craig Muldrew, B.A., M.A. (Alberta), Ph.D. (Cantab.), (Early Mod. Brit. Econ. & Soc. Hist.) [Credit; food], jcm11@cam.ac.uk

Richard A.W. Rex, M.A., Ph.D. (Cantab.), Fellow & Director of Stud. (Early Mod. Brit. & Eur. Hist., esp. Relig. & Intellectual) [Henry VIII; Lollardy; Renaissance humanism; Reformation theology], rawr1@cam.ac.uk

Andrew C. Thompson, M.A., M.Phil., Ph.D. (Cantab.), Fellow (18th & 19th c. Brit & Eur. Hist.) [Hanoverian monarchy; international Protestantism; international relations], act25@cam.ac.uk

Robinson College CB3 9AN. 01223 339100. Fax 01223 351794

Martin Brett, M.A., D.Phil. (Oxon.), Emeritus Fellow (10th–13th c. Brit. & Eur.) [Canon law in Britain & Europe; diplomatic], mb110@cam.ac.uk

Peter Newman Brooks, M.A., Ph.D. (Cantab.), Emeritus Fellow (Reformation)

Amy L. Erickson, B.A. (Calif. at Berkeley), Ph.D. (Cantab.), Fellow [Early modern economic history], ale25@cam.ac.uk

Sarah M.S. Pearsall, B.A. (Yale), M.A. (Cantab.), M.A., Ph.D. (Harv.), Fellow (U.S.) [History of N. America in the early modern era], smsp100@cam.ac.uk

Mikulas Teich, M.A., Ph.D. (Leeds), Emeritus Fellow (16th–20th c. Hist. of Sc.)

Deborah Thom, M.A., Ph.D. (C.N.A.A.), Fellow & Director of Stud., Hist. & Soc. & Pol. Sc. (20th c. Brit. Soc. & Econ. Hist.) [Psychology & punishment of children in 20th c.], dt111@cam.ac.uk

David Woodman, M.A., Ph.D. (Cantab.), Fellow & Director of Stud., Hist. & Soc. (10th–12th c. Eng.) [Charters & chronicles]

St. Catharine's College CB2 1RL. 01223 338300. Fax 01223 338340
Nora Berend, B.A. (L. Eötvös), M.A. (Paris), Ph.D. (Columbia), Fellow & Director of Stud.,
Hist. (Med. Eur.) [Social & religious history; frontier societies; cultural interaction; medieval
Hungary], nb213@cam.ac.uk
Simon Layton (World Hist.) [Piracy, Indian Ocean, British empire], sl501@cam.ac.uk

St. John's College CB2 1TP. 01223 338600. Fax 01223 337720
Andrew K. Arsan, M.A., Ph.D. (Cantab.), Fellow & Director of Stud. & Lect. (Mid. E.) [Middle
Eastern & world history], aka25@cam.ac.uk
John Iliffe, M.A., Ph.D., Litt.D. (Cantab.), Fellow, Supervisor & Emeritus Prof. (Afric. Hist.)
[African History]
Peter A. Linehan, M.A., Ph.D. (Cantab.), F.B.A., Fellow (Med. Eur.) [History of medieval Spain
& Portugal; history of medieval canon law], pal35@cam.ac.uk
Mark Nichols, M.A., Ph.D. (Cantab.), Fellow, Tutor, Supervisor & Librarian (Early Mod. Brit.)
[Elizabeth & early Stuart govt. & politics; conspiracies; treason trials; Sir Walter Raleigh;
history of the British Empire], amn1000@cam.ac.uk
Sylvana P. Tomaselli, B.A. (Brit. Col.), M.A. (York, Canada & Cantab.), Fellow & Sir Harry
Hinsley Lect. (Pol. Thought) [History, social & political sciences; Enlightenment political
theory & conjectural history], st240@cam.ac.uk

Selwyn College CB3 9DQ. 01223 335846. Fax 01223 335837
Christopher Briggs, B.A. (Oxon.), Ph.D. (Cantab.), University Lect. (Med. Brit. Soc. & Econ.
Hist.) [Society, economy & law in England & Europe 1200–1500], cdb23@cam.ac.uk
Eoin Devlin, B.A. (N.U.I.), M.A. (Dublin), M.Phil., Ph.D. (Cantab.), British Academy Fellow
[Early modern cultural, religious & political history in Britain & Europe, esp. Baroque
culture, social interaction & confessional identities in the late 17th & early 18th c.],
eld31@cam.ac.uk
Michael J. Sewell, M.A., Ph.D. (Cantab.), Fellow, Director of Stud. in Hist., Tutor & Admissions
Tutor (Arts) (Mod. Amer., Int. Rel.) [History of U.S. foreign relations & the international
history of the Cold War], mjs1001@cam.ac.uk
David L. Smith, M.A., Ph.D. (Cantab.), Fellow, College Lect. & Director of Stud. in Hist. (Early
Mod. Brit. Hist.) [British political, constitutional & legal history in the early modern period,
esp. 17th c.; history of Parliament; monarchy & royalism; the career of Oliver Cromwell],
dls10@cam.ac.uk

Sidney Sussex College CB2 3HU. 01223 338800. Fax 01223 338884
Derek E.D. Beales, M.A., Ph.D. (Cantab.), F.B.A., Fellow & Emeritus Prof. (Mod. Brit. & Eur.)
[Joseph II; Enlightened absolutism; secularisation & monasteries 18th–19th c.; music in
society], deb1000@cam.ac.uk
Helen R. Castor, M.A., Ph.D. (Cantab.), Fellow (Med. Eng.) [Politics, governance & political
society in later medieval England], hrc12@cam.ac.uk

Trinity College CB2 1TQ. 01223 338400. Fax 01223 338564
Joya Chatterji, M.A., Ph.D. (Cantab.), Fellow (Mod. Extra-Eur. Hist.) [History of S. Asia;
decolonisation; migration & diaspora], jc280@cam.ac.uk
Simon D. Keynes, M.A., Ph.D. (Cantab.), Elrington & Bosworth Prof. of Anglo-Saxon
(5th–11th c. Brit.) [Anglo-Saxon history], sdk13@cam.ac.uk
Sachiko Kusukawa, M.Phil., Ph.D. (Cantab.), Fellow (Early Mod. Hist.) [History of science
1450–1750; cultural & intellectual history; history of the book], sk111@cam.ac.uk
Peter A.V. Sarris, M.A., D.Phil. (Oxon.), Fellow (Early Med. Hist.) [Late Roman history;
Byzantine history; early medieval social, economic & legal history], pavs2@cam.ac.uk

Richard W. Serjeantson, B.A. (York), Ph.D. (Cantab.), Fellow (Early Mod. Intellectual Hist.)
[History of political thought; history of scholarship; history of the sciences; Francis Bacon],
rws1001@cam.ac.uk
M. Teresa J. Webber, M.A. (Oxon. & Lond.), D.Phil. (Oxon.), Fellow (Med. Palaeography)
[Medieval libraries & book production], mtjw2@cam.ac.uk

Trinity Hall CB2 1TJ. 01223 332500. Fax 01223 332537
J. Clare L. Jackson, M.A. (Cantab.), M.Phil. (Wales), Ph.D. (Cantab.), Staff Fellow & Director
of Stud. (17th c. Brit.) [History of ideas in early modern Britain, esp. Scotland; legal history;
politics of the Stuart multiple monarchy], jclj1@cam.ac.uk
William O'Reilly, B.A. (N.U.I.), M.St., D.Phil. (Oxon.), Staff Fellow (Early Mod. Eur.) [Early
modern Habsburg Europe; Spanish-Austrian relations; history of migration, colonialism &
imperialism; Atlantic history], wto21@cam.ac.uk
Pedro Ramos Pinto, B.A., M.Phil., Ph.D. (Cantab.), Staff Fellow (Int. Econ. Hist.) [Modern
European history; economic history; social movements; history of welfare; social
citizenship; history of inequality], prr211@cam.ac.uk
John F. Pollard, M.A. (Cantab.), Ph.D. (Read.), Staff Fellow (19th–20th c. Eur. Hist.)
[History of modern Italy & the papacy, esp. its diplomatic & financial aspects; European
fascist & present-day neo-Nazi movements; social & political Catholicism in Europe],
jfp32@cam.ac.uk

Wolfson College CB3 9BB. 01223 335900. Fax 01223 335908
Marguerite W. Duprée, M.A., Ph.D. (Cantab.), Fellow [Medical profession; Scottish hydros;
urban social welfare; family; cotton industry], mdupree@arts.gla.ac.uk
Charles A. Jones, Ph.D. (Cantab.), Fellow (Int. Hist.) [Civil-military relations],
caj26@cam.ac.uk
Marie B. Lovatt, Ph.D. (Cantab.), Fellow & Tutor (Med. Eng. Eccles. Hist.), mbl20@cam.ac.uk
Susan Oosthuizen, Ph.D. (Cantab.), Fellow (Landscape Hist.), smo23@cam.ac.uk
Christina Skott, Ph.D. (Cantab.), Fellow (18th c.) [Southeast Asia, esp. the Malay world; early
modern European expansion in Asia; cultural & scientific exchanges between Europe &
Southeast Asia; colonial agriculture], mcg27@cam.ac.uk

CANTERBURY CHRIST CHURCH UNIVERSITY

North Holmes Road, Canterbury, Kent, CT1 1QU. 01227 767700. Fax 01227 470442
www.canterbury.ac.uk
Department of History & American Studies

John M. Bulaitis, B.A., M.A., Ph.D. (Lond.), Sen. Lect. (19th–20th c. Eur.) [20th c. France;
history of the French Communist party], John.Bulaitis@canterbury.ac.uk
Paul Dalton, B.A., Ph.D. (Sheff.), Princ. Lect. (Med. Eng. & Eur.) [Political, social &
ecclesiastical history of England & Normandy 11th–12th c.]
Jacqueline S. Eales, B.A., Ph.D. (Lond.), Prof. (Local Hist., 17th c. Soc. & Pol.) [Kent & the
English civil wars, 1640–60], Jackie.Eales@canterbury.ac.uk
Thomas W. Hennessey, B.A. (Surrey), M.A., Ph.D. (Belf.), Prof. (19th–20th c. Brit. & Irish
Hist.) [Conflict in Ireland, 1886–1998], Thomas.Hennessey@canterbury.ac.uk
*Stephen A. Hipkin, B.A. (Kent), D.Phil. (Oxon.), Head of Dept. (16th–17th c. Soc. Hist.)
[Crime, custom & conflict in Kent 1550–1750], Stephen.Hipkin@canterbury.ac.uk

David J. Hitchcock, B.A., M.A. (Ottawa), Ph.D. (Warwick), Lect. (16th–18th c. Eur.) [Social & cultural history of vagrancy in early modern England], David.Hitchcock@canterbury.ac.uk
Stephen J.K. Long, B.A., M.Phil., Ph.D. (Birm.), Sen. Lect. (20th c. U.S. Foreign Policy) [The C.I.A., covert operations & U.S. policy in the Cold War, 1945–60], Steve.Long@canterbury.ac.uk
Lydia J. Plath, B.A., M.A., Ph.D. (Warwick), Sen. Lect. (19th–20th c. U.S.) [History of slavery, race & racial violence], Lydia.Plath@canterbury.ac.uk
Kevin J. Ruane, B.A., Ph.D. (Kent), Prof. (20th c. U.S. Foreign Policy) [Anglo-American relations & the Cold War in S.E. Asia 1945–60], Kevin.Ruane@canterbury.ac.uk
Louise J. Wilkinson, M.A., Ph.D. (Lond.), Lect. (Med. Eng. & Eur.) [Women & gender in 13th c. England & Wales], Louise.Wilkinson@canterbury.ac.uk
Nick Witham, B.A., M.Res., Ph.D. (Nott.), Sen. Lect. (20th c. U.S. Soc. & Cultural Hist.) [Popular protest & dissent; historiography & memory studies], Nick.Witham@canterbury.ac.uk
Sara J. Wolfson, B.A., M.A., Ph.D. (Dunelm.), Lect. (Early Mod. Brit. & Eur.) [Gender, court & political history in 17th c. Britain & Europe], Sara.Wolfson@canterbury.ac.uk

CARDIFF UNIVERSITY

Cardiff, CF10 3XU. 029 2087 4000
www.cardiff.ac.uk
Cardiff School of History, Archaeology & Religion
John Percival Building, Colum Drive, Cardiff, CF10 3EU. 029 2087 4259. Fax 029 2087 4929
www.cardiff.ac.uk/share/
History & Welsh History 029 2087 4313. **Ancient History** 029 2087 4821
Archaeology 029 2087 4470
Cardiff Business School
Aberconway Building, Colum Drive, Cardiff, CF10 3EU. 029 2087 4256. Fax 029 2087 4419
Cardiff Centre for Lifelong Learning
Senghennydd Road, Cardiff, CF24 4AG. 029 2087 4831. Fax 029 2066 8935
www.cardiff.ac.uk/learn/
Cardiff School of European Studies
65–68 Park Place, Cardiff, CF10 3YQ. 029 2087 4889. Fax 029 2087 4946
Welsh School of Architecture
Bute Building, Cardiff, CF10 3NB. 029 2087 4430. Fax 029 2087 4926

Padma J. Anagol, B.A. (Mysore), M.A., M.Phil. (Delhi), Ph.D. (Lond.), Sen. Lect. in Mod. Hist. (Mod. Asia, Gender Hist.) [Gender & women's history], anagol@cardiff.ac.uk
*Nicholas J. Baker-Brian, M.A., Ph.D. (Wales), Sen. Lect. in Anc. Hist., Head of Rel. Stud. (Later Roman Empire, Early Med. Stud.) [Latin & Greek Patristic texts; Manichaeism; early medieval Ireland & Wales], baker-briannj1@cardiff.ac.uk
Jenny Benham, B.A., M.A., Ph.D. (East Anglia), Lect. in Med. Hist. (Int. Rel. & Diplomacy, c.900–1250, Eng. Legal Codes) [Peacemaking in the middle ages; law, treaties & international relations], benhamj@cardiff.ac.uk
Gerrit-Jan Berendse, B.A., M.A., D.Phil. (Utrecht), Prof. of Mod. Eur. Literature & Culture, Sch. of Eur. Stud. (20th c. Culture) [East German culture; political violence in literature & visual arts], berendsegj@cardiff.ac.uk

Cardiff

David E.G. Boucher, B.A. (Wales), M.Sc. (Lond.), Ph.D. (Liv.), Prof. in Eur. Stud., Sch. of Eur. Stud. (Pol. Phil.) [History of natural/human rights; British idealism; methodology], boucherde@cardiff.ac.uk

Lloyd Bowen, B.A. (Exeter), M.A., Ph.D. (Wales), Sen. Lect. in Welsh Hist. (Early Mod. Wales) [Civil war; Wales & the British state], bowenl@cardiff.ac.uk

Trevor Boyns, B.Sc. (Warwick), Ph.D. (Wales), Prof. in Business Hist., Business Sch. (Business Hist.), boyns@cardiff.ac.uk

Guy J. Bradley, B.A., M.A., Ph.D. (Lond.), Sen. Lect. in Anc. Hist. [Italy in the 1st millennium B.C.; Roman history in the monarchic & republican periods], bradleygj@cardiff.ac.uk

David J. Broughton, B.A. (Sussex), M.Sc. (Strathclyde), Ph.D. (Essex), Sen. Lect. in Pol., Sch. of Eur. Stud. (20th c. Brit.) [British parties & elections; European politics], broughton@cardiff.ac.uk

Augustine Casiday, B.A., B.Sc. (Alabama), M.A. (Washington in St. Louis), Ph.D. (Dunelm.), Lect. [History of monasticism; early Christian thought; history of theology; history of ideas], casidaya@cardiff.ac.uk

Alistair M. Cole, B.Sc.(Econ.) (Lond.), D.Phil. (Oxon.), Prof. in Eur. Stud., Sch. of Eur. Stud. (French Pol.) [Politics & contemporary history of France], colea@cardiff.ac.uk

Max Deeg, Dr.phil., Dr.phil.habil (Vienna), Prof. of Buddhist Stud. [History of Buddhism in India, Central Asia & China], deegm1@cardiff.ac.uk

Mark P. Donovan, B.A. (C.N.A.A. & Open), M.Sc., Ph.D. (Lond.), Sen. Lect. in Pol., Sch. of Eur. Stud. (20th c. Italy) [Italian party system; political parties; electoral reform & referendum], donovan@cardiff.ac.uk

Peter Dorey, B.A. (Sussex), M.A. (Leeds), Ph.D. (Hull), Reader in Pol., Sch. of Eur. Stud. (20th c. Brit.) [British politics since 1945], dorey@cardiff.ac.uk

Andrew Dowling, B.A. (Kent), M.A. (Lond.), Ph.D. (Southampton), Lect. in Hispanic Stud., Sch. of Eur. Stud. (Mod. Spain) [Catalan nationalism], dowlinga@cardiff.ac.uk

Kenneth H.F. Dyson, B.Sc.(Econ.), M.Sc.(Econ.) (Lond.), Ph.D. (Liv.), F.B.A., Res. Prof. in Eur. Stud., Sch. of Eur. Stud. (Eur. Pol.) [Politics of E.U.; politics of the euro; Germany & Europe], dysonkh@cardiff.ac.uk

Peter W. Edbury, M.A., Ph.D. (St. And.), Prof. in Med. Hist. (Med. Brit. & Eur., Crusades) [Crusades & Latin East], edbury@cardiff.ac.uk

Heiko M. Feldner, Diplom (Halle-Wittenberg), Sen. Lect. in Mod. German Hist., Sch. of Eur. Stud. (Mod. Germany) [Intellectual history; historiography & theory], feldnerhm@cardiff.ac.uk

Federica Ferlanti, M.Phil. (Cantab.), Ph.D. (Cagliari), Lect. in Chinese Hist. [19th & 20th c. Chinese history], ferlantif@cardiff.ac.uk

*Paul Furlong, Ph.L. (Gregoriana), M.A. (Oxon.), Ph.D. (Read.), Prof. of Eur. Stud., Head of Sch. of Eur. Stud. (Italian Pol.) [Politics & contemporary history of Italy], furlongp@cardiff.ac.uk

Kate M. Gilliver, B.A., Ph.D. (Lond.), Sen. Lect. in Anc. Hist. (Rome) [Roman warfare; atrocities in Roman warfare], gilliverk@cardiff.ac.uk

Claire J. Gorrara, B.A. (Leeds), M.St., D.Phil. (Oxon.), Prof. in French, Sch. of Eur. Stud. (French Literature, Feminist Theory) [World War II & women's writing, memory & identity; Occupation of France; film], gorrara@cardiff.ac.uk

Peter Guest, B.A., Ph.D. (Lond.), Sen. Lect. in Archaeol. (Roman World) [Roman Britain; numismatics; later Roman empire; impact of Roman customs on indigenous societies], guestp@cardiff.ac.uk

Bruce A. Haddock, B.A. (Leicester), D.Phil. (Oxon.), Prof. in Mod. Eur. Soc. & Pol. Thought, Sch. of Eur. Stud. (Pol. Thought) [Modern European federal theory; politics & culture in Italy & Romania], haddockba@cardiff.ac.uk

David L. Hanley, M.A. (Oxon.), Ph.D. (Warwick), Prof. in Pol., Sch. of Eur. Stud. (Mod. France) [Political parties in modern France; development of transnational parties], hanleydl@cardiff.ac.uk

James Hegarty, M.A., Ph.D. (Manc.), Sen. Lect. in Indian Relig. [Indian cultural history; philology], hegartyj@cardiff.ac.uk

John Hines, M.A., D.Phil. (Oxon.), Prof. in Med. Stud. (Early Med. Brit. & Eur.) [Interrelationship of ethnic, political, linguistic & cultural change], hines@cardiff.ac.uk

William D. Jones, B.A., Ph.D. (Wales), Prof. of Mod. Hist. (19th–20th c. Brit. & Wales) [Welsh migrant communities in U.S. & Australia], joneswd@cardiff.ac.uk

Bronach Kane, B.A., M.A., Ph.D. (York), Lect. in Med. Hist. (Cultural & Soc. Hist. of Late Med. England, Gender Relations, Concepts of Identity & Belonging, Eng. Eccles. Courts) [Gender & testimony in church courts of England, 1200–1500], kaneb@cardiff.ac.uk

Stephen Lambert, M.A., D.Phil. (Oxon.), Reader in Anc. Hist. (Greek Hist.) [Greek epigraphy; Greek religion], lamberts@cardiff.ac.uk

Alan M. Lane, M.A. (Glas.), Ph.D. (Lond.), Sen. Lect. in Archaeol. (Dark Age Brit. Archaeol.) [Dark age settlement], lanea@cardiff.ac.uk

Judi D. Loach, Ph.D. (Cantab.), Prof. in Architecture, Welsh Sch. of Architecture (Architectural Hist.) [17th c. French architecture; Le Corbusier; Jesuits], loachj@cardiff.ac.uk

Josef Lössl, Ph.D. (Regensburg), Dr.habil. (Münster), Prof. of Hist. Theol. [Early Christianity; Latin & Greek patristics], losslj@cardiff.ac.uk

Tracey Loughran, B.A., M.A., Ph.D. (Lond.), Lect. in Medical Hist. [Health & gender in Britain; dissemination of medical knowledge; history of psychology & psychiatry; shell shock], loughrantl@cf.ac.uk

Derek Matthews, B.Sc.(Econ.), M.A. (Leeds), Ph.D. (Hull), Prof. in Business & Econ. Hist., Business Sch. (Econ. Hist.) [History of accountants; business & labour history], matthewsdr@cardiff.ac.uk

Steve F. Mills, B.A., M.A., Ph.D. (Wales), Lect. in I.T. Applications (I.T. Applications in Hist. & Archaeol.) [Auditory archaeology; Cornish tin mining], millssf1@cardiff.ac.uk

Janett Morgan, M.A., Ph.D. (Cardiff), Lect. in Anc. Hist. [Domestic space in ancient Greece], morganj56@cardiff.ac.uk

Scott C. Newton, M.A. (Cantab.), Ph.D. (Birm.), Prof. of Mod. Hist. (20th c. Brit.) [The global economy, 1944–2000; Wilson governments, 1964–70; Keynes], newtonsc@cardiff.ac.uk

*Helen J. Nicholson, M.A. (Oxon.), Ph.D. (Leicester), Prof. of Med. Hist., Head of Hist. (Med. Brit. & Eur., Crusades) [The military orders; crusades; gender; monasticism; Templars], nicholsonhj@cardiff.ac.uk

Paul T. Nicholson, B.A., Ph.D. (Sheff.), Reader in Archaeol. (Sc. Archaeol., Egyptology) [Ancient Egypt; faience & glass], nicholsonpt@cardiff.ac.uk

Jonathan P. Osmond, M.A., D.Phil. (Oxon.), Prof. of Mod. Eur. Hist. (Mod. Eur., Germany) [Modern German art & politics], osmond@cardiff.ac.uk

Kevin Passmore, B.A., Ph.D. (Warwick), Prof. of Mod. Hist. (20th c. Eur., France) [The Right & extreme Right in France since 1870], passmore@cardiff.ac.uk

R. Denys Pringle, B.A. (Southampton), D.Phil. (Oxon.), Prof. of Archaeol. (Crusader Archaeol.) [Crusader churches; medieval & Ottoman Ramla], pringlerd@cardiff.ac.uk

Louis P. Rawlings, B.A., Ph.D. (Lond.), Sen. Lect. in Anc. Hist. (Greece, Rome, Anc. & Med. Warfare) [Ethos, warfare & society in Graeco-Roman world; Carthage], rawlings@cf.ac.uk

*Niall M. Sharples, M.A. (Glas.), Prof. of Archaeol. (Iron Age Brit. & Eur.) [Brochs; hillforts; chambered tombs; history of archaeology], sharples@cardiff.ac.uk

Gerwin A. Strobl, M.Phil., D.Phil. (Salzburg), Lect. in Mod. Hist. (20th c. Eur.) [Britain in Nazi propaganda; Nazi theatre], stroblg@cardiff.ac.uk

Toby Thacker, B.A. (Oxon.), Ph.D. (Wales), Sen. Lect. in Mod. Eur. Hist. (Mod. Germany) [Music & politics in 20th c. Germany; occupation of Germany 1945–9], thackeret@cardiff.ac.uk

Laurence Totelin, B.A. (Brussels), M.Phil. (Cantab.), Ph.D. (Lond.), Lect. in Anc. Hist. [Greek & Roman science & medicine; gender history; history of sexuality; Greek history], totelinlm@cardiff.ac.uk

Shaun F. Tougher, B.A. (Belf.), Ph.D. (St. And.), Sen. Lect. in Anc. Hist. (Greece, Rome, Byzantium) [Leo VI; eunuchs in antiquity], toughersf@cardiff.ac.uk

*Frank Trombley, M.A., Ph.D. (Calif.), Prof. of Relig. Stud. (Early Islam, Classical Arabic & Byz. Hist.) [Near East c.500–1075], trombley@cardiff.ac.uk

Keir Waddington, B.A. (East Anglia), M.A., Ph.D. (Lond.), Prof. of Mod. Hist. (Mod. Brit. Soc. & Medical Hist.) [Rural health in Wales; social history of medicine; literature & science], waddingtonk@cardiff.ac.uk

Garthine M. Walker, B.A., Ph.D. (Liv.), Reader in Mod. Hist. (Early Mod. Brit. & Eur., Gender Hist.) [Power, gender & law in early modern England; social impact of civil wars & revolution in Britain], walkergm@cardiff.ac.uk

Stephanie Ward, M.A., Ph.D. (Wales), Lect. in Welsh Hist. (19th & 20th c. Welsh Hist.) [Unemployment & social policy in 20th c. Wales]

Ruth C. Westgate, M.A. (Cantab.), Ph.D. (Manc.), Sen. Lect. in Anc. Hist. & Archaeol. (Anc. Greece) [Greek archaeology & social history, esp. domestic architecture, ancient mosaics], westgater@cardiff.ac.uk

A. James M. Whitley, M.A., Ph.D. (Cantab.), Prof. of Archaeol. (Greek Archaeol.) [Literacy; Crete & Greece in Archaic period; art & narrative; hero cults], whitleya@cardiff.ac.uk

Alasdair W.R. Whittle, M.A., D.Phil. (Oxon.), F.B.A., Distinguished Res. Prof. in Archaeol. (Neolithic Brit. & Eur.) [Neolithic settlement & society in Britain & Europe], whittle@cardiff.ac.uk

*Chris Williams, B.A., Ph.D. (Wales), Prof. of Hist, Head of Sch. of Hist., Archaeol. & Relig. (19th & 20th c. Brit.) [South Wales coalfield], williamsc92@cardiff.ac.uk

Mark R.F. Williams, B.A., M.Phil., D.Phil. (Oxon.), Lect. in Early Mod. Hist. (Early Mod. Brit. & Ireland) [Royalist exile of 1650s; cultural interaction between Britain, Ireland & France], williamsm64@cardiff.ac.uk

Martin Wright, B.A., M.Phil., Ph.D. (Wales), Welsh Medium Lect. in Hist. [British socialism; socialist tradition in Wales], wrightmk@cardiff.ac.uk

David R. Wyatt, B.A., M.A., Ph.D. (Wales), Sen. Lect. (Early Med. Brit. & Ireland) [Slavery in medieval Britain & Ireland; community & engagement]

CARDIFF METROPOLITAN UNIVERSITY

Cyncoed Centre, Cyncoed Road, Cardiff, CF2 6XD. 029 2050 6570. Fax 029 2074 7665
www.uwic.ac.uk
School of Education

Colin Sowden, (Victorian & Edwardian Hist.)

Charlie Whitham, B.A., M.A. (W. of Eng.), Ph.D. (Wales), (Amer. & Brit. Pol. Hist.)

Sian R. Williams, B.A., Ph.D. (Wales), Sen. Lect. (15th–16th c. Welsh & Brit. Hist., 19th–20th c. Women)

UNIVERSITY OF **CENTRAL LANCASHIRE**

Preston, Lancashire, PR1 2HE
School of Education & Social Science 01772 893090. Fax 01772 893922
www.uclan.ac.uk/ahss/education_social_sciences/history/history.php

Stephen Caunce, B.A. (Lond.), Ph.D. (Leeds), Sen. Lect. (18th–20th c. Econ. & Soc. Hist.)
[History of N. England 1550–1950], sacaunce@uclan.ac.uk
Jonathan Colman, B.A., M.A. (Leeds), Ph.D. (Liv.), Lect. (Int. Hist.) [British & American Cold
War foreign policies; intelligence studies], jcolman@uclan.ac.uk
Philip Constable, M.A. (Cantab. & Michigan), Ph.D. (Lond.), Sen. Lect. (S. & S.E. Asian Hist.),
pconstable@uclan.ac.uk
Billy Frank, B.A. (Edge Hill), M.A. (York), Ph.D. (Edge Hill), Sen. Lect. (Afric. Hist.) [De-
colonisation in southern Africa], bfrank@uclan.ac.uk
Andrew Gritt, B.A., Ph.D. (Central Lancs.), Sen. Lect. (Mod. Brit. Hist. 1600–1900) [Rural
history; history of welfare; popular politics; public history], ajgritt1@uclan.ac.uk
John Manley, M.A., M.Litt. (Edin.), Ph.D. (Dalhousie), Sen. Lect. (N. Amer. Hist.) [Canadian
Communist party], jmanley@uclan.ac.uk
Nicholas Mansfield, B.A. (Manc.), B.Phil. (Exeter), Ph.D. (Wolverhampton), Sen.
Res. Fellow (Rural Labour Hist.) [Class, politics & the military; material culture],
nmansfield@uclan.ac.uk
Stephen Meredith, B.A., M.A., M.Sc. (Lond.), Ph.D. (Sheff.), Sen. Lect. (Mod. & Contemp.
Brit. Hist. & Pol.) [History of the Labour party; social democracy & 20th c. British
'progressive' politics], scmeredith@uclan.ac.uk
Mairtin O'Cathain, B.A., Ph.D. (Ulster), Lect. (Irish Hist.) [Fenianism; Irish in Scotland],
mso-cathain@uclan.ac.uk
Sally Pilkington, B.A. (Central Lancs.), Sen. Lect. (Brit. Soc. & Cultural Hist.) [Built
environment; gender; design history], sapilkington@uclan.ac.uk
David Stewart, M.A., Ph.D. (Glas.), Sen. Lect. (20th c. Soc. & Pol.) [20th c. Scotland],
dstewart@uclan.ac.uk
Keith Vernon, B.Sc., M.Sc. (Leicester), Ph.D. (Manc.), Sen. Lect. (Mod. Soc. Hist.) [British
universities in 20th c.], kvernon@uclan.ac.uk
Wendy Webster, B.A., M.Litt. (Cantab.), M.A. (York), Emeritus Prof. (Women's Hist.) [20th c.
women's history; personal narratives; oral history; life-writing], wwebster@uclan.ac.uk

UNIVERSITY OF **CHESTER**

Parkgate Road, Chester, CH1 4BJ. 01244 511000
www.chester.ac.uk
Department of History & Archaeology 01244 512151. Fax 01244 511150

Hannah E. Ewence, B.A., M.A., Ph.D. (Southampton), Lect. (Mod. Hist.) [Immigration history;
British minority history], h.ewence@chester.ac.uk
Peter G.I. Gaunt, B.A. (Wales), Ph.D. (Exeter), Prof. of Early Mod. Hist. (Early Mod.,
Architecture/Landscape) [Oliver Cromwell; the Cromwell family; the Civil War],
p.gaunt@chester.ac.uk
Meggen Gondek, B.A. (Tufts), M.Phil., Ph.D. (Glas.), Reader (Archaeol.) [Archaeology; early
medieval Britain & Ireland], m.gondek@chester.ac.uk

Tim Grady, B.A. (Keele), M.A., Ph.D. (Southampton), Sen. Lect. (Mod. Hist.) [Modern German history; German-Jewish history], t.grady@chester.ac.uk

Amy Gray Jones, B.Sc. (Lond.), M.Sc. (Bradford), Ph.D. (Manc.), Lect. in Archaeol. (Archaeol.) [Funerary archaeology; human osteology; Mesolithic archaeology of Britain & Europe], a.grayjones@chester.ac.uk

Michael Huggins, B.A., M.A., Ph.D. (Liv.), Sen. Lect. in Mod. Hist. [Modern Ireland; nationalism; popular protest & culture], m.huggins@chester.ac.uk

Donna R. Jackson, B.A., M.A., (East Anglia), Ph.D. (Cantab.), Sen. Lect. (Mod. Hist.) [Modern American history; American constitutional history; Cold War foreign policy], d.jackson@chester.ac.uk

*Keith A.J. McLay, M.A. (Glas.), M.Sc. (Lond.), Ph.D. (Glas.), Sen. Lect. (Early Mod. Brit. & Eur. Hist.) [Early modern amphibious warfare; politics & diplomacy during the reigns of William III, Queen Anne & George I], k.mclay@chester.ac.uk

James H. Pardoe, B.Sc.(Econ.) (Lond.), M.Sc. (Edin.), Ph.D. (Manc.), Sen. Lect. (Landscape Hist., Heritage Management, 20th c. Int. Hist.) [Architecture; heritage studies; museology], j.pardoe@chester.ac.uk

Thomas Pickles, M.A., M.St., D.Phil. (Oxon.), Lect. (Med. Hist.) [Early medieval British history, archaeology & place-names], t.pickles@chester.ac.uk

Barry Taylor, B.A., M.A. (Dunelm.), Ph.D. (Manc.), Lect. (Archaeol.) [European late upper Palaeolithic & Mesolithic; environmental archaeology & palaeo-ecology], b.taylor@chester.ac.uk

Howard M.R. Williams, B.Sc. (Sheff.), M.A., Ph.D. (Read.), Prof. of Archaeol. [Early medieval archaeology; mortuary archaeology; history of archaeology], howard.williams@chester.ac.uk

Katherine A. Wilson, M.A., Ph.D. (Glas.), Lect. (Med. Hist.) [Late medieval Burgundian Netherlands; material culture & society], k.wilson@chester.ac.uk

UNIVERSITY OF CHICHESTER

Bishop Otter Campus, College Lane, Chichester, West Sussex, PO19 6PE.
01243 816000. Fax 01243 816080
www.chi.ac.uk

Department of History

Mark Bryant, B.A., Ph.D. (Lond.), Sen. Lect. in Hist. [Early modern Europe; French court life; cultural history], m.bryant@chi.ac.uk

Andrew Chandler, B.A. (Birm.), Ph.D. (Cantab.), Sen. Lect. in Mod. Relig. & Anglo-German Hist.

*Hugo Frey, B.A., M.A., Ph.D. (Surrey), Princ. Lect. in 20th c. Eur. Hist. [French cultural, social & political history], h.frey@chi.ac.uk

Keith W. Jenkins, B.A., Ph.D. (Nott.), Prof. Emeritus of Hist. Theory (Hist. of Ideas) [Historical method; philosophy of history], k.jenkins@chi.ac.uk

Susan Morgan, B.A., M.A., Ph.D. (Brist.), Reader in 19th & 20th c. Hist. & Women's Hist. [19th c. women, religion & social reform], s.morgan@chi.ac.uk

Amanda Richardson, B.A. (Winchester), Ph.D. (Southampton), Lect. in Hist. & Heritage Stud. [Landscape history; local history; heritage studies], a.richardson@chi.ac.uk

Danae Tankard, B.A., Ph.D. (Lond.), Lect. in Hist. [Rural social history; local history], d.tankard@chi.ac.uk

CITY UNIVERSITY

www.city.ac.uk
Cass Business School 106 Bunhill Row, London, EC1Y 8TZ. 020 7040 8600
www.cass.city.ac.uk

Forrest H. Capie, B.A. (Auckland), M.Sc., Ph.D. (Lond.), Emeritus Prof. of Econ. Hist.
(Monetary & Finance Hist.) [Monetary & financial developments in Britain 1850–1990]

COVENTRY UNIVERSITY

Priory Street, Coventry, CV1 5FB. 024 7688 7688
www.coventry.ac.uk
Department of International Studies & Social Science
024 7688 8256/8176. Fax 024 7688 8679

Neil Forbes, B.A. (Hull), M.A. (Lond.), Ph.D. (Kent), (Mod. Brit. Hist.) [British external
economic policy in the 1930s], n.forbes@coventry.ac.uk
Peter J. Gallagher, B.Sc., M.A. (Wolverhampton), Sen. Lect. [French political history;
nationalism; the far Right; questions of identity], p.gallagher@coventry.ac.uk
Cathy Hunt, B.A. (Warwick), Ph.D. (Coventry), Sen. Lect. in Hist. (20th c. Brit. Hist.) [British
labour politics 1900–50], c.hunt@coventry.ac.uk
Frank D. Magee, B.A., Ph.D. (Leeds), Assoc. Head of Dept. (19th & 20th c. Int. Hist.) [British
foreign policy 1918–39], f.magee@coventry.ac.uk
Brett Sanders, B.A., M.A. (Coventry), Lect. in Hist. (Environmental Hist.),
b.sanders@coventry.ac.uk
Andrew D. Smith, B.A. (Queen's, Ont.), Ph.D. (Western Ontario), Sen. Lect. in Hist. (N. Amer.)
[Business & global history], ab0352@coventry.ac.uk

DE MONTFORT UNIVERSITY

The Gateway, Leicester, LE1 9BH. 0116 255 1551. Fax 0116 257 7199
www.dmu.ac.uk
School of Humanities

Neil Carter, B.A. (C.N.A.A.), Ph.D. (Warwick), Res. Fellow [Sports history],
necarter@dmu.ac.uk
Robert Colls, B.A. (Sussex), D.Phil. (York), Prof. of Cultural Hist. [National & regional
identities; George Orwell; sports history], rmcolls@dmu.ac.uk
David Dee, B.A., M.A. (De Montfort), Lect. (Mod. Hist.) [Jews & sport], ddee@dmu.ac.uk
Richard Holt, M.A., Ph.D. (Oxon.), Prof. of Hist. (Sport), rholt@dmu.ac.uk
Pierre Lanfranchi, Ph.D. (E.U.I.), Res. Prof. of Hist. (Sport & Soc.), planfranchi@dmu.ac.uk
John F. Martin, B.Sc., M.Phil. (Loughborough), Ph.D. (Read.), Reader (Agrarian Hist.)
[Impact of government policies on British agriculture 1850; U.K. economy since 1939],
jfmartin@dmu.ac.uk

Kenneth Morrison, M.A. (Aberd.), Ph.D. (Stirling), Reader in Mod. S. East Eur. Hist. [20th c. Balkan history & politics], kmorrison@dmu.ac.uk

*Panikos Panayi, B.A. (C.N.A.A.), Ph.D. (Sheff.), Prof. of Eur. Hist., Subject Leader, Hist. (Mod. Brit. & Eur.) [Ethnicity & racism in modern Europe], ppanayi@dmu.ac.uk

Dilwyn Porter, B.A., Ph.D. (Manc.), Prof. (Mod. Brit.) [Financial journalism in Britain since c.1850; mail order retailing in Britain; social history of Association Football in Britain since 1945]

Matthew Taylor, B.A. (York), Ph.D. (De Montfort), Prof. [Sports history, esp. British football], mtaylor@dmu.ac.uk

Pippa Virdee, B.A., Ph.D. (Coventry), Sen. Lect. [S. Asian communities in Britain; partition of India, 1947], pvirdee@dmu.ac.uk

Jean Williams, B.A. (Open & Loughborough), M.A. (Leicester), Ph.D. (De Montfort), Sen. Res. Fellow [Gender & education; gender & sport history; children's literature; literature & sport], jwilliams@dmu.ac.uk

UNIVERSITY OF DERBY

Derby, DE22 1GB.
www.derby.ac.uk
School of Humanities: Literary, Historical & Cultural Studies
Faculty of Arts, Design & Technology 01332 593216. Fax 01332 591736
www.derby.ac.uk/history/

Paul Elliott, B.A., M.A. (Nott.), Ph.D. (Leicester), Lect. in Hist. (18th & 19th c. Brit. Hist.) [18th & 19th c. urban history; scientific & intellectual history; history of education], p.elliott@derby.ac.uk

Catherine Feely, B.A., M.A., Ph.D. (Manc.), Lect. in Hist. (Mod. Brit. & Eur. Hist.) [19th & 20th c. British cultural & intellectual history; history of Marxism; history of reading, writing & publishing; history of the press], c.feely@derby.ac.uk

Robert Hudson, B.A. (Lond.), M.Phil. (Exeter), Ph.D. (Derby), University Reader in Contemp. Eur. Hist. & Cultural Pol. (Mod. & Contemp. Eur. Hist. & Cultural Pol.) [Identity politics & conflict studies in contemporary Europe, esp. with regard to French society & conflict (1939–62); history & cultural politics of Yugoslavia & successor states], r.c.hudson@derby.ac.uk

Ruth Larsen, B.A., M.A., Ph.D. (York), Lect. in Hist. (Country House, Hist. of the Family, Gender Hist.) [Domestic & social roles of aristocratic women in the long 18th c.; state of the church in mid 19th c. Yorkshire], r.larsen@derby.ac.uk

Tom Neuhaus, B.A. (Essex), M.Phil., Ph.D. (Cantab.), Lect. in Hist. (Mod. Eur. & Int. Hist.) [European representations of Tibet; history of imperialism; travel; Chinese history], t.neuhaus@derby.ac.uk

*Ian Whitehead, B.A., Ph.D. (Leeds), Head of Literary, Hist. & Cultural Stud. (Mod. Brit. Hist., Hist. of 20th c. Warfare) [Medical history of the two world wars], i.whitehead@derby.ac.uk

UNIVERSITY OF DUNDEE

Dundee, DD1 4HN. 01382 223181. Fax 01382 386794
www.dundee.ac.uk
Department of History

Zoe A. Colley, B.A., M.A., Ph.D. (Newcastle), Lect. (19th–20th c. Amer.) [Civil rights movement in America], z.a.colley@dundee.ac.uk

Murray Frame, M.A., M.Litt. (Aberd.), Ph.D. (Cantab.), Sen. Lect. (19th–20th c. Eur. & Int.) [19th & 20th c. Russian history], m.frame@dundee.ac.uk

Matthew Graham, B.A., M.A., Ph.D. (Sheff.), Lect. in Hist. & Pol. (Mod. Afric.) [South African history; national liberation struggles; international relations; post-colonial governance], m.v.graham@dundee.ac.uk

Anja Johansen, B.A., Cand.mag. (Copenhagen), Ph.D. (Florence), Sen. Lect. (18th–20th c. Eur.) [Crime & criminal justice in France & Germany], a.m.johansen@dundee.ac.uk

William Kenefick, B.A., Ph.D. (Strathclyde), Sen. Lect. (19th–20th c. Scot. & Brit.) [British labour & industrial history; the role of the Irish in the Scottish dock labour force], w.kenefick@dundee.ac.uk

James Livesey, B.A., M.A. (N.U.I.), Ph.D. (Harv.), Prof. of Global Hist. [Global history; French revolution; Atlantic history; conceptual history], j.livesey@dundee.ac.uk

Alan Ross MacDonald, M.A., Ph.D. (Edin.), Sen. Lect. (Early Mod. Scot.) [Parliament in the 16th–17th c.; environmental history], a.r.macdonald@dundee.ac.uk

Graeme Morton, M.A., Ph.D. (Edin.), Prof. (19th–20th c. Scot. Identity) [Scottish diaspora], g.l.morton@dundee.ac.uk

Derek J. Patrick, M.A., Ph.D. (St. And.), Lect. (17th–18th c. Scot.) [Causes & consequences of the Union of 1707; late 17th c. Scottish parliament], d.j.patrick@dundee.ac.uk

John M. Regan, B.A. (Ulster), Ph.D. (Belf.), Lect. in Hist. (19th–20th c. Ireland & Brit.) [Revolution & settlement in 20th c. Ireland; state formation & political violence], j.regan@dundee.ac.uk

*Christopher D. Storrs, B.A. (Oxon.), M.A., Ph.D. (Lond.), Reader (16th–18th c. Eur.) [Early modern history, esp. Spain, Italy & Portugal; international relations; war; state formation; diplomacy; nobility], c.d.storrs@dundee.ac.uk

Annie Tindley, M.A., M.Sc., Ph.D. (Edin.), Sen. Lect. (19th–20th c. Brit. & Scot. Hist.) [Landed elites & estates; imperial history], a.tindley@dundee.ac.uk

Martine J. van Ittersum, B.A. (Amsterdam), M.A., Ph.D. (Harv.), Sen. Lect. (Early Mod. Eur.) [Britain & The Netherlands in the 17th c.], m.j.vanittersum@dundee.ac.uk

Matthew C. Ward, B.A. (Dunelm.), M.A. (Ohio State), Ph.D. (William & Mary), Sen. Lect. (18th–20th c. Amer.) [Colonial American history; Native American history], m.c.ward@dundee.ac.uk

Christopher A. Whatley, B.A., Ph.D. (Strathclyde), Prof. of Scot. Hist. (17th–20th c. Scot. & Brit.) [Scottish economic & social history c.1690–1850; causes & consequences of the Union of 1707; order & disorder; the industrial city, esp. Dundee], c.a.whatley@dundee.ac.uk

Perry Willson, B.Sc. (Manc.), Ph.D. (Essex), Prof. of Mod. Eur. Hist. [20th c. Italian gender history & Italian fascism], p.r.willson@dundee.ac.uk

UNIVERSITY OF **DURHAM**

University Offices, Old Shire Hall, Durham, DH1 3HP. 0191 334 2000. Fax 0191 334 3740
www.dur.ac.uk
Department of History 43 North Bailey, Durham, DH1 3EX.
0191 334 1040/1072. Fax 0191 334 1041
www.dur.ac.uk/History/
Department of Archaeology South Road, Durham, DH1 3LE.
0191 334 1100.Fax 0191 334 1101
www.dur.ac.uk/Archaeology/
Department of Classics 38 North Bailey, Durham, DH1 3EU.
0191 334 1670. Fax 0191 334 7338
www.dur.ac.uk/Classics/
Department of Geography South Road, Durham, DH1 3LE.
0191 334 1800. Fax 0191 334 1801
www.geography.dur.ac.uk
Department of Theology Abbey House, Palace Green, Durham, DH1 3RS.
Fax 0191 374 4744
www.dur.ac.uk/Theology/
School of Government & International Relations
The Al-Qasimi Building, Elvet Hill Road, Durham, DH1 3TU.
0191 334 2822. Fax 0191 334 2830
www.dur.ac.uk/imeis/

Paul Bailey, B.A. (Leeds), M.A. (Lond.), Ph.D. (Brit. Col.), Prof. of Hist. [Social & economic history of modern China], Paul.Bailey@durham.ac.uk
Alex Barber, B.A., Ph.D. (Lond.), Lect. in Hist. (Early Mod.) [Intellectual & religious history; the transmission of ideas in 17th c. Britain], A.W.Barber@durham.ac.uk
Christopher W. Brooks, B.A. (Princeton), D.Phil. (Oxon.), Prof. of Hist. (Early Mod. Brit.) [Law, politics & society in England, 1485–1660], C.W.Brooks@durham.ac.uk
John-Henry Clay, B.A., Ph.D. (York), Lect. in Hist. (Med.) [Anglo-Saxon & Frankish history], J.W.Clay@durham.ac.uk
David M. Craig, B.A. (Lond.), Ph.D. (Cantab.), Lect. in Hist. (19th c.) [Political & intellectual history of modern Britain], D.M.Craig@durham.ac.uk
Sarah R. Davies, M.A. (St. And.), M.A. (Lond.), D.Phil. (Oxon.), Sen. Lect. in Hist. (20th c. Eur.) [Soviet/Russian history], S.R.Davies@durham.ac.uk
Ben Dodds, B.A., M.A., Ph.D. (Dunelm.), Sen. Lect. in Hist. (Med.) [Late medieval economic & social history], Benjamin.Dodds@durham.ac.uk
Joanne C. Fox, B.A., Ph.D. (Kent), Prof. of Hist. (Mod. Eur.) [Film & propaganda history, esp. Germany & Britain], J.C.Fox@durham.ac.uk
Helen Foxhall Forbes, M.A., M.Phil, Ph.D. (Cantab.), Lect. in Hist. (Med.) [Anglo-Saxon history & theology], H.G.FoxhallForbes@durham.ac.uk
Richard Gameson, M.A., D.Phil. (Oxon.), Prof. [History of the book, esp. medieval manuscripts & illumination], Richard.Gameson@durham.ac.uk
Giles E.M. Gasper, M.A., M.St., D.Phil. (Oxon.), Sen. Lect. in Hist. (Med.) [Intellectual life & culture, 1000–1300], G.E.M.Gasper@durham.ac.uk
Adrian G. Green, B.A. (Oxon.), M.A., Ph.D. (Dunelm.), Lect. in Hist. (16th–18th c.) [Social & economic history of Britain, 1500–1800, esp. housing], A.G.Green@durham.ac.uk
Howell J. Harris, M.A., D.Phil. (Oxon.), Prof. of Hist. (Amer.) [American labour & business; the cast-iron stove in Victorian America], H.J.Harris@durham.ac.uk

Carol Harrison, M.A., D.Phil. (Oxon.), Prof. of Hist. [History & theology of the early church]

Matthew Johnson, M.A., M.St., D.Phil (Oxon.), Lect. in Hist. [British political history since 1850], Matthew.Johnson@durham.ac.uk

Ludmilla J. Jordanova, M.A. (Cantab.), M.A. (Essex), Ph.D. (Cantab.), Prof. of Hist. & Visual Culture (Mod.) [Portraiture & identity; history of science & medicine; gender; historiography; public history], Ludmilla.Jordanova@durham.ac.uk

James Koranyi, B.A., M.A., Ph.D. (Exeter), Lect. in Hist. [East-Central Europe, 19th & 20th c.], James.Koranyi@durham.ac.uk

Cherry Leonardi, B.A., M.A. (Lond.), Ph.D. (Dunelm.), Sen. Lect. in Hist. [Eastern Africa; Sudan; governance, traditional authority & conflict in Africa], D.C.Leonardi@durham.ac.uk

Christian D. Liddy, B.A. (Lond.), M.A., D.Phil. (York), Sen. Lect. in Hist. (Med.) [Cities, English government & politics 13th–15th c.], C.D.Liddy@durham.ac.uk

Andrew Louth, M.A. (Cantab. & Oxon.), M.Th. (Edin.), D.D. (Oxon.), Prof. of Patristics (Late Antique & Byz.) [John of Damascus & Byzantine theology], Andrew.Louth@durham.ac.uk

Jennifer Luff, Ph.D. (William & Mary), Lect. in Hist. [Modern American working-class politics; history of conservatism], Jennifer.Luff@durham.ac.uk

Cathy McClive, B.A., M.A. (Lond.), Ph.D. (Warwick), Lect. in Hist. (Early Mod. Eur.) [Social & cultural history of gender, medicine & sexuality in early modern France], Cathy.Mcclive@durham.ac.uk

Natalie Mears, M.A. (Cantab.), M.Litt., Ph.D. (St. And.), Sen. Lect. in Hist. (Early Mod.) [16th c. politics & religion, esp. Elizabeth I], Natalie.Mears@durham.ac.uk

Ranald C. Michie, M.A., Ph.D. (Aberd.), Prof. of Hist. (Econ.) [Modern British economic history; City of London; stock exchanges; banking], R.C.Michie@durham.ac.uk

Andrzej J. Olechnowicz, B.A., D.Phil. (Oxon.), Lect. in Hist. (19th c.) [British social history; the modern British monarchy], A.J.Olechnowicz@durham.ac.uk

Toby Osborne, M.A., D.Phil. (Oxon.), Sen. Lect. in Hist. (Early Mod.) [International relations & dynastic politics 16th–17th c.], Toby.Osborne@durham.ac.uk

Nicole Reinhardt, M.A. (Freiburg), Ph.D. (E.U.I. Florence), Sen. Lect. in Early Mod. Hist. [Religious & political culture; 17th c. Spain, Italy & France], Nicole.Reinhardt@durham.ac.uk

Alec Ryrie, M.A. (Cantab.), M.Litt., D.Phil. (Oxon.), Prof. of the Hist. of Christianity (Early Mod.) [Political, religious & social history of 16th & early 17th c. England & Scotland]

Len E. Scales, B.A., Ph.D. (Manc), Sen. Lect. in Hist. (Med. Eur.) [Medieval Europe, esp. Germany], L.E.Scales@durham.ac.uk

Kay Schiller, M.A. (Munich), Ph.D. (Chicago), Reader in Hist. (Mod. Eur.) [20th c. Germany, esp. intellectual & sports history], Kay.Schiller@durham.ac.uk

Tom Stammers, M.A., M.Phil, Ph.D. (Cantab.), Lect. in Hist. (Mod. Eur. Cultural Hist.) [France c.1700–1900; French Revolution & its afterlives; European Romanticism], T.E.Stammers@durham.ac.uk

Julia Stapleton, B.A. (Wales), M.A., D.Phil. (Sussex), Reader in Pol. (20th c. Brit.) [British intellectual history], Julia.Stapleton@durham.ac.uk

*Stephen J.C. Taylor, M.A., Ph.D. (Cantab.), Prof. in the Hist. of Early Mod. England (Early Mod.) [Politics & religion in England 17th–19th c.; monarchy & religion in Britain since 1660], S.J.C.Taylor@durham.ac.uk

Gabriella A. Treglia, M.A., M.Phil., Ph.D. (Cantab.), Lect. in Hist. (19th & 20th c. Amer. Race Hist., Native Amer. Hist.) [Native Americans in the 20th c.; the Indian New Deal], G.A.Treglia@durham.ac.uk

Chris Vaughan, Ph.D. (Dunelm.), Lect. in Afric. Hist. (Afric.Hist.) [20th c. East African history], Christopher.Vaughan@durham.ac.uk

Philip A. Williamson, M.A., Ph.D. (Cantab.), Prof. of Hist. (20th c. Brit.) [Politics & government since 1850; state prayers & religion since 16th c.], P.A.Williamson@durham.ac.uk

Justin Willis, B.A., Ph.D. (Lond.), Prof. of Hist. [Eastern African history, including Sudan; ethnicity; alcohol in Africa; governance & authority in colonial Africa], Justin.Willis@durham.ac.uk

Christine Woodhead, B.A. (Oxon.), Ph.D. (Edin.), Teaching Fellow in Hist. (Early Mod.) [The Ottoman empire & Mediterranean world], C.M.Woodhead@durham.ac.uk

Julian Wright, M.A., D.Phil. (Oxon.), Sen. Lect. in Hist. (Mod. Eur.) [France 1789–1940: politics, intellectual history, culture], Julian.Wright@durham.ac.uk

UNIVERSITY OF EAST ANGLIA

University Plain, Norwich, NR4 7TJ. 01603 456161. Fax 01603 458553
www.uea.ac.uk
School of History 01603 592070. Fax 01603 250434
www.uea.ac.uk/his/
Centre of East Anglian Studies 01603 592070. Fax 01603 250434
School of American Studies 01603 592280. Fax 01603 507728
School of World Art Studies & Museology Fax 01603 593642

Edward D.J. Acton, B.A. (York), Ph.D. (Cantab.), Prof. of Mod. Eur. Hist. [Russian Revolution of 1917 & its historiography; Stalin & power], E.Acton@uea.ac.uk

Louise Atherton, M.A., Ph.D. (East Anglia), Sen. Lect. in Landscape Hist. [Espionage; the secret state], L.Atherton@uea.ac.uk

Mark Bailey, B.A. (Dunelm.), Ph.D. (Cantab.), Prof. of Late Med. Hist. [Economic & social history of the middle ages]

David Bates, B.A., Ph.D. (Exeter), Prof. of Med. Hist., Director, Centre of East Anglian Stud. [10th–13th c. Britain & France; William the Conqueror; Anglo-Norman charters], David.Bates@uea.ac.uk

*Catherine D. Carmichael, B.A. (Lond.), Ph.D. (Bradford), Reader. in Eur. Hist. [National identity & state formation in the Balkans; ethnicity & violence], Cathie.Carmichael@uea.ac.uk

John D. Charmley, B.A., D.Phil. (Oxon.), Prof. of Eng. Hist., Head of Sch. of Hist. [International history 1870–1990], J.Charmley@uea.ac.uk

Steven Cherry, B.A., M.A., Ph.D. (East Anglia), Reader in Econ. & Soc. Hist. [Medical services & hospitals; labour movement; welfare], S.Cherry@uea.ac.uk

Roy A. Church, B.A., Ph.D. (Nott.), Emeritus Prof. of Econ. & Soc. Hist. [Industrial relations in coal industry; business finance in coal & iron industries; industrial design], R.Church@uea.ac.uk

Joanne T. Clarke, B.A. (Sydney), Ph.D. (Edin.), Lect. in Archaeol. [Pre- & proto-historic eastern Mediterranean & the Levant; material culture studies], Joanne.Clarke@uea.ac.uk

Richard D.G. Crockatt, M.A. (Edin.), D.Phil. (Sussex), Emeritus Prof. of Amer. Hist. [Cold War; contemporary U.S. foreign policy], R.Crockatt@uea.ac.uk

Jennifer Davey, B.A., Ph.D. (East Anglia), Lect. in Mod. Brit. Hist. [19th c. British history], Jennifer.Davey@uea.ac.uk

Ferdinand de Jong, Ph.D. (Amsterdam), Lect. in Anthr. [History, memory & identity], F.Jong@uea.ac.uk

*Simon Dell, B.A., Ph.D. (Lond.), [Modernism; history of photography; France between the wars; 20th c. art & architecture], S.Dell@uea.ac.uk

Hugh Doherty, B.A. (Lond.), D.Phil. (Oxon.), Lect. in Med. Hist. [Medieval history], hugh.doherty@uea.ac.uk

Silvia Evangelisti, B.A., Ph.D. (E.U.I.), Lect. in Eur. Hist. [Female monastic institutes in 16th & 17th c. Italy; gender & citizenship in early modern Europe], S.Evangelisti@uea.ac.uk

Ian Farr, B.A. (Dunelm.), Sen. Lect. in Eur. Hist. [Social & political history of modern Germany, esp. peasant society; Bavaria], I.Farr@uea.ac.uk

Jacqueline Fear-Segal, B.A. (East Anglia), M.A. (Harv.), Ph.D. (Lond.), Reader in Amer. Hist. [Native Americans; immigration; Americanisation; race; education; visual & spatial history], J.Fear-Segal@uea.ac.uk

Rebecca Fraser, B.A., M.A., Ph.D. (Warwick), Lect. in Amer. Hist. [Gender & sexuality in the antebellum South; the cultural world of the enslaved], Becky.Fraser@uea.ac.uk

Malcolm J. Gaskill, M.A., Ph.D. (Cantab.), Prof. of Early Mod. Hist. [Early modern English society & culture: witchcraft, crime, mentalities], M.Gaskill@uea.ac.uk

John Gregory, M.A., Ph.D. (East Anglia), Sen. Lect. in Landscape Hist., J.Gregory@uea.ac.uk

Emma A. Griffin, M.A. (Lond.), Ph.D. (Cantab.), Lect. in Mod. Brit. Hist. [English social history & popular culture in the 18th & 19th c.], E.Griffin@uea.ac.uk

Polly Ha, B.A. (Yale), Ph.D. (Cantab.), Lect. in Early Mod. Hist. [The Puritan world; the Reformation; religious & social dynamics of early modern England], P.Ha@uea.ac.uk

Christopher Harper-Bill, B.A., Ph.D. (Lond.), Prof. of Hist. (Med. Hist.) [Medieval church in England; medieval history of East Anglia; medieval ecclesiastical records], C.Harper-Bill@uea.ac.uk

T.A. (Sandy) Heslop, B.A. (Lond.), Prof. of Hist. of Art [Social context of art & architecture c.1000–1200], T.Heslop@uea.ac.uk

G.M. Hicks, B.A. (East Anglia), M.A. (Lond.), Ph.D. (East Anglia), Lect. in Mod. Brit. Hist. [British politics & foreign policy in the 19th & 20th c., esp. 1830–80], G.Hicks@uea.ac.uk

Richard Hodges, O.B.E., B.A., Ph.D. (Southampton), Prof. of Visual Arts & Director of Inst. of World Archaeol. [Material culture, history & social mentality in late antiquity & early medieval Europe], R.Hodges@uea.ac.uk

Steven Hooper, B.Sc., Ph.D. (Cantab.), Prof. [Anthropology; the arts of the Pacific & N. America; exchange; ethnohistory], S.Hooper@uea.ac.uk

Anthony C. Howe, B.A., D.Phil. (Oxon.), Prof. of Mod. Hist. [Britain in the 19th & early 20th c., esp. politics, culture & economy], A.C.Howe@uea.ac.uk

Benjamin Jones, B.A., D.Phil. (Sussex), Lect. in Mod. Brit. Hist. [20th c. Britain; the working classes], B.Jones5@uea.ac.uk

Anthony Kemp-Welch, B.Sc., Ph.D. (Lond.), Reader in Hist. [Poland & the Cold War; Nikolai Bukharin], A.Kemp-Welch@uea.ac.uk

Vassiliki Koutrakou, B.A. (Athens), M.A., Ph.D. (Cantab.), Lect. in Contemp. Eur. Stud. [International relations; mediation & conflict resolution], V.Koutrakou@uea.ac.uk

George F. Lau, B.A. (Yale), Lect. in the Arts of the Americas [S. America; Andes; prehistory & archaeology], George.Lau@uea.ac.uk

Tom O. Licence, M.A., M.Phil., Ph.D. (Cantab.), Lect. in Med. Hist. [Monasticism; religious history; the Norman Conquest]

Robert E. Liddiard, B.A., M.A., Ph.D. (East Anglia), Sen. Lect. in Med. Landscape Hist. [Landscape history, 500–1500; castles & high status landscapes; Norman Conquest], Rob.Liddiard@uea.ac.uk

John Mack, M.A. (Sussex), D.Phil. (Oxon.), [Anthropology of art; the arts of Africa; museums & cultural institutions; cultural 'heritage'], John.Mack@uea.ac.uk

Malcolm McLaughlin, B.A., M.A., Ph.D. (Essex), Lect. in Amer. Hist. [History of race, class & racial violence in 20th c. U.S.], M.Mclaughlin@uea.ac.uk

Richard Maguire, B.A. (Warwick), M.A., Ph.D. (East Anglia), Lect. in Public Hist. & Engagement [Heritage; local history; atomic energy], R.C.Maguire@uea.ac.uk

Richard Mills, B.A., Ph.D. (East Anglia), Lect. in Mod. Eur. Hist. [History of sport, politics & nationalism; socialist Yugoslavia & its successor states], R.Mills@uea.ac.uk

John B. Mitchell, B.A. (Swarthmore), Reader in Hist. of Art [Art, architecture & material culture of early medieval Europe], John.Mitchell@uea.ac.uk

Victor F.G. Morgan, B.A., Ph.D. (East Anglia), Sen. Lect. in Eng. Soc. Hist. [Cambridge University; civic ritual; concept of fame], Victor.Morgan@uea.ac.uk

Matthias Neumann, M.A. (Dresden), Ph.D. (East Anglia), Lect. in Med. Hist. [Russian & European history since 1800], M.Neumann@uea.ac.uk

John B. Onians, B.A. (Cantab.), Ph.D. (Lond.), Prof. of Visual Art [Classical art & Renaissance architecture; biological basis of artistic activity], J.Onians@uea.ac.uk

Thomas Otte, M.A., Ph.D. (Birm.), Sen. Lect. in Int. & Diplomatic Hist. [British foreign policy from the Crimean War to the Great War; Lord Salisbury; Anglo-German relations before 1914], T.Otte@uea.ac.uk

Carole Rawcliffe, B.A., Ph.D. (Sheff.), Prof. of Hist. [Social history of medicine; medieval women; medieval hospitals; leprosy in the middle ages], C.Rawcliffe@uea.ac.uk

Christina Riggs, B.A. (Brown), M.A. (Calif. at Berkeley), D.Phil. (Oxon.), [Visual & material culture of ancient Egypt, including Hellenistic & Roman Egypt], C.Riggs@uea.ac.uk

Daniel J. Rycroft, B.A. (East Anglia), D.Phil. (Sussex), Lect. in Arts & Cultures of Asia [Art & myth; colonial cultures; de-colonisation & visual culture; subalternity & representation], D.Rycroft@uea.ac.uk

Camilla Schofield, B.A. (Washington), M.Phil., Ph.D. (Yale), Lect. in Mod. Brit. Hist. [Modern British, imperial & European history], Camilla.Schofield@uea.ac.uk

Jessica Sharkey, M.A. (St. And.), Ph.D. (Cantab.), Lect. in Early Mod. Hist. [Wolsey; Tudor religion & politics; England & the Vatican], Jessica.Sharkey@uea.ac.uk

Sarah Spooner, M.A., Ph.D. (East Anglia), Lect. in Landscape Hist., S.Spooner@uea.ac.uk

Margit Thøfner, B.A., M.A. (Lond.), D.Phil. (Sussex), [Visual culture of early modern Europe; gender], M.Thofner@uea.ac.uk

Jan Vermeiren, Ph.D. (Lond.), Lect. in Mod. Eur. Hist. (Mod. German & Eur. Hist.) [19th & 20th c. German & European history, esp. nationalism & geopolitics; the late Habsburg monarchy; World War I; populism & right-wing extremism; European integration], j.vermeiren@uea.ac.uk

Nicholas C. Vincent, M.A., M.Phil., D.Phil. (Oxon.), F.B.A., Prof. of Med. Hist. (Med. Eng. & Eur. Hist.) [12th–13th c. Church & politics], N.Vincent@uea.ac.uk

Peter Waldron, B.A., Ph.D. (Lond.), Prof. of Hist. (Russian & E. Eur. Hist.) [Russia since 1800], P.Waldron@uea.ac.uk

Paul S. Warde, B.A., Ph.D. (Cantab.), Reader in Early Mod. Hist. (Early Mod. German Econ., Soc. & Environmental Hist.) [Peasant society; forest history; common lands], p.warde@uea.ac.uk

Fiona C. Williamson, B.A., M.A. (East Anglia), Lect. in Early Mod. Hist. [English social & political history, 1500–1700], F.Williamson@uea.ac.uk

Tom M. Williamson, B.A., Ph.D. (Cantab.), Prof. of Landscape Archaeol. [English landscape archaeology & East Anglian history], T.Williamson@uea.ac.uk

UNIVERSITY OF **EAST LONDON**

University Way, London, E16 2RD. 020 8223 3000
www.uel.ac.uk
School of Arts & Digital Industries
Docklands Campus, 4–6 University Way, London, E16 2RD.
020 8223 2742. Fax 020 8223 2898

Catherine Blackford, D.Phil. (East Lond.), Sen. Lect. (19th–20th c. Brit. Hist.) [19th–20th c. feminism], C.M.A.Blackford@uel.ac.uk
Toby Butler, Ph.D. (Open), Lect. [London history; digital heritage], T.Butler@uel.ac.uk
Rosalind Carr, B.A. (Monash), Ph.D. (Glas.), Lect. [18th–19th c. cultural & gender history; Scottish history; empire], R.J.Carr@uel.ac.uk
Katharine Hodgkin, B.A., D.Phil. (Sussex), Princ. Lect. (Early Mod. Cultural Hist.) [Autobiography], K.Hodgkin@uel.ac.uk

EDGE HILL UNIVERSITY

St. Helen's Road, Ormskirk, Lancs., L39 4QP. 01695 575171. Fax 01695 579997
www.edgehill.ac.uk
Department of History
www.edgehill.ac.uk/Faculties/FAS/history/index.htm

Alyson Brown, B.A., M.A., Ph.D. (Hull), Reader in Criminal Hist. (Hist. of Crime & Punishment) [English penal history; English prison violence; history of child prostitution & abuse, 1880s–1970s], browna@edgehill.ac.uk
Daniel A. Gordon, B.A. (Oxon.), M.A., D.Phil. (Sussex), Lect. [Immigrant protest & anti-racism in France since 1961; the international movements of 1968], gordond@edgehill.ac.uk
Bob Nicholson, B.A., M.A., Ph.D. (Manc.), [19th c. Britain & America; popular culture; transatlantic relations; press history; print culture; humour; crime; digital humanities], bob.nicholson@edgehill.ac.uk
James Renton, B.A. (Manc. Met.), Ph.D. (Lond.), Sen. Lect. (Brit. Imp. Hist.) [British empire in the Middle East; Orientalism; Britain & the origins of the Arab-Israeli conflict; anti-Semitism & Islamophobia], renjobj@edgehill.ac.uk
*Roger H. Spalding, B.A., M.Phil. (East Anglia), Sen. Lect. (Oral Hist., Labour Party, National Identity) [Relationship between formation of national identity & popular perceptions of the past], spaldr@edgehill.ac.uk
Nicky Tsougarakis , B.A., M.A., Ph.D. (Leeds), Lect. in Med. Hist. [The Greco-Latin East in the Crusader period; monasticism]
Kevern J. Verney, B.A., M.A. (Cantab.), M.A., Ph.D. (Keele), Prof. of Amer. Hist. (U.S.A., Afric.-Amer. Hist.) [Booker T. Washington; the N.A.A.C.P.; African-American history & U.S. popular culture], verneyk@edgehill.ac.uk
Charlie Whitham, B.A., M.A., Ph.D. (Swansea), Sen. Lect. in Amer. Hist. [U.S. foregin policy; World War II; Anglo-American relations; U.S. foreign economic policy; U.S. business elites]

UNIVERSITY OF **EDINBURGH**

Old College, South Bridge, Edinburgh, EH8 9YL. 0131 650 1000
www.ed.ac.uk
School of History, Classics & Archaeology
William Robertson Wing, Old Medical School, Teviot Place, EH8 9AG.
0131 650 6693. Fax 0131 651 3070
History of Art, Edinburgh College of Art 20 Chambers Street, EH1 1JZ.
0131 650 4124. Fax 0131 650 8019
Centre for the Study of Christianity in the Non-Western World
New College, Mound Place, EH1 2LX. 0131 650 8952. Fax 0131 650 6579
Centre for the Study of Modern Conflict
William Robertson Wing, Old Medical School, Teviot Place, EH8 9AG. 0131 651 1254
School of Divinity New College, Mound Place, EH1 2LX. 0131 650 8900
School of Law Old College, South Bridge, EH8 9YL. 0131 650 2006. Fax 0131 650 6317
School of Literatures, Languages & Cultures
Islamic & Middle Eastern Studies 7–8 Buccleuch Place, EH8 9LW.
0131 650 4182. Fax 0131 650 6804
Sanskrit 7 Buccleuch Place, EH8 9LW. 0131 650 4227. Fax 0131 650 1258
School of Social & Political Science
Chrystal Macmillan Building, 15a George Square, EH8 9LD. 0131 650 1000
Centre of African Studies 21 George Square, EH8 9LL. 0131 650 3878

Paul Addison, M.A., D.Phil. (Oxon.), Hon. Fellow [Social & political history of Britain since 1945], Paul.Addison@ed.ac.uk

Talat Ahmed, B.A. (Leeds), M.A., Ph.D. (Lond.), Lect. in Mod. S. Asian Hist. [Colonial & postcolonial India; Pakistan; cultural movements & intellectual trends; cinema & society], T.Ahmed@ed.ac.uk

Thomas Ahnert, M.A., Ph.D. (Cantab.), Sen. Lect. in Early Mod. Intellectual Hist. [History of the Enlightenment], Thomas.Ahnert@ed.ec.uk

Pertti Ahonen, B.A., M.A. (Oregon), M.Phil., Ph.D. (Yale), Sen. Lect. in Eur. Hist. [20th c. & esp. post-1945 Europe; modern Germany], P.Ahonen@ed.ac.uk

William M. Aird, M.A., Ph.D. (Edin.), Lect. in Med. Hist. [11th c. & 12th c.; the Normans in northern & southern Europe; medieval saints' cults; medieval gender; political culture], William.M.Aird@ed.ac.uk

Michael Anderson, O.B.E., M.A., Ph.D. (Cantab.), F.B.A., Hon. Fellow & Emeritus Prof. of Econ. Hist. [Scottish population; western families & life-cycles], M.Anderson@ed.ac.uk

Robert D. Anderson, M.A., D.Phil. (Oxon.), Prof. of Mod. Hist. (Mod. Eur.) [19th c. France; history of education in 19th & 20th c. Scotland & Europe], R.D.Anderson@ed.ac.uk

Michael J. Angold, B.A., D.Phil. (Oxon.), Hon. Fellow & Emeritus Prof. [Political, social & religious history of the Byzantine empire; 17th c. travellers to Greece], Michael.Angold@ed.ac.uk

Monica Azzolini, M.A. (Milan), M.Phil., Ph.D. (Cantab.), Sen. Lect. in Eur. Hist., 1500–1800 [History of science & medicine in the Renaissance & early modern period; gender & sexuality], M.Azzolini@ed.ac.uk

Judith M. Barringer, B.A., Ph.D. (Yale), Prof. [Greek sculpture & vase painting; Greek mythology & religion], J.M.Barringer@ed.ac.uk

Laszlo Bartosiewicz, M.A., Ph.D., D.Sc., Reader, p/t [Zooarchaeology; man-animal relationships; animal domestication], Laszlo.Bart@ed.ac.uk

Crispin P. Bates, M.A., Ph.D. (Cantab.), Prof. in Mod. S. Asian Hist. [Economic, social & political history of modern India; orientalism & colonial discourse; postcolonial S. Asia; Indian tribes & colonial migration], Crispin.Bates@ed.ac.uk

Cordelia Beattie, B.A. (Birm.), M.A., D.Phil. (York), Sen. Lect. in Med. Hist. [Social & cultural history of England & Europe in the later middle ages; women & gender; towns; lawcourts; households & work], Cordelia.Beattie@ed.ac.uk

Dominic Berry, M.A., D.Phil. (Oxon.), Sen. Lect. [Cicero; Roman history; numismatics], D.H.Berry@ed.ac.uk

Sandra Bingham, B.A. (Alberta), M.A., Ph.D. (Brit. Col.), Sen. Teaching Fellow [Roman imperial history], S.Bingham@ed.ac.uk

Donald Bloxham, B.A. (Keele), Ph.D. (Southampton), Richard Pares Prof. of Eur. Hist. [Third Reich; the Holocaust; war crimes trials; post-war Europe; Armenian genocide], Donald.Bloxham@ed.ac.uk

Stephen I. Boardman, M.A., Ph.D. (St. And.), Reader in Scot. Hist. [Scottish kingship; Clan Campbell; saints' cults in late medieval Scotland; heraldry], Steve.Boardman@ed.ac.uk

Felix Boecking, B.A., Ph.D. (Cantab.), Lect. in Econ. & Pol. Hist. of Mod. China, Felix.Boecking@ed.ac.uk

Claudia Bolgia, Ph.D. (Warwick), [Art & architectural history of medieval Rome], C.Bolgia@ed.ac.uk

Clive Bonsall, Prof. of Early Prehist. & Archaeol., C.Bonsall@ed.ac.uk

Stephen Bowd, M.A., Ph.D. (Edin.), Reader in Eur. Hist., 1500–1800 [Renaissance Italy], Stephen.Bowd@ed.ac.uk

Esther Breitenbach, M.A., Ph.D. (Edin.), Hon. Fellow (Econ. & Soc. Hist.), Esther.Breitenbach@ed.ac.uk

*John L. Brockington, M.A., D.Phil. (Oxon.), Reader in Sanskrit (Hist. of Anc. India, Muslim India, Hinduism) [History of Vaishnavism]

*Stewart J. Brown, B.A. (Illinois), M.A., Ph.D. (Chicago), Prof. of Eccles. Hist. (Relig. & Soc. in Mod. Brit. & Eur.), S.J.Brown@ed.ac.uk

Thomas S. Brown, M.A. (Edin.), Ph.D. (Nott.), Reader in Med. Hist. [Early medieval Italy; Byzantium & the West; Britain & the continent c.500–c.1100], T.S.Brown@ed.ac.uk

Adam Budd, B.A., M.A., D.F.A., Ph.D. (Toronto), Sen. Teaching Fellow (18th c. Cultures) [18th c. cultural history], Adam.Budd@ed.ac.uk

Jill Burke, B.A. (Oxon.), M.A., Ph.D. (Lond.), Lect. in Hist. of Art [Art & patronage in 15th & 16th c. Italy], Jill.Burke@ed.ac.uk

Douglas L. Cairns, M.A., Ph.D. (Glas.), Prof. [Early Greek poetry; Greek society & ethics], Douglas.Cairns@ed.ac.uk

John W. Cairns, LL.B., Ph.D. (Edin.), Reader in Private Law [Legal profession & legal education in early modern Scotland]

Ewen A. Cameron, M.A. (Aberd.), Ph.D. (Glas.), Sir William Fraser Prof. of Scot. Hist. & Palaeography (Scot. Hist. & Palaeography) [Scottish history 18th–20th c., esp. 20th c.; Scotland & Ireland, esp. 19th c.], E.Cameron@ed.ac.uk

Lilah Canevaro, B.A., M.A., Ph.D (Dunelm), Leverhulme Early Career Fellow [Archaic Greek poetry, epic & didactic; connections between Greek literature & other cultures & time periods; Victorian poetry & art], L.G.Canevaro@ed.ac.uk

Mirko Canevaro, B.A., M.A., Ph.D. (Dunelm.), Chancellor's Fellow in Classics [Classics & ancient history; political & legal institutions of the ancient poleis down to the Hellenistic period, in Greek epigraphy & Attic oratory], Mirko.Canevaro@ed.ac.uk

Emile Chabal, B.A., M.Phil., Ph.D. (Cantab.), Chancellor's Fellow in Hist. [Modern European history; French political history], Emile.Chabal@ed.ac.uk

Martin J. Chick, M.A. (Cantab.), Ph.D. (Lond.), Prof. of Econ. & Soc. Hist. [Economic planning of Attlee governments 1945–51; 20th c. business history; 20th c. government; energy & environmental policy], Martin.Chick@ed.ac.uk

Sarah D.P. Cockram, M.A., M.Phil., Ph.D., Leverhulme Early Career Fellow [Renaissance Italy; human-animal relations], S.Cockram@ed.ac.uk

Francis D. Cogliano, B.A. (Tufts), M.A., Ph.D. (Boston), Prof. of Amer. Hist. [The American Revolution; 18th c. New England], F.Cogliano@ed.ac.uk

Viccy Coltman, B.A., M.A., Ph.D. (Lond.), Lect. in Hist. of Art [Visual & material culture of 18th c. Britain, esp. Scotland], Viccy.Coltman@ed.ac.uk

Neil Cox, Ph.D. (St. And.), Prof. of Mod. & Contemp. Art [Picasso; Braque; 20th c. art in France], Neil.Cox@ed.ac.uk

Jeremy A. Crang, B.A. (Stirling), Ph.D. (Edin.), Sen. Lect. in Brit. Hist. [Britain & the Second World War], J.A.Crang@ed.ac.uk

*James Crow, B.A. (Birm.), M.Litt. (Newcastle), Prof. of Classical Archaeol., Head of Archaeol. [Roman frontiers; Byzantine archaeology], Jim.Crow@ed.ac.uk

Robert Crowcroft, B.A., M.A., Ph.D., Lect. in Hist. [Impact & consequences of war in 1930–50s Britain], R.G.Crowcroft@ed.ac.uk

Roger Davidson, M.A., Ph.D. (Cantab.), Emeritus Prof. of Econ. & Soc. Hist., Leverhulme Emeritus Fellow [The social history of venereal disease], Roger.Davidson@ed.ac.uk

Glenys M. Davies, B.A., Ph.D. (Lond.), Sen. Lect. in Classical Art & Archaeol. [Roman funerary art], G.M.Davies@ed.ac.uk

Gayle Davis, M.A., M.Phil. (Glas.), Ph.D. (Edin.), Wellcome Sen. Lect. in the Hist. of Medicine [Social history of health & medicine], gayle_davis79@hotmail.com

Jane E.A. Dawson, B.A., Ph.D. (Dunelm.), John Laing Prof. of Reformation Hist. [Politics & Reformation in 16th c.; the Scottish Highlands], J.Dawson@ed.ac.uk

Alan F. Day, B.A. (Southampton), M.A. (McMaster & Johns Hopkins), Ph.D. (Johns Hopkins), Hon. Fellow [Social history of early N. America to 1800; development of political parties & ideology], Alan.F.Day@ed.ac.uk

Enda Delaney, B.A., M.A. (N.U.I.), Ph.D. (Belf.), Reader in Mod. Hist. [Social & cultural history of modern Ireland & the Irish diaspora], Enda.Delaney@ed.ac.uk

T.M. Devine, O.B.E., B.A., Ph.D., D.Litt. (Strathclyde), F.B.A., Personal Sen. Res. Prof. in Hist. (Mod. Scot. Hist.), T.M.Devine@ed.ac.uk

Harry T. Dickinson, B.A., M.A. (Dunelm.), Ph.D. (Newcastle), D.Litt. (Edin.), Emeritus Prof. & Hon. Prof. Fellow in Brit. Hist. [National & local politics, political debate & organisations, 1688–1832; radical & popular politics; Britain & the American & French Revolutions], Harry.Dickinson@ed.ac.uk

Angela Dimitrakaki, Ph.D. (Read.), Lect. in Contemp. & 20th c. Art, Angela.Dimitrakaki@ed.ac.uk

Robert Dinnis, B.A., M.Sc., Ph.D., Early Career Fellow in Archaeol. [Middle-Upper Palaeolithic transition, esp. in northern Europe; the palaeogeography of northern Europe; Upper Palaeolithic technology, typology & function; the use of chronometric data in archaeological reconstructions], rdinnis@staffmail.ed.ac.uk

Frances D. Dow, M.A. (Edin.), D.Phil. (York), Hon. Fellow (Brit.) [Radicalism in England 1600–60, including puritanism; English Revolution 1640–60], Dr.F.D.Dow@ed.ac.uk

Matthew Dziennik, Ph.D. (Edin.), Early Career Fellow in Hist. [Military labour in the early British empire; political, social, & cultural structures of colonial rule], Matthew.Dziennik@ed.ac.uk

Owen Dudley Edwards, B.A. (N.U.I.), Hon. Fellow (N. Amer. & Irish) [History & literature of modern Ireland, Britain & North America]

Andrew W. Erskine, M.A., D.Phil. (Oxon.), Prof. of Anc. Hist. [Hellenistic history; Roman imperialism; political thought, esp. Stoicism], Andrew.Erskine@ed.ac.uk

Manuel Fernández-Götz, Ph.D., Chancellor's Fellow in Archaeol. [Iron Age societies in central & western Europe; archaeology of identities], M.Fernandez-Gotz@ed.ac.uk

Linda Fibiger, B.A. (Dublin), M.Sc. (Bradford), D.Phil. (Oxon.), Lect. in Bioarchaeol. (Archaeol.) [Neolithic Europe; conflict archaeology, interpersonal violence & cranial trauma], Linda.Fibiger@ed.ac.uk

Frances Fowle, M.A., M.Sc., Ph.D. (Edin.), Lect. in Hist. of Art [Art in France & Britain in the 19th & 20th c.], Frances.Fowle@ed.ac.uk

Adam P. Fox, B.A., Ph.D. (Cantab.), Reader in Econ. & Soc. Hist. [Oral traditions & the impact of literacy in early modern England], Adam.Fox@ed.ac.uk

James E. Fraser, B.A. (Toronto), M.A. (Guelph), Ph.D. (Edin.), Sen. Lect. in Early Scot. Hist. & Culture [War, Church & society in early medieval Britain & Ireland], James.E.Fraser@ed.ac.uk

Victoria Gardner, D.Phil. (Oxon.), Lect. in Soc. Hist. (Soc. Hist.) [Economics & culture in the 18th & 19th c.], Victoria.Gardner@ed.ac.uk

Alain George, D.Phil. (Oxon.), [Islamic art; Koranic inscriptions; calligraphy], A.George@ed.ac.uk

Julian Goodare, M.A., Ph.D. (Edin.), Reader in Scot. Hist. [Government, finance & politics in early modern Scotland; the witch hunt in Scotland & Europe], J.Goodare@ed.ac.uk

John E. Gooding, M.A. (Oxon.), Hon. Fellow [Political, social & cultural history of Russia 1801–1991; Perestroika & revolution of 1991; Leo Tolstoy], John.Gooding@ed.ac.uk

Anthony Gorman, (Mod. Mid. E.) [History of modern Egypt]

Benjamin Gray, M.A., D.Phil. (Oxon.), Chancellor's Fellow in Classics [Ancient Greek city-state; political & ethical thought], Benjamin.Gray@ed.ac.uk

David G. Greasley, B.A., B.Phil., Ph.D. (Liv.), Prof. of Econ. Hist. [Economic & industrial growth], David.Greasley@ed.ac.uk

Felicity Green, Ph.D. (Cantab.), Chancellor's Fellow in Hist. [Early modern European intellectual history; late 16th & early 17th c. moral & political thought], Felicity.Green@ed.ac.uk

Judith A. Green, B.A. (Lond.), D.Phil. (Oxon.), Emeritus Prof. of Med. Hist. [English history 11th & 12th c.; Ducal Normandy & the Normans; history of medieval women], Judith.Green@ed.ac.uk

*Trevor Griffiths, M.A., D.Phil. (Oxon.), Reader in Econ. & Soc. Hist., Head of Hist. [Leisure in Britain since 1750; technological change of British textile industry], Trevor.Griffiths@ed.ac.uk

Lucy H. Grig, B.A. (Cantab.), M.A. (York), Ph.D. (Cantab.), Lect. [Late antiquity; early Christianity], Lucy.Grig@ed.ac.uk

Anna Groundwater, M.A. (Cantab.), Ph.D. (Edin.), Co-ordinator of Graduate Methods Training (Brit. & Scot. Hist.) [Early modern British & Scottish government & society; the Union of the Crowns], Anna.Groundwater@ed.ac.uk

Erika Hanna, B.A., M.A. (Brist.), D.Phil. (Oxon.), Chancellor's Fellow in Hist. [20th c. Ireland; urban history; history of photography; historiography & research methodologies], Erika.Hanna@ed.ac.uk

Chris Harding, D.Phil. (Oxon.), Lect. in Asian Hist. [Asian & European religious cultures], Christopher.Harding@ed.ac.uk

Susan M. Hardman Moore, M.A. (Cantab.), M.A.R. (Yale), Ph.D. (Kent), Sen. Lect. in Div. [Early modern religious history; theology; spirituality, esp. Reformed tradition; puritanism in England & New England], S.HardmanMoore@ed.ac.uk

Bill Hare, Visiting Lect., p/t [20th c. Scottish art], billhare@ed.ac.uk

Fabian Hilfrich, M.A. (St. Louis), Ph.D. (Berlin), Sen. Lect. in Amer. Hist. [19th & 20th c. diplomatic history; German history; European history; cultural history; ideology], Fabian.Hilfrich@ed.ac.uk

Carole Hillenbrand, M.A. (Cantab. & Oxon.), Ph.D. (Edin.), Emeritus Prof. of Islamic Hist. [Medieval Islamic history; Sufism; historiography; political thought; history of Middle East 1050–1150]

Claudia Hopkins, Ph.D. (Edin.), Visiting Lect., p/t [Golden Age Spanish art; Goya], C.Hopkins@ed.ac.uk

Alvin Jackson, B.A., D.Phil. (Oxon.), Sir Richard Lodge Prof. of Brit. Hist. [19th & 20th c. Irish & British political history; British-Irish relations; the Union & Home Rule], Alvin.Jackson@ed.ac.uk

Louise Jackson, B.A. (Oxon.), M.A. (Exeter), Ph.D. (Surrey), Reader in Econ. & Soc. Hist. [Women in gender; crime & policing; childhood & child welfare], Louise.Jackson@ed.ac.uk

Ine Jacobs, M.A., Ph.D., Chancellor's Fellow in Classics [4th & 7th c. Eastern Roman Empire], Ine.Jacobs@ed.ac.uk

Rhodri Jeffreys-Jones, B.A. (Wales), Ph.D. (Cantab.), Emeritus Prof. of Amer. Hist. [U.S. foreign policy & intelligence 1898–2001; F.B.I.; women, African Americans, labour, students & the Vietnam War], R.Jeffreys-Jones@ed.ac.uk

David Kaufman, B.A., Ph.D., Lect. in Hist. [East-Central Europe between the end of the 19th c. & the Second World War], D.Kaufman@ed.ac.uk

Gavin Kelly, B.A. (Cantab.), M.A., D.Phil. (Oxon.), Sen. Lect. [Latin literature & politics; history of the Roman empire], Gavin.Kelly@ed.ac.uk

Elena Kranioti, M.D., Ph.D. (Crete), Lect. in Forensic Anthr.

Iain Lauchlan, B.A., Ph.D. (Leeds), Lect. in Eur. Hist. [Russia; espionage; revolutions; Stalinism], Iain.Lauchlan@ed.ac.uk

Robert Leighton, M.A., Ph.D. (Edin.), Sen. Lect. in Archaeol. (Eur. & Mediterranean Archaeol.), Robert.Leighton@ed.ac.uk

Dmitri Levitin, B.A., M.Phil. (Cantab.), Chancellor's Fellow in Hist. [British & European early modern intellectual, religious & cultural history], Dmitri.Levitin@ed.ac.uk

David Lewis, B.A., M.A., Ph.D. (Dunelm.), Early Career Fellow in Classics [Social & economic history of ancient Greece], David.Lewis@ed.ac.uk

Lloyd J. Llewellyn-Jones, B.A. (Hull), M.A., Ph.D. (Wales), Sen. Lect. [Gender in antiquity; dress; Persia; reception of antiquity in art, drama & film], L.Llewellyn-Jones@ed.ac.uk

Amy J. Lloyd, B.A. (Toronto), M.Phil., Ph.D. (Cantab.), Leverhulme Trust Early Career Fellow [Modern British & Canadian social, cultural & economic history; British emigration], Amy.Lloyd@ed.ac.uk

Francesca Locatelli, B.A. (Rome), M.A., Ph.D. (Lond.), Lect. in the Hist. of Sub-Saharan Afric. [Urban cultures; migration & diaspora; crime; gender relations], F.Locatelli@ed.ac.uk

Calum Maciver, M.A., M.Sc., Ph.D. (Edin.), Lect. in Classics (Greek & Latin) [Greek literature written in the Roman Empire, 1st–3rd c.], Calum.Maciver@ed.ac.uk

Eoin McLaughlin, Ph.D. (N.U.I.), Leverhulme Early Career Fellow [Irish land reform; sovereign debt; market responses, 1890–1938], Eoin.McLaughlin@ed.ac.uk

Kathleen McSweeney, M.A., Ph.D., Sen. Lect. in Human Osteology [Skeletal evidence; taphonomy of human remains]

Robert J. Mason, B.A., D.Phil. (Oxon.), Reader in Amer. Hist. (Contemp. U.S.), Robert.Mason@ed.ac.uk

Magdalena S. Midgley, M.A., Ph.D. (Edin.), Prof. of Archaeol. [Early farming; megaliths; Neolithic society], Magda.Midgley@ed.ac.uk

Robert J. Morris, B.A., D.Phil. (Oxon.), Emeritus Prof. of Econ. & Soc. Hist. [Social structure in 19th c. towns; gender & property], R.J.Morris@ed.ac.uk

Alexander J. Murdoch, B.A. (George Washington), Ph.D. (Edin.), Sen. Lect. in Scot. Hist. (18th c.) [British emigration 1600–1900; Scottish settlement in North America], Alex.Murdoch@ed.ac.uk

Stana S. Nenadic, B.A. (Strathclyde), M.A., Ph.D. (Glas.), Prof. of Soc. & Cultural Hist. [Material culture in Britain 18th–19th c.; women in business in 19th c.], Stana.Nenadic@ed.ac.uk

Andrew Newman, B.A., Ph.D. (Calif.), Reader in Persian & Islamic Stud. [Shi'ism; Islamic medicine; Persian literature], Andrew.Newman@ed.ac.uk

Mark Newman, B.A. (Leicester), M.A. (Wales), Ph.D. (Mississippi), Reader in Amer. Hist. [African-American history; the civil rights movement; religion & race relations; southern white liberals], M.Newman@ed.ac.uk

Paul C. Nugent, B.A. (Cape Town), M.A. (Lond.), Prof. of Comparative Afric. Hist. & Director of Centre of Afric. Stud. [Artificial boundaries & formation of identities in Africa; 20th c. political history of Ghana & Togo; African agriculture], Paul.Nugent@ed.ac.uk

Donncha O'Rourke, B.A., Ph.D., Lect. in Classics [Latin poetry, 1st c. B.C.], donncha.orourke@ed.ac.uk

Sara Parvis, B.A. (Oxon.), Ph.D. (Edin.), Lect. in Patristics in Eccles. Hist. [Early Christian history & doctrine], S.Parvis@ed.ac.uk

Andrew Patrizio, Ph.D. (Edin.), Prof. of Scot. Visual Culture [Scottish visual culture since 1945], A.Patrizio@ed.ac.uk

Edgar J. Peltenburg, B.A., Ph.D. (Birm.), Hon. Prof. Fellow in Archaeol. (Near E.) [Later bronze & iron ages of Cyprus & the Near East], E.Peltenburg@ed.ac.uk

Gordon Pentland, B.A. (Oxon.), Ph.D. (Edin.), Reader in Brit. Hist. [Radicalism & reform in 19th c. Britain], Gordon.Pentland@ed.ac.uk

Heather Pulliam, Ph.D. (St. And.), [Celtic & early medieval art], H.Pulliam@ed.ac.uk

Gianluca Raccagni, Ph.D., Chancellor's Fellow in Hist. [Political culture & political structures in the central middle ages], Gianluca.Raccagni@ed.ac.uk

*Ian B.M. Ralston, M.A., Ph.D. (Edin.), Abercromby Chair of Archaeol. (Prehistoric Eur.) [Iron age France; Scottish archaeology], Ian.Ralston@ed.ac.uk

*Carol M. Richardson, Ph.D. (St. And.), Head of Hist. of Art [Rome & institutional patronage], C.M.Richardson@ed.ac.uk

Richard Rodger, M.A., Ph.D. (Edin.), Prof. of Econ. & Soc. Hist. [Social & economic structure of towns since 1780; property relations; public health & public policy in the 19th c.], Richard.Rodger@ed.ac.uk

*Ulrike Roth, B.A., M.A., Ph.D., Sen. Lect., Head of Classics [Roman republican history; ancient slavery; gender in history], U.Roth@ed.ac.uk

Julius Ruiz, B.A. (Wales), M.St., D.Phil. (Oxon.), Lect. (19th–20th c. Spain), J.Ruiz@ed.ac.uk

Benjamin Russell, B.A., M.St., M.Phil. (Oxon.), Lect. in Classics (Classical Archaeol.) [Roman art; architecture; the ancient economy], Ben.Russell@ed.ac.uk

Eberhard W. Sauer, M.St., D.Phil. (Oxon.), Prof. [Archaeology of the Roman empire], Eberhard.Sauer@ed.ac.uk

Ulf-Dietrich Schoop, M.A., Ph.D. (Tübingen), Lect. in Near E. Archaeol. [Early prehistory of Anatolia; Hittites], Ulf.Schoop@ed.ac.uk

W. David H. Sellar, B.A. (Oxon.), LL.B. (Edin.), Hon. Fellow [History of family; Scottish legal history; Highland clans]

Lisa-Marie Shillito, B.A. (Oxon.), M.Sc., Ph.D. (Reading), Chancellor's Fellow in Archaeol. [Bioarchaeology & human origins], lshillit@staffmail.ed.ac.uk

David Silkenat, B.A. (Duke), Ph.D. (N. Carolina), Lect. in Hist. (Amer. Hist.) [Social & cultural history of the American South during the 19th century], David.Silkenat@ed.ac.uk

Catherine Spencer, M.A., Lect. [North American & British art, post 1945], Catherine.Spencer@ed.ac.uk

David A.T. Stafford, M.A. (Cantab.), Ph.D. (Lond.), Leverhulme Emeritus Prof., Project Director, Centre for the Study of the Two World Wars [20th c. British, European & international history], David.Stafford@ed.ac.uk

Jill R. Stephenson, M.A., Ph.D. (Edin.), Emeritus Prof. of Mod. Hist. (Eur.) [Society & politics in modern Germany to 1945], J.Stephenson@ed.ac.uk

Gordon D. Thomas, M.A., M.Litt., Ph.D. (Edin.), Sen. Lect. in Archaeol. [Prehistory of Cyprus; experimental archaeology; archaeological illustration; Roman Scotland], Gordon.Thomas@ed.ac.uk

T. Jack Thompson, B.A. (Belf.), Ph.D. (Edin.), Sen. Lect. in World Christianity [History of African Christianity], T.Jack.Thompson@ed.ac.uk

Richard I. Thomson, M.A. (Oxon.), M.A., Ph.D. (Lond.), Watson Gordon Prof. of Fine Art [19th & early 20th c. visual culture in France], R.Thomson@ed.ac.uk

Thomas S. Tolley, B.A., Ph.D. (East Anglia), Sen. Lect. in Hist. of Art [Visual culture in 14th–15th c. N. Europe; music & the visual arts], Tom.Tolley@ed.ac.uk

Simon Trépanier, B.A. (Ottawa), M.A., Ph.D. (Toronto), Lect. [Greek literature & philosophy], Simon.Trepanier@ed.ac.uk

Tamara Trodd, Ph.D. (Lond.), Lect. [20th c. & contemporary art], Tamara.Trodd@ed.ac.uk

Wendy Ugolini, M.A. (Cantab.), Ph.D. (Edin.), Lect. in Mod. Brit. Hist., Wendy.Ugolini@ed.ac.uk

Andrew F. Walls, O.B.E., M.A., B.Litt. (Oxon.), Director Emeritus of the Centre for the Study of Christianity in the Non-Western World [Christianity in non-western settings; history of missionary movement], Andrew.Walls@ptsem.edu

Genevieve Warwick, B.A., Ph.D. (Johns Hopkins), Lect. [Italian Renaissance; early modern European art], G.Warwick@ed.ac.uk

Tom Webster, B.A. (East Anglia), Ph.D. (Cantab.), Lect. in Brit. Hist. [17th c. English religious history; early modern ecclesiastical architecture; philosophy of history], Tom.Webster@ed.ac.uk

Richard Williams, M.A., Ph.D. (Manc.), Sen. Lect. in Hist. of Art [Contemporary art, architecture & urbanisation], R.J.Williams@ed.ac.uk

Stephanie Winder, Lect. in Classics [Greek literature & culture; Hellenistic poetry], Stephanie.Winder@ed.ac.uk

Jenny Wormald, M.A., Ph.D., Hon. Fellow (Scot. Hist.) [Late medieval & early modern Scotland & Britain], Jenny.Wormald@ed.ac.uk

David F. Wright, M.A. (Cantab.), D.D. (Edin.), Hon. Fellow (Early Church) [Augustine; baptism; Bucer, Calvin, Knox; homosexuality]

Chia-Ling Yang, Ph.D. (Lond.), Lect. [19th & 20th c. Chinese painting], C.Yang@ed.ac.uk

Nuala Zahedieh, B.Sc., M.Sc., Ph.D. (Lond.), Reader in Econ. & Soc. Hist. [Economic history of early modern Britain; British Atlantic economy c.1607–1770], N.Zahedieh@ed.ac.uk

UNIVERSITY OF ESSEX

Wivenhoe Park, Colchester, Essex, CO4 3SQ. 01206 873333. Fax 01206 873598
www.essex.ac.uk
Department of History 01206 872302. Fax 01206 873757

D. Hugh V. Brogan, M.A. (Cantab.), Res. Prof. [John F. Kennedy; U.S. machine politics; Alexis de Tocqueville; history of Repton School], hbrogan@essex.ac.uk

Pamela M. Cox, B.A., Ph.D. (Cantab.), Reader in Soc. Hist. (19th–20th c. Brit.) [Crime; comparative public policy; voluntary sector; gender; youth culture; governmentality; cultural & social history], pamcox@essex.ac.uk

Catherine Crawford, B.A. (Brit. Col.), M.Sc. (Sussex), D.Phil. (Oxon.), Lect. in Hist. (17th–19th c. Eng., Hist. of Medicine) [Medicine & the law; illness & culture; community activism in 20th c. London; cultural & social history], crawc@essex.ac.uk

Joan M. Davies, B.A., Ph.D. (Lond.), Visiting Fellow (16th–18th c. Eur.) [Early modern French aristocracy & patronage; Montmorency family; urban society & Reformation in Toulouse], davjo@essex.ac.uk

Amanda Flather, B.A., Ph.D. (Essex), Lect. in Hist. (16th–18th Eng.) [Social & cultural history; social space; gender & sexuality; local history], flatak@essex.ac.uk

Thomas S. Freeman, B.A., Ph.D. (Rutgers), Lect. in Hist. (16th–17th c. Eng. Relig. Cultural & Soc.) [Persecution; martyrdom; historiography; exorcism & demonism; John Foxe the martyrologist & reign of Mary I], tfreeman@essex.ac.uk

Mark R. Frost, B.A. (Oxon.), M.Phil., Ph.D. (Cantab.), Lect. in Hist. (18th–20th c. Asian & Colonial) [Port cities; migration; the colonial public sphere; nationalism, cosmopolitanism & decolonisation], mrfrost@essex.ac.uk

Matthew Grant, B.A., M.A., Ph.D. (Lond.), Lect. in Hist. (Mod. Brit.) [Cold war Britain; Second World War; citizenship; memory; political culture], mgranta@essex.ac.uk

Peter J. Gurney, B.A., M.A., D.Phil. (Sussex), Sen. Lect. (Mod. Brit.) [Social history; mass consumption], pjgurney@essex.ac.uk

Laila Haidarali, B.A. (Western Ont.), M.A. (Windsor), Ph.D. (York, Canada), Lect. in U.S. Hist. [20th c. U.S.A., African American history; women & gender history; beauty culture; Harlem Renaissance literature; identity politics; cultural & social history; consumer culture], lhaid@essex.ac.uk

Brian R. Hamnett, M.A., Ph.D. (Cantab.), Res. Prof. of Hist. [Iberian & Ibero-American history; comparative empires & post-imperial crises; cultural history; literary representations of history]

John Haynes, B.A., M.A., Ph.D. (Manc.), Lect. in Film Stud. [Film theory & history; cinemas, societies & the cultural politics of film in the Soviet Union & U.S.A.; oral history & documentary film], jhaynes@essex.ac.uk

Edward J. Higgs, B.A., D.Phil. (Oxon.), Prof. of Hist. (16th–20th c. Eng.) [State surveillance of the citizen; technologies of identification; history of statistics, censuses & surveys], ejhiggs@essex.ac.uk

Elena Hore, B.A. (Moscow), M.A., Ph.D. (Essex), Lect. in Russian & Contemp. Hist. [Russia; the U.S.S.R.; post-Soviet history; history of the Cold War], ehore@essex.ac.uk

Jeremy M. Krikler, B.A. (Cape Town), D.Phil. (Oxon.), Reader in Hist. (20th c. S. Afric., 18th c. Eng. Slave Trade, 19th & 20th c. Imp.) [Race & class; agrarian history; labour movements; the slave trade; literature & empire], jeremy@essex.ac.uk

Andrew J. Priest, B.A., Ph.D. (Birm.), Lect. in Hist. (19th & 20th c. U.S.A.) [History of U.S. foreign policy; rise & decline of American power; relationship between domestic & foreign policy; the Vietnam war], apriest@essex.ac.uk

James R. Raven, M.A. (Cantab.), M.A. (Oxon.), Ph.D., Litt.D. (Cantab.), Prof. of Hist. (17th–19th c. Brit. & Colonial) [17th–19th c. literary & cultural, British & colonial history, with particular emphasis on book & communications history]

Matthias Röhrig Assunção, B.A., M.A. (Paris), Ph.D. (Berlin), Reader in Hist. (Latin Amer.) [Colonial history of Latin America; slavery & post-emancipation in Brazil & the Caribbean; political history of 19th & 20th c. Latin America]

Michael S. Roper, B.A. (Melb.), M.A. (Monash), Ph.D. (Essex), Prof. of Soc. & Cultural Hist. (20th c. Brit.) [Family relationships & the First World War; masculinity & subjectivity; children & the aftermath of the First World War; psychoanalysis & historical research], mrop@essex.ac.uk

Nadine Rossol, M.A. (St. And.), Ph.D. (Limerick), Lect. in Hist. (20th c. German Hist.) [20th c. German history, political culture & cultural representation; police history; Weimar & Nazi Germany], nrossol@essex.ac.uk

*Alison Rowlands, B.A. (Oxon.), Ph.D. (Cantab.), Sen. Lect. in Eur. Hist. (16th–18th c. Eur.) [Women, gender, crime & witchcraft in early modern Germany; history of Rothenburg ob der Tauber; witchcraft in Essex & East Anglia, 16th–20th c.], alisonc@essex.ac.uk

David Rundle, M.A., D.Phil. (Oxon.), Lect. in Hist. (15th–17th c. Brit. & Eur.) [Renaissance, esp. humanism; history of books & libraries; political thought], drundle@essex.ac.uk

Rainer U.W. Schulze, M.A., Ph.D. (Göttingen), Prof. of Hist. (19th–20th c. Eur.) [20th c. German history; the Holocaust; forced migration movements in 20th c. Europe; collective memory & individual experience; Bergen-Belsen concentration camp; Roma & Sinti in Europe after 1945], rainer@essex.ac.uk

E. Anthony Swift, M.A., Ph.D. (Calif. at Berkeley), Sen. Lect. in Hist. (19th–20th c. Russia) [Russian popular culture; world's fairs & international expositions], swift@essex.ac.uk

Fiona M. Venn, B.A., Ph.D. (Brist.), Visiting Fellow (20th c. U.S.A., Int. Hist.) [Oil diplomacy; Anglo-American relations], vennf@essex.ac.uk

John D. Walter, M.A. (Cantab. & Penn.), Prof. of Hist. (Brit. & Irish Early Mod. Hist.) [Popular protest & political culture in early modern England; English civil war/revolution; food in history; history of gesture], jwalter@essex.ac.uk

Neil Younger, B.A., M.Phil., Ph.D. (Birm.), Lect. in Hist. (16th c. Eng.) [Politics; government; local government; warfare], nyounger@essex.ac.uk

Xun Zhou, B.A. (Sichuan), M.A., Ph.D. (Lond.), Lect. in Hist. (19th–20th c. China) [Cultural nationalism in 20th c. China; Chinese historiography & history of sinology; health in Mao's China; opium & empire, 16th–20th c.; race & ethnicity in China since 17th c.], xzhoug@essex.ac.uk

UNIVERSITY OF **EXETER**

Exeter, Devon, EX4 4RJ. 01392 661000. Fax 01392 263108
www.exeter.ac.uk
History 01392 264297. Fax 01392 263305
http://humanities.exeter.ac.uk/history/
Continuing Education 01392 262828. Fax 01392 262829
Archaeology 01392 724350. Fax 01392 724358
Classics & Ancient History 01392 264202. Fax 01392 264377
http://humanities.exeter.ac.uk/archaeology
Medical History 01392 263289. Fax 01392 263305
Institute of Cornish Studies 01326 371811

Kristofer M. Allerfeldt, B.A., Ph.D. (Exeter), Sen. Lect. in Hist. (19th & 20th c. U.S. Hist.) [U.S. immigration policy; American nationalism & nativism; U.S. in Great War; crime & deviancy in early 20th c. America; Ku Klux Klan; organised crime], K.M.Allerfeldt@exeter.ac.uk

Sara Barker, B.A. (Dunelm.), M.A. (York), Ph.D. (St. And.), Lect. in Hist. (Early Mod. Eur.) [French religious wars & reformation; religious identity & theology; poetry & drama], S.K.Barker@exeter.ac.uk

Jonathan Barry, M.A., D.Phil. (Oxon.), Prof. of Hist. (17th–18th c. Brit.) [Bristol; S.W. England; provincial towns; middling sort; witchcraft; civic culture], J.Barry@exeter.ac.uk

Helen Birkett, B.A. (Lond.), M.A., Ph.D. (York), Lect. in Med. Hist. [Medieval religious history; intellectual & cultural history in the 12th & 13th c.]

Jeremy M. Black, M.A. (Cantab. & Oxon.), Ph.D. (Dunelm.), Prof. of Hist. (Early Mod. & Mod.) [Warfare; international relations; historical atlases]

Alan E. Booth, B.A., Ph.D. (Kent), Prof. (20th c. Brit., 19th–20th c. Developing World) [Economic thought & policy; technical change; British industry since 1945], A.E.Booth@exeter.ac.uk

Bruce Bradley, B.A. (Arizona), Ph.D. (Cantab.), Prof. of Prehist. (Prehist.) [Experimental archaeology; flaked stone technology], B.A.Bradley@exeter.ac.uk

David C. Braund, M.A., Ph.D. (Cantab.), Prof. of Mediterranean & Black Sea Hist. (Hist. of Early Roman Empire)

Roger Burt, B.Sc.(Econ.), Ph.D. (Lond.), Emeritus Prof. of Mining Hist. (18th–20th c. Brit. & U.S.A., Tech.) [Investment in metal mining: Britain & abroad 1870–1914], R.Burt@exeter.ac.uk

Isabelle Charmantier, B.A. (Montpellier), Ph.D. (Sheff.), Assoc. Res. Fellow (Medical Hist.) [Scientific taxonomies; Linnaeus; history of ornithology, 17th–18th c.], I.Charmantier@exeter.ac.uk

Nandini Chatterjee, B.A. (Calcutta), M.A., M.Phil. (J. Nehru), Ph.D. (Cantab.), Lect. in Hist. (Hist. of India) [Law & cultural exchanges in British & Mughal empires], N.Chatterjee@exeter.ac.uk

James Clark, B.A. (Brist.), M.A., D.Phil. (Oxon.), Prof. of Hist. (Hist.) [Religious, intellectual & cultural history, esp. monasticism 1300–1600], J.G.Clark@exeter.ac.uk

Timothy Cooper, B.A. (Oxon.), Ph.D. (Cantab.), Sen. Lect. in Hist. (Mod. Brit.) [British environmental history & politics], T.Cooper@exeter.ac.uk

Freyja Cox Jensen, B.A., M.St., D.Phil. (Oxon.), Lect. in Early Mod. Hist. [The study of classical culture & the book in early modern England & Europe]

Oliver H. Creighton, B.A. (Exeter), M.A., Ph.D. (Leicester), Assoc. Prof. of Archaeol. (Medieval Archaeol., Landscape Stud., Castle Stud.), O.H.Creighton@exeter.ac.uk

Gareth Curless, B.A., Ph.D. (Exeter), E.S.R.C. Future Leaders Fellow & Lect. in Hist. (Hist.) [Emergence of organised labour & unrest in British empire during decolonisation], G.M.Curless@exeter.ac.uk

Robin W. Dennell, M.A., Ph.D. (Cantab.), Prof. of Archaeol. [Asia; Palaeolithic; Pleistocene; human evolution world heritage], R.W.Dennell@exeter.ac.uk

Kate Fisher, B.A. (Cantab.), M.Sc., Ph.D. (Oxon.), Prof. of Hist. [19th & 20th c. sexuality & medicine, esp. birth control & abortion; modern reception of ancient cultures as shaping attitudes towards sexuality], K.Fisher@exeter.ac.uk

Robert Fletcher, B.A., M.St., D.Phil. (Oxon.), Lect. in Global/Imp. Hist. [British imperialism & desert administration, 1929–36]

*Henry French, B.A., Ph.D. (Cantab.), Prof. of Soc. Hist. [Rural society & the 'middle sort' in early modern England], H.French@exeter.ac.uk

Jana Funke, M.A. (Cologne), M.St. (Oxon.), Ph.D. (Edin.), Res. Fellow (Medical Hist.) [Sexual science; constructions of sexual knowledge in Britain & Germany, 19th–20th c.], J.Funke@exeter.ac.uk

Maria Fusaro, Ph.D. (Cantab.), Sen. Lect. in Hist., Director, Centre for Maritime Hist. Stud. [Early modern social & economic history; early modern Mediterranean; mercantile networks], M.Fusaro@exeter.ac.uk

Alison Haggett, B.A., M.A., Ph.D. (Exeter), Lect. in Hist. (Medical Hist.) [20th c. social & cultural history; history of mental illness; gender; psychopharmacology], A.N.Haggett@exeter.ac.uk

Sarah M. Hamilton, B.A. (Cantab.), M.A., Ph.D. (Lond.), Prof. of Hist. [Central medieval social history of religion, esp. penance & excommunication; medieval liturgy; heresy], S.M.Hamilton@exeter.ac.uk

Anthony Harding, B.A., M.A., Ph.D., Prof. (Prehist.) [European bronze age], A.F.Harding@exeter.ac.uk

Hajnalka Herold, Dip. in Archaeol. (Budapest), Ph.D. (Vienna), Lect. in Historic Archaeol. [Early medieval archaeology, 400–1100 A.D.; archaeometry; experimental archaeology], H.Herold@exeter.ac.uk

Linda M. Hurcombe, B.A. (Southampton), Ph.D. (Sheff.), Sen. Lect. in Archaeol. (Prehist.) [Material culture; lithics; usewear analysis], L.M.Hurcombe@exeter.ac.uk

Stacey Hynd, M.A., D.Phil. (Oxon.), Lect. in Afric. Hist. [Crime & punishment in British Africa], S.Hynd@exeter.ac.uk

José Iriarte, Lic. (Montevideo), Ph.D. (Kentucky), Assoc. Prof. of Archaeol. [South America; prehistoric palaeoethnobotany], J.Iriarte@exeter.ac.uk

Elena Isayev, B.A. (York, Ont.), M.A. (Brit. Col.), Ph.D. (Lond.), [Italic communities 4th–1st c. B.C.]

Mark A. Jackson, B.Sc., M.B., B.S. (Lond.), Ph.D. (Leeds), Prof. of Hist. of Medicine, Director, Centre for Medical Hist., M.A.Jackson@exeter.ac.uk

Justin Jones, B.A., Ph.D. (Cantab.), Lect. in Hist. (Mod. S. Asia) [Islam; Muslim society; religious change in India], J.R.Jones@exeter.ac.uk

Gill Juleff, B.Sc., Ph.D. (Lond.), Sen. Lect. in Archaeol. (Prehist.) [Archaeometallurgy], G.Juleff@exeter.ac.uk

Chris Knüsel, B.A. (Wisconsin-Madison), M.A. (York), Ph.D. (Simon Fraser), Assoc. Prof. (Bioarchaeology) [Social archaeology & skeletal biology; funerary archaeology], C.J.Knusel@exeter.ac.uk

Marisa Lazzari, Lic. (Buenos Aires), Ph.D. (Columbia), Sen. Lect. (Archaeol.) [Archaeology of circulation & social interaction in the south central Andes], M.Lazzari@exeter.ac.uk

Tehyun Ma, B.A. (Penn.), Ph.D. (Brist.), Lect. in Hist. (Hist. of Mod. China) [State-building in China & Taiwan, 1945–55], T.Ma@exeter.ac.uk

James A. Mark, B.A., M.Phil., D.Phil. (Oxon.), Prof. of Hist. (20th c. Central-E. Eur.) [Social history of communism; social, cultural & political memory; oral history], J.A.Mark@exeter.ac.uk

Joseph L. Melling, B.Soc.Sc. (Bradford), Ph.D. (Glas.), Prof. of Hist. of Medicine & Industry (19th–20th c. Brit., Soc. Management) [History of industrial supervision; lunacy], J.L.Melling@exeter.ac.uk

Lynette G. Mitchell, B.A. (Northeastern), Ph.D. (Dunelm.), Lect. in Classics

Robert G. Morkot, B.A., Ph.D. (Lond.), Sen. Lect. in Archaeol. [Egypt; Sudan; Libya; Near East; ancient economies]

Roger Morriss, B.Sc. (Southampton), Ph.D. (Lond.), Sen. Lect. in Hist. (Early Mod. & Mod. Maritime & Naval Hist.), R.A.Morriss@exeter.ac.uk

Staffan Müller-Wille, M.Sc. (Berlin), Ph.D. (Bielefeld), Sen. Lect. in Hist. [History of heredity, natural history & racial anthropology, 18th–20th c.], S.E.W.Mueller-Wille@exeter.ac.uk

Jonathan D. Nichol, M.A., Ph.D. (Cantab.), Sen. Lect. in Educ., Sch. of Educ.

Richard Noakes, M.A., Ph.D. (Cantab.), Sen. Lect. in Hist. (Hist. of Mod. Sc. & Tech.) [19th c. physical sciences; science & the occult; 19th & 20th c. telecommunications; science & the media], R.J.Noakes@exeter.ac.uk

Daniel Ogden, M.A., D.Phil. (Oxon.), Prof. of Anc. Hist. [Greek social history]

Ioana Oltean, M.A. (Cluj Napoca, Romania), Ph.D. (Glas.), Sen. Lect. [Archaeology of the Roman empire], I.A.Oltean@exeter.ac.uk

Bryony Onciul, B.A. (Nott.), M.A., Ph.D. (Newcastle), Lect. in Public Hist. (Public Hist.) [Public history; culture & heritage; indigenous postcolonial history], B.A.Onciul@exeter.ac.uk

*Alan K. Outram, B.A., Ph.D. (Dunelm.), M.Sc. (Sheff.), Assoc. Prof. of Archaeol. Sc. (Prehist.) [Zooarchaeology; palaeoeconomics; Central Asia], A.K.Outram@exeter.ac.uk

Mark Overton, B.A. (Exeter), M.A., Ph.D. (Cantab.), Prof. of Econ. & Soc. Hist. (Brit. Econ. & Soc.) [Rural history; English economic & social history 16th–19th c.], M.Overton@exeter.ac.uk

Richard J. Overy, M.A., Ph.D. (Cantab.), F.B.A., Prof. of Hist. (Mod.) [20th c. Germany; air power history], R.Overy@exeter.ac.uk

Marc-William Palen, B.A., M.A., Ph.D. (Texas), Lect. in Hist. (Imp./Global Hist.) [British & American imperialism; free trade ideology & political economy since 1800], M.Palen@exeter.ac.uk

Philip J. Payton, B.Sc. (Brist.), Ph.D. (Adelaide & C.N.A.A.), Emeritus Prof. of Cornish & Australian Stud. [Emigration; mining; place & identity; biography; First World War], P.J.Payton@exeter.ac.uk

Catriona Pennell, B.A. (Dublin), M.Sc. (Lond.), Ph.D. (Dublin), Sen. Lect. in Hist. (First World War Stud., Mod. Brit., Mod. Mid. E.) [First World War; British imperialism in Middle East; war studies; Anglo-Irish relations], C.L.Pennell@exeter.ac.uk

Yolanda Plumley, M.A., Ph.D. (Exeter), Prof. of Hist. (Med. Eur.) [History of late medieval music & courtly culture; French songs & lyrics 14th & 15th c., esp. Guillaume de Marchaut], Y.M.Plumley@exeter.ac.uk

Timothy J. Rees, M.A. (Lond.), D.Phil. (Oxon.), Sen. Lect. in Hist. (Mod. Eur.) [Rural history of Spain; Franco regime & Spanish Communist party], T.J.Rees@exeter.ac.uk

Matthias Reiss, M.A. (Cincinnati), Ph.D. (Hamburg), Sen. Lect. in Hist. (Mod.) [19th & 20th c. American, British & German social history; PoWs; unemployment; protest marches], M.Reiss@exeter.ac.uk

Matthew Rendle, B.A., M.A., Ph.D. (Exeter), Lect. in Hist. (Mod. Eur.) [Russian political & social history, 18th–20th c., particularly Russian nobility], M.Rendle@exeter.ac.uk

Catherine R. Rider, M.A., Ph.D. (Lond.), Sen. Lect. in Hist. (Med. Brit. & Eur.) [Late medieval Britain & Europe; history of magic, religion & medicine], C.R.Rider@exeter.ac.uk

Stephen J. Rippon, B.A., Ph.D. (Read.), Prof. of Landscape Archaeol. (Late Roman & Early Med. Hist.) [History of landscape; wetland archaeology], S.J.Rippon@exeter.ac.uk

Levi Roach, B.A., M.Phil., Ph.D. (Cantab.), Lect. in Med. Hist. [European history *c*.400–1200, esp. kingship & the state; penitential/apocalyptic thought]

Laura Rowe, B.A., M.St. (Oxon.), Ph.D. (Lond.), Lect. in Naval Hist. (19th & 20th c. Soc. & Cultural Hist.), L.Rowe@exeter.ac.uk

Laura Sangha, M.A., Ph.D. (Warwick), Lect. in Hist. (Early Mod. Brit.) [Angels & popular belief in English religious cultures, *c*.1480–1700], L.S.Sangha@exeter.ac.uk

Nicholas Terry, B.A., M.Phil., Ph.D. (Lond.), Lect. in Mod. Hist. [European history; wartime knowledge of the Holocaust]

David Thackeray, M.St. (Oxon.), Ph.D. (Cantab.), Lect. in Hist. (Mod. Brit.) [British political history 19th & 20th c.; Conservative party; popular political participation & organisation], D.Thackeray@exeter.ac.uk

Martin C. Thomas, B.A., D.Phil. (Oxon.), Prof. of Hist. (20th c. France & Eur.) [French foreign & defence policy 1930s–50s; French imperial history; decolonisation; Vichy empire], Martin.C.Thomas@exeter.ac.uk

Andrew Thompson, M.A., D.Phil. (Oxon.), Prof. of Mod. Hist. [Relations between British & imperial history in the 19th & 20th c.; 'imperial' migration before & after 1945]

Andrew Thorpe, B.A. (Birm.), Ph.D. (Sheff.), Prof. of Mod. Pol. Hist. [20th c. British political history; history of party & policy making; international community], A.J.Thorpe@exeter.ac.uk

Sarah Toulalan, B.A., Ph.D. (Lond.), Sen. Lect. in Hist. (Early Mod. Brit. & Eur.) [The body, gender, sex & sexuality; health & medicine; the family in 17th c. Britain], S.D.Toulalan@exeter.ac.uk

Richard Toye, B.A., M.Phil., Ph.D. (Cantab.), Prof. of Hist. (19th–20th c. Brit. & Int.) [Economic thought & policy; politics; empire; the United Nations], R.Toye@exeter.ac.uk

Garry H. Tregidga, B.A., M.Phil., Ph.D. (Exeter), Director, Inst. of Cornish Stud. [19th & 20th c. Liberalism in the S.W.; oral history; regional politics & religion], G.H.Tregidga@exeter.ac.uk

Robert van de Noort, B.A. (Utrecht), Drs. (Amsterdam), Ph.D. (Exeter), Prof. of Wetland Archaeol. [Landscape archaeology; wetlands & prehistoric boats], R.van-de-Noort@exeter.ac.uk

Jane C. Whittle, B.A. (Manc.), D.Phil. (Oxon.), Prof. of Hist. (Late Med. & Early Mod. Brit. Econ. & Soc.) [14th–17th c. rural society & economy of England; gender history], J.C.Whittle@exeter.ac.uk

Nicola Whyte, B.A., M.A., Ph.D. (East Anglia), Sen. Lect. in Hist. (Early Mod. Brit.) [Landscape, environment & society *c*.1500–1800], N.M.Whyte@exeter.ac.uk

*John M. Wilkins, M.A., Ph.D. (Cantab.), Prof. of Greek Culture (Anc. Greek Hist.), J.M.Wilkins@exeter.ac.uk

T. Peter Wiseman, M.A., D.Phil. (Oxon.), D.Litt. (Dunelm.), F.B.A., Emeritus Prof. of Classics (Hist. of Late Roman Republic) [Roman republican history & mythology]

UNIVERSITY OF **GLASGOW**

Glasgow, G12 8QQ. 0141 339 8855. Fax 0141 330 4889
www.gla.ac.uk
School of Humanities
www.gla.ac.uk/schools/humanities/
History 0141 330 4509. Fax 0141 330 5000
www.gla.ac.uk/schools/humanities/history/
Economic & Social History 0141 330 5992. Fax 0141 330 4889
Centre for the History of Medicine 0141 339 6071. Fax 0141 330 8011
Archaeology 0141 330 5690. Fax 0141 330 3544
www.gla.ac.uk/subjects/archaeology/
Classics 0141 330 5695. Fax 0141 339 4459
Hispanic Studies 0141 330 5335. Fax 0141 329 1119
History of Art 0141 330 5677. Fax 0141 330 3513
Theology & Religious Studies 0141 330 6524
Institute of Central & East European Studies 0141 330 5585

Lynn C. Abrams, B.A., Ph.D. (East Anglia), Prof. of Gender Hist. (Mod. Germany, Women, Children) [Gender relations, marriage, divorce & the law in 19th c. Germany; child welfare; women in Scotland], l.abrams@glasgow.ac.uk

Stuart R. Airlie, M.A. (Glas.), D.Phil. (Oxon.), Sen. Lect. in Med. Hist. (Early Med. Eur. & Brit.) [Carolingian political history & culture], s.airlie@glasgow.ac.uk

Colleen Batey, B.A., Ph.D. (Dunelm.), Sen. Lect. in Archaeol. [Scandinavian & North Atlantic archaeology, particularly artefact studies], c.batey@glasgow.ac.uk

John Bonehill, B.A., Ph.D. (Leicester), Lect. [18th & 19th c. European art, esp. British art & culture; relationship between the imagery of warfare & emergent conceptions of British national identity], john.bonehill@glasgow.ac.uk

Karin Bowie, B.A., M.B.A., M.Phil., Ph.D. (Glas.), Lect. in Scot. Hist. (16th–18th c.), k.bowie@glasgow.ac.uk

Maude Bracke, Ph.D. (E.U.I.), Lect. in Eur. Hist. (Eur. Hist. post-1800), m.bracke@glasgow.ac.uk

Kenneth E. Brophy, B.Sc., Ph.D. (Glas.), Lect. in Archaeol. [Neolithic Britain; theoretical archaeology], k.brophy@glasgow.ac.uk

Dauvit E. Broun, B.A., Ph.D. (Edin.), Prof. of Med. Scot. Hist. (6th–15th c. Scot. Hist., Early Med. Ireland) [Medieval Scottish historiography & identity; Scottish charters & literacy to 13th c.], d.broun@glasgow.ac.uk

Ewan N. Campbell, B.Sc. (Glas.), Ph.D. (Wales), Sen. Lect. in Archaeol. [Early medieval Celtic Britain; trade & economy; artefact studies], e.campbell@glasgow.ac.uk

Samuel K. Cohn, Jr., B.A. (Union), M.A. (Wis.), Ph.D. (Harv.), Prof. of Med. Hist. [Late medieval Italy; history of medicine; Black Death; comparative rebellion; history of human immunity], s.cohn@glasgow.ac.uk

Christopher Dalglish, M.A., Ph.D. (Glas.), Lect. [Historical archaeology; landscape archaeology; archaeology of Scotland in British, European & world contexts], c.dalglish@glasgow.ac.uk

Patricia de Montfort, B.F.A. (Cork), M.Litt., Ph.D. (St. And.), Lect. [Exhibition culture in London 1878–1908], patricia.de-montfort@glasgow.ac.uk

Stephen T. Driscoll, B.A., M.Sc. (Penn.), Ph.D. (Glas.), Prof. of Hist. Archaeol. [Medieval Scotland], s.driscoll@glasgow.ac.uk

Marilyn Dunn, M.A., Ph.D. (Edin.), Sen. Lect. in Med. Hist. (Med. Eur., Relig. & Monasticism, Byz.), m.dunn@glasgow.ac.uk

Marguerite W. Duprée, B.A. (Mt. Holyoke Coll., Mass.), M.A. (Princeton), D.Phil. (Oxon.), Prof. of Soc. & Medical Hist. [Medical profession; Scottish hydropathic establishments; family; cotton industry; National Health Service], marguerite.dupree@glasgow.ac.uk

Nyree J. Finlay, M.A. (Edin.), Ph.D. (Read.), Lect. in Archaeol. [Gatherer/hunter archaeology in northern Europe; lithic technology; archaeology of gender], n.finlay@glasgow.ac.uk

Michael J. French, B.A. (East Anglia), M.Sc., Ph.D. (Lond.), Prof. of Econ. & Soc. Hist. (19th–20th c. U.S.A., Business) [American business since 1970s; commercial travellers], michael.french@glasgow.ac.uk

Michael J.M. Given, B.A. (Oxon.), Ph.D. (Cantab.), Sen. Lect. [Archaeological survey; landscape archaeology; eastern Mediterranean; imperialism & postcolonial theory; history of archaeology], m.given@glasgow.ac.uk

Claudia Glatz, B.A., M.A., Ph.D. (Lond.), Lect. in Prehist. Mediterranean Archaeol.

Eleanor J. Gordon, M.A. (Edin.), Ph.D. (Glas.), Prof. of Gender & Soc. Hist. (19th–20th c. Brit., Gender, Labour) [History of middle classes; family history; women's labour history], eleanor.gordon@glasgow.ac.uk

Elizabeth Hancock, B.A. (Sheff.), Director, Decorative Arts & Design Hist. [European furnishing textiles; research & grant development], liz.hancock@glasgow.ac.uk

William S. Hanson, B.A., Ph.D. (Manc.), Prof. of Roman Archaeol. [Impact of Roman occupation on frontier provinces of Roman empire; aerial archaeology], w.hanson@glasgow.ac.uk

W. Ian P. Hazlett, B.A. (Belf.), B.D. (St. And.), D.Litt. (St. And.), Dr.theol. (Münster), Prof. of Eccles. Hist. [16th c. text editing – Martin Bucer; Scottish Reformation; confessions of faith; 18th c. Irish church history], i.hazlett@glasgow.ac.uk

Erma Hermens, M.A., Ph.D. (Leiden), Lect. [Historical painting techniques, with an emphasis on 16th & 17th c. Italian art & Dutch & Flemish painting], erma.hermens@glasgow.ac.uk

David Hopkins, B.A. (C.N.A.A.), M.A., Ph.D. (Essex), Prof. of Hist. of Art [Dada & surrealism; Duchamp; 20th c. photography], david.hopkins@glasgow.ac.uk

Rupert A. Housley, B.Sc. (Leicester), M.Sc. (Southampton), Ph.D. (Cantab.), Lect. in Archaeol. Sc. [Early prehistoric archaeology; scientific dating methods; environmental & wetland archaeology; archaeobotany], r.housley@glasgow.ac.uk

*Jeremy W. Huggett, B.A. (Leeds), Ph.D. (C.N.A.A.), Sen. Lect. in Archaeol. [Anglo-Saxon England; social & economic archaeology; computing in archaeology], j.huggett@glasgow.ac.uk

Annmarie Hughes, B.A., Ph.D. (Strathclyde), Lect. in Econ. & Soc. Hist. (19th–20th c. Brit Hist. & Popular Culture) [Gender, feminism & domestic violence], annemarie.hughes@glasgow.ac.uk

Richard E. Jones, B.Sc. (Kent), M.Sc. (Warwick), Ph.D. (Wales), Sen. Lect. in Archaeol. [Archaeological science in Scotland & E. Mediterranean], r.jones@glasgow.ac.uk

Debbie Lewer, B.A., Ph.D. (Manc. Met.), Lect. (20th c. Eur. Art) [German art, architecture & politics], deborah.lewer@glasgow.ac.uk

*Catriona M.M. Macdonald, M.A. (St. And.), Ph.D. (Strathclyde), Reader in Late Mod. Scot. Hist. [Socio-political & cultural history of late modern Scotland in a U.K. & global context], catriona.macdonald@glasgow.ac.uk

Margaret F. MacDonald, B.A. (Leeds), D.Litt. (Glas.), Hon. Prof. Res. Fellow [Etchings of James NcNeill Whistler], margaret.macdonald@glasgow.ac.uk

Martin D.W. MacGregor, M.A., Ph.D. (Edin.), Lect. in Scot. Hist. (Scotland 1707–1999) [Gaelic Scotland c.1200–c.1700: society, culture, politics & identity, with particular reference to the relationship with Ireland & to the use of literary sources; migration, emigration & Irish immigration; Highlands], m.macgregor@glasgow.ac.uk

Stephen Marritt, B.A. (Belf.), M.Phil., Ph.D. (Glas.), Lect. in Med. Hist. [British Isles & northern European 11th & 12th c. political & ecclesiastical history]

Alexander Marshall, M.A. (Glas.), M.A. (Lond.), Ph.D. (Glas.), Sen. Lect. in Med. Hist. [Russian/Soviet military & political history]

Charlotte Methuen, B.A., M.A. (Cantab.), B.D., Ph.D. (Edin.), Lect. in Eccles. Hist. & Reformation Stud., charlotte.methuen@glasgow.ac.uk

Marina Moskowitz, B.A., M.A., Ph.D. (Yale), Reader in Mod. Hist. [Material culture; American middle-class culture], m.moskowitz@glasgow.ac.uk

Michael S. Moss, M.A. (Glas.), Prof. [University history & historiography], m.moss@glasgow.ac.uk

Sumita Mukherjee, B.A. (Dunelm.), M.St., D.Phil. (Oxon.), Lect. in Econ. & Soc. Hist. [19th & 20th c. south Asia; British empire; south Asian migration], sumita.mukherjee@glasgow.ac.uk

Thomas Munck, M.A. (St. And.), Ph.D. (East Anglia), Prof. of Early Mod. Eur. Hist. (Early Mod. Eur., French Revolution) [Social history of the Enlightenment; 17th–18th c. Denmark], t.munck@glasgow.ac.uk

Paul P. Musselwhite, B.A., M.A., Ph.D. (William & Mary), Lect. in Amer. Hist. [17th c. American south; early modern Atlantic; civic & political culture], paul.musselwhite@glasgow.ac.uk

Simon Newman, B.A. (Nott.), M.A. (Wis.), M.A., Ph.D. (Princeton), Sir Denis Brogan Prof. of Amer. Stud., Director of Amer. Stud. (Amer. Hist.) [Early American social & cultural history], s.newman@glasgow.ac.uk

Malcolm A. Nicolson, B.Sc. (Aberd.), Ph.D. (Edin.), Prof. in the Hist. of Medicine [History of diagnosis; history of biomedical science; history of ecology], malcolm.nicolson@glasgow.ac.uk

Phillips P. O'Brien, B.A., Ph.D. (Cantab.), Reader in Mod. Hist. (Mod. Amer.), p.o'brien@glasgow.ac.uk

Nick Pearce, B.A. (C.N.A.A.), M.A. (Lond.), Prof. of Chinese Art [Chinese decorative arts 10th–19th c.; Chinese art in the West], nick.pearce@glasgow.ac.uk

Jim Phillips, M.A. (Aberd.), Ph.D. (Edin.), Sen. Lect. in Econ. & Soc. Hist. [Labour, class & industrial relations; Scotland & Britain in the 20th c.; coal mining; deindustrialisation], james.phillips@glasgow.ac.uk

Tony Pollard, M.A., Ph.D., Sen. Lect. in Hist./Battlefield Archaeol. [Conflict archaeology; Jacobite wars; 20th c. warfare], tony.pollard@glasgow.ac.uk

Steven Reid, M.A., Ph.D. (St. And.), Lect. in Scot. Hist. [The European Renaissance & Reformation]

John C. Richards, M.A., Ph.D. (Glas.), Sen. Lect. in Hist. of Art [Humanism & visual arts in Italian trecento], john.richards@glasgow.ac.uk

Andrew P. Roach, M.A. (Cantab. & Read.), D.Phil. (Oxon.), Sen. Lect. in Hist. (12th–13th c. Church, Med. Towns) [Heresy & response of the church in 12th–13th c.], a.roach@glasgow.ac.uk

Neil Rollings, B.Sc., Ph.D. (Brist.), Prof. of Econ. & Business Hist. (20th c. Brit., Econ. Policy) [British economic policy post-1945; British industry & European integration 1945–73], neil.rollings@glasgow.ac.uk

Duncan M. Ross, M.A. (Glas.), Ph.D. (Lond.), Sen. Lect. in Econ. & Soc. Hist. (20th c. Business Hist.) [Bank-industry relations in Britain; history of savings banks; Scottish economy], duncan.ross@glasgow.ac.uk

Sally Rush, M.A. (Edin.), Ph.D. (Glas.), Sen. Lect. [19th–20th c. decorative art, with particular reference to stained glass], sally.rush@glasgow.ac.uk

Catherine R. Schenk, B.A., M.A. (Toronto), Ph.D. (Lond.), Prof. of Int. Econ. Hist. (20th c. Int. Monetary Relations) [Post-war international financial relations; east Asia & Europe], catherine.schenk@glasgow.ac.uk

Alexandra Shepard, M.A. (Cantab.), M.Phil. (Yale), Ph.D. (Cantab.), Reader (Early
Mod. Brit.) [Gender; violence; perceptions of worth & social status, 1550–1750],
a.shepard@glasgow.ac.uk

Julia M.H. Smith, M.A. (Cantab.), D.Phil. (Oxon.), Edwards Prof. of Med. Hist. [Late Roman
& early medieval history, including politics; women & gender; saints' cults & religion],
jmhs@glasgow.ac.uk

Donald A. Spaeth, B.A. (Reed Coll.), M.A., Ph.D. (Brown), Sen. Lect. in Hist. Computing
(Soc. Hist., Early Mod. Eur. & Eng., Hist. Computing) [Social history of religion; Church of
England in 17th & 18th c.], d.spaeth@glasgow.ac.uk

Raymond G. Stokes, B.A. (S. Florida), M.A., Ph.D. (Ohio State), Prof. of Business Hist.
[German business history; comparative industrial history; history of science & technology],
ray.stokes@glasgow.ac.uk

Matthew J. Strickland, M.A., Ph.D. (Cantab.), Prof. of Med. Hist. (Anglo-Norman &
Angevin Pol. & Milit. Hist., Chivalry) [Chivalry & conduct in warfare; baronial rebellion],
m.strickland@glasgow.ac.uk

Peter van Dommelen, B.A., Ph.D. (Leiden), Prof. of Mediterranean Archaeol.
[Theory in archaeology; Mediterranean, Italian & Phoenician archaeology],
p.vandommelen@glasgow.ac.uk

Sabine Wieber, B.A., M.A. (Brit. Col.), Ph.D. (Chicago), Lect. [Austrian & German art,
architecture & design 1800–1930, esp. the modern interior, gender & nationalism],
sabine.wieber@glasgow.ac.uk

Clare A. Willsdon, M.A., Ph.D. (Cantab.), Reader in Hist. of Art (19th & 20th c. painting),
clare.willsdon@glasgow.ac.uk

GLASGOW CALEDONIAN UNIVERSITY

Glasgow School for Business & Society
City Campus, Cowcaddens Road, Glasgow, G4 0BA. 0141 331 3253. Fax 0141 331 3439
www.gcu.ac.uk/gsbs/historyandpolitics/

Janet Greenlees, B.A. (St. Olaf Coll., Minn.), M.A., D.Phil. (York), Lect. (Health Hist., Mod.
Amer. Hist, Mod. Brit. Hist.) [Maternal healthcare; employer provision of healthcare; textile
industries], janet.greenlees@gcu.ac.uk

S. Karly Kehoe, B.A. (St. Mary's U., Canada), Ph.D. (Glas.), Lect. (Mod. Brit., Scot.
& Irish Hist.) [19th–early 20th c. national identity; Catholicism; citizenship; gender],
karly.kehoe@gcu.ac.uk

*Peter Kirby, B.A. (Liv.), Ph.D. (Sheff.), Prof. [Children; industrialisation; poverty; coal mining;
health], peter.kirby@gcu.ac.uk

Vicky Long, B.A., M.A., Ph.D. (Warwick), Lect. (Mod. Brit. Hist. & Hist. of Medicine) [19th &
20th c. British occupational health services; 19th & 20th c. British mental health; disability
history], victoria.long@gcu.ac.uk

Elaine W. McFarland, M.A., Ph.D. (Glas.), Prof. of Hist. (19th–20th c. Brit. & Scot. Hist.,
20th c. Eur.) [Religion in modern Scotland; Scottish military tradition; war & memory],
e.mcfarland@gcal.ac.uk

Ben Shepherd, B.A. (East Anglia), M.A. (Essex), Ph.D. (Birm.), Reader (20th c. Eur.
Milit. Hist.) [Germany & Austrian military history; counter-insurgency warfare],
b.shepherd@gcal.ac.uk

Fiona Skillen, M.A., M.Phil.,Ph.D. (Glas.), Lect. (Sports Hist., Management & Gender)
[19th–20th c. sports history; gender history; popular culture], fiona.skillen@gcu.ac.uk

John Stewart, B.A. (C.N.A.A.), M.Phil (Lond.), Prof. of Health Hist. (Health Hist.) [History of medicine; childhood; welfare], john.stewart@gcal.ac.uk

Oonagh Walsh, B.A. (Dublin), M.A., Ph.D., Prof. of Gender [Medical history; gender history; Irish history], oonagh.walsh@gcu.ac.uk

UNIVERSITY OF **GLOUCESTERSHIRE**

School of Humanities
Francis Close Hall, Cheltenham, Glos., GL50 4AZ. 01242 532747. Fax 01242 43314
www.glos.ac.uk/schools/humanities/

Anna French, B.A., Ph.D. (Birm.), Sen. Lect. in Early Mod. Eur. Hist. [Early modern European history, esp. religion & culture in England], afrench@glos.ac.uk

Melanie J. Ilic, B.A. (Manc.), M.Phil., Ph.D. (Birm.), Prof. of Soviet Hist. (Russia & U.S.S.R., Women) [Soviet women's history], milic@glos.ac.uk

Vicky Morrisroe, B.A., M.A., Ph.D. (Manc.), Sen. Lect. in Mod. Hist. [19th c. intellectual & socio-cultural history of Britain], vmorrisroe@glos.ac.uk

Christian O'Connell, B.A. (Leeds), M.A. (Lond.), Ph.D. (Glos.), Lect. in Amer. Hist. (Amer. Hist.) [20th c. socio-cultural history & music], coconnell@glos.ac.uk

Iain J.M. Robertson, B.A. (C.N.A.A.), Ph.D. (Brist.), Reader (Cultural & Landscape Hist.) [20th c. social protest in the Scottish Highlands; the role of heritage in the making of landscape], irobertson@glos.ac.uk

Neil A. Wynn, M.A. (Edin.), Ph.D. (Open), Prof. of 20th c. Amer. Hist. (20th c. U.S. Soc., Race) [The 1920s; World War II], nwynn@glos.ac.uk

UNIVERSITY OF **GREENWICH**

Old Royal Naval College, Park Row, Greenwich, London, SE10 9LS. 020 8331 8000.
Fax 020 8316 8876
www.greenwich.ac.uk
School of Humanities 020 8331 8800. Fax 020 8331 8805
Greenwich Maritime Institute 020 8331 7688. Fax 020 8331 7690
www.gre.ac.uk/about/schools/gmi/
Department of Education & Community Studies 020 8331 8590. Fax 020 8331 8145

*June Balshaw, B.A., M.A., Ph.D. (Greenwich), Princ. Lect., University Teaching Fellow (Gender & Family Hist.) [Gender & family history], j.m.balshaw@gre.ac.uk

*Chris Bellamy, B.A. (C.N.A.A.), M.A. (Oxon. & Lond.), Ph.D. (Edin.), Director, Greenwich Maritime Inst. & Prof. of Maritime Security (Maritime Security, Naval & Milit. Hist., Security & Defence Stud.) [Naval & military history; piracy & response to it; peace support operations; terrorism; Russia], c.d.bellamy@gre.ac.uk

Andrew Dawson, B.Sc.(Econ.) (Wales), Ph.D. (Sheff.), Sen. Lect. (U.S. Soc. & Econ., Hollywood) [Machine building in Philadelphia 1830–90; U.S. film industry], a.dawson@gre.ac.uk

Sandra Dunster, B.A., M.A., Ph.D. (Nott.), Sen. Res. Fellow/Lect. [16th–18th c. England & Europe; local history], s.a.dunster@gre.ac.uk

Emma Hanna, B.A., Ph.D. (Kent), Sen. Lect. (19th–20th c. Brit. & Eur. Hist.) [Social & cultural aspects of World War I & II, esp. the representation & dissemination of historical information in the British media], e.l.mahoney@gre.ac.uk

Roger Knight, M.A. (Dublin), Ph.D. (Lond.), Visiting Prof. of Naval Hist. (18th–20th c. Pol./ Naval Hist.) [Naval history, 18th–early 19th c.; Napoleonic Wars]

Mary Clare H. Martin, B.A. (York), Ph.D. (Lond.), Sen. Lect. (Hist. of Childhood, Youth & Educ.) [18th–19th c. children, education & religion; charity & the Poor Law, esp. in Walthamstow & Leyton, Essex; women & philanthropy 1740–1940; children's illness in the 19th c.], m.c.h.martin@gre.ac.uk

Vanessa Taylor, B.A., M.A., Ph.D. (Lond.), Res. Fellow (Environmental Hist. & the Sea) [Water & water supplies; governance & ecology of riverine systems & coastal areas; oral history; coastal communities], v.j.taylor@gre.ac.uk

Chris Ware, M.A., Ph.D. (Greenwich), Sen. Lect. in Naval Hist. (Naval Hist., 1700–1990) [The Royal Navy, 1688–1739, both operational & administrative], c.j.ware@gre.ac.uk

Martin Wilcox, M.A., Ph.D. (Hull), Sen. Res. Fellow & Lect. in Maritime Hist. (Brit. & Int. Merchant Shipping & Fisheries since the 18th c., Mod. Econ. & Soc. Hist.) [The British maritime economy since the 18th c., esp. maritime labour, the history of fisheries & the Royal Navy], m.h.wilcox@gre.ac.uk

UNIVERSITY OF **HERTFORDSHIRE**

College Lane, Hatfield, Herts., AL10 9AB. 01707 284000. Fax 01707 284115
www.herts.ac.uk
School of Humanities
de Havilland Campus, Hatfield, Herts., AL10 9AB

Owen Davies, B.A. (Wales), Ph.D. (Lancaster), Prof. of Soc. Hist. (Early Mod. Brit. & Eur.) [Witchcraft & magic], o.davies@herts.ac.uk

Jennifer Evans, B.A., M.A., Ph.D. (Exeter), Lect. in Hist. [17th c. gender, medicine & sexuality], j.evans5@herts.ac.uk

Christine Garwood, M.A., Ph.D. (Leicester), Lect. in Public Hist. [19th c. social history; science & religion; heritage studies & public history], c.garwood@herts.ac.uk

Alix Green, M.A., M.Phil. (Cantab.), Ph.D. (Herts.), Lect. in Hist. & Policy [Public history; history & public policy; historiography & theory; higher education; historical skills & practices], a.r.green@herts.ac.uk

Christopher Krantz, B.A. (Columbia), M.A. (N.Y.), Ph.D. (Lond.), Lect. in Hist. [The transatlantic slave trade; 18th c. Africa; 18th–19th c. American history], c.krantz@herts.ac.uk

Sarah Lloyd, B.A., D.Phil. (Oxon.), Reader (18th c. Brit.) [18th c. poverty, charity, gender & sexuality; public history], s.v.lloyd@herts.ac.uk

Simon Martin, B.A., M.A., Ph.D. (Lond.), Sen. Res. Fellow in Mod. Italian Hist. [Modern Italy; identity; fascism; sport]

Ciara Meehan, B.A., Ph.D. (N.U.I.), Lect. in Hist. [20th c. Ireland: identity & state building; social change; women's history], c.meehan2@herts.ac.uk

Julie Moore, B.A. (Open), M.A., Ph.D. (Herts.), Co-Director, Heritage Hub [19th c. British regional & social history], j.p.2.moore@herts.ac.uk

Jonathan Morris, M.A., Ph.D. (Cantab.), Res. Prof. in Mod. Eur. Hist. [19th & 20th c. Italian history; retailing; consumption; petite bourgeoisie], j.2.morris@herts.ac.uk

Anne Murphy, B.A., M.A., Ph.D. (Leicester), [18th c. financial history], a.l.murphy@herts.ac.uk
Katrina Navickas, B.A., M.St., D.Phil. (Oxon.), [19th c. radicalism; 19th c. regional & social history], k.navickas@herts.ac.uk
Tony Shaw, B.A. (Leeds), D.Phil. (Oxon.), Prof. of Contemp. Hist. (20th c. Int. Hist.) [Communications & politics; Cold War; film & history], a.t.shaw@herts.ac.uk
John Styles, M.A. (Cantab.), Res. Prof. in Hist. (18th c. Brit. Hist.) [Material culture; consumption; design & manufacturing], j.a.styles@herts.ac.uk

UNIVERSITY OF HUDDERSFIELD

Queensgate, Huddersfield, HD1 3DH. 01484 472359. Fax 01484 472655
www.hud.ac.uk
School of Music, Humanities & Media: Division of History
www.hud.ac.uk/mh/history/

Paul Atkinson, B.A. (Oxon.), Ph.D. (Leeds), [Economic & social history of Britain & other industrialised countries, 1850–1960], p.d.atkinson@hud.ac.uk
*Sarah Bastow, B.A., Ph.D. (Huddersfield), Head of Dept. (Med. & Early Mod.) [16th & 17th c. religious history; English Catholicism; history of the North of England], s.l.bastow@hud.ac.uk
Patricia H. Cullum, B.A. (Keele), D.Phil. (York), (Med.) [Hospitals & charity; piety of lay women; clergy & masculinity], p.c.cullum@hud.ac.uk
Lindsey Dodd, B.A., M.A. (Sussex), Ph.D. (Reading), [Allied bombing of France; children in war; modern French history], l.dodd@hud.ac.uk
Barry Doyle, B.A., Ph.D. (East Anglia), (Mod. Brit.) [Urban history; hospitals; popular culture], barry.doyle@hud.ac.uk
Robert J. Ellis, B.A., Ph.D., (Mod. Brit.) [History of mental health care in Britain since 1800], r.j.ellis@hud.ac.uk
Rebecca Gill, B.A. (Lond.), M.A., Ph.D. (Manc.), Lect. (Mod. Hist.) [British & British imperial history, 19th–20th c.; humanitarian organisations], r.gill@hud.ac.uk
Jonathan Gledhill, B.A., M.A. Ph.D. (Lancaster), [History of Scotland, 1100–1500; history of north of England & the Anglo-Scottish border; lordship & local identities in medieval Scotland; regional history], j.gledhill@hud.ac.uk
Martin Hewitt, B.A. (Oxon.), M.B.A. (Warwick), M.A. (New Brunswick), D.Phil. (Oxon.), Prof. of Hist. (19th c. Brit.) [Intellectual & literary culture of the 19th c. city; life writing, esp. autobiographical narratives & their relation to historical memory; the Victorian press; Victorian reading cultures & the histories of print], m.hewitt@hud.ac.uk
Keith Laybourn, B.Sc. (Bradford), M.A., Ph.D. (Lancaster), Prof. (Mod. Brit.) [Labour history; philanthropy; welfare state & social policy], k.laybourn@hud.ac.uk
Daryl Leeworthy, M.A. (Oxon.), M.A. (St Mary's), Ph.D. (Swansea), [Welsh, Irish & Canadian 19th–20th c. history; labour history; history of sport], d.leeworthy@hud.ac.uk
Katherine J. Lewis, B.A. (Warwick), M.A., D.Phil. (York), Sen. Lect. (Med.) [Saints' cults; concepts of gender; kingship & masculinity], k.lewis@hud.ac.uk
Janette Martin, B.A., Ph.D. (York), Lect. [19th c. radical history & political oratory], j.martin@hud.ac.uk
David Taylor, B.A., D.Phil. (Oxon.), Prof. Emeritus (Mod. Brit.) [Crime & policing in modern Britain], d.taylor2@hud.ac.uk

Timothy J. Thornton, M.A., D.Phil. (Oxon.), Prof. & Pro Vice-Chancellor (Med. & Early
   Mod.) [Palatinates of Chester & Durham; Isle of Man; Channel Islands; prophecy],
   t.j.thornton@hud.ac.uk
Paul J. Ward, B.A., Ph.D. (Lond.), Prof. (Mod. Brit.) [British national identities late
   19th–20th c.; Americanisation; Welsh history], p.j.ward@hud.ac.uk

UNIVERSITY OF HULL

Hull, HU6 7RX. 01482 346311. Fax 01482 466205
www.hull.ac.uk
Department of History 01482 465344. Fax 01482 465192
www.hull.ac.uk/history/
Department of American Studies 01482 465303
www.hull.ac.uk/amstuds/

Andrew C. Ayton, B.A., Ph.D. (Hull), Sen. Lect. in Hist. (Later Med. Soc. & Milit.)
   [The organisation of war & the military community in late medieval England],
   A.C.Ayton@hull.ac.uk
David V.N. Bagchi, M.A., D.Phil. (Oxon.), Sen. Lect. in the Hist. of Christian Thought [Early
   church history; 16th c. religious history; Martin Luther], D.V.Bagchi@hull.ac.uk
Catherine Baker, M.A., Ph.D. (Lond.), Lect. in 20th c. Hist. [Southeast Europe; music &
   politics; peace operations; languages & conflict], Catherine.Baker@hull.ac.uk
Greg Bankoff, B.A. (Portsmouth), Ph.D. (Murdoch), Prof. of Hist. (Mod.) [Environment;
   disasters; animals; S.E. Asia], G.Bankoff@hull.ac.uk
Michaela Barnard, B.A., M.A. (Hull), Lect. in Hist. [Maritime business history],
   M.G.Barnard@hull.ac.uk
John G. Bernasconi, B.A. (Brist.), M.A. (Lond.), Director of Fine Art [Narrative painting of
   Venetian *scuole*], J.G.Bernasconi@hull.ac.uk
Thomas Biskup, M.Phil., Ph.D. (Cantab.), Lect. in Hist. (Early Mod.) [18th–19th c. monarchy;
   Anglo-German Enlightenment], T.Biskup@hull.ac.uk
P. Glenn Burgess, B.A., M.A. (Wellington), Ph.D. (Cantab.), Prof. of Hist. (17th c. Pol.
   Thought) [Tudor & Stuart political thought], P.G.Burgess@hull.ac.uk
Amanda L. Capern, B.A. (Lond.), M.A., Ph.D. (Sydney), Lect. in Hist. (Early Mod., Women's
   Hist.), A.L.Capern@hull.ac.uk
David B. Crouch, B.A., Ph.D. (Wales), Prof. of Med. Hist. (Med.) [12th–13th c. aristocracy;
   12th c. political history; reign of King Stephen], D.Crouch@hull.ac.uk
Nicholas J. Evans, B.A. (Leicester), Ph.D. (Hull), Lect. in Diaspora Hist. [19th–20th c.
   migration], N.J.Evans@hull.ac.uk
Helen Fenwick, B.A. (York), Ph.D. (Hull), Lect. in Archaeol. [Medieval settlement; landscape
   archaeology & G.I.S.], H.Fenwick@hull.ac.uk
Richard C. Gorski, B.A., Ph.D. (Hull), Philip Nicholas Memorial Sen. Lect. in Maritime Hist.,
   R.C.Gorski@hull.ac.uk
Peter E. Grieder, M.A., Ph.D. (Cantab.), Lect. in Mod. Eur. Hist. [East German Communist
   party, 1985–9], P.E.Grieder@hull.ac.uk
A. Peter M. Halkon, B.A. (Liv.), M.A. (Dunelm.), Ph.D. (Hull), Lect. in Archaeol. [Landscape
   archaeology; iron age & Roman east Yorkshire], A.P.Halkon@hull.ac.uk
Douglas J. Hamilton, M.A., Ph.D. (Aberd.), Sen. Lect. in Hist. (Mod.) [18th c. Atlantic world;
   slavery; British empire], D.Hamilton@hull.ac.uk

Julian P. Haseldine, M.A. (Oxon.), Ph.D. (Cantab.), Sen. Lect. in Med. Hist. [Medieval Europe; the central middle ages; cultural & religious history], J.P.Haseldine@hull.ac.uk

Karl T. Hoppen, M.A. (N.U.I.), Ph.D. (Cantab.), F.B.A., Emeritus Prof. of Hist. (Victorian Pol., 19th c. Ireland) [19th c. Ireland], K.T.Hoppen@hull.ac.uk

Howell A. Lloyd, B.A. (Wales), D.Phil. (Oxon.), Emeritus Prof. of Hist. (16th c. Eng. & French Govt. & Soc.) [History of European political thought], H.A.Lloyd@hull.ac.uk

V. Alan McClelland, M.A. (Birm. & Sheff.), Ph.D. (Sheff.), Emeritus Prof. of Educ. [R.C. Church history 1850–1945; the Irish diaspora since 1845]

Jenny Macleod, M.A. (Edin.), M.Phil, Ph.D. (Cantab.), Lect. in 20th c. Hist. [Britain & Australia; cultural history of World War I], J.Macleod@hull.ac.uk

Philip J. Morgan, M.A. (Cantab.), Ph.D. (Read.), Sen. Fellow [Italian fascism 1919–45; comparative fascism in inter-war Europe], P.J.Morgan@hull.ac.uk

David E. Omissi, B.A. (Lancaster), M.A., Ph.D. (Lond.), Sen. Lect. in Hist. (19th c. Imp. & Milit.) [Later colonial India; British imperial & military history], D.E.Omissi@hull.ac.uk

John J.N. Palmer, B.A., B.Litt. (Oxon.), Ph.D. (Lond.), Emeritus Prof. of Hist. (Med.) [Domesday Book; Hundred Years' War; Richard II; medieval chroniclers; British bibliography], J.J.Palmer@hull.ac.uk

Robin Pearson, M.A. (Edin.), Ph.D. (Leeds), Prof. of Econ. & Soc. Hist. (19th c. Brit., Germany) [History of insurance industry], R.Pearson@hull.ac.uk

Joy Porter, M.A., Ph.D. (Nott.), Prof. of Indigenous Hist. [North America; indigenous history, culture & literature], Joy.Porter@hull.ac.uk

J. Leslie Price, B.A., Ph.D. (Lond.), Emeritus Reader in Hist. (17th c. Dutch) [History of Dutch Republic in 17th c.; Anglo-Dutch relations], J.L.Price@hull.ac.uk

Alison Price-Moir, B.A. (Hull), M.A. (Lond.), Lect. in Hist. of Art [Modern & 19th c. art], A.J.Price-Moir@hull.ac.uk

Charles W.A. Prior, B.A. (Queen's, Ont.), M.A. (Toronto), Ph.D. (Queen's, Ont.), Sen. Lect. in Early Mod. Brit. Hist (16th–18th c. Brit.) [Political thought; religious debates; historiography; early British empire], C.Prior@hull.ac.uk

Douglas A. Reid, B.A., Ph.D. (Birm.), Sen. Lect. in Soc. Hist. (17th–20th c. Brit., India) [Leisure & popular culture, esp. in 19th c. towns; holiday patterns & railway excursions], D.A.Reid@hull.ac.uk

David Richardson, M.A. (Manc.), Prof. of Econ. Hist. (Amer., Brit. & Japanese Econ.) [Transatlantic slavery, incl. Africa], P.D.Richardson@hull.ac.uk

Alan G.V. Simmonds, B.A. (Sussex), M.A. (Lond.), Ph.D. (Leeds), Lect. (Mod. Hist.) [20th c. government policy in Britain; British society during the First World War; social & political context of welfare policy in post-war Britain], A.Simmonds@hull.ac.uk

Simon C. Smith, B.A., Ph.D. (Lond.), Prof. of Mod. Hist. (Mod. Brit.) [British imperialism; S.E. Asia; Middle East], S.C.Smith@hull.ac.uk

*David J. Starkey, B.A. (Leeds), M.A., Ph.D. (Exeter), Wilson Family Prof. in Maritime Hist. [Modern British maritime history], D.J.Starkey@hull.ac.uk

Sarah E. Thomas, M.A. (St. And.), M.Phil. (Oslo), Ph.D. (Glas.), Lect. in Med. Hist. (Med. Hist.) [Britain & Scandinavia; religious & social archaeology; history of the late middle ages], S.E.Thomas@hull.ac.uk

Michael E. Turner, B.Sc. (Lond.), Ph.D. (Sheff.), Emeritus Prof. of Econ. & Soc. Hist. (20th c. Brit., U.S.S.R.) [Farm output & production in England 1700–1914], M.E.Turner@hull.ac.uk

Colin Veach, M.A., Ph.D. (Dublin), Lect. in Med. Hist. [Britain & Ireland; social & political history of 12th & 13th c. British Isles], C.Veach@hull.ac.uk

Jenel Virden, B.A., M.A. (Washington State), Ph.D. (Washington), Sen. Lect. in Amer. Hist. (Contemp., Immigration) [Immigration; war & society], J.Virden@hull.ac.uk

John Walker, B.A., M.A., Ph.D. (St. And.), Lect. in Hist. [Medieval Yorkshire; the Templars], J.Walker@hull.ac.uk

Rosemary Wall, B.A. (Liv.), M.A., Ph.D. (Lond.), Lect. in Global Hist. [History of medicine in Britain & internationally, 19th & 20th c.], R.Wall@hull.ac.uk

Peter Wilson, B.A., Ph.D. (Cantab.), G.F. Grant Prof. of Hist. (Early Mod.) [Early modern Germany; war in European history], P.H.Wilson@hull.ac.uk

UNIVERSITY OF **KEELE**

Keele, Staffs., ST5 5BG. 01782 732000
www.keele.ac.uk
Department of History 01782 733196. Fax 01782 583195
www.keele.ac.uk/history/
Department of American Studies 01782 733010. Fax 01782 583195
www.keele.ac.uk/americanstudies/
School of Politics, International Relations & Philosophy
01782 733088. Fax 01782 733592
www.keele.ac.uk/spire/

Ben M. Anderson, B.A., M.A., Ph.D. (Manc.), Lect. in Mod. Eur. Hist. [Urban history; landscape & tourism], b.anderson@keele.ac.uk

Ian J. Atherton, B.A., Ph.D. (Cantab.), Sen. Lect. in Hist. [Staffordshire; early Stuart religion & politics; post-Reformation cathedrals; English Civil War; commemoration of war], i.j.atherton@keele.ac.uk

Rachel K. Bright, B.A., Ph.D. (Lond.), Lect. in Mod. Hist. [British empire & Africa; migration & information networks; race, violence & colonial identity], r.k.bright@keele.ac.uk

Malcolm H. Crook, B.A. (Wales), Ph.D. (Lond.), Prof. of French Hist. (Mod. Eur.) [French elections & voting behaviour 1789–1889; French Revolution & early 19th c. France], m.h.crook@keele.ac.uk

Kathleen G. Cushing, B.A. (Sarah Lawrence Coll.), Lic. in Med. Stud. (Toronto), M.Phil., D.Phil. (Oxon.), Reader in Med. Hist. [Medieval history, c.900–1250; Church history & canon law], k.g.cushing@keele.ac.uk

Christoph Dieckmann, M.A. (Hamburg), Ph.D. (Freiburg), Lect. in Mod. Eur. Hist. [Inter-war Europe; German occupation policy in Europe; the Holocaust], c.dieckmann@keele.ac.uk

Bülent Gokay, Ph.D. (Cantab.), Prof. of Int. Rel. [Soviet foreign policy; Turkish political history; oil politics & energy security; political economy of the waning U.S. influence], b.gokay@keele.ac.uk

Robert W.B. Gray, B.A. (Leeds), M.A., Ph.D. (Lond.), Lect. in Mod. Eur. Hist. [The Habsburg monarchy & successor states from c.1700; rural history; landscape & environment; spatial history], r.w.b.gray@keele.ac.uk

Ann L. Hughes, B.A., Ph.D. (Liv.), Prof. of Early Mod. Brit. Hist. (17th c. Eng., Women) [Political, cultural & religious history of Britain mid 17th c.], a.l.hughes@keele.ac.uk

Karen Hunt, B.A. (Kent), M.A., Ph.D. (Manc.), Prof. of Mod. Brit. Hist. [Gender & politics 19th–20th c.; politics of food], k.hunt@keele.ac.uk

Anthony Kauders, B.A. (Hamilton Coll.), M.A. (Lond.), D.Phil. (Oxon.), Lect. in Eur. Hist. [German-Jewish history from 1780 to the present; anti-semitism in the 20th c.; modern German history; history of psychology, psychoanalysis & hypnosis], a.d.kauders@keele.ac.uk

Lorna Lloyd, B.Sc.(Econ.), Ph.D. (Lond.), Reader in Int. Rel. [Diplomatic, political, legal & historical aspects of the League of Nations, the Commonwealth & the U.N.], l.lloyd@keele.ac.uk

Philip J. Morgan, B.A., Ph.D. (Lond.), Sen. Lect. in Med. Hist. [Reign of Henry IV; gentry; war & society; history of water], p.j.morgan@keele.ac.uk

Helen Parr, B.A. (Cantab.), M.A., Ph.D. (Lond.), Lect. in Int. Rel. [British politics & foreign policy since 1945; Britain & the Cold War; Britain & European integration], h.parr@keele.ac.uk

Laura Sandy, B.A., M.A., Ph.D. (Manc.), Lect. in Amer. Hist. [Colonial/antebellum American history], l.r.sandy@keele.ac.uk

Axel R. Schäfer, M.A. (Oregon), Ph.D. (Washington), Prof. of Amer. Hist. [20th c. U.S. political & intellectual history], a.schaefer@keele.ac.uk

Shalini Sharma, B.A., M.A. (Cantab.), M.Phil. (J. Nehru), Ph.D. (Lond.), Lect. in Colonial/ Post-Colonial Hist. [South Asian history; Indian & American relations in the 20th c.], s.sharma@keele.ac.uk

*Alannah E. Tomkins, B.A. (Keele), D.Phil. (Oxon.), Sen. Lect. in Hist. [Social history of medicines; poverty/poor relief & charity], a.e.tomkins@keele.ac.uk

Nigel J. Tringham, B.A. (Wales), M.Litt., Ph.D. (Aberd.), Sen. Lect. in Hist. & County Editor, *V.C.H. Staffs.* [Staffordshire; medieval secular cathedrals; palaeography], n.j.tringham@keele.ac.uk

UNIVERSITY OF **KENT**

Canterbury, Kent, CT2 7NZ. 01227 764000. Fax 01227 827258
www.kent.ac.uk
School of History
www.kent.ac.uk/history/

Julie Anderson, Ph.D. (Leicester), Sen. Lect. (Hist. of Medicine) [Cultural & social history of 20th c. medicine], J.P.Anderson@kent.ac.uk

Ian Beckett, B.A. (Lancaster), Ph.D. (Lond.), Prof. of Milit. Hist. [British auxillary forces in the First World War & late Victorian army], I.Beckett@kent.ac.uk

Barbara Bombi, M.A., Ph.D., Reader in Med. Hist. (Med. Hist.) [Ecclesiastical & religious history 1200–1400], B.Bombi@kent.ac.uk

Philip C. Boobbyer, M.A. (Cantab. & Georgetown), Ph.D. (Lond.), Reader in Mod. Eur. Hist. [Soviet history; Russian intellectual history], P.C.Boobbyer@kent.ac.uk

Alixe Bovey, B.A. (Victoria), M.A., Ph.D. (Lond.), Sen. Lect. (Med. Hist.) [Late medieval visual culture; illuminated manuscripts], A.Bovey@kent.ac.uk

Timothy Bowman, B.A. (Belf.), Ph.D. (Luton), Sen. Lect. (Mod. Brit. Milit. Hist.) [The British army from c.1800; Irish history from c.1770], T.Bowman@kent.ac.uk

Ambrogio A. Caiani, Ph.D. (Cantab.), Lect. (Early Mod. Eur. Hist.) [Revolutionary France & Napoleonic Italy], A.A.Caiani@kent.ac.uk

James P. Carley, Ph.D. (Toronto), Prof. of Hist. of the Book [Old & Middle English; history of manuscripts; bibliography & the early Tudor period], J.P.Carley@kent.ac.uk

Pratik Chakrabarti, Ph.D. (J. Nehru), Reader (Mod. Medicine) [History of imperial medicine & science], P.Chakrabarti@kent.ac.uk

Mark L. Connelly, B.A., Ph.D. (Lond.), Prof. (Mod. Brit. Milit. Hist.) [British military history from 1800], M.L.Connelly@kent.ac.uk

George R. Conyne, B.A. (Haverford Coll.), J.D. (Tulane), Ph.D. (Cantab.), Lect. (Amer. Hist.) [American constitutional, political & diplomatic history], G.R.Conyne@kent.ac.uk

Grayson M. Ditchfield, B.A. (Dunelm.), Ph.D. (Cantab.), Prof. of 18th c. Hist. [Political & religious history of 18th c. Britain], G.M.Ditchfield@kent.ac.uk

Peter Donaldson, Ph.D. (Kent), Lect. (Milit. Hist.) [Cultural impact of the First World War], P.Donaldson@kent.ac.uk

*Kenneth C. Fincham, M.A. (Oxon.), Ph.D. (Lond.), Prof. of. Early Mod. Hist. (Early Mod. Brit.) [Politics, religion & culture of early modern Europe], K.C.Fincham@kent.ac.uk

Helen Gittos, D.Phil. (Oxon.), Lect. (Med. Hist.) [Social & cultural history of the early middle ages], H.B.Gittos@kent.ac.uk

Stefan P. Goebel, M.Phil., Ph.D. (Cantab.), Sen. Lect. (Mod. Brit. Hist.) [Comparative history & cultural history of war], S.P.Goebel@kent.ac.uk

David I. Grummitt, Ph.D. (Lond.), Sen. Lect. (Early Mod. Hist.) [Political, administrative & military history of late-medieval & early Tudor England], D.I.Grummitt@kent.ac.uk

Rebekah Higgitt, B.A., M.A. (Dunelm.), Ph.D. (Imp.), Lect. (Hist. of Sc.) [Relationship between science & the public in 18th & 19th c. Britain], R.Higgitt@kent.ac.uk

Gaynor L. Johnson, Ph.D. (Wales), Prof. of Hist. [Origins & consequences of war in the modern era], G.L.Johnson@kent.ac.uk

Karen R. Jones, B.A. (Warwick), M.A., Ph.D. (Brist.), Sen. Lect. (Amer. Hist.) [The American West; environmental history], K.R.Jones@kent.ac.uk

Jan Loop, Ph.D. (Berne), Lect. (Early Mod. Hist.) [Intellectual, religious & cultural history of Europe & the Near East], J.Loop@kent.ac.uk

Giacomo Macola, Ph.D. (Cantab.), Sen. Lect. (Afric. Hist.) [Post-18th c. Central African political & intellectual history], G.Macola@kent.ac.uk

Emily Manktelow, Ph.D. (Lond.), Lect. (Colonial/Imp. Hist.) [Colonial & postcolonial social & cultural history], E.Manktelow@kent.ac.uk

David J. Ormrod, B.Sc.(Econ.) (Lond.), Ph.D. (Cantab.), Prof. of Econ. & Cultural Hist. (Early Mod. Econ. Hist.) [Early modern economic & cultural history], D.J.Ormrod@kent.ac.uk

Juliette Pattinson, Ph.D. (Lancaster), Reader (Mod. Eur. Hist.) [Socio-cultural history of the Second World War], J.Pattinson@kent.ac.uk

William Pettigrew, Ph.D. (Oxon.), Reader (Amer. Hist.) [Transatlantic slave trade], W.Pettigrew@kent.ac.uk

David L. Potter, B.A. (Dunelm.), Ph.D. (Cantab.), Reader (Early Mod. Eur.) [War, the Crown & aristocracy in 15th & 16th c. France], D.L.Potter@kent.ac.uk

Ulf I.D. Schmidt, D.Phil. (Oxon.), Prof. of Mod. Hist. [Medicine in Weimar & Nazi Germany; history of medical ethics; history of medical film], U.I.Schmidt@kent.ac.uk

Phil Slavin, Ph.D. (Toronto), Lect. (Med. Hist.) [Late-medieval environmental, economic & social history of the British Isles], P.Slavin@kent.ac.uk

Charlotte L. Sleigh, M.A., M.Phil., Ph.D. (Cantab.), Reader (Hist. & Cultural Stud. of Sc.) [Life sciences in 19th & 20th c.; metaphors in science], C.L.Sleigh@kent.ac.uk

Crosbie W. Smith, M.A., Ph.D. (Cantab.), Prof. of Hist. of Sc. [Science & technology in 19th c. Britain; literature & science], C.Smith@kent.ac.uk

Danielle van den Heuvel, Ph.D. (Utrecht), Lect. (Early Mod. Hist.) [Early modern social & economic history], D.Vandenheuvel@kent.ac.uk

David A. Welch, B.A. (Wales), Ph.D. (Lond.), Prof. of Mod. Eur. Hist. (20th c.) [20th c. political propaganda], D.A.Welch@kent.ac.uk

Leonie Wells-Furby, Ph.D. (Kent), Lect. (Early Mod. Hist.) [Early modern English & Scottish history], L.Wells-Furby@kent.ac.uk

John Wills, M.A., Ph.D. (Brist.), Sen. Lect. (Amer. Hist.) [Environmental history; California; cyberculture; 1950s America; Disney], J.Wills@kent.ac.uk

KINGSTON UNIVERSITY

Faculty of Arts & Social Sciences: Economics, History & Politics
Penrhyn Road, Kingston upon Thames, Surrey, KT1 2EE.
020 8417 9000
http://fass.kingston.ac.uk/schools/economics/politics-history/

Peter J. Beck, B.Sc.(Econ.), Ph.D. (Lond.), Emeritus Prof. of Int. Hist. [Britain & Germany in 1930s; history of international organisation; British politicians & history; British politics & sport], P.Beck@kingston.ac.uk

*John R. Davis, M.A., Ph.D. (Glas.), Prof. of Hist. & Int. Rel. [Anglo-German relations 19th–20th c.; commercial & foreign policy], J.Davis@kingston.ac.uk

Christopher J. French, B.A., M.A., Ph.D. (Exeter), Emeritus Reader in Soc. & Econ. Hist. [Trade & shipping in 18th c.; local history], C.French@kingston.ac.uk

Keith R. Grieves, B.Ed., Ph.D. (Manc.), Prof. of Hist. & Educ. [World War I: Britain; government policy; local consequences; aftermath & remembrance], K.Grieves@kingston.ac.uk

Sue Hawkins, B.Sc. (Manc.), M.Sc. (Lond.), Ph.D. (Kingston), Lect. in Hist. [Nursing history; 19th c. social history; women's history; history of healthcare; digital history], S.E.Hawkins@kingston.ac.uk

Marko Hoare, B.A. (Cantab.), M.A., M.Phil., Ph.D. (Yale), Reader [Balkan history & politics; genocide & genocide prevention]

Marisa A. Linton, B.A., M.A., D.Phil. (Sussex), Reader in Eur. Hist. [18th–19th c. French political culture; Enlightenment & the French Revolution], M.Linton@kingston.ac.uk

Jeremy Nuttall, B.A. (Belf.), M.A. (Manc), D.Phil. (Oxon.), Sen. Lect. in Hist. [20th c. Britain, esp. the Labour party], J.Nuttall@kingston.ac.uk

Craig Phelan, B.A., M.A., Ph.D. (Ohio State), Prof. of Mod. Hist. [U.S. political & economic history; labour & trade union history worldwide], C.Phelan@kingston.ac.uk

Nicola Phillips, B.A., M.A., Ph.D. (Lond.), Lect. in Hist. [British & American women's history; 18th c. social & legal history; public history], N.Phillips@kingston.ac.uk

John Stuart, B.A. (Open), M.A., Ph.D. (Lond.), Princ. Lect. in Hist., Director of the Centre for Local Hist. Stud. [History of the British empire; history of Christian missions in Africa], J.Stuart@kingston.ac.uk

Mark A. Williams, B.A., M.A., Ph.D. (Sussex), Lect. in Hist. [18th c. Britain, esp. national identities; crime & punishment; early modern European cultural history], M.Williams@kingston.ac.uk

Steven A. Woodbridge, B.A. (Kingston), M.Sc. (Lond.), Ph.D. (Kingston), Lect. in Hist. [20th c. Britain, esp. fascism & far-right extremism], S.Woodbridge@kingston.ac.uk

UNIVERSITY OF **LANCASTER**

Bailrigg, Lancaster, LA1 4YW. 01524 65201
www.lancs.ac.uk
Department of History 01524 593155. Fax 01524 846102
www.lancs.ac.uk/fass/history/
Department of Economics 01524 594601 Fax 01524 594244
www.lums.lancs.ac.uk/econ/
Department of European Languages & Cultures 01524 593483
www.lancs.ac.uk/fass/eurolang/
Department of Continuing Education 01524 592623. Fax 01524 592448
www.lancs.ac.uk/depts/conted/
Lancaster Institute for Contemporary Arts (L.I.C.A.) 01524 594151
www.liveatlica.org
The Law School 01524 592465 Fax: 01524 848137
www.lancs.ac.uk/fass/law/

Sarah E. Barber, B.A., Ph.D. (Dublin), Sen. Lect. in Hist. [17th c. republicanism; comparative European attitudes to minorities], s.barber@lancaster.ac.uk

Michael Beckerman, B.A., M.A., Ph.D. (Columbia), Distinguished Prof. of Hist. [Czech & East European music; nationalism; gypsies; film music]

Mercedes Maroto Camino, Ph.D. (Auckland & San Diego), Prof. of Hist. [Cultural history; 17th & 20th c. Spain]

Allyson Fidler, B.A., Ph.D. (Southampton), Prof. of German & Austrian Stud. [Cultural history; 20th c. Germany & Austria], a.fidler@lancaster.ac.uk

Cornelia Graebner, M.A. (Bonn), Ph.D. (Amsterdam), Lect. in Hispanic Stud. [Cultural history; 20th c. Mexico], s.graebner@lancaster.ac.uk

Ian Gregory, Ph.D. (Lond.), Reader in Hist. [Digital humanities], i.gregory@lancaster.ac.uk

Patrick Hagopian, B.A. (Sussex), M.A. (Penn.), Ph.D. (Johns Hopkins), Sen. Lect. in Hist. [U.S. social & cultural history; memorials, museums & Vietnam], p.hagopian@lancaster.ac.uk

Paul Hayward, B.A., M.A. (Auckland), Ph.D. (Cantab.), Sen. Lect. in Hist. [Lives of Anglo-Saxon saints & martyrs; historical writing in the middle ages], p.hayward@lancaster.ac.uk

Timothy Hickman, B.S. (Oregon), Ph.D. (Calif.), Sen. Lect. in Hist. [American cultural history; technology & medicine], t.a.hickman@lancaster.ac.uk

Michael J. Hughes, B.A. (Read.), M.Sc., Ph.D. (Lond.), Prof. of Russian Hist. [Russian & international history; Anglo-Russian relations; role of religion in international affairs], m.hughes1@lancaster.ac.uk

Theodora Jim, B.A., D.Phil. (Oxon.), Academic Fellow [Ancient Greek religion; history & culture; comparative ancient religions], t.jim@lancaster.ac.uk

*Andrew Jotischky, B.A. (Cantab.), M.Phil., Ph.D. (Yale), Prof. of Med. Hist. [Medieval Church; Crusading & the Near East; Carmelite order], a.jotischky@lancaster.ac.uk

Aristotle Kallis, B.A. (Athens), Ph.D. (Edin.), Prof. of Hist. [Cultural & political history; 20th c. Italy, Spain & Greece], a.kallis@lancaster.ac.uk

Alex Metcalfe, B.A. (Oxon. & Leeds), M.A. (Oxon.), Ph.D. (Leeds), Sen. Lect. in Hist. [Social, administrative & linguistic history of the medieval Middle East & Mediterranean; Islam], a.metcalfe@lancaster.ac.uk

Jonathan Munby, B.A. (Exeter), Ph.D. (Minn.), Sen. Lect. [Cinema & society in the U.S.; history & theory of American mass/popular culture, esp. role in mediation of race & ethnicity], j.munby@lancaster.ac.uk

Paolo Palladino, B.A. (Columbia), Ph.D. (Minn.), Prof. of Hist. & Theory [History of 20th c. science, technology & medicine; historiographical methods & sociology of knowledge], p.palladino@lancaster.ac.uk

Corinna Peniston-Bird, M.A., Ph.D. (St And.), Sen. Lect. in Hist. [Gender identities; tourism & national identity; Austrian national identity in the inter-war period], c.m.peniston-bird@lancaster.ac.uk

Stephen P. Pumfrey, B.A. (Cantab.), Ph.D. (Lond.), Sen. Lect. in Hist. [Cultural history of scientific revolution; experimental philosophy; William Gilbert (1544–1603)], s.pumfrey@lancaster.ac.uk

Jeffrey M. Richards, M.A. (Cantab.), Prof. of Cultural Hist. [National identity; monarchy; music & imperialism]

Samantha Riches, B.A. (Keele), M.A. (York), Ph.D. (Leicester), Director of Stud. for Hist. & Archaeol. [Late medieval cultural history; saints' cults], s.riches@lancaster.ac.uk

Thomas Rohkramer, B.A., M.A., Ph.D. (Freiburg), Sen. Lect. in Hist. [Modern Germany; cultural history], t.rohkramer@lancaster.ac.uk

*Derek Sayer, B.A. (Essex), Ph.D. (Dunelm.), Prof. of Cultural Hist. [20th c. Prague as a mirror on modernity], d.sayer@lancaster.ac.uk

John Strachan, B.A., M.A. (Warwick), Ph.D. (Manc.), Lect. in Hist. [Social & cultural history; 19th c. France], j.strachan@lancaster.ac.uk

Keith J. Stringer, B.A. (Newcastle), M.A., Ph.D. (Cantab.), Prof. of Med. Brit. Hist. [Kingship & nobility in medieval England & Scotland; regional & national identity], k.stringer@lancaster.ac.uk

Deborah Sutton, B.A. (York), M.Sc. (Sheff.), Ph.D. (New Delhi), Lect. in Hist. [S. Asia; agrarian & environmental history], d.sutton@lancaster.ac.uk

James C. Taylor, B.A., M.A., Ph.D. (Kent), Sen. Lect. in Hist. [Economic & business history; public perceptions of business activity in 19th c. Britain], james.taylor@lancaster.ac.uk

Amit Thakkar, B.A. (Birm.), M.A. (Lond.), Ph.D. (Liv.), Lect. in Spanish Amer. Stud. [Cultural history; 20th c. Spain & Latin America], a.thakkar@lancaster.ac.uk

Alan Warburton, B.A., M.A., Ph.D. (Lancaster), Teaching Fellow in Hist. [World War I; modern security issues; missile & space programmes; weapons of mass destruction], a.warburton@lancaster.ac.uk

John Welshman, B.A. (York), D.Phil. (Oxon.), Sen. Lect. in Hist. [Health care & social policy in 20th c. Britain]

Angus J.L. Winchester, B.A., Ph.D. (Dunelm.), Sen. Lect. in Hist. [Landscape & environmental history; local & regional history], a.winchester@lancaster.ac.uk

Yoke-Sum Wong, B.A., Ph.D. (Alberta), Lect. in Hist. [History of the built environment; 19th c. Singapore; 20th c. Japan], y.wong@lancaster.ac.uk

UNIVERSITY OF LEEDS

Leeds, LS2 9JT. 0113 243 1751. Fax 0113 244 3923
www.leeds.ac.uk
School of History 0113 343 3610. Fax 0113 234 2759
www.leeds.ac.uk/history/

Holger H.W. Afflerbach, M.A., Dr.phil.habil (Dusseldorf), Prof. of Central Eur. Hist. [International relations before 1914; history of the two world wars; naval history], H.H.W.Afflerbach@leeds.ac.uk

Stephen A. Alford, M.A., Ph.D. (St. And.), Prof. of Early Mod. Brit. Hist. [Early modern, esp. Tudor, politics & political thought; William Cecil, Lord Burghley; espionage; early modern travel & exploration], S.Alford@leeds.ac.uk

Peter P. Anderson, B.A. (C.N.A.A.), M.A., Ph.D. (Lond.), Lect. in 20th c. Eur. Hist. [Spain; civil war; repression; humanitarianism], P.P.Anderson@leeds.ac.uk

Anyaa Anim-Addo, Ph.D. (Lond.), Lect. in Caribbean Hist. [Mobility, identity & culture in post-emancipation Caribbean; labour & leisure in 19th c. Caribbean port towns; empire & colonialism; gender; business history], A.Anim-Addo@leeds.ac.uk

Nir Arielli, B.A., M.A. (Jerusalem), Ph.D. (Leeds), Lect. in Int. Hist. (20th c.) [European & Middle Eastern history; war volunteering; transnational military service], N.Arielli@leeds.ac.uk

Simon J. Ball, M.A. (Oxon.), Ph.D. (Cantab.), Prof. of Int. Hist. [British defence policy, colonial policy & politics; the Cold War], S.J.Ball@leeds.ac.uk

Alexandra E. Bamji, B.A., M.Phil., Ph.D. (Cantab.), Lect. in Early Mod. Hist. (16th & 17th c.) [Venice; religion, disease & death in early modern Europe], A.Bamji@leeds.ac.uk

Julia S. Barrow, M.A. (St. And.), D.Phil. (Oxon.), Prof. of Med. Stud. (8th–13th c.) [Clergy; bishops; charters; historical writing], J.S.Barrow@leeds.ac.uk

Robert D. Black, B.A. (Chicago), Ph.D. (Lond.), Prof. of Renaissance Hist. (Early Mod.) [Medieval & Renaissance Italy], R.D.Black@leeds.ac.uk

Regina Blaszczyk, M.A., Ph.D. (Delaware), Prof. of the Hist. of Business & Soc. [History of innovation; consumer culture in comparative perspective; fashion, colour & retailing], R.Blaszczyk@leeds.ac.uk

F. Roy Bridge, B.A., Ph.D. (Lond.), Emeritus Prof., Hon. Lect. in Int. Hist. (19th c.) [Great Powers]

Sarah Burgin, M.A., Ph.D. (Leeds), Teaching Fellow in Amer. Hist. (Amer. Hist.) [White anti-racism in 1960s & 1970s; race, gender & US cultural protest since 1865], S.Burgin@leeds.ac.uk

Adam Cathcart, Ph.D., Lect. (Chinese Hist.) [Early Cold War in North East Asia (1945–60); Manchuria], A.Cathcart@leeds.ac.uk

Emma S. Cavell, B.A., M.A. (Tasmania), D.Phil. (Oxon.), Hon. Lect. in Med. Hist., E.Cavell@leeds.ac.uk

Hugh P. Cecil, M.A., D.Phil. (Oxon.), Hon. Lect. in Hist. (Later Mod. Brit.)

John A. Chartres, M.A., D.Phil. (Oxon.), Emeritus Prof. of Soc. & Econ. Hist. [19th c. rural trades & crafts; 18th c. fiscal data as sources], J.A.Chartres@leeds.ac.uk

Malcolm S. Chase, B.A. (York), M.A., D.Phil. (Sussex), Prof. of Soc. Hist. [19th–20th c. British social & labour history], M.S.Chase@leeds.ac.uk

John C.R. Childs, B.A. (Hull), Ph.D. (Lond.), Emeritus Prof. of Milit. Hist. [War in modern world 1500–1995], J.C.R.Childs@leeds.ac.uk

Wendy R. Childs, M.A., Ph.D. (Cantab.), Emerita Prof. of Later Med. Hist. [English overseas trade; reign of Edward II], W.R.Childs@leeds.ac.uk

Catherine E.B. Coombs, B.A., M.A., Ph.D. (Leeds), Teaching Fellow in Mod. Imp. Hist. (19th & 20th c.) [Punjab; colonialism, nationalism & the state in northern India], C.E.B.Coombs@leeds.ac.uk

Kate M. Dossett, B.A. (Oxon.), M.A. (Warwick), Ph.D. (Cantab.), Lect. in Hist. (N. Amer.) [African-American history; women's history; Harlem Renaissance], K.M.Dossett@leeds.ac.uk

Shane D. Doyle, M.A. (Cantab. & Lond.), Ph.D. (Cantab.), Sen. Lect. in Wider World Hist. (Afric.) [Demographic history; medical history; environmental history], S.D.Doyle@leeds.ac.uk

William Flynn, B.Mus. (Rochester), M.Mus. (Edin.), M.A., Ph.D. (Duke), Lect. in Med. Latin. [Interactions among liturgy, music & theology; elementary music & grammar instruction to 1200; music & Latin palaeography; music theory to 1300; Hildegard of Bingen], W.Flynn@leeds.ac.uk

Gordon C.F. Forster, B.A. (Leeds), Hon. Lect. in Hist., Sen. Life Fellow (Early Mod. Brit., Local) [Yorkshire & York 16th–17th c.; Leeds 1600–1720]

Matthew Frank, B.A. (Lond.), M.St., D.Phil. (Oxon.), Lect. in Int. Hist. (20th c.) [Population transfer in post-war Europe], M.Frank@leeds.ac.uk

John Gooch, B.A., Ph.D. (Lond.), Emeritus Prof. of Int. Hist. (19th–20th c.) [Military & foreign policy in liberal & fascist Italy], J.Gooch@leeds.ac.uk

William R. Gould, B.A., M.Phil., Ph.D. (Cantab.), Prof. of Indian Hist. (Mod. India) [20th c. India; Hindu nationalism], W.R.Gould@leeds.ac.uk

Simon J.D. Green, M.A., D.Phil. (Oxon.), Prof. of Mod. Brit. Hist. (Later Mod. Brit., Local & Regional) [Religion in 20th c. Britain], S.J.D.Green@leeds.ac.uk

Simon D. Hall, M.A. (Sheff.), Ph.D. (Cantab.), Sen. Lect. in N. Amer. Hist. [American South; African American history; post-1945 social & political history, esp. the 1960s], S.D.Hall@leeds.ac.uk

Raphael J.L. Hallett, B.A. (Cantab.), M.A., D.Phil. (Sussex), Teaching Fellow in Early Mod. Hist. (Early Mod. Hist.) [Printing revolution; language arts; history of ideas], R.Hallett@leeds.ac.uk

James R. Harris, B.A., M.A. (Toronto), Ph.D. (Chicago), Sen. Lect. in Mod. Hist. (Mod. Eur., 20th c. Russia) [Stalin & Stalinism], J.R.Harris@leeds.ac.uk

William E.H. Jackson, B.A., M.Sc. (Lond.), Ph.D. (Leeds), Lect. in Imp. Hist. [Imperial history], W.Jackson@leeds.ac.uk

Emilia M. Jamroziak, B.A. (Poznan), M.A. (C.E.U. Budapest), Ph.D. (Leeds.), Sen. Lect. in Med. Hist. [12th–14th c. British social & religious history; Cistercian order in medieval Europe; medieval frontier societies], E.M.Jamroziak@leeds.ac.uk

Laura King, B.A., M.A., Ph.D. (Sheff.), Arts Engaged Postdoctoral Fellow [Family; masculinity; fatherhood in 20th c. Britain], L.King@leeds.ac.uk

Kevin Linch, B.A., M.A., Ph.D. (Leeds), Sen. Teaching Fellow (18th c. Brit.), K.B.Linch@leeds.ac.uk

*Graham A. Loud, M.A., D.Phil. (Oxon.), Prof. of Med. Hist., Head of Sch. (Med.) [S. Italy & Sicily 950–1250: political, social & ecclesiastical history; Germany, political & ecclesiastical history 1050–1250; Crusades], G.A.Loud@leeds.ac.uk

Iona McCleery, M.A., Ph.D. (St. And.), Lect. in Hist. [Medieval medicine; saints' lives & miracles; Portugal], I.McCleery@leeds.ac.uk

Andrea Major, M.A., M.Sc., Ph.D. (Edin.), Sen. Lect. in Wider World Hist. [Early colonial India; British imperialism & social/gender issues], A.Major@leeds.ac.uk

Peter Maw, Ph.D., Lect. (18th c. Hist.) [Early industrial revolution in northern England; Atlantic trade in 18th c.], P.Maw@leeds.ac.uk

Jessica Meyer, B.A. (Yale), Ph.D. (Cantab.), Wellcome Trust Fellow in Hist. of Medicine [History of masculinity; war; disability; popular fiction], J.K.Meyer@leeds.ac.uk

Alan V. Murray, M.A., Ph.D. (St. And.), Sen. Lect. in Med. Stud., Editor, *International Medieval Bibliography* (Med. Hist.) [Crusades & the Latin East; warfare & chivalry], A.V.Murray@leeds.ac.uk

David M. Palliser, M.A., D.Phil. (Oxon.), Emeritus Prof. of Med. Hist. (Brit., Local & Regional Hist.) [English urban history *c.*600–1540], David.Palliser@btinternet.com

Guy Perry, M.A., M.St., D.Phil. (Oxon.), Lect. in Med. Hist. [Social & geographical mobility in the central medieval period, esp. French-speaking world & Crusades], G.J.M.Perry@leeds.ac.uk

Mark B Smith, B.A. (Oxon.), M.A., Ph.D. (Lond.), Lect. in Mod. Hist. (19th & 20th c.) [Late imperial Russia & the Soviet Union; history of welfare], M.B.Smith@leeds.ac.uk

Edward M. Spiers, M.A., Ph.D. (Edin.), Prof. of Strategic Stud. (19th–20th c.) [Chemical warfare; Scottish soldiers & 2nd Sudan war], E.M.Spiers@leeds.ac.uk

Martin Thornton, B.A. (Southampton), M.A. (Kent), Ph.D. (Lond.), Sen. Lect. in Int. Hist. [Canadian foreign policy post-1945], M.Thornton@leeds.ac.uk

P. Ellis Tinios, B.A. (Harv.), M.Phil. (Leeds), Ph.D. (Michigan), Hon. Lect. in Hist. (Japan) [Printing & popular culture in early modern Japan], P.E.Tinios@leeds.ac.uk

Steven W. Tolliday, M.A., Ph.D. (Cantab.), Prof. of Econ. Hist. (Mod. Econ., Business) [Business history, U.K.; automobile industry; Japan since 1945], S.W.Tolliday@leeds.ac.uk

Rachel E. Utley, B.A., M.A., Ph.D. (Leeds), Lect. in Int. Hist. [French foreign & defence policies since 1958; Cold War & post-Cold War international history; United Nations], R.E.Utley@leeds.ac.uk

Geoffrey T.P. Waddington, B.A., Ph.D. (Leeds), Sen. Lect. in Int. Hist. [Nazi foreign policy 1933–45; Axis diplomacy], G.T.P.Waddington@leeds.ac.uk

Lorna L. Waddington, B.A., M.A., Ph.D. (Leeds), Lect. in Int. Hist. [Weimar & Nazi Germany; anti-communist propaganda & politics; ethnic cleansing & genocide], L.L.Waddington@leeds.ac.uk

Richard C. Whiting, M.A., D.Phil. (Oxon.), Prof. of Mod. Hist. (Later Mod. Brit.) [History of trade unions; empire & politics], R.C.Whiting@leeds.ac.uk

Keith M. Wilson, B.A., D.Phil. (Oxon.), Emeritus Prof. of the Hist. of Int. Pol. (19th–20th c.), K.M.Wilson@leeds.ac.uk

Ian N. Wood, M.A., D.Phil. (Oxon.), Prof. of Early Med. Hist. (Med.) [Missionary hagiography; transformation of the Roman world; modern historiography of late antiquity; Bede's hagiography], I.N.Wood@leeds.ac.uk

Anthony D. Wright, M.A., D.Phil. (Oxon.), Emeritus Prof. in Eccles. Hist. (Early Mod. Eur. & Brit.) [History of the papacy], A.D.Wright@leeds.ac.uk

LEEDS METROPOLITAN UNIVERSITY

Civic Quarter, Leeds, LS1 3HE. 0113 812 0000
www.leedsmet.ac.uk
Faculty of Arts & Society
School of Cultural Studies Broadcasting Place, Woodhouse Lane, Leeds, LS2 9EN.
0113 812 5931. 0113 812 3403

Simon Blanchard, B.A., M.A. (Oxon.), Ph.D. (Lincoln), Sen. Lect. [19th & 20th c. media &
cultural history], s.blanchard@leedsmet.ac.uk
Matthew Caygill, B.A. (Leeds), M.A. (York), Sen. Lect. [Politics & culture in the eras of
depression & war; Vietnam War], m.caygill@leedsmet.ac.uk
Helen Dampier, B.A., M.A. (Rhodes), Ph.D. (Newcastle), Sen. Lect. [Colonial history; South
Africa; history & memory; life writing; Olive Schreiner], h.dampier@leedsmet.ac.uk
Shane Ewen, B.A., M.A., Ph.D. (Leicester), Sen. Lect. [Social & cultural history; British urban
history; municipal history; transnational history], s.ewen@leedsmet.ac.uk
Grainne Goodwin, B.A. (Edin.), M.A., Ph.D. (York), Sen. Lect. [Women & empire; British India;
19th c. literary history; the British suffragette movement], g.goodwin@leedsmet.ac.uk
Kelly Hignett, B.A., M.Phil., Ph.D. (Keele), Lect. [20th c. central & eastern Europe; Russia/
U.S.S.R.; organised crime; crime & deviance], k.l.hignett@leedsmet.ac.uk
Simon Morgan, B.A. (Oxon.), M.A. (Warwick), D.Phil. (York), Sen. Lect. [Victorian Britain;
political culture; radicalism; gender; women; urban elites], s.j.morgan@leedsmet.ac.uk
Stephen Mosley, B.A. (Manc. Met.), M.A., Ph.D. (Lancaster), Sen. Lect. [Social & cultural
history; urban history; environmental history], s.mosley@leedsmet.ac.uk
Alison Oram, B.A. (C.N.A.A.), M.Sc. (Brist.), Ph.D. (Lond.), Prof. of Soc. & Cultural
Hist. [Social & cultural history; gender history; history of sexuality in 20th c. Britain],
a.oram@leedsmet.ac.uk
Rachel Rich, B.A. (McGill), M.A., Ph.D. (Essex), Sen. Lect. (Soc. & Cultural Hist.)
[Social & cultural history; history of food in France & England; gender history],
R.Rich@leedsmet.ac.uk
Heather Shore, B.A. (North Lond.), M.A., Ph.D. (Lond.), Sen. Lect. [Social & cultural history,
1750–1914; history of crime in Britain, 1700–1945], h.shore@leedsmet.ac.uk

LEEDS TRINITY UNIVERSITY COLLEGE

(Accredited by the University of Leeds)
Brownberrie Lane, Horsforth, Leeds, LS18 5HD
www.leedstrinity.ac.uk
Department of Humanities 0113 283 7100. Fax 0113 283 7200

Diane K. Drummond, B.Soc.Sc. (Birm.), Ph.D. (Lond.), Reader in Mod. Hist.
(19th–20th c. Brit. Hist., 20th c. World) [Railways & British imperialism; women & railways],
d.drummond@leedstrinity.ac.uk
*Maureen A. Meikle, M.A., Ph.D. (Edin.), Prof. of Early Mod. Hist. (Early Mod.) [Social history;
Scottish history; women's history], m.meikle@leedstrinity.ac.uk
Rosemary A. Mitchell, B.A., D.Phil. (Oxon.), Reader in Victorian Stud. (18th–20th c. Brit.
Hist.) [Women's history; gender history; text & image studies; 19th c. cultural history],
r.mitchell@leedstrinity.ac.uk

Leeds Trinity

Karen A. Sayer, B.A. (C.N.A.A.), D.Phil. (Sussex), Prof. of Soc. & Cultural Hist.
(18th–19th c. Brit. & Eur., 20th c. Amer. Hist.) [Rural society; women; 19th c. cultural
history; environmental history], k.sayer@leedstrinity.ac.uk

UNIVERSITY OF **LEICESTER**

University Road, Leicester, LE1 7RH. 0116 252 2522. Fax 0116 252 2200
www.le.ac.uk
School of Historical Studies 0116 252 2587. Fax 0116 252 3986
www.le.ac.uk/history/
Centre for English Local History 0116 252 2762. Fax 0116 252 5769
www.le.ac.uk/elh/
Centre for Urban History 0116 252 2762. Fax 0116 252 5769
www.le.ac.uk/urbanhist/
Department of History of Art & Film 0116 252 2866. Fax 0116 252 5128
Department of Politics 0116 252 2702. Fax 0116 252 5082
School of Archaeology & Ancient History 0116 252 2611. Fax 0116 252 5005
www.le.ac.uk/ar/

Penelope Allison, M.A., Ph.D. (Sydney), Reader in Archaeol. & Anc. Hist. [Roman
archaeology, esp. domestic space], pma9@le.ac.uk
Clare Anderson, Ph.D. (Edin.), Prof. of Hist. [19th & 20th c. Indian Ocean; history of
confinement], ca26@le.ac.uk
J. Appleby, B.A. (Cantab.), M.A. (Southampton), Ph.D. (Cantab.), Lect. in Archaeol. & Anc.
Hist. [Human bioarchaeology; bronze age Eurasia], ja253@le.ac.uk
Nigel R. Aston, B.A. (Dunelm.), D.Phil. (Oxon.), Reader in Early Mod. Hist. [History of
religion in western Europe 1650–1830; the place of the clergy in politics & intellectual life;
universities 1650–1830; Anglo-French relations in religion & politics], na47@le.ac.uk
Bernard P. Attard, B.A., M.A. (Melb.), D.Phil. (Oxon.), Lect. in Econ. Hist. [History of the
international economy; British settler society], bpa1@le.ac.uk
Stuart R. Ball, M.A., Ph.D. (St. And.), Reader in Hist. (Mod. Brit.) [Conservative party; history
of parliament], bal@le.ac.uk
Guy Barefoot, B.A., Ph.D. (East Anglia), Lect. in Film Stud. [U.S. & British cinema],
gb80@le.ac.uk
Huw J. Barton, B.A., Ph.D. (Sydney), Lect. in Bioarchaeol. [Hunter-gatherer archaeology;
Australian archaeology; lithics; archaeobotany], hjb15@le.ac.uk
James S. Bothwell, B.A., M.A. (Alberta), Ph.D. (St. And.), Lect. in Hist. (Med. Brit.) [Kings &
nobility; royal favourites; patronage; social history], jsb16@le.ac.uk
Anthony E. Brown, M.A. (Oxon.), Ph.D. (Leicester), University Fellow in Archaeol.
(Landscape) [Domesday Book & the landscape], aeb10@le.ac.uk
James Campbell, B.A., M.A. (Warwick), Ph.D. (Nott.), Lect. in Amer. Hist. [Slavery in the
Americas; 19th c. African American history; race; crime & punishment], jmc62@le.ac.uk
*James R. Chapman, B.A., M.A. (East Anglia), Ph.D. (Lancaster), Prof. of Film Stud. [British
cinema & television history; film propaganda; media representations of the past; the cultural
politics of popular fictions], jrc28@le.ac.uk
Neil J. Christie, B.A., Ph.D. (Newcastle), Reader in Archaeol. (Late Roman & Med. Italy)
[Barbarian Europe; late Roman–early medieval Italy], njc10@le.ac.uk

Craig Cipolla, B.A., M.A. (Mass.), Ph.D. (Penn.), Lect. in Archaeol. [Historical archaeology; comparative colonialism; North America], cc363@le.ac.uk

Elizabeth J. Clapp, B.A., Ph.D. (Lond.), Sen. Lect. in Hist. (Amer.) [Women & social welfare reforms in progressive era America; women & party politics in early 19th c. America], ejc12@le.ac.uk

John R.D. Coffey, B.A., Ph.D. (Cantab.), Prof. of Early Mod. Hist. [17th–18th c. British religion, politics & ideas], jrdc1@le.ac.uk

Nicholas J. Cooper, B.Sc. (Leicester), Lect., p/t (Roman Brit., Roman Ceramics), njc9@le.ac.uk

Peter Darby, B.A. (Reading), M.A. (Dunelm.), Ph.D. (Birm.), British Academy Postdoctoral Fellow (Early Med.) [Early middle ages, esp. development of the Church in the medieval west], pd24@le.ac.uk

Martin L. Davies, M.A. (Oxon.), Reader in Hist. (Mod. Eur.) [History of ideas; construction & ramifications of historical knowledge], mld@le.ac.uk

David N. Edwards, B.A. (York), M.Litt. (Newcastle), Ph.D. (Cantab.), Lect. in Archaeol. [African archaeology; landscape archaeology], dne1@le.ac.uk

David P.M. Ekserdjian, B.A. (Cantab.), M.A., Ph.D. (Lond.), Prof. of Hist. of Art & Film [Italian Renaissance art], dpme1@le.ac.uk

Lin Foxhall, M.B.E., B.A. (Bryn Mawr), M.A. (Penn.), Ph.D. (Liv.), Prof. of Greek Hist. & Archaeol. [Greek farming systems; masculinity; clothing & textiles], lf4@le.ac.uk

Thomas Frangenberg, Ph.D. (Cologne), Reader in Hist. of Art [Art; art theory; perspective theory 15th–18th c.], tf6@le.ac.uk

David C. Gentilcore, B.A. (Toronto), M.A. (McMaster), Ph.D. (Cantab.), Prof. of Hist. [Social & cultural history of early modern Italy; history of medicine; food history], dcg2@le.ac.uk

Miriam C. Gill, B.A. (Oxon.), Ph.D. (Lond.), Director of Certificates in Architectural & Art Hist. (Med. Art Hist., Wall Paintings), mcg9@le.ac.uk

Mark Gillings, B.Sc., Ph.D. (Bradford), Reader in Archaeol. (Landscape, G.I.S.) [Archaeological survey; geographical information systems (G.I.S.); virtual reality], mg41@le.ac.uk

Simon Gunn, Ph.D. (Manc.), Prof. of Urban Hist., Director of Centre for Urban Hist. [English industrial cities c.1800–1980; history & cultural theory], sg201@le.ac.uk

Mary Harlow, B.A., Ph.D. (Leicester), Sen. Lect. in Anc. Hist. [Roman social history; dress; history of the family in late antiquity], mh385@le.ac.uk

Ian Harris, M.A., Ph.D. (Cantab.), Lect. in Early Mod. Hist. [Intellectual history; British history], ich1@le.ac.uk

Oliver Harris, B.A., M.A., Ph.D. (Cardiff), Lect. in Archaeol. [Neolithic Britain & Europe; archaeological theory; the archaeology of the body], ojth1@le.ac.uk

*Colin C. Haselgrove, B.Sc. (Sussex), M.A., Ph.D. (Cantab.), Prof. of Archaeol., Head of Sch. [Later prehistoric archaeology; iron age/Roman transition; Celtic coins], cch7@le.ac.uk

John Hayward, B.A., M.A. (Manc.), Ph.D. (Liv.), Teaching Fellow in Anc. Hist. [Herodotus; Greek history & society], jlth1@le.ac.uk

Terence Hopkinson, M.A., Ph.D. (Cantab.), Lect. in Archaeol. (Palaeolithic) [Palaeolithic ecology, settlement & stone tool technology], th46@le.ac.uk

Andrew J. Hopper, B.A., M.A., D.Phil. (York), Lect. in Eng. Local Hist. [Religion & political culture in 17th c. England], ajh69@le.ac.uk

Sally Horrocks, M.A. (Cantab.), Ph.D. (Manc.), Lect. in Mod. Brit. Hist. [Science & technology in 20th c. Britain; women scientists, technologists & technicians], smh4@le.ac.uk

Norman J. Housley, M.A., Ph.D. (Cantab.), Prof. of Hist. (Med. Eur.) [The Crusades], hou@le.ac.uk

Elizabeth T. Hurren, B.A., Ph.D. (Leicester), Reader in Medical Hum. [18th & 19th c. history of medicine; rural society; poverty & welfare; history of anatomy & the body from early modern birthing room to modern incubator], eh14@le.ac.uk

Simon T. James, B.Sc., Ph.D. (Lond.), Reader in Archaeol. [Roman warfare; reconstruction & re-enactments], stj3@le.ac.uk

Olaf Jensen, M.A., Ph.D. (Hanover), Lect. in Holocaust Stud. [National Socialism; Holocaust; history & memory], oj6@le.ac.uk

Andrew Johnstone, B.A. (Liv.), M.Phil., Ph.D. (Birm.), Lect. in Amer. Hist. [U.S. foreign policy], aej7@le.ac.uk

Richard L.C. Jones, B.A., D.Phil., Lect. in Landscape Hist. [Landscape archaeology; medieval rural settlement development; farming practices, esp. manuring], rlcj1@le.ac.uk

Prashant Kidambi, B.A. (Osmania), M.A., M.Phil. (J. Nehru), D.Phil. (Oxon.), Sen. Lect. in Brit. Imp. & World Hist. [Social & urban history of south Asia; social history of modern Spain, esp. the relationship between sport & British imperialism], pk64@le.ac.uk

Peter J.R. King, B.A. (Kent), B.Phil. (Exeter), Ph.D (Cantab.), Prof. of Eng. Local Hist. [18th & 19th c. criminal justice history; history of welfare & poverty], pk180@le.ac.uk

Steven A. King, B.A. (Kent), Ph.D. (Liv.), Prof. of Econ. & Soc. Hist. [History of European industrialisation 1650–1900; history of British & European welfare systems from 1601; social history of medicine], sak28@le.ac.uk

Turi King, B.A. (Cantab.), M.Sc., Ph.D. (Leicester), Lect. in Genetics & Archaeol. [Viking ancestry & identities; surnames; Y chromosome; D.N.A.], tek2@le.ac.uk

Zoe Knox, B.A. (Griffith & Monash), Ph.D. (Monash), Lect. in Mod. Russian Hist. [Religion in modern Russia], zk15@le.ac.uk

George Lewis, B.A., M.A., Ph.D. (Newcastle), Reader in U.S. Hist. [Civil rights; white supremacy; race & ethnicity; anti-communism], gdgl1@le.ac.uk

Toby Lincoln, D.Phil. (Oxon.), Lect. in Chinese Urban Hist. [Modern Chinese urban history, esp. urban morphology, the changing urban-rural relationship & daily life in different environments], tl99@le.ac.uk

Phillip G. Lindley, M.A., Ph.D. (Cantab.), Reader in Hist. of Art [Late medieval & early modern art & architecture], pgl1@le.ac.uk

Naoise MacSweeney, B.A. (Cantab.), M.A. (Lond.), Ph.D. (Cantab.), Lect. in Anc. Hist. [Greek world & the Near East; migration & cultural contact], nms241@le.ac.uk

Rebecca Madgin, B.A., M.A., Ph.D. (Leicester), Lect. in Eur. Planning Hist. [Redevelopment of European cities during the 19th & 20th c.], rmm13@le.ac.uk

Lydia Matthews, B.A., M.A. (Natal), D.Phil. (Oxon.), Teaching Fellow in Anc. Hist. [Late Roman Republic; gender]

*David J. Mattingly, B.A., Ph.D. (Manc.), Prof. of Roman Archaeol. (Roman, Landscape) [Landscape archaeology; archaeology of Roman empire; Roman farming economy], djm7@le.ac.uk

Andrew Merrills, B.A. (Oxon.), M.A., Ph.D. (Cantab.), Res. Fellow in Anc. Hist. [Geography & travel in the classical world; late antiquity; north Africa; perceptions of the Nile], shm11@le.ac.uk

James Moore, B.A. (Oxon.), Ph.D. (Manc.), Teaching Fellow in Mod. Brit. Soc. Hist. [19th & early 20th c. British history], jm68@le.ac.uk

Deirdre O'Sullivan, B.A. (N.U.I.), M.Phil. (Dunelm.), Lect. in Archaeol. (Med. Brit. & Ireland) [Early Northumbria; Viking-age Ireland], dmo@le.ac.uk

Claudia Prestel, M.A., Ph.D. (Munich), Reader in Hist. (Jewish Hist.) [Women's history; social history], cp59@le.ac.uk

Simon Richards, M.A., Ph.D. (Essex), Lect. [History & theory of architecture & town-planning; aesthetics; theory of art], sr148@le.ac.uk

Eliza Riedi, M.A. (Cantab.), Ph.D. (St. And.), Lect. in Imp. Hist. [British women & the British empire 1880–1914; South African War; sport & the military], er48@le.ac.uk

Sarah A. Scott, B.Sc. (Leicester), D.Phil. (Oxon.), Lect. in Archaeol., p/t [Prehistoric & Roman art], sas11@le.ac.uk

Caroline Sharples, B.A., M.A., Ph.D. (Southampton), Lect. in Mod. Eur. Hist. [History of modern Germany; legacy of National Socialism], cs383@le.ac.uk

*D. Graham J. Shipley, M.A., D.Phil. (Oxon.), Prof. of Anc. Hist. (Greek & Roman) [Sparta; landscapes; Hellenistic history], gjs@le.ac.uk

Keith D.M. Snell, M.A., Ph.D. (Cantab.), Prof. of Rural & Cultural Hist. [Cultural & agrarian history], kdm@le.ac.uk

Dan Stewart, B.A. (Memorial, Newfoundland), M.A. (Brit. Col.), Ph.D. (Leicester), Lect. in Anc. Hist. [Greek history, esp. social history, landscapes, Hellenistic & Roman Greece], ds120@le.ac.uk

Joanna E. Story, B.A., Ph.D. (Dunelm.), Prof. of Med. Hist. [8th–9th c. Britain & Europe], js73@le.ac.uk

*Rosemary H. Sweet, M.A., D.Phil. (Oxon.), Prof. of Urban Hist. [18th c. urban history], rhs4@le.ac.uk

Sarah A. Tarlow, B.A. (Sheff.), M.Phil., Ph.D. (Cantab.), Sen. Lect. in Archaeol. [Death & burial; post-medieval archaeology; ethics], sat12@le.ac.uk

Jeremy Taylor, B.A., Ph.D. (Dunelm.), Lect. [Landscape archaeology; iron age-Roman rural social organisation], jt38@le.ac.uk

Richard M. Thomas, B.A., Ph.D. (Birm.), Sen. Lect. in Archaeol. (Archaeozoology) [Medieval & post-medieval animal husbandry; diet & status; animal palaeopathology], rmt12@le.ac.uk

Deborah Toner, B.A., M.A., Ph.D. (Warwick), Lect. in Mod. Hist. [Mexican history & literature], dt151@le.ac.uk

Marijke van der Veen, Kand.doct. (Groningen), M.A., Ph.D. (Sheff.), Prof. of Archaeol. (Archaeobotany) [Environmental archaeology; archaeobotany], mvdv1@le.ac.uk

Pragya Volva, B.A., M.A. (Mumbai), M.A., Ph.D. (York), Teaching Fellow in Early Med. Hist. [Medieval history, esp. the Viking Age], pv51@le.ac.uk

Ian K. Whitbread, B.A. (Brist.), Ph.D. (Southampton), Lect. [Archaeological science; ceramic production & exchange; Greek archaeology], ikw3@le.ac.uk

Mark Williams, B.A. (Ontario), M.Phil., D.Phil. (Oxon.), Lect. in Early Mod. Hist. [17th c. cultural, religious & political history in Britain, Ireland & France], mw272@le.ac.uk

Ruth L. Young, B.Sc., M.Phil. (Bradford), Sen. Lect. in Archaeol., p/t [Iron age archaeology in S. Asia; environmental archaeology; mobility], rly3@le.ac.uk

UNIVERSITY OF **LINCOLN**

Brayford Pool, Lincoln, LN6 7TS. 01522 882000
www.lincoln.ac.uk
Department of Humanities
www.lincoln.ac.uk/humanities/

Sue Bestwick, B.A. (Lincolnshire & Humberside), M.A. (Nott.), Sen. Lect. in Hist. (Mod. Brit. & Eur., Communication Skills) [Environmental history; post-colonial Australian identity], sbestwick@lincoln.ac.uk

Krista Cowman, B.A. (Keele), M.A. (Lond.), D.Phil. (York), Prof. of Hist. (Women's Hist., Gender, Mod. Brit.) [Suffrage; feminism; socialism; World War I], kcowman@lincoln.ac.uk

Pietro Dipaola, B.A. (Venice), Ph.D. (Lond.), Lect. in Hist. (Mod. Brit. & Eur. Pol. & Soc. Hist.) [Anarchism; political migration; labour & social movements], pdipaola@lincoln.ac.uk

Christine Grandy, B.A. (Dalhousie), M.A. (York, Canada), D.Phil. (York), Lect. (Film Hist., Gender & Mod. Brit.) [Mass culture; censorship; inter-war], cgrandy@lincoln.ac.uk

Cairo Hickman, B.A. (Nott.), Ph.D. (Lond.), Lect. in Hist. (Med., Mod., Theory of Hist., Hist. of Journalism) [Roman & medieval religion; cartography; popular culture], chickman@lincoln.ac.uk

Kate Hill, B.A. (Warwick), Ph.D. (Lancaster), Princ. Lect. in Hist. (19th c. Brit. Culture & Soc., Med.) [Victorian musems; material culture], khill@lincoln.ac.uk

Philippa M. Hoskin, M.A., D.Phil. (Oxon.), Reader in Hist. (Med. Brit. & Eur.) [Ecclesiastical history; diplomatic & palaeography; sanctity], phoskin@lincoln.ac.uk

Heather Hughes, B.A. (Witwatersrand), Ph.D. (Lond.), Prof. of Hist. (Tourism, Southern Afric. Stud.) [Links between tourism & heritage; southern African political history], hhughes@lincoln.ac.uk

Joanna Huntington, B.A. (Newcastle), M.A., Ph.D. (York), Lect. in Hist. (Med. Brit. & Eur.) [Anglo-Norman England; Normandy; medieval masculinities; sanctity; queenship; kingship; uses of history in the early/high middle ages], jhuntington@lincoln.ac.uk

*Ian Packer, M.A. (Cantab.), D.Phil. (Oxon.), Reader in Hist. (Mod. Brit. Pol. & Soc. Hist.) [British politics in late 19th & early 20th c.; politics & literature], ipacker@lincoln.ac.uk

Finn Pollard, M.A., M.Sc., Ph.D. (Edin.), Lect. in Hist. (Mod. U.S.) [Literary representations of U.S. national character; 'independence' in early American politics], fpollard@lincoln.ac.uk

Anna Marie E. Roos, B.A., M.H., Ph.D. (Colo.), Sen. Lect. in Hist. (Early Mod. Hist., Sc. & Medicine) [History of natural history; history of chemistry; gender; history of scientific institutions], aroos@lincoln.ac.uk

Antonella Liuzzo Scorpo, B.A. (Catania), Ph.D. (Exeter), Lect. in Hist. (Cultural & Med. Hist. of Iberia & Western Mediterranean) [Friendship; history of emotions; power & authority], aliuzzoscorpo@lincoln.ac.uk

Pete Shinner, B.A. (Humberside), Ph.D. (Lincoln), Sen. Lect. in Hist. (English Civil War, 19th & 20th c. Brit., 20th c. Russia) [Victorian middle classes; brewing & railway industries], pshinner@lincoln.ac.uk

Jamie Wood, B.A., M.A., Ph.D. (Manc.), Lect. in Hist. (Med. & Roman Hist., Spain) [Identity; pedagogy; historiography; violence], jwood@lincoln.ac.uk

Harry Ziegler, M.A. (Stuttgart), Cert. d'études politiques (Paris), Sen. Lect. in Hist. (Mod. Eur.) [Weimar & Third Reich; cultural history], hziegler@lincoln.ac.uk

UNIVERSITY OF **LIVERPOOL**

P.O. Box 147, Liverpool, L69 3BX. 0151 794 2000. Fax 0151 708 6502
www.liv.ac.uk
School of History 0151 794 2396/2413. Fax 0151 794 2366
www.liv.ac.uk/history/
School of Archaeology, Classics & Egyptology
12–14 Abercromby Square, Liverpool, L69 7WZ.
0151 794 2438 (Classics & Ancient History). 0151 794 2467 (Archaeology & Egyptology)
Hartley Building, Brownlow Street, Liverpool, L69 3GS. 0151 794 5044 (Archaeology)
www.liv.ac.uk/sacos/

Zosia H. Archibald, M.A., D.Phil. (Oxon.), Lect. in Anc. Hist. & Classical Archaeol.,
z.archibald@liv.ac.uk
William J. Ashworth, B.Sc., M.A., Ph.D., Sen. Lect. in Hist. [Science, technology & taxation],
w.j.ashworth@liv.ac.uk
John C. Belchem, B.A., D.Phil. (Sussex), Prof. of Mod. Hist. (Mod. Brit. & Irish Hist.) [Irish in
Liverpool; modern history of Isle of Man], j.c.belchem@liv.ac.uk
Harald Braun, M.A. (Heid.), D.Phil. (Oxon.), Lect. in Eur. Hist. [Late medieval/early modern
political thought; history of early colonial empires], h.e.braun@liv.ac.uk
Alexandrina Buchanan, B.A., M.Sc., Ph.D., Lect. in Archive Stud. [Archival theory &
methodology; history of record-keeping & historiography], alexandrina.buchanan@liv.ac.uk
Marios Costambeys, B.A. (Lond.), Ph.D. (Cantab.), Sen. Lect. in Hist. (Eur. Soc., Relig.,
Landscapes & Culture, 4th–10th c.), costa@liv.ac.uk
Andrew M. Davies, B.A., Ph.D. (Cantab.), Sen. Lect. in Econ. & Soc. Hist. [Youth gangs &
street violence 1870–1940], a.m.davies@liv.ac.uk
Alex Drace-Francis, M.A., Ph.D. (Lond.), Lect. in Mod. Eur. Hist. [Cultural & social history of
Romania & south-east Europe], a.drace-francis@liv.ac.uk
Marianne Elliott, B.A. (Belf.), D.Phil. (Oxon.), Andrew Geddes & John Rankin Prof. of Mod.
Hist. (Irish, French & 18th c. Eur. Hist.) [A history of Catholics of Ulster], melliot@liv.ac.uk
Charles J. Esdaile, B.A., Ph.D. (Lancaster), Prof. of Mod. Hist. (19th–20th c. Eur., esp. Spain)
[History of Spain 1808–1939], epsom@liv.ac.uk
C.J. Eyre, M.A., D.Phil. (Oxon.), Lect. in Egyptology (Hist. of Anc. Egypt) [Ancient Egypt;
socio-economic history]
John R. Fisher, B.A., M.Phil. (Lond.), Ph.D. (Liv.), Prof. of Mod. Hist. & Latin-Amer. Stud.
[Spanish imperial policy; Peru 18th–19th c.]
Robert Foley, B.A., M.A. (N.Y.), Ph.D. (Lond.), Sen. Lect. in Mod. Eur. Hist. [Military history,
esp. Germany before 1914], robert.foley@liv.ac.uk
Philip W.M. Freeman, B.A., Ph.D. (Sheff.), Lect. in Roman Archaeol. [Historiography of the
Roman empire frontiers], p.w.m.freeman@liv.ac.uk
Alan M. Greaves, B.A. (Dunelm.), Ph.D. (Leeds), Lect. in Archaeol. & Greek Hist. [History &
archaeology of Asia Minor], greaves@liv.ac.uk
Charlotte Harrison, B.A., M.A.R.M., Lect. in Records & Archive Management [Historical
development of record-keeping; legal/social contexts; land tenure; conveyancing &
litigation], charlotte.harrison@liv.ac.uk
Martin R.V. Heale, B.A. (Exeter), M.Phil., Ph.D. (Cantab.), Lect. in Med. Hist. [Late medieval
England; religious orders; popular religion], mrvheale@liv.ac.uk
Jonathan Hogg, B.A., M.A., Ph.D. (Liv.), Lect. in 20th c. Hist. [Nuclear culture; science fiction;
intellectual history; political thought], j.g.hogg@liv.ac.uk
Michael F. Hopkins, B.A., M.A., Ph.D., Sen. Lect. in Amer. Foreign Policy [American foreign
policy; British foreign policy; international history], michael.hopkins@liv.ac.uk

Damien Kempf, B.A. (Paris), M.A. (E.H.E.S.S.), Ph.D. (Johns Hopkins), Lect. in Med.
  Hist. [Cultural & intellectual history; medieval historiography; history of books],
  damien.kempf@liv.ac.uk
Anne McLaren, B.A. (Washington), M.A., Ph.D. (Johns Hopkins), Sen. Lect. (Early Mod.)
  [Kingship in early modern Britain], a.mclaren01@liv.ac.uk
Keith Mason, B.A. (Oxon.), M.A., Ph.D. (Johns Hopkins), Lect. in Mod. Hist. (18th c. N. Amer.
  & Caribbean) [Loyalism; U.S. constitution; slavery], mason@liv.ac.uk
Christopher B.E. Mee, B.A. (Brist.), Ph.D. (Lond.), Charles W. Jones Prof. in Anc. Hist. &
  Classical Archaeol. [Aegean & Greek archaeology]
Graeme Milne, M.A., Ph.D., Lect. in Mod. Hist. [Urban, maritime & business history;
  international trade & shipping; Victorian globalisation; port cities], g.j.milne@liv.ac.uk
Alexander Morrison, M.A., D.Phil. (Oxon.), Lect. in Imp. Hist. [Comparative imperial history;
  Russian empire in central Asia; British empire in India], a.s.morrison@liv.ac.uk
Mark Peel, B.A., M.A. (Flinders), M.A. (Johns Hopkins), Ph.D. (Melbourne), Prof. of Mod.
  Cultural & Soc. Hist. [Comparative history of charity & social work; social mobility; domestic
  service], mark.peel@liv.ac.uk
Margaret Procter, B.A. (Dunelm.), [Perceptions of the use & management of records &
  administration], mprocter@liv.ac.uk
Brigitte Resl, M.Phil., Ph.D. (Vienna), Prof. of Med. Hist. (Med. Hist.) [Representation &
  significance of animals in medieval discourse], b.resl@liv.ac.uk
*Robin J. Seager, M.A. (Oxon.), Reader in Anc. Hist. [5th–4th c. B.C. Greek history; 2nd–1st
  c. Roman history; Constantine & Ammianus], rseager@liv.ac.uk
Sally B. Sheard, B.A., Ph.D. (Liv.), Lect. in Hist. [19th c. public health], sheard@liv.ac.uk
Nigel J. Swain, B.A., Ph.D. (Cantab.), Lect. in Econ. & Soc. Hist. (Mod. Eastern Eur., esp.
  Hungary), swainnj@liv.ac.uk
Mark Towsey, M.A., M.Litt., Ph.D., Lect. in Mod. Brit. Hist. [History of reading in 18th & 19th
  c.], m.r.m.towsey@liv.ac.uk
*Christopher J. Tuplin, M.A., D.Phil. (Oxon.), Reader in Anc. Hist. & Classical Archaeol.
  [Achaemenid Persian empire; Xenophon], c.j.tuplin@liv.ac.uk
Dmitri van den Bersselaar, M.A., Ph.D. (Leiden), Sen. Lect. in Afric. Hist. [West Africa;
  the Atlantic world; migrant communities; identity, ethnicity, (trans-)nationalism, (post-)
  colonialism], dvdb@liv.ac.uk

LIVERPOOL HOPE UNIVERSITY

Hope Park, Liverpool, L16 9JD. 0151 291 3000. Fax 0151 291 3160
www.hope.ac.uk
Department of Politics, History, Media & Communication
www.hope.ac.uk/politicshistoryandmedia/

John C. Appleby, B.A., Ph.D. (Hull), Sen. Lect. (Early Mod.) [English trade & colonisation in N.
  America], applebj@hope.ac.uk
Bryce Evans, B.A. (Warwick), M.A., Ph.D. (Dublin), Lect. (Mod.) [Modern Europe; modern
  Irish history; economic history], evansb1@hope.ac.uk
Eric Grove, M.A. (Aberd.), M.A. (Lond.), Ph.D. (Hull), Prof. of Naval Hist. (Mod.) [Naval
  history; maritime strategy & security; modern military history; military technology;
  terrorism & insurgency; contemporary security studies; nuclear weapons & strategy],
  grovee@hope.ac.uk

Stephen Kelly, B.A., M.A., Ph.D. (N.U.I.), Lect. (Mod.) [Modern European history; British-Irish relations; John Henry Newman; Anglo-Irish relations], kellys@hope.ac.uk

Fiona Pogson, B.A., Ph.D. (Liv.), Sen. Lect. (Early Mod.) [Early Stuart political & administrative history], pogsonf@hope.ac.uk

Sonja Tiernan, Cert., H.Dip., M.A., Ph.D. (N.U.I.), Lect. in Mod. Hist. (Mod.) [British & Irish gender & women's history; crime & punishment], tiernas@hope.ac.uk

*Christopher Williams, B.A. (Portsmouth), M.Sc.(Econ.) (Swansea), Ph.D. (Essex), Prof. of Mod. Hist., Head of Dept. (Mod.) [Russian social & cultural history; modern European history], williac7@hope.ac.uk

LIVERPOOL JOHN MOORES UNIVERSITY

0151 231 2121
www.ljmu.ac.uk
School of Humanities & Social Science
68 Hope Street, Liverpool, L1 9BZ. 0151 231 5144

Mike Benbough-Jackson, B.A. (Glamorgan), M.A. (Cardiff), Ph.D. (Wales), Sen. Lect. (18th–20th c. Soc. & Cultural Hist.)

David Clampin, B.A. (Coventry), M.A. (Kent), Ph.D. (Aberystwyth), Lect. (20th c. Brit.) [Propaganda; home front during World War II], d.j.clampin@ljmu.ac.uk

Sam Davies, B.Sc. (Brist.), Ph.D. (L.J.M.U.), Prof. of Hist. (19th–20th c. Soc. Hist., Labour Hist.) [Inter-war municipal elections], r.s.davies@ljmu.ac.uk

Francis X. McDonough, M.A. (Oxon.), Ph.D. (Lancaster), Prof. of Int. Hist. (20th c. Pol.), f.x.mcdonough@ljmu.ac.uk

Lucinda Matthews-Jones, B.A., Ph.D. (Manc.), [19th c. cultural history; religion, esp. Anglicanism; gender history; Christian domesticity]

Alex Miles, LL.B., M.A. (Keele), Ph.D. (Salford), [20th–21st c. American foreign relations; presidential decision-making]

Gillian O'Brien, M.A. (Dublin), Ph.D. (Liv.), [18th–19th c. Irish history; urban history; commemoration]

Nicholas J. White, B.A., Ph.D. (Lond.), Reader in Imp. & C'wealth Hist. (20th c. Imp. Hist., Decolonisation) [Business-government relations & end of empire], n.j.white@ljmu.ac.uk

UNIVERSITY OF **LONDON**

Birkbeck, University of London   Malet Street, WC1E 7HX. 020 7631 6000.
Fax 020 7631 6270
www.bbk.ac.uk
Department of History, 28 Russell Square, WC1B 5DQ.
020 3073 8093.
www.bbk.ac.uk/history/
Department of Politics & Sociology
Department of Geography

Sunil Amrith, Ph.D. (Cantab.), Reader in Mod. Asian Hist. (Mod. Asian Hist.) [Cultural &
political history of south Indian migration to Southeast Asia, esp. Burma, Malaysia &
Singapore], s.amrith@bbk.ac.uk
Frederick Anscombe, B.A. (Yale), Ph.D. (Princeton), Sen. Lect. [Balkans & Middle East],
f.anscombe@bbk.ac.uk
*John Arnold, B.A., D.Phil. (York), Head of Dept. & Prof. of Med. Hist. (Med. Hist.) [Medieval
history], j.arnold@bbk.ac.uk
Jennifer Baird, B.A. (Newfoundland), M.A. (Brit. Col.), Ph.D. (Leicester), Sen. Lect. in
Archaeol. (Roman Archaeol.) [Roman provincial archaeology; ancient housing & the history
of Classical archaeology], j.baird@bbk.ac.uk
Joanna Bourke, B.A., M.A. (Auckland), Ph.D. (A.N.U.), Prof. of Hist. (Brit. & Irish
Soc. & Cultural Hist.) [War; gender; masculinity; emotions; working-class cultures],
j.bourke@bbk.ac.uk
Sean Brady, B.A., M.A., Ph.D. (Lond.), Lect. in Mod. Brit. & Irish Hist. (Mod. Brit. & Irish Hist.)
[Religion, the family & sexuality in 19th c. Britain & Ireland], s.brady@bbk.ac.uk
Christy Constantakopoulou, M.A., Ph.D. (Oxon.), Sen. Lect. in Anc. Hist. (Anc. Hist.) [History
of the Aegean world & its islands; Greek historiography], c.constantakopoulou@bbk.ac.uk
Matt Cook, Sen. Lect. in Hist. & Gender Stud. (Gender Theory) [History of sexuality & the
history of London in the 19th & 20th c.], m.cook@bbk.ac.uk
Serafina Cuomo, B.A. (Naples), Ph.D. (Cantab.), Reader in Roman Hist. (Greek & Roman
Hist.) [Ancient Greek & Roman cultures], s.cuomo@bbk.ac.uk
Filippo De Vivo, B.A. (Cantab.), D.E.A. (E.H.E.S.S, Paris), Ph.D. (Cantab.), Lect. in Early
Mod. Eur. Hist. (Early Mod. Eur. Hist.) [Early modern Italy & the Republic of Venice],
f.de-vivo@bbk.ac.uk
Catharine H. Edwards, M.A., Ph.D. (Cantab.), Prof. of Classics & Anc. Hist. (Roman Hist.)
[Social & cultural history of ancient Greece; receptions of antiquity in later periods],
c.edwards@bbk.ac.uk
David Feldman, M.A., Ph.D. (Cantab.), Sen. Lect. in Hist. (Mod. Brit.) [History of minorities in
British society since 1600; British Jewish history], d.feldman@bbk.ac.uk
Orlando G. Figes, B.A., Ph.D. (Cantab.), Prof. of Hist. (18th–20th c. Eur.) [History of Russia
since 1800], o.figes@bbk.ac.uk
Caroline Goodson, Ph.D. (Columbia), R.C.U.K. Academic Fellow [Medieval history &
archaeology; architecture in southern Italy in the middle ages], c.goodson@bbk.ac.uk
Vanessa A. Harding, M.A., Ph.D. (St. And.), Prof. of Hist. (Brit. Hist.) [Medieval & early
modern London history; death; the family], v.harding@bbk.ac.uk
John Henderson, B.A. (Newcastle), M.A. (Cantab.), Ph.D. (Lond.), Prof. of Italian
Renaissance Hist. [Italian Renaissance & early modern European history],
j.henderson@bbk.ac.uk

Sarah Howard, M.A., M.Phil., Ph.D. (Cantab.), Lect. in Mod. Eur. Hist. (Mod. Eur. Hist.) [20th c. French history; The Algerian War, 1954–62; France & its empire; families & state welfare in contemporary France], s.howard@bbk.ac.uk

Caroline Humfress, B.A., M.A., Ph.D. (Cantab.), Reader in Hist. [Late antique & early medieval history], c.humfress@bbk.ac.uk

Matthew J. Innes, M.A., Ph.D. (Cantab.), Prof. of Med. Hist. [Politics, society & culture of medieval Europe, 700–1100], m.innes@bbk.ac.uk

Julia Laite, B.A., Ph.D. (Cantab.), Lect. in Brit. Hist. (Brit. Hist) [Modern history of women, gender, & sexuality; migration & transnational history; crime & criminal justice], j.laite@bbk.ac.uk

Julia Lovell, B.A., M.A., M.Phil., Ph.D., Sen. Lect. in Mod. Chinese Hist. (Mod. East Asia.) [Modern Asian history], j.lovell@bbk.ac.uk

Lesley McFadyen, M.A. (Glas.), M.A. (Southampton), Ph.D. (Wales), Lect. in Archaeol. [Architecture in prehistory; history of ideas between archaeology & architecture], l.mcfadyen@bbk.ac.uk

Caspar Meyer, B.A. (Lond.), D.Phil. (Oxon.), Lect. in Classical Archaeol. [Greek art & archaeology], h.meyer@bbk.ac.uk

Daniel Pick, M.A., Ph.D. (Cantab.), Prof. of Hist. [19th & 20th c. European culture, thought & the human sciences], d.pick@bbk.ac.uk

April Pudsey, B.A., M.A., Ph.D. (Manc.), Lect. in Anc. Hist. [Rome; Greece; Egypt], a.pudsey@bbk.ac.uk

Jessica Reinisch, Leverhulme Early Career Fellow (Mod. Eur. Hist.) [Modern European & German history], j.reinisch@bbk.ac.uk

Tim Reynolds, B.A., M.A., Ph.D. (Cantab.), Sen. Lect. in Archaeol. [Human prehistory adaptations], te.reynolds@bbk.ac.uk

Jan Rueger, Ph.D. (Cantab.), Leverhulme Res. Fellow & Lect. in Mod. Eur. Hist. [German, British & European history in the 19th & 20th c.], j.rueger@bbk.ac.uk

Hilary J. Sapire, B.A. (Cape Town), Ph.D. (Witwatersrand), Lect. in Hist. (Imp. & C'wealth) [Social history of South Africa in 20th c.], h.sapire@bbk.ac.uk

Chandak Sengoopta, M.D. (Calcutta), M.A. (Cornell), Ph.D. (Johns Hopkins), Prof. of Hist. of Medicine & Sc. [History of European medicine; history of modern science in India; cultural history of modern India], c.sengoopta@bbk.ac.uk

Adam Shapiro, Ph.D. (Chicago), Lect. in Intellectual & Cultural Hist. [History of science; history of religion; U.S. history; history of education], a.shapiro@bbk.ac.uk

Naoko Shimazu, B.A. (Manitoba), M.Phil., D.Phil. (Oxon.), Lect. in Japanese Hist. (Mod. Japan) [Cultural history of the Russo-Japanese war], n.shimazu@bbk.ac.uk

Laura Stewart, M.A., (St And.), M.Sc., Ph.D. (Edin.), Lect. in Early Mod. Brit. Hist. [Political & fiscal history of early modern Scotland; comparative history of Scotland in the context of early modern Europe], l.stewart@bbk.ac.uk

Julian Swann, B.A. (Lancaster), Ph.D. (Cantab.), Prof. of Hist. (Early Mod. Eur.) [Estates General of Burgundy 1661–1790], j.swann@bbk.ac.uk

Becky Taylor, (20th c. Soc. Hist.) [19th & 20th c. social history, especially migration, minorities, poverty & the state], r.taylor@bbk.ac.uk

Frank Trentmann, B.A. (Lond.), M.A., Ph.D. (Harv.), Prof. of Hist. (Mod. Brit.) [Political culture; political economy; consumption], f.trentmann@bbk.ac.uk

Nikolaus D. Wachsmann, B.Sc. (Lond.), M.Phil. (Cantab.), Ph.D. (Lond.), Reader in Mod. Eur. Hist. (Mod. Eur.) [20th c. German history], n.wachsmann@bbk.ac.uk

Brodie Waddell, B.A., M.A. (Victoria, Canada), Ph.D. (Warwick), Lect. in Early Mod. Hist. (Early Mod. Hist.) [England c.1550–1750], b.waddell@bbk.ac.uk

Courtauld Institute of Art Somerset House, Strand, WC2R 0RN.
020 7848 2777. Fax 020 7848 2410
www.courtauld.ac.uk

Rebecca Arnold, B.A., M.A., Ph.D. (Lond.), Lect. in Hist. of Dress & Textiles [20th c. dress & fashion; modernity & the body], rebecca.arnold@courtauld.ac.uk

Caroline H. Arscott, B.A. (Cantab.), M.A., Ph.D. (Leeds), Prof. of Hist. of Art [British art & society in Victorian period, esp. urbanism & images of the city], caroline.arscott@courtauld.ac.uk

Sussan Babaie, B.A. (Tehran), M.A. (Amer. Uni. Washington), Ph.D. (N.Y.), Lect. in Hist. [Islamic & Iranian art], sussan.babaie@courtauld.ac.uk

Martin Caiger-Smith, B.A. (Cantab.), M.A. (Lond.), Programme Leader for M.A. in Curating the Art Museum [Curating; modern & contemporary museums & galleries; history of exhibitions & display], martin.caiger-smith@courtauld.ac.uk

Joanna L. Cannon, B.A., Ph.D. (Lond.), Reader in Hist. of Art [W. European art 13th–14th c.; central Italian art & architecture, esp. associated with the mendicant orders], joanna.cannon@courtauld.ac.uk

*Georgia M. Clarke, M.A. (Cantab.), Ph.D. (Lond.), Reader in Hist. of Architecture [15th–17th c. architecture, particularly Italian; architecture & texts; urbanism; Italian Renaissance palaces; Bologna; Rome], georgia.clarke@courtauld.ac.uk

Antony Eastmond, B.A. (Oxon.), M.A., Ph.D. (Lond.), Reader in Hist. of Art (Byz.) [Medieval & Byzantine art & culture; interchange between Christianity & Islam], antony.eastmond@courtauld.ac.uk

*John Lowden, M.A. (Cantab. & Lond.), Ph.D. (Lond.), Prof. of Hist. of Art & Head of Stud. for the Med. & Byz. Period [Medieval art, esp. the illuminated manuscript between late antiquity & the end of the middle ages], john.lowden@courtauld.ac.uk

Sheila McTighe, B.A. (Georgetown), M.A., Ph.D. (Yale), Sen. Lect. in Hist. of Art [17th c. Italian & French art; the relationship of painting, poetry & music; reception history], sheila.mctighe@courtauld.ac.uk

Susie M. Nash, B.A., Ph.D. (Read.), Debby Loeb Brice Prof. of Hist. of Renaissance Art [14th–16th c. N. European art, esp. French & Flemish illuminated manuscripts; panel paintings; relationships between different media; devotional images], susie.nash@courtauld.ac.uk

Scott Nethersole, B.A., M.A., Ph.D. (Lond.), Lect. in Hist. of Art [Italian art of the 15th c.; representations of violence in art; altarpieces], scott.nethersole@courtauld.ac.uk

Tom Nickson, B.A. (Cantab.), M.A., Ph.D. (Lond.), Lect. in Hist. of Art [Art, architecture & exchange in medieval Europe & the Mediterranean, esp. Spain], tom.nickson@courtauld.ac.uk

*Mignon Nixon, A.B. (Harv.), Ph.D. (City Univ., N.Y.), Prof. of Hist. of Art [Post-1945 American art; feminism; theory & criticism], mignon.nixon@courtauld.ac.uk

Satish Padiyar, B.A., M.A., Ph.D. (Lond.), Lect. in Hist. of Art [Late 18th & 19th c. French art; European neoclassical sculpture], satish.padiyar@courtauld.ac.uk

Gavin Parkinson, B.A. (Manc.), M.A., Ph.D. (Lond.), Lect. in Eur. Modernism [Art in France; surrealism; science; linguistics], gavin.parkinson@courtauld.ac.uk

Guido Rebecchini, B.A. (Università degli Studi di Roma La Sapienza), M.A. (Università degli Studi di Siena), Ph.D. (Warburg), Lect. in Hist. of Art [16th c. southern European art], guido.rebecchini@courtauld.ac.uk

Robin Schuldenfrei, B.A. (Brown), M.A. (Williams Coll., Mass.), Ph.D. (Harv.), Lect. in Hist. of Art [European & American modern architecture & design], robin.schuldenfrei@courtauld.ac.uk

London

Katie Scott, M.A. (Cantab.), Ph.D. (Lond.), Prof. of Hist. of Art [City as sign of polite culture in 18th c. France; 17th–18th c. French architecture: decoration], katie.scott@courtauld.ac.uk
*David H. Solkin, A.B. (Harv.), M.A. (Lond.), Ph.D. (Yale), Walter H. Annenberg Prof. of Hist. of Art [British art c.1660–1840; the politics of representation], david.solkin@courtauld.ac.uk
Julian P. Stallabrass, B.A. (Oxon.), M.A., Ph.D. (Lond.), Prof. of Hist. of Art [20th c. art, esp. British post-war; photography; contemporary art], julian.stallabrass@courtauld.ac.uk
Christine Stevenson, B.A. (Victoria), M.A., Ph.D. (Lond.), Lect. in the Hist. of Brit. Architecture, christine.stevenson@courtauld.ac.uk
Wenny Teo, B.A. (York), M.A., Ph.D. (Lond.), Lect. in Hist. of Art [Modern & contemporary Asian art, esp. China], wenny.teo@courtauld.ac.uk
Sarah G. Wilson, B.A. (Oxon.), M.A., Ph.D. (Lond.), Prof. of Hist. of Art [School of Paris; surrealism; art & politics in Europe & the Soviet bloc after 1945; international contemporary art], sarah.g.wilson@courtauld.ac.uk
*Joanna W. Woodall, B.A. (York), M.A., Ph.D. (Lond.), Prof. of Hist. of Art [Netherlandish art & European portraiture c.1530–17th c.; court of Philip II; Antonis Mor], joanna.woodall@courtauld.ac.uk

Goldsmiths, University of London   New Cross, SE14 6NW. 020 7919 7171
www.goldsmiths.ac.uk
Department of History 020 7919 7490.
Fax 020 7919 7398

Tobias Abse, M.A., Ph.D. (Cantab.), Lect. in Hist. (Mod. Eur.) [20th c. Italian history], t.abse@gold.ac.uk
Dejan Djokic, B.A., Ph.D. (Lond.), Reader in Hist. [Modern history of the Balkans, esp. political, social & cultural history of former Yugoslavia; rise & development of national ideologies in 19th c. Europe; democracy & dictatorship in inter-war Europe; Cold War history], d.djokic@gold.ac.uk
*Richard Grayson, B.A. (East Anglia), D.Phil (Oxon.), Prof. of 20th c. Hist. & Head of Dept. [20th c. British & Irish history; First World War], r.grayson@gold.ac.uk
Ariel Hessayon, B.A. (Oxon.), Ph.D. (Cantab.), Sen. Lect. in Hist [Early modern Britain & Europe; radical religion & ideas], a.hessayon@gold.ac.uk
Sarah Lambert, B.A., M.A. (Lond.), Lect. in Hist. [Gender in medieval history & literature], s.lambert@gold.ac.uk
Rebekah Lee, B.A. (Harv.), M.Phil., D.Phil. (Oxon.), Sen. Lect. in Hist. (Afric.) [Southern African social & cultural history; gender & urbanisation; religion & identity], r.lee@gold.ac.uk
Stephen Pigney, M.A., Ph.D. (Lond.), Lect. in Hist. [Early modern British intellectual, cultural, literary & religious history], s.pigney@gold.ac.uk
Jan Plamper, B.A. (Brandeis), Ph.D. (Calif. at Berkeley), Prof. of Hist. [Modern European & Russian history; politics & visual history; history of emotions], j.plamper@gold.ac.uk
John Price, B.A., Ph.D. (Lond.), Lect. in Hist. [19th & 20th c. British social history], j.price@gold.ac.uk
Vivienne Richmond, B.A., M.Res., Ph.D. (Lond.), Lect. in Hist., Deputy Head of Dept. [British proletarian dress since the 18th c., esp. its use in the construction of identity & the various modes by which clothing has been acquired; history of death & bodily disposal; research methodology & interdisciplinary approaches], v.richmond@gold.ac.uk
Anastasia Stouraiti, B.A., M.A., Ph.D. (Athens), Lect. in Hist. [Social, political & cultural history of the republic of Venice; history of books & readers in early modern Europe; colonialism & its forms of knowledge; the comparative history of early modern empires], a.stouraiti@gold.ac.uk

Erica Wald, B.A. (Smith Coll.), M.Sc. (Lond.), Ph.D. (Cantab.), Lect. in Hist. [Imperial, social & medical history], e.wald@gold.ac.uk

Alexander Watson, B.A., D.Phil. (Oxon.), Lect. in Hist. [Social, cultural & military history of central Europe & Britain during the First World War], a.watson@gold.ac.uk

Ronit Yoeli-Tlalim, B.A., M.A. (Tel Aviv), Ph.D. (Lond.), Wellcome Trust Lect. [History of Asian medicine; interactions between medicine & religion], r.yoeli-tlalim@gold.ac.uk

Heythrop College Kensington Square, W8 5HQ. 020 7795 6600.
Fax 020 7795 4200
www.heythrop.ac.uk
Department of Theology

*Richard M. Price, M.A., D.Phil. (Oxon.), B.D., M.Th. (Lond.), Prof. of the Hist. of Christianity (Church Hist. & Patristics) [Early church councils], r.price@heythrop.ac.uk

Oliver P. Rafferty, B.A. (Lond.), M.Phil. (Dublin), M.Sc (Oxon.), M.Th. (Lond.), D.Phil. (Oxon.), Lect. in the Hist. of Christianity [19th & 20th c. Irish history], o.rafferty@heythrop.ac.uk

Institute of Commonwealth Studies Senate House, WC1E 7HU.
020 7862 8844. Fax 020 7862 8820
http://commonwealth.sas.ac.uk/

*Philip V. Murphy, B.A., D.Phil. (Oxon.), Prof. of Brit. & C'wealth Hist., Director (Mod. Brit.) [Colonialism; history of the secret service], philip.murphy@sas.ac.uk

Sue Onslow, B.Sc., Ph.D. (Lond.), Sen. Res. Fellow/Co-Investigator, C'wealth Hist. Project [Oral history; decolonisation in sub-Saharan Africa; Britain & the Cold War], sue.onslow@sas.ac.uk

Damien Short, LL.B. (Wales), M.A. (Cardiff), Ph.D. (Essex), Sen. Lect. in Human Rights [Australian Aboriginal history; colonialism; genocide studies], damien.short@sas.ac.uk

Institute of Education 20 Bedford Way, WC1H 0AL.
020 7612 6543. Fax 020 7612 6366
www.ioe.ac.uk
Department of Humanities & Social Sciences
Department of Lifelong & Comparative Education

Vincent Carpentier, M.A., Ph.D. (Montpellier), Reader in Hist. of Educ. [Education & the social & economic history of Europe & the U.S.A. in the 19th & 20th c.; funding in higher education; quantitative history; international perspectives], v.carpentier@ioe.ac.uk

Steven Cowan, M.A., Ph.D. (Lond.), Lect. in Educ. [History of literacy; global issues in history of education], s.cowan@ioe.ac.uk

Mark Freeman, M.A. (Oxon.), M.Phil, Ph.D. (Glas.), Sen. Lect. in Educ. [History of education in modern Britain; adult education; youth movements; voluntary sector; informal education; heritage], m.freeman@ioe.ac.uk

*Gary McCulloch, M.A., Ph.D. (Cantab.), Brian Simon Prof. of Hist. of Educ. [Secondary education; teachers & curriculum; international & comparative perspectives], g.mcculloch@ioe.ac.uk

Tom Woodin, M.A. (Sussex), Ph.D. (Manc.), Sen. Lect. in Educ. [Historical approaches to educational research; social movements; widening participation], t.woodin@ioe.ac.uk

London

Institute of Historical Research Senate House, WC1E 7HU.
020 7862 8740. Fax 020 7862 8745
www.history.ac.uk

Matthew Davies, M.A., D.Phil. (Oxon.), Prof. of Urban Hist., Director of the Centre for
Metropolitan Hist. [Medieval & early modern London; crafts & guilds in the later middle
ages; late medieval English social & economic history], matthew.davies@sas.ac.uk
*Miles Taylor, B.A. (Lond.), M.A., Ph.D. (Cantab.), Prof. of Hist., Director [19th & 20th c.
British history; the history of parliamentary representation since 1760; the British Raj,
c.1858–1947; Victorian culture & historiography], miles.taylor@sas.ac.uk
Jane Winters, M.A. (Oxon.), M.A., Ph.D. (Lond.), Reader in Digital Humanities [Big data; web
archives; peer review; open access; digital history], jane.winters@sas.ac.uk

Institute of Latin American Studies Senate House, Malet Street WC1E 7HU.
020 7862 8844. Fax 020 7862 8886
http://ilas.sas.ac.uk/

*Linda Newson, B.A., Ph.D., Prof., Director [Latin America & the Philippines during the
Spanish colonial period; the impact of colonial rule on indigenous societies; the Portuguese
slave trade to Latin America; history of medicine in early colonial Spanish America],
linda.newson@sas.ac.uk

King's College Strand, WC2R 2LS. 020 7836 5454
www.kcl.ac.uk
Department of History 020 7848 1078
www.kcl.ac.uk/artshums/depts/history/
Centre for Hellenic Studies & Department of Classics
020 7848 2343. Fax 020 7848 2545
Centre for the History of Science, Technology & Medicine
020 7848 1078.
Department of Theology & Religious Studies 020 7848 2339.
Fax 020 7848 2255
Department of Geography 020 7848 2632. Fax 020 7848 2287
Department of War Studies 020 7836 2178.
Fax 020 7848 2026
Menzies Centre for Australian Studies 020 7240 0220.
Fax 020 7240 8292

Lindsay Allen, B.A. (Oxon.), Ph.D. (Lond.), Lect. in Greek & Near E. Hist. [Near East,
esp. the Achaemenid Persian empire; history of scholarship & reception studies],
lindsay.allen@kcl.ac.uk
Jennifer Altehenger, Ph.D. (Heid.), Lect. in Contemp. Chinese Hist. [Social & cultural history
of People's Republic of China], jennifer.altehenger@kcl.ac.uk
Stephen D. Baxter, B.A., M.St., D.Phil. (Oxon.), Reader in Hist. (Med.) [Land
tenure, prosopography & politics in late Anglo-Saxon & early Norman England],
stephen.baxter@kcl.ac.uk
Francisco Bethencourt, M.A. (Universidade Nova de Lisboa), Ph.D. (E.U.I.), Charles Boxer
Prof. of Hist. [Racism in European expansion; Inquisition in southern Europe & overseas],
francisco.bethencourt@kcl.ac.uk

James E. Bjork, Ph.D. (Chicago), Sen. Lect. in Mod. Eur. Hist. [Social history of religion; history of nationalisation], james.bjork@kcl.ac.uk

*Robert Blackburn, B.A., M.Sc., Ph.D., LL.D., Prof., Director of the Inst. of Contemp. Brit. Hist. (Brit. Pol.) [English constitutional history], robert.blackburn@kcl.ac.uk

Andrew Blick, B.Sc., M.A., Ph.D. (Lond.), Lect. in Pol. & Contemp. Hist. [British prime ministers; civil servants & special advisers; constitutional reform in the U.K.]

Hugh Bowden, B.A., D.Phil. (Oxon.), Sen. Lect. in Anc. Hist. [Practice of ancient religion, esp. in ancient Greece], hugh.bowden@kcl.ac.uk

*Carl Bridge, B.A. (Sydney), Ph.D. (Flinders), Prof. & Head of Menzies Centre for Australian Stud. [Domestic politics & diplomacy; Australia in World War II], carl.bridge@kcl.ac.uk

Arthur Burns, M.A., D.Phil. (Oxon.), Prof. of Hist. (Later Mod.) [Reform of Church of England early/mid 19th c.; church parties; reform; clergy], arthur.burns@kcl.ac.uk

Peter Busch, M.Sc., Ph.D. (Lond.), Lect. in War Stud. [Cold War; Vietnam War]

David A. Carpenter, M.A., D.Phil. (Oxon.), Prof. of Hist. (Med.) [English political, social & architectural history 12th–14th c.], david.carpenter@kcl.ac.uk

Patrick Chabal, Ph.D. (Cantab.), Chair in African Hist. & Pol. [Modern & contemporary history of Africa], patrick.chabal@kcl.ac.uk

David J. Crankshaw, M.A., Ph.D. (Cantab.), Lect. in Hist. of Early Mod. Christianity [Tudor & Stuart religions; political & social history, esp. Elizabethan privy council; Matthew Parker, archbishop of Canterbury, & St. Paul's Cathedral; confessionalisation; early modern political thought], david.crankshaw@kcl.ac.uk

Julia Crick, Ph.D. (Cantab.), Prof. of Palaeography & Manuscript Stud. [Medieval Britain to 1200], julia.crick@kcl.ac.uk

Lucy Delap, B.A., M.Phil., Ph.D. (Cantab.), Reader in 20th c. Brit. Hist. (Mod. Brit.) [British history since 1840; gender history; history of feminism; history of emotions; oral history], lucy.delap@kcl.ac.uk

Christopher Dillon, Ph.D. (Lond.), Lect. in Early Mod. Hist. [Modern Germany], christopher.dillon@kcl.ac.uk

Michael L. Dockrill, M.A. (Illinois), B.Sc.(Econ.), Ph.D. (Lond.), Emeritus & Visiting Prof. of Diplomatic Hist. [British & U.S. foreign & defence policy in the 20th c.]

Richard Drayton, Ph.D. (Yale), Rhodes Prof. of Imp. Hist. [British empire; French expansion c.1500–1850; global & transnational history; history of the Caribbean], richard.drayton@kcl.ac.uk

Anne J. Duggan, B.A., Ph.D. (Lond.), Emerita Visiting Res. Prof. of Hist. (Med.) [Thomas Becket; conflict of laws; Becket cult], anne.duggan@kcl.ac.uk

David E.H. Edgerton, B.A. (Oxon.), Ph.D. (Lond.), Hans Rausing Prof. of Hist. of Sc. & Tech. [History of 20th c. Britain; global histories of technology; material histories of modernity], david.edgerton@kcl.ac.uk

Max Edling, Ph.D. (Cantab.), Lect. in North Amer. Hist. [North American history 1500–1865; American founding; U.S. early republic], max.edling@kcl.ac.uk

Serena Ferente, B.A., M.A., Ph.D. (E.H.E.S.S., Paris), Lect. in Med. Hist. [Italian political history, 14th & 15th c.; women's history & history of European political ideas], serena.ferente@kcl.ac.uk

Eliza Filby, B.A. (Dunelm.), M.A. (Lond.), Ph.D. (Warwick), Lect. in Mod. Brit. Hist. [Religion & politics in 1980s Britain; history of multiculturalism; religious diversity & secularisation in post-war Britain], liza.filby@kcl.ac.uk

Lawrence D. Freedman, K.C.M.G., C.B.E., B.A.(Econ.) (Manc.), B.Phil. (York), D.Phil. (Oxon.), Prof. of War Stud. [American decisions on military intervention 1945–95]

Caitjan Gainty, Ph.D. (Chicago), Lect. in Hist. of Sc., Tech. & Medicine [History of medicine; American 20th c. cultural history; history of film], catherine.gainty@kcl.ac.uk

Anne H. Goldgar, B.A. (Princeton), M.A., Ph.D. (Harv.), Reader in Hist. (Early Mod.) [European cultural & social history; France & Netherlands], anne.goldgar@kcl.ac.uk

Michael S. Goodman, B.A. (Leicester), M.A. (Nott.), Ph.D., Lect. in War Stud. [Nuclear weapons history; intelligence; Cold War history]

Laura Gowing, M.A. (Oxon.), Ph.D. (Lond.), Prof. of Early Mod. Brit. Hist. (Early Mod.) [Women's history; the body in early modern England], laura.gowing@kcl.ac.uk

Toby Green, Ph.D. (Birm.), Lect. in Lusophone Afric. Hist. & Culture [History of race & slavery in the Atlantic; African engagement with the early Atlantic world], toby.green@kcl.ac.uk

Edith Hall, D.Phil. (Oxon.), Prof. of Classics [Ancient Greek social & intellectual history], edith.hall@kcl.ac.uk

Peter J. Heather, M.A., D.Phil. (Oxon.), Prof. of Hist. (Med.) [Late Roman & early medieval history c.250–600, esp. imperialism, bureacracies, migration & ethnicity], peter.heather@kcl.ac.uk

Judith Herrin, M.A. (Cantab.), Ph.D. (Birm.), Prof. Emeritus, Constantine Leventis Sen. Res. Fellow of Late Antique & Byz. Stud. [Women in Byzantium; Byzantium in relation to Islam & the west; history of the city of Ravenna in late antiquity], judith.herrin@kcl.ac.uk

Vincent Hiribarren, Ph.D. (Leeds), Lect. in World Hist. [African & world history; cartography; digital humanities], vincent.hiribarren@kcl.ac.uk

Brian Holden Reid, B.A. (Hull), M.A. (Sussex), Ph.D. (Lond.), Prof. of Amer Hist. & Milit. Institutions [British & U.S. military thought in the 20th c.; American Civil War]

Jan Willem Honig, Doctorall (Amsterdam), Ph.D. (Lond.), Sen. Lect. in War Stud. [Warfare in the middle ages; European security]

Alan James, B.A., M.A. (Alberta), Ph.D. (Manc.), Sen. Lect. in War Stud. [Early modern naval warfare; early European overseas expansion]

Michael D. Kandiah, B.A. (Victoria, Canada), Ph.D. (Exeter), Director of the Witness Seminar Programme (20th c. Brit.) [Politics & diplomacy, esp. Cold War & Anglo-American relations; elite oral history; the role of British embassies & High Commissions], michael.kandiah@kcl.ac.uk

Lucy E. Kostyanovsky, M.A., D.Phil. (Oxon.), Lect. in Hist. (Early Mod.) [English Reformation], lucy.wooding@kcl.ac.uk

Andrew D. Lambert, LL.B., M.A., Ph.D. (Lond.), Prof. of Naval Hist. [19th c. naval history, strategy, politics, technology]

Michael Ledger-Lomas, M.A., Ph.D. (Cantab.), Lect. in Hist. of Mod. Christianity [History of religion & theology in 19th c. Britain & Europe], michael.ledger-lomas@kcl.ac.uk

Stephen Lovell, B.A. (Cantab.), M.A., Ph.D. (Lond.), Prof. of Mod. Hist. (Mod. Hist.) [18th–20th c. Russian history; old age in Russia], stephen.lovell@kcl.ac.uk

Sophie Lunn-Rockliffe, B.A. (Oxon.), Ph.D. (Cantab.), Lect. in Roman Hist. [History of late antiquity; early Christianity; history of ideas], sophie.lunn-rockliffe@kcl.ac.uk

Ian R. McBride, B.A. (Oxon.), Ph.D. (Lond.), Prof. of Irish & Brit. Hist. (Early Mod.) [Irish history; 18th c. political & religious thought], ian.mcbride@kcl.ac.uk

David A. McLean, B.A. (Hull), M.A., Ph.D. (Cantab.), Prof. of Hist. (Later Mod.) [Educational change & ideas in early Victorian England], david.a.mclean@kcl.ac.uk

Anna Maerker, Lect. in World Hist. [Material & visual culture of medicine & science since the 18th c.], anna.maerker@kcl.ac.uk

Joseph Maiolo, B.A., M.A. (Toronto), Ph.D. (Lond.), Sen. Lect. in War Stud. [20th c. international history; Second World War; history of intelligence; naval warfare]

Peter J. Marshall, D.Phil. (Oxon.), Emeritus Prof. & Visiting Res. Fellow (Imp. & C'wealth Hist.) [India; imperial history], history@kcl.ac.uk

Daniel Matlin, B.A., M.A., Ph.D. (Cantab.), Lect. in the Hist. of the U.S. since 1865 [Race & intellectual life in 20th c. U.S.A.], daniel.matlin@kcl.ac.uk

Roger Mortimore, M.A., D.Phil. (Oxon.), Prof. of Public Opinion & Pol. Analysis [Modern British public opinion & elections], roger.mortimore@kcl.ac.uk

Henrik Mouritsen, B.A. (Odense), Ph.D. (Copenhagen), Prof. of Roman Hist. [Roman social & political history; slavery & manumission; Latin epigraphy], henrik.mouritsen@kcl.ac.uk

Janet L. Nelson, D.B.E., B.A., Ph.D. (Cantab.), F.B.A., Emerita & Visiting Res. Prof. of Med. Hist. (Med.) [Earlier medieval social & political history; medieval women & gender], janet.nelson@kcl.ac.uk

Niall O'Flaherty, Ph.D. (Cantab.), Lect. in the Hist. of Eur. Pol. Thought [18th & 19th c. British & European political ideas], niall.o'flaherty@kcl.ac.uk

William J. Philpott, B.A., D.Phil. (Oxon.), Sen. Lect. in Hist. (19th c. Brit. & Eur.) [Military & international history, esp. two world wars; Anglo-French relations; 19th–20th c. European political & social history; naval history], william.philpott@kcl.ac.uk

Irene Polinskaya, B.A. (St. Petersburg), Ph.D. (Stanford), R.C.U.K. Fellow in Greek Hist. [Ancient Greek religion; ancient Greek social history; Greek epigraphy], irene.polinskaya@kcl.ac.uk

Andrew N. Porter, M.A., Ph.D. (Cantab.), Emeritus & Visiting Res. Prof. of Imp. Hist. (Later Mod.) [Christian missions; religion, economics & empire from 1750; decolonisation], andrew.porter@kcl.ac.uk

Virginia Preston, B.A. (Oxon.), Ph.D. (Greenwich), Deputy Director, Inst. of Contemp. Brit. Hist. [19th c. social history; 19th & 20th c. naval & maritime history], virginia.preston@kcl.ac.uk

Dominic Rathbone, M.A., Ph.D. (Cantab.), Prof. of Anc. Hist. [Early Roman republic; the political & agrarian history of the middle republic; effects of Roman rule on Egypt], dominic.rathbone@kcl.ac.uk

Alice Rio, B.A., M.A., Ph.D. (Lond.), Lect. in Med. Eur. Hist. [History of late antique & early medieval Europe], alice.rio@kcl.ac.uk

Richard Roberts, B.A. (Lond.), Ph.D. (Cantab.), Prof. of Contemp. Hist. (Mod. Financial & Econ. Hist.) [Finance & banking in the 19th–21st c.], richard.roberts@kcl.ac.uk

Michael P. Rowe, B.A., Ph.D. (Lond.), Sen. Lect. in Hist. (Mod.) [State & nation building in revolutionary & Napoleonic Europe], michael.rowe@kcl.ac.uk

Philip A.G. Sabin, M.A. (Cantab.), Ph.D. (Lond.), Prof. of Strategic Stud. [Air power; British defence policy; technology & military affairs; ancient warfare]

Alexandra Sapoznik, Ph.D. (Cantab.), Lect. in Late Med. Hist. [Peasant land use & agricultural productivity in late medieval England], alexandra.sapoznik@kcl.ac.uk

Simon Sleight, M.A. (Lond.), Ph.D. (Monash), Lect. in Australian Hist. [Australian history; history of children & young people; urban history], simon.sleight@kcl.ac.uk

Dionysios Stathakopoulos, B.A. (Münster), Ph.D. (Vienna), Lect. in Byz. Stud. [Wealth & its uses in the late Byzantine empire (1261–1453); poverty & social stratification], dionysios.stathakopoulos@kcl.ac.uk

Sarah E. Stockwell, M.A. (Cantab.), M.St., D.Phil. (Oxon.), Sen. Lect. in Hist. (Later Mod.) [Decolonisation; W. Africa], sarah.stockwell@kcl.ac.uk

*Adam D. Sutcliffe, B.A., Ph.D. (Lond.), Sen. Lect. in Early Mod. Eur. Hist. [Intellectual history of western Europe; Jewish history], adam.sutcliffe@kcl.ac.uk

Alice Taylor, B.A., M.A., D.Phil. (Oxon.), Lect. in Med. Hist. [Law & legal compilations; medieval Scotland; social rituals & rank relations], alice.taylor@kcl.ac.uk

Patricia Thane, M.A. (Oxon.), Ph.D. (Lond.), Res. Prof. in Contemp. Brit. Hist. (20th c. Brit.) [Social welfare & social policy; old age & ageing; gender], pat.thane@kcl.ac.uk

David Todd, Diplôme (Paris), Ph.D. (Cantab.), Lect. in World Hist. [French & British imperial history, 18th–20th c.; political economy since 1700; the impact of the world on Europe since 1500], david.todd@kcl.ac.uk

London

Richard H. Trainor, B.A. (Brown), M.A. (Oxon. & Princeton), D.Phil. (Oxon.), Prof. of Soc. Hist., Principal [Social history of British middle class & its urban elites 1850–1950; universities in urban context since 1850], principal@kcl.ac.uk
AbdoolKarim Vakil, B.A. (York), Lect. in Contemp. Portuguese Hist. [19th & 20th c. Portuguese intellectual & cultural history], abdoolkarim.vakil@kcl.ac.uk
Richard C. Vinen, M.A., Ph.D. (Cantab.), Prof. of Hist. (Later Mod.) [20th c. French history], richard.vinen@kcl.ac.uk
Evelyn Welch, Ph.D. (Warburg), Prof. of Renaissance Stud. [Renaissance & early modern material cutlure], evelyn.welch@kcl.ac.uk
Jon E. Wilson, B.A. (Oxon.), M.A. (New Sch. for Soc. Res.), D.Phil. (Oxon.), Sen. Lect. in Hist. (Later Mod.) [South Asian & British imperial history], jon.wilson@kcl.ac.uk
Abigail Woods, M.A., M.Sc., Ph.D. (Manc.), Vet. M.B. (Cantab.), Reader in Hist. of Human & Animal Health [Science; practice & policy of animal health & welfare], abigail.woods@kcl.ac.uk
Reza Zia-Ebrahimi, D.Phil. (Oxon.), Lect. in 20th c. Mid. E. Hist. [Nationalism & race; Iran, 1860–1940], reza.zia-ebrahimi@kcl.ac.uk

London School of Economics Houghton Street, Aldwych WC2A 2AE.
020 7405 7686. Fax 020 7242 0392
www.lse.ac.uk
Department of Economic History 020 7955 7084.
Department of International History 020 7955 7548.
Fax 020 7955 6800
Department of Economics
Department of Government 020 7955 7204.
Fax 020 7955 1707
Department of International Relations 020 7955 7404.
Fax 020 7955 7446

Olivier Accominotti, B.A. (Paris), M.A., Ph.D. (Sciences Po, Paris), Lect. in Econ. Hist. [Monetary & financial history of the 19th & 20th c.], o.accominotti@lse.ac.uk
Kirsten Ainley, B.A. (Oxon.), M.Sc., Ph.D. (Lond.), Lect. in Int. Rel., k.a.ainley@lse.ac.uk
J. Chris Alden, B.A. (Reed Coll.), M.A.L.D., Ph.D. (Tufts), Reader in Int. Rel., j.c.alden@lse.ac.uk
Roham Alvandi, B.A. (Sydney), M.A.L.D. (Tufts), M.Phil., D.Phil. (Oxon.), Assistant Prof. of Int. Hist. [Iran; Persian Gulf; Cold War], r.alvandi@lse.ac.uk
*Nigel J. Ashton, M.A., Ph.D. (Cantab.), Prof. of Int. Hist. [Anglo-American relations since 1945; modern Middle East], n.ashton@lse.ac.uk
Leonardo Baccini, Laurea (Florence), M.A. (Bologna), Ph.D. (Dublin), Lect. in Int. Rel., l.baccini@lse.ac.uk
Marc D. Baer, B.A. (Northwestern), Ph.D. (Chicago), Prof. of Int. Hist. (Int. Hist.) [Christians, Jews & Muslims in Europe & the Middle East, early modern to modern eras], m.d.baer@lse.ac.uk
Dudley E. Baines, B.Sc.(Econ.) (Lond.), Emeritus Reader in Econ. Hist. [20th c. London labour market; 18th–19th c. European migration: overseas & internal], d.e.baines@lse.ac.uk
Gerben Bakker, B.A., M.Sc. (Grönigen), Ph.D. (E.U.I.), Sen. Lect. in Econ. Hist. & Accounting [Film & entertainment industry in Europe & the U.S. since 1890; multinationals in the music industry; evolution of markets, industries & firms & their impact on economic development], g.bakker@lse.ac.uk

Rodney S. Barker, B.A. (Cantab.), Ph.D. (Lond.), Reader in Govt. (19th–20th c. Brit. Pol.) [Political thought in Britain 19th–20th c.]

A. John L. Barnes, M.A. (Cantab.), Lect. in Pol. Sc. (19th–20th c. Brit. Pol.)

Alan J. Beattie, B.Sc.(Econ.) (Lond.), Sen. Lect. in Pol. Sc. [18th–19th c. British constitutional history]

Antony M. Best, B.A. (Leeds), Ph.D. (Lond.), Assoc. Prof. of Int. Hist. (20th c. E. Asia, Japan) [Anglo-Japanese relations 1858–present], a.best@lse.ac.uk

Federica Bicchi, Ph.D., Lect. in Int. Rel., f.c.bicchi@lse.ac.uk

Lars Boerner, B.A., M.A. (Zurich), M.A. (Tilburg), Ph.D. (Humboldt), Lect. in Econ. Hist. [History of markets; market clearing mechanisms], l.boerner@lse.ac.uk

Robert W.D. Boyce, B.A. (Wilfrid Laurier), M.A., Ph.D. (Lond.), Emeritus Lect. in Int. Hist. (20th c.) [Franco-British relations 1918–40], r.boyce@lse.ac.uk

Stephen Broadberry, Prof. of Econ. Hist. [Global economic history; very long run economic growth; international comparisons of growth & productivity performance since 1870], s.n.broadberry@lse.ac.uk

Chris J. Brown, B.Sc.(Econ.), Ph.D. (Kent), Prof. of Int. Rel., c.j.brown@lse.ac.uk

Steven Casey, B.A. (East Anglia), D.Phil. (Oxon.), Prof. of Int. Hist. [U.S. foreign policy; World War II; the Korean War], s.casey@lse.ac.uk

Jeffrey Chwieroth, Ph.D., Reader in Int. Rel., j.m.chwieroth@lse.ac.uk

Christopher Coker, B.A. (Cantab.), D.Phil. (Oxon.), Prof. of Int. Rel., c.coker@lse.ac.uk

Janet Coleman, B.A., M.Phil., Ph.D. (Yale), Prof. of Anc. & Med. Pol. Thought [Ancient, medieval & Renaissance political history; pre-modern theories of state & church], j.coleman@lse.ac.uk

Michael Cox, B.A. (Read.), Prof. of Int. Rel. [Cold War history; international history of the 20th c.; American foreign policy], m.e.cox@lse.ac.uk

Neil Cummins, B.Sc. (Dublin), M.Sc., Ph.D. (Lond.), Lect. in Econ. Hist. [Historical demography; social mobility], n.j.cummins@lse.ac.uk

Katerina Dalacoura, B.A., M.A., Ph.D. (Lond.), Sen. Lect. in Int. Rel., k.dalacoura@lse.ac.uk

Kent G. Deng, B.A. (Beijing), Ph.D. (La Trobe), Reader in Econ. Hist. [Pre-modern Chinese maritime & economic history; role of the literati; economic role of the Chinese peasantry], k.g.deng@lse.ac.uk

Lord Desai, M.A. (Bombay), Ph.D. (Penn. & London Guildhall), Prof. of Econ.

Toby Dodge, Ph.D. (Lond.), Reader in Int. Rel., b.t.dodge@lse.ac.uk

Timothy P.G. Dyson, B.Sc., M.Sc. (Lond.), Prof. of Population Stud. [Indian historical demography, esp. of famines, Berar & the Ludhiana district], t.dyson@lse.ac.uk

Spyros Economides, B.Soc.Sc. (Birm.), M.Sc., Ph.D. (Lond.), Sen. Lect. in Int. Rel., s.economides@lse.ac.uk

Robert Falkner, D.Phil. (Oxon.), Sen. Lect. in Int. Rel., r.falkner@lse.ac.uk

Leigh Gardner, Lect. in Econ. Hist. [Economic & fiscal history of the British empire, esp. Africa; political economy of medieval kingship; economic origins of political institutions], l.a.gardner@lse.ac.uk

Fawaz Gerges, M.A. (Lond.), D.Phil. (Oxon.), Prof. of Int. Rel., f.a.gerges@lse.ac.uk

Terence R. Gourvish, B.A., Ph.D. (Lond.), Director of the Business Hist. Unit, t.r.gourvish@lse.ac.uk

Jürgen Haacke, Ph.D., Sen. Lect. in Int. Rel., j.haacke@lse.ac.uk

Tanya Harmer, B.A. (Leeds), M.A., Ph.D. (Lond.), Assistant Prof. of Int. Hist. [20th c. Latin America & the U.S.; the Cold War], t.harmer@lse.ac.uk

Janet M. Hartley, B.A., Ph.D. (Lond.), Prof. of Int. Hist. (18th–19th c. Russia) [Social history of Russia c.1650–1825], j.m.hartley@lse.ac.uk

Timothy J. Hochstrasser, M.A., Ph.D. (Cantab.), Assoc. Prof. of Int. Hist. (18th c.) [European Enlightenment; physiocracy/cameralism; music in 18th c. Europe], t.hochstrasser@lse.ac.uk

Mark J. Hoffman, B.A. (Mass.), M.Sc.(Econ.) (Lond.), Lect. in Int. Rel., m.hoffman@lse.ac.uk
W. Peter Howlett, B.A. (Warwick), M.Phil., Ph.D. (Cantab.), Sen. Lect. in Econ. Hist.
[British economy in the 20th c.; human capital: railway workers in the 19th c.],
w.p.howlett@lse.ac.uk
Chris Hughes, B.A. (Kingston), M.Sc., M.A. (Lond.), Ph.D., Prof. of Int. Rel.,
c.r.hughes@lse.ac.uk
Janet E. Hunter, B.A. (Sheff.), D.Phil. (Oxon.), Saji Res. Prof. of Japanese Econ. & Soc.
Hist. [Female labour market in pre-war Japan; communications in pre-war Japan],
j.e.hunter@lse.ac.uk
*Kimberley Hutchings, B.A., M.Sc., Ph.D., Prof. of Int. Rel., k.hutchings@lse.ac.uk
Alejandra Irigoin, Ph.D. (Lond.), Sen. Lect. in Econ. Hist. [Latin American economic history],
m.a.irigoin@lse.ac.uk
Jennifer Jackson-Preece, B.A., M.A., D.Phil. (Oxon.), Sen. Lect. in Int. Rel.,
j.jackson-preece@lse.ac.uk
George W. Jones, M.A., D.Phil. (Oxon.), Prof. of Govt. (20th c. Cabinet & Parliamentary Hist.)
[Prime ministers' advisory networks]
Heather S. Jones, B.A., Ph.D. (Dublin), Assoc. Prof. of Int. Hist. [First World War studies],
h.s.jones@lse.ac.uk
Matthew C. Jones, B.A. (Sussex), D.Phil. (Oxon.), Prof. of Int. Hist. (Int. Hist.) [British foreign
& defence policy; American history since 1945; Anglo-American relations; modern S.E.
Asia], m.c.jones@lse.ac.uk
Paul Keenan, B.A. (Belf.), M.A. (York), Ph.D. (Lond.), Assistant Prof. of Int. Hist. [St.
Petersburg; the Russian court; 18th c. Russia], p.keenan@lse.ac.uk
Paul Kelly, B.A. (York), Ph.D. (Lond.), Lect. in Pol. Theory (18th–20th c. Pol. Thought,
Utilitarians)
C. John Kent, M.A., Ph.D. (Aberd.), Reader in Int. Rel. (20th c. Mid. E. & Afric.) [British
defence policy 1945–58, with special reference to the Middle East], j.c.kent@lse.ac.uk
MacGregor Knox, B.A. (Harv.), Ph.D. (Yale), Emeritus Prof. of Int. Hist. [Comparative history
of fascism & Nazism; fascist foreign policy], m.knox@lse.ac.uk
Mathias Koenig-Archibugi, Ph.D. (Florence), Sen. Lect. in Global Pol.,
m.koenig-archibugi@lse.ac.uk
Tomila V. Lankina, B.A. (Tashkent), M.A. (Mass.), D.Phil. (Oxon.), Sen. Lect. in Int. Rel.,
t.lankina@lse.ac.uk
George Lawson, B.A. (Manc.), M.Sc., Ph.D. (Lond.), Lect. in Int. Rel., g.lawson@lse.ac.uk
Timothy C. Leunig, M.A., M.Phil., D.Phil. (Oxon.), Reader in Econ. Hist. [Comparative
industrial history 1880–1939], t.leunig@lse.ac.uk
Colin M. Lewis, B.A., Ph.D. (Exeter), Emeritus Prof. of Latin Amer. Econ. Hist. [Economic
policy since 1920 in Brazil & Argentina], c.m.lewis@lse.ac.uk
Joanna E. Lewis, B.A. (Bath), M.Phil., Ph.D. (Cantab.), Assistant Prof. of Int. Hist. (Mod.
Afric.) [Mau Mau (Kenya); Angola; Mozambique; eastern Africa], j.e.lewis1@lse.ac.uk
N. Piers Ludlow, B.A., D.Phil. (Oxon.), Assoc. Prof. of Int. Hist. [History of European
integration; post-1945 western Europe], n.p.ludlow@lse.ac.uk
Debin Ma, Ph.D. (N. Carolina), Sen. Lect. in Econ. Hist. [Growth & development; institutions;
economic history of China & E. Asia], d.ma1@lse.ac.uk
Jens Meierhenrich, D.Phil. (Oxon.), Sen. Lect. in Int. Rel. [Genocide in Rwanda; war crimes;
international law; conflict resolution], j.meierhenrich@lse.ac.uk
Chris Minns, B.A. (Belf.), M.A. (Alberta), Ph.D. (Essex), Sen. Lect. in Econ. Hist. [North
American economic history; labour history; migration], c.minns@lse.ac.uk
Mary S. Morgan, B.Sc.(Econ.), Ph.D. (Lond.), F.B.A., Prof. of Hist. & Phil. of Econ. [History of
economic model-building], m.morgan@lse.ac.uk
Sönke Neitzel, Ph.D., Habil. (Mainz), Prof. of Int. Hist. [Imperialism; First & Second World
Wars; history of international relations; war studies], s.neitzel@lse.ac.uk

Iver B. Neumann, Cand.mag, Cand.polit., Ph.D. (Oslo), Prof. of Int. Rel.,
iver.neumann@lse.ac.uk

Lauren M. Phillips, M.A. (Stanford), Ph.D. (Lond.), Lect. in Int. Rel. [International political
economy], l.m.phillips@lse.ac.uk

Anita J. Prazmowska, B.A. (Birm.), Ph.D. (Lond.), Prof. of Int. Hist. (20th c. E. Eur.) [Origins of
communism in Poland 1943–8], a.j.prazmowska@lse.ac.uk

Paul Preston, M.A., D.Phil. (Oxon.), M.A. (Read.), F.B.A., Príncipe de Asturias Prof. of
Contemp. Spanish Hist. (20th c. Eur.) [Fascism; Spain: republic, civil war, Franco
dictatorship, transition to democracy], p.preston@lse.ac.uk

Svetozar Rajak, M.Sc., Ph.D. (Lond.), Assoc. Prof. of Int. Hist. (Int. Hist.) [Balkans in the 20th
c.; Third World & non-aligned in the Cold War], s.rajak@lse.ac.uk

Albrecht O. Ritschl, B.A., Ph.D. (Munich), Prof. of Econ. Hist. [20th c. monetary history, esp.
Germany], a.o.ritschl@lse.ac.uk

Maria-José Rodriguez-Salgado, B.A. (Dunelm.), Ph.D. (Hull), McRah Prof. of Int.
Hist. (16th c.) [Charles V; Philip II of Spain; international relations 15th–17th c.],
m.j.rodriguez-salgado@lse.ac.uk

Joan R. Rosés, B.Sc. (Barcelona), M.Sc., Ph.D. (Madrid), Prof. of Econ. Hist. [Modern &
contemporary economic history], j.r.roses@lse.ac.uk

Tirthankar Roy, B.A. (Visva-Bharati), Ph.D. (J. Nehru), Prof. of Econ. Hist. [Industrialisation in
India, with reference to the role of artisans], t.roy@lse.ac.uk

Thomas Sattler, Ph.D. (Gerzensee), Ph.D. (E.T.H. Zurich), Lect. in Int. Pol. Econ.,
t.sattler@lse.ac.uk

Kirsten E. Schulze, B.A. (Maine), M.Phil., Ph.D. (Oxon.), Assoc. Prof. of Int. Hist. [Israeli
foreign & defence policy; minorities in Lebanon], k.e.schulze@lse.ac.uk

*Max-Stephan H.J. Schulze, Dip.VW. (Freiburg), Ph.D. (Lond.), Prof. of Econ. Hist. [Economic
development of Austria-Hungary & Germany since 1800], m.s.schulze@lse.ac.uk

Ulrich Sedelmeier, M.A., Ph.D. (Sussex), Sen. Lect. in Int. Rel., u.sedelmeier@lse.ac.uk

Taylor C. Sherman, B.Sc. (Lond.), M.A., Ph.D. (Cantab.), Assoc. Prof. of Int. Hist. [South
Asia], t.c.sherman@lse.ac.uk

Elizabeth H. Shlala, B.S.F.S., M.A., Ph.D. (Georgetown), Fellow in Int. Hist. [International
history; modern Middle East & north Africa], e.shlala@lse.ac.uk

John Sidel, B.A., M.A. (Yale), Ph.D. (Cornell), Prof. of Int. Rel., j.t.sidel@lse.ac.uk

Nicholas R.A. Sims, B.Sc.(Econ.) (Lond.), Emeritus Reader in Int. Rel., n.sims@lse.ac.uk

Alan Sked, M.A. (Glas.), D.Phil. (Oxon.), Prof. of Int. Hist. (19th–20th c. Eur.),
a.sked@lse.ac.uk

Karen E. Smith, B.A. (Wellesley Coll.), M.A. (Johns Hopkins), Ph.D. (Lond.), Prof. of Int. Rel.,
k.e.smith@lse.ac.uk

Gagan D.S. Sood, M.A., Ph.D. (Yale), Assistant Prof. in Early Mod. Hist. (Early Mod. Hist.)
[Early modern India & the Islamic world; transition to modern colonialism; pre-modern
globalisation], g.sood1@lse.ac.uk

A.R. Kristina Spohr, B.A. (East Anglia), M.Phil., Ph.D. (Cantab.), Assoc. Prof. of Int. Hist.
(Mod. Eur., Int. Rel.) [Post-Cold War security developments; 20th c. German history],
k.spohr-readman@lse.ac.uk

David Stevenson, M.A., Ph.D. (Cantab.), Stevenson Prof. of Int. Hist. (20th c. Eur.) [Arms
races in 19th–20th c.], d.stevenson@lse.ac.uk

Paul Stock, B.A., M.Sc., Ph.D. (Lond.), Assistant Prof. of Early Mod. Int. Hist. (1500–1850)
[18th & 19th c. intellectual history], p.stock@lse.ac.uk

Oliver Volckart, M.A., Ph.D. (Berlin), Dr.phil.rer.pol.habil. (Jena), Reader in Econ. Hist. [Late
medieval & early modern economic history, esp. institutional change & monetary history],
o.j.volckart@lse.ac.uk

Tamás Vonyó, B.Sc. (Budapest), M.Phil., D.Phil. (Oxon.), Lect. in Econ. Hist. [Economic growth in Germany & east-central Europe in the 20th c.], t.vonyo@lse.ac.uk
Patrick Wallis, B.A. (York), M.Sc., D.Phil. (Oxon.), Reader in Econ. Hist. [Developments in medicine & pharmacy in London 1580–1720; professional, social & ethical responses to epidemics; guilds & the organisation of pre-modern work], p.h.wallis@lse.ac.uk
Laurent Warlouzet, M.A., Ph.D., Postdoctoral Fellow in Int. Hist. (Int. Hist.) [European integration since 1945], l.d.warlouzet@lse.ac.uk
Arne Westad, B.A. (Oslo), Ph.D. (Chapel Hill, N.C.), Prof. in Int. Hist. [Cold War history; international history of E. Asia], a.westad@lse.ac.uk
Peter C. Wilson, B.A. (Keele), M.Sc. (Southampton), Ph.D. (Lond.), Sen. Lect. in Int. Rel. [History of 20th c. international thought], p.c.wilson@lse.ac.uk
Stephen B. Woolcock, B.Sc., M.Phil. (Edin.), Ph.D. (Lond.), Lect. in Int. Rel., s.b.woolcock@lse.ac.uk
Vladislaw Zubok, B.A., Ph.D. (Moscow), Prof. of Int. Hist. (Int. Hist.) [Cold War; Soviet Union; Stalinism; Russia's intellectual history in the 20th c.], v.m.zubok@lse.ac.uk

London School of Hygiene and Tropical Medicine   Keppel Street, WC1E 7HT.
020 7927 2434
www.lshtm.ac.uk
Centre for History in Public Health
020 7927 2434.
Fax 020 7927 2701

Stuart C. Anderson, B.Sc., M.A., Ph.D. (Lond.), Reader in the Soc. Hist. of Pharmacy [History of 20th c. pharmacy; policy & practice; medicines], stuart.anderson@lshtm.ac.uk
*Virginia S. Berridge, B.A., Ph.D. (Lond.), Prof. of Hist. (20th c. Hist. of Medicine) [20th c. health policy: A.I.D.S., drugs, smoking, alcohol; media; public health: evidence & policy], virginia.berridge@lshtm.ac.uk
Martin Gorsky, B.A. (Essex), Ph.D. (Brist.), Reader in the Hist. of Health Policy [Voluntary hospitals; mutual health insurance; British welfare state; the N.H.S.; comparative health systems], martin.gorsky@lshtm.ac.uk
Anne Hardy, M.A., D.Phil. (Oxon.), Hon. Prof. of Hist of Public Health [History of discourse & epidemiology in 19th & 20th c.], anne.hardy@lshtm.ac.uk
Alex Mold, B.A., Ph.D. (Birm.), Lect. [History of illegal drugs; voluntary sector & health; consumerism & health], alex.mold@lshtm.ac.uk
Sarah Walters, B.A., M.Sc., Ph.D. (Cantab.), Lect. [African history; historical demography; history of medicine & public health; population health; health inequalities; socio-economic determinants of health], sarah.walters@lshtm.ac.uk

Queen Mary, University of London   Mile End Road, E1 4NS. 020 7882 5555.
Fax 020 7975 5500
www.qmul.ac.uk
Department of History 020 7882 8351.
Fax 020 8980 8400

Thomas S. Asbridge, B.A. (Wales), Ph.D. (Lond.), Sen. Lect. (Early Med.) [Crusading history], T.S.Asbridge@qmul.ac.uk
Richard Bourke, B.A. (Dublin), Ph.D. (Cantab.), Sen. Lect. (Pol. Thought) [Intellectual history; Irish history], R.Bourke@qmul.ac.uk
Joanna Cohen, B.A. (Cantab.), M.A. (Northwestern), Ph.D. (Penn.), Lect. in Hist., J.Cohen@qmul.ac.uk

Mark Curran, Lect. in Early Mod. Hist. [Enlightenment studies; 18th c. media; book history; digital humanities]

Jon Davis, B.A., M.A., Ph.D. (Lond.), Lect. (Constitutional Hist.) [Contemporary British history], J.M.Davis@qmul.ac.uk

*Virginia G. Davis, B.A., Ph.D. (Dublin), Prof. of Hist (Later Med. Brit., Hist. Computing) [English medieval clergy], V.G.Davis@qmul.ac.uk

Peter R. Denley, M.A., D.Phil. (Oxon.), Sen. Lect. (Later Med. Eur., Hist. Computing) [History of universities, esp. in Italy], P.R.Denley@qmul.ac.uk

Thomas M. Dixon, B.A., Ph.D. (Cantab.), Sen. Lect. (Hist. of Sc. & Relig.) [19th c. British history; U.K.-U.S. modern philosophy; history of emotions], T.M.Dixon@qmul.ac.uk

Saul Dubow, B.A. (Cape Town), D.Phil. (Oxon.), Prof. [History of modern South Africa from the early 19th c. to the present]

James R.V. Ellison, B.A., Ph.D. (Kent), Sen. Lect. (Later Mod. Brit. & Eur.) [Britain & Europe since 1945], J.R.V.Ellison@qmul.ac.uk

Martyn Frampton, B.A., Ph.D. (Cantab.), Lect. in Hist., M.Frampton@qmul.ac.uk

H. Mark Glancy, B.A. (Lancaster), M.A., Ph.D. (East Anglia), Sen. Lect. (U.S. Hist., Cinema) [British & American film industry], H.M.Glancy@qmul.ac.uk

Raphael Gross, Reader in Hist. [German & German-Jewish history]

Rhodri Hayward, B.A., Ph.D. (Lancaster), Lect. (Hist. of Medicine), R.Hayward@qmul.ac.uk

Peter J. Hennessy, M.A., Ph.D. (Cantab.), F.B.A., Attlee Prof. of Contemp. Brit. Hist. (Later Mod. Brit.) [History of office of U.K. premier; British history since 1945], P.J.Hennessy@qmul.ac.uk

Tristram Hunt, B.A., Ph.D. (Cantab.), Sen. Lect. (Victorian Brit. Hist.) [Civic pride; urban identity], T.Hunt@qmul.ac.uk

Maurizio Isabella, B.A. (Milan), M.Phil., Ph.D. (Cantab.), Lect. in Mod. Eur. Hist., M.Isabella@qmul.ac.uk

Julian T. Jackson, M.A., Ph.D. (Cantab.), F.B.A., Prof. of Mod. Hist. (Later Mod. Eur.) [20th c. French history], J.T.Jackson@qmul.ac.uk

Colin D.H. Jones, B.A., D.Phil. (Oxon.), Prof. of Hist., C.D.H.Jones@qmul.ac.uk

Kate J.P. Lowe, B.A., Ph.D. (Lond.), Prof. of Renaissance Hist. & Culture (Renaissance Italy) [Sub-Saharan Africans in Europe], K.J.P.Lowe@qmul.ac.uk

Helen McCarthy, B.A. (Cantab.), M.A., Ph.D. (Lond.), Lect. in Hist., H.McCarthy@qmul.ac.uk

J. Andrew Mendelsohn, B.A. (Harv.), M.A., Ph.D. (Princeton), Reader in Hist. of Sc. & Medicine [Life sciences; European science], A.Mendelsohn@qmul.ac.uk

Catherine Merridale, B.A. (Cantab.), Ph.D. (Birm.), Prof. of Contemp. Hist. (Russia) [Cultural history of the Kremlin], C.Merridale@qmul.ac.uk

Daniel Peart, Lect. in Amer. Hist. [The relationship between the American people & their government from the ratification of the Constitution to the Civil War]

Michael C. Questier, D.Phil. (Sussex), Prof. of Hist. (Early Mod. Brit. & Eur.) [Politics of religion in Britain between the Reformation & Civil War], M.C.Questier@qmul.ac.uk

Yossef Rapoport, B.A. (Tel Aviv), Ph.D. (Princeton), Lect. (Soc. Hist.) [Medieval history], Y.Rapoport@qmul.ac.uk

Miri E. Rubin, M.A. (Hebrew Univ., Jerusalem), Ph.D. (Cantab.), Prof. of Late Med. Eur. [Social relations & religious culture; Jewish-Christian relations], M.E.Rubin@qmul.ac.uk

Donald Sassoon, M.A. (Penn. State), B.Sc., Ph.D. (Lond.), Prof. of Comparative Eur. Hist. (Later Mod. Eur.) [European socialist & communist parties], D.Sassoon@qmul.ac.uk

Quentin Skinner, Barber Beaumont Prof. of Hum. [Intellectual history of early modern Europe; political philosophy in the 17th c.; Thomas Hobbes]

Jonathan D. Smele, B.A. (Leeds), M.Phil. (Glas.), Ph.D. (Wales), Sen. Lect. (Later Mod. Eur.) [Bibliography & history of Russian Revolution & civil war; history of Siberia], J.D.Smele@qmul.ac.uk

Gareth Stedman Jones, Prof. of the Hist. of Ideas [Political thought after the French Revolution; 19th c. socialism; the thought of Karl Marx]

Iain Stewart, Lect. in Mod. Eur. Hist. [Raymond Aron in the context of the reorientation of French philosophy & social science in the 1930s & the context of his relationship with Jean-Paul Sartre; post-war crisis of western political philosophy]

Tilli Tansey, Prof. of the Hist. of Mod. Medical Sc. [History of modern biomedicine]

Barbara Taylor, Prof. of Hist. [British Enlightenment; feminist thought; theories & histories of subjectivity]

Daniel W. Todman, B.A. (Lond.), M.Phil. (Cantab.), Sen. Lect. (Later Mod. Brit.) [Cultural impact of modern war], D.W.Todman@qmul.ac.uk

Georgios Varouxakis, Ph.D. (Lond.), Reader (Hist. of Pol. Thought), G.Varouxakis@qmul.ac.uk

Amanda Vickery, Prof. of Early Mod. Hist. [British society & culture; gender & family; words & objects]

Christina von Hodenberg, M.A. (Munich), Ph.D. (Bielefeld), Reader [Social & cultural history of Germany], C.Hodenberg@qmul.ac.uk

Mark J. White, B.A. (Nott.), M.A. (Wis.), Ph.D. (Rutgers), Prof. of Amer. Hist. (Amer.) [Kennedy presidency], M.J.White@qmul.ac.uk

Daniel Wildmann, Lect. in Hist. [Modern German-Jewish history & culture; history of the Third Reich; anti-Semitism; history of masculinities; history of the body; film]

Royal Holloway, University of London

Egham Hill, Egham, Surrey, TW20 0EX.
01784 434455. Fax 01784 437520
www.rhul.ac.uk
Department of History 01784 443314.
Fax 01784 433032
Bedford Centre for the History of Women
Founder's Building
Centre for the History of Bodies &
Material Culture
Centre for South Asian Studies
Centre for Minority Studies
Centre for Public History, Heritage &
Engagement with the Past
Departments of Classics, Geography
Italian, Management
The Hellenic Institute 01784 443791
Holocaust Research Centre

Richard Alston, B.A. (Leeds), Ph.D. (Lond.), Prof. of Anc. Hist. (Roman Empire) [Urbanisation & cultural change in Roman Egypt], r.alston@rhul.ac.uk

K. Humayun Ansari, O.B.E., B.Sc. (Exeter), Ph.D. (Lond.), Prof. of Hist. [Islam & cultural diversity; migration], k.ansari@rhul.ac.uk

*Sarah F.D. Ansari, B.A., Ph.D. (Lond.), Reader (World & Mod. Indian Hist.) [Muslim South Asia], s.ansari@rhul.ac.uk

Akil N. Awan, B.Sc., M.A., Ph.D. (Lond.), Lect. [History of terrorism; contemporary Islam], akil.awan@rhul.ac.uk

Caroline M. Barron, M.A. (Oxon.), Ph.D. (Lond.), Emerita Prof. of Hist. of London (Later Med.) [Medieval London; women; gentry & aristocracy; reign of Richard II], c.barron@rhul.ac.uk

Daniel Beer, Ph.D. (Cantab.), Sen. Lect. (Mod. Eur.) [Late 19th & early 20th c. intellectual history], daniel.beer@rhul.ac.uk

Ilker Evrim Binbas, B.A. (M.E.T.U.), M.A. (Hacettepe), Ph.D. (Chicago), Lect. in Early Mod. Asian Empires [Late medieval & early modern Islamic intellectual history], evrim.binbas@rhul.ac.uk

Rai Brown, B.A., M.A. (Malaysia), Ph.D. (Lond.), Lect. in Asia Pacific Hist. & Management [Chinese business; Asian economic growth], r.brown@rhul.ac.uk

Clive R. Burgess, M.A., D.Phil. (Oxon.), Sen. Lect. [Church music in medieval English towns; late medieval & Reformation piety], c.burgess@rhul.ac.uk

Sandra Cavallo, Laurea (Turin), D.E.A. (Lyon), Dott. (Turin), Ph.D. (Lond.), Prof. (Early Mod. Eur.) [Early modern Italy: body, health, family & homes], s.cavallo@rhul.ac.uk

David Cesarani, O.B.E., B.A. (Cantab.), M.A. (N.Y.), D.Phil. (Oxon.), Res. Prof. [Jewish history; Holocaust studies; history of migration], david.cesarani@rhul.ac.uk

Justin A.I. Champion, M.A., Ph.D. (Cantab.), Prof. of Hist. (17th c. Brit., Pol. Thought) [Cultural & material history of the Bible 1500–1800], j.champion@rhul.ac.uk

Gregory R. Claeys, B.A., M.A. (Montreal), Ph.D. (Cantab.), Prof. of Hist. of Pol. Thought (Mod.), g.claeys@rhul.ac.uk

Mary Cowling, B.A., Ph.D. (Leeds), Lect. in Victorian Art [Pre-Raphaelite landscape & scientific perception; art & physiognomy]

Markus Daechsel, M.A., Ph.D. (Lond.), Lect. in Mod. Islamic Societies, markus.daechsel@rhul.ac.uk

Charalambos Dendrinos, M.A., Ph.D. (Lond.), Sen. Lect. in Byz. Literature & Greek Palaeography [Editing of Byzantine texts from manuscripts], ch.dendrinos@rhul.ac.uk

*Felix F. Driver, B.A., Ph.D. (Cantab.), Prof. of Human Geog. (Brit. & Imp.) [Cultural history of exploration & empire], f.driver@rhul.ac.uk

Robert Fitzgerald, B.A., Ph.D. (Lond.), Reader in Business Hist. [Modern business & economic history], r.fitzgerald@rhul.ac.uk

Dawn-Marie Gibson, B.A., Ph.D. (Ulster), Lect. in Mod. U.S. Hist. (Amer.) [Nation of Islam; civil rights; contemporary African American religion], dawn-marie.gibson@rhul.ac.uk

Helen E. Graham, B.A. (Lond.), D.Phil. (Oxon.), Prof. (20th c. Eur., esp. Spain) [Spanish Civil War; social history of Francoism 1939–51], h.graham@rhul.ac.uk

Stephen Gundle, B.A. (Liv.), M.A. (N.Y. & Oxon.), Ph.D. (Cantab.), Sen. Lect., Dept. of Italian (Mod. Italy) [Cinema & society in Italy 1930–60], s.gundle@rhul.ac.uk

David M. Gwynn, B.A. (Massey), M.A. (Auckland), Ph.D. (Oxon.), Reader [Ancient & late antique history], david.gwynn@rhul.ac.uk

Jane Hamlett, M.A., Ph.D. (Lond.), Lect. in Mod. Brit. Hist. [Material culture, domesticity, family life & institutions in 19th & 20th c. Britain], jane.hamlett@rhul.ac.uk

Jonathan P. Harris, B.A., M.A., Ph.D. (Lond.), Prof. of the Hist. of Byz. [Byzantium & the West, esp. the Crusades & the Italian Renaissance], jonathan.harris@rhul.ac.uk

J.N. Peregrine B. Horden, M.A. (Oxon.), Prof. in Hist. of Medicine [Healthcare in N.W. Europe & E. Mediterranean c.250–c.850], p.horden@rhul.ac.uk

Emm Barnes Johnstone, B.A., Ph.D. (Cantab.), Teaching & Res. Fellow [History of medicine], emm.johnstone@rhul.ac.uk

Zoë Laidlaw, B.A., B.Sc. (Melb.), D.Phil. (Oxon.), Reader in Brit. Imp. & Colonial Hist. [Political, social & intellectual history of 19th c. British empire], zoe.laidlaw@rhul.ac.uk

Peter Longerich, M.A., Dr.phil.habil (Munich), Prof. (20th c. Germany, Holocaust), p.longerich@rhul.ac.uk

Andrea Mammone, Laurea (Siena), Ph.D. (Leeds), Lect. in Hist. (Mod. Eur.) [Transnational history; far right in western Europe; modern & contemporary Italy], andrea.mammone@rhul.ac.uk

Chi-Kwan Mark, M.Phil. (Hong Kong), D.Phil. (Oxon.), Lect. (E. Asian Int. Hist.) [The Cold War in Asia; Hong Kong in Sino-British relations; the American community on China's periphery], chi-kwan.mark@rhul.ac.uk

Vanessa A. Martin, B.A., Ph.D. (Lond.), Prof. of Mod. Mid. E. Hist. (Mod. Mid. E., esp. Iran) [The emergence of the Khumaini state], v.martin@rhul.ac.uk

Stella M. Moss, B.A., M.A. (Manc.), D.Phil. (Oxon.), Teaching Fellow (Mod. Brit.) [Modern British popular culture & gender], stella.moss@rhul.ac.uk

Rudolf Muhs, M.A. (Freiburg), Lect. in 20th c. Eur. Hist. (Mod. Germany), r.muhs@rhul.ac.uk

Jonathan P. Phillips, B.A. (Keele), Ph.D. (Lond.), Prof. of Hist. (Med.) [Crusades & Latin East, esp. Second Crusade 1145–9; English & Flemish relations 11th–12th c.], j.p.phillips@rhul.ac.uk

N. Boris Rankov, M.A., D.Phil. (Oxon.), Prof. of Anc. Hist. (Roman) [Praetorian guard; Athenian trireme], b.rankov@rhul.ac.uk

Francis C.R. Robinson, C.B.E., M.A., Ph.D. (Cantab.), Prof. of Hist. of S. Asia (Int. & Mod. Islamic) [Islamic S. Asia; transmission of Islamic knowledge], f.robinson@rhul.ac.uk

Nigel E. Saul, M.A., D.Phil. (Oxon.), Prof. of Med. Hist. (Later Eng. Med.) [The reign of Richard II; the English gentry], n.saul@rhul.ac.uk

Florian Schui, M.A. (Bochum & N.Y.), Ph.D. (Cantab.), Lect. in Mod. Eur. Hist. [History of political & economic ideas; economic history], florian.schui@rhul.ac.uk

Graham Smith, B.A. (Stirling), M.A. (Essex), Ph.D. (Stirling), Sen. Lect. (Oral Hist.) [History of medicine; public history], graham.smith@rhul.ac.uk

Dan Stone, M.A., D.Phil. (Oxon.), Prof. of Hist. (20th c Eur.) [Holocaust; fascism; philosophy of history], d.stone@rhul.ac.uk

R. Emmett Sullivan, B.A. (Kent), M.Sc.(Econ.) (Lond.), Ph.D. (A.N.U.), Sen. Teaching Fellow (Mod. Int. Econ.) [Inter-war unemployment; neo-classical political economy; trade & customs unions], emmett.sullivan@rhul.ac.uk

Weipin Tsai, M.A. (Hull), M.Sc. (Lond.), Ph.D. (Leeds), Lect. in Mod. Chinese Hist. [Chinese postal service; history of journalism], weipin.tsai@rhul.ac.uk

Alex Windscheffel, B.A. (Oxon.), Ph.D. (Lond.), Sen. Lect. (Mod. Brit.) [British political history post-1832], a.windscheffel@rhul.ac.uk

School of Oriental and African Studies

Thornhaugh Street, Russell Square, WC1H 0XG.
020 7637 2388. Fax 020 7436 3844
www.soas.ac.uk
Department of History 020 7898 4600.
Fax 0207 898 4699

Teresa Bernheimer, B.A., (Lond.), M.Phil., D.Phil. (Oxon.), Lect. (Hist. of the Near & Mid. E.) [Social history of early Islam], tb31@soas.ac.uk

Ian G. Brown, B.A. (Brist.), M.A., Ph.D. (Lond.), Prof. of Econ. Hist. of S.E. Asia [1930s Depression in rural S.E. Asia], ib@soas.ac.uk

Michael Charney, B.A. (Michigan-Flint), M.A. (Michigan & Ohio), Ph.D. (Michigan), Reader in S.E. Asian & Imp. Hist. [The history of Buddhist societies in S. & S.E. Asia; culture, technology & warfare in colonial Africa & Asia]

William G.R. Clarence-Smith, M.A. (Cantab.), Dip.Pol. (Paris), Ph.D. (Lond.), Prof. of Econ. Hist. of Asia & Afric. [Tropical tree crops; commercial diasporas], wc2@soas.ac.uk

Wayne L. Dooling, B.A., M.A. (Cape Town), Ph.D. (Cantab.), Sen. Lect. in Hist. of S. Afric., wd2@soas.ac.uk

Roy S. Fischel, B.A., M.A. (Jerusalem), M.A., Ph.D. (Chicago), Lect. in the Hist. of S. Asia [History of precolonial South Asia, esp. Muslim politics & societies; the Deccan, 1300–1700]

Benjamin C. Fortna, B.A. (Yale), M.A. (Columbia), Ph.D. (Chicago), Sen. Lect. in Hist. of Mod. Mid. E. [Modern Middle East; Ottoman history], bf7@soas.ac.uk

Nelida Fuccaro, M.A. (Venice), Ph.D. (Dunelm.), Reader in Mod. Hist. of the Arab Mid. E. [Urban history of Bahrain & other Gulf & Indian Ocean towns], nf2@soas.ac.uk

Christopher Gerteis, B.A. (Calif.), M.A., Ph.D. (Iowa), Lect. in Hist. of Contemp. Japan [Modern Japan; labour; gender], cg24@soas.ac.uk

Konrad Hirschler, M.A., Ph.D. (Lond.), Sen. Lect. in Hist. of Near Mid. E. [Historiography & Islam in the Middle East], kh20@soas.ac.uk

Andrea Janku, MA., Ph.D. (Heid.), Sen. Lect. in Hist. of China, aj7@soas.ac.uk

Lars Laamann, B.A. (Freiburg), M.A., Ph.D. (Lond.), Lect. in the Hist. of China [18th–20th c. China], ll10@soas.ac.uk

George Lane, B.A., M.A., Ph.D. (Lond.), Sen. Teaching Fellow in the Hist. of the Near & Mid. E. [The Ilkhanate], gl1@soas.ac.uk

Angus Lockyer, B.A. (Cantab.), M.A. (Washington), Ph.D. (Stanford), Lect. in the Hist. of Japan [Social & cultural history of modern Japan], al21@soas.ac.uk

Eleanor Newbigin, B.A., M.Phil., Ph.D (Cantab.), Lect. in the Hist. of S. Asia in the Mod. Period [Modern South Asia, especially gender, the family & law], en2@soas.ac.uk

*John Parker, B.A., Ph.D. (Lond.), Sen. Lect. in Hist. of Afric. [Social history of colonial Ghana], jp23@soas.ac.uk

Richard Reid, B.A. (Stirling), Ph.D. (Lond.), Reader in Hist. of Afric. [Warfare in E. Africa; politics of the Horn], rr15@soas.ac.uk

Peter G. Robb, B.A. (Wellington), Ph.D. (Lond.), Prof. of Hist. of India [Rural India, 18th–20th c.: law; surveys; economy], pr4@soas.ac.uk

Marie Rodet, Dip.Pol. (Rennes), Ph.D. (Vienna), Lect. in the Hist. of Afric. [Modern West African history, esp. social & gender history of western Mali; slavery & emancipation], mr28@soas.ac.uk

Mandy Sadan, M.A. (Oxon.), Ph.D. (Lond.), Lect. in Hist. of S.E. Asia [Colonial & post-colonial S.E. Asia; Burma], ms114@soas.ac.uk

Shabnum S. Tejani, B.A. (Oberlin), M.A., M.Phil., Ph.D. (Columbia), Sen. Lect. in Hist. of Mod. S. Asia [Nationalism & communalism; intellectual history of secularism; social history of Bombay Presidency], st40@soas.ac.uk

University College   Gower Street, WC1E 6BT. 020 7679 2000
www.ucl.ac.uk
Department of History 020 7679 1340. Fax 020 7413 8394
Department of Anthropology 020 7679 7085.
Fax 020 7679 7728
Department of Dutch 020 7679 3113.
Fax 020 7209 1026
Department of Geography 020 7679 5500. Fax 020 7679 7565
Department of German 020 7679 7120. Fax 020 7679 0157
Department of Hebrew & Jewish Studies 020 7679 7171.
Fax 020 7209 1026
Department of History of Art 020 7679 7514.
Fax 020 7916 5939
Department of Italian 020 7679 7784. Fax 020 7209 0638
Department of Scandinavian Studies 020 7679 7176.
Fax 020 7679 7750
Department of Science & Technology Studies 020 7679 1328.
Fax 020 7916 2425
Institute of the Americas 020 3108 9716
Institute of Archaeology 020 7679 7495. Fax 020 7383 2572
Department of Information Studies 020 7679 7204.
Fax 020 7383 0557
School of Slavonic & East European Studies 020 7679 8774.
Fax 020 7679 8777
Wellcome Trust Centre for the History of Medicine
020 7679 8100. Fax 020 7679 8194

Bojan Aleksov, M.A., Ph.D. (Budapest), Lect. in Mod. S.E. Eur. Hist. [Religion & nationalism],
b.aleksov@ucl.ac.uk
Haki Antonsson, Ph.D. (St. And.), Lect. in Med. Scandinavian Stud. [History & culture of
Scandinavia c.900–c.1300; Christianisation of Scandinavia], h.antonsson@ucl.ac.uk
Valentina Arena, Laurea (Florence), Perfezionamento (Florence & Pisa), Ph.D. (Lond.), Lect.
in Anc. Hist. [Roman republic; politics & ancient political thought; Greek & Roman coins],
v.arena@ucl.ac.uk
Guy Attewell, B.A., M.A., Ph.D. (Lond.), Lect. in Hist. of Medicine [History of yunani tibb;
'Greco-Islamic' medicine], g.attewell@ucl.ac.uk
Brian Balmer, D.Phil. (Sussex), Reader in Sc. Policy Stud. [Policies for biotechnology
& genetics; military technology & arms limitation; the sociology of science],
b.balmer@ucl.ac.uk
Michael Berkowitz, B.A. (Hobart Coll., N.Y.), M.A., Ph.D. (Wis.), Prof. of Mod. Jewish Hist.
[Modern Jewish identity formation], m.berkowitz@ucl.ac.uk
Sergei Bogatyrev, Ph.D. (Helsinki), Sen. Lect. in Early Russian Hist. [Medieval Russia;
Muscovite culture; Ivan the Terrible], s.bogatyrev@ucl.ac.uk
Iain Borden, B.A., M.Sc., M.A., Ph.D., Prof. of Architecture & Urban Culture [Architectural
history], i.borden@ucl.ac.uk
Wendy Bracewell, M.A., Ph.D. (Stanford), Prof. of S.E. Eur. Hist. [South-eastern Europe &
the Balkans; early modern frontiers; social & national identities; travel & travel-writing;
historiography; post-colonial studies; inter-disciplinarity], w.bracewell@ucl.ac.uk
Victor Bulmer-Thomas, B.A., M.A., D.Phil. (Oxon.), Prof. [Economic history of Latin America &
the Caribbean since the Napoleonic Wars]

Richard Butterwick-Pawlikowski, M.A. (Cantab.), D.Phil. (Oxon.), Prof. of Polish-Lithuanian Hist. [Polish-Lithuanian history, esp. 1730–1830; the Enlightenment & its critics], r.butterwick@ucl.ac.uk

Joe Cain, B.S., M.A., Ph.D., Sen. Lect. in Hist. & Phil. of Biology [20th c. evolutionary studies; history of natural history], j.cain@ucl.ac.uk

Hasok Chang, B.S., Ph.D., Reader in Phil. of Sc. [History & philosophy of the physical sciences], h.chang@ucl.ac.uk

Hugh Clout, B.A., M.Phil., Ph.D. (Lond.), F.B.A., Prof. of Geog. [Rural & historical geography; regional development; France; Western Europe; London; history of geography], h.clout@geog.ucl.ac.uk

Michael P. Collins, B.Sc., M.Sc. (Lond.), M.Phil. (Cantab.), D.Phil. (Oxon.), Lect. in 20th c. Brit. Hist. [British political & intellectual history], michael.collins@ucl.ac.uk

*Stephen R. Conway, B.A. (Leeds), Ph.D. (Lond.), Prof. of Hist. (17th–20th c. Brit., 17th–18th c. Amer.) [British political & constitutional history from 1688; theories of peace & war; American War of Independence; Britain & continental Europe in 18th c.], s.conway@ucl.ac.uk

Simon Corcoran, M.A., D.Phil. (Oxon.), M.Ar.Ad. (Liv.), Res. Fellow [Ancient history (Rome); Roman law], s.corcoran@ucl.ac.uk

David L. d'Avray, M.A. (Cantab.), D.Phil. (Oxon.), F.B.A., Prof. of Hist. (Med., Relig. Hist.) [Medieval marriage preaching; medieval papacy], d.d'avray@ucl.ac.uk

T.J. Demos, Ph.D., Lect. in Mod. & Contemp. Art [20th c. American & European art], tj.demos@ucl.ac.uk

Richard Dennis, B.A., Ph.D. (Cantab.), Reader in Geog. ['Modernity' of cities in the late 19th & early 20th c.], r.dennis@geog.ucl.ac.uk

John Dickie, B.A., M.A., D.Phil. (Oxon.), Reader in Mod. Italian Stud. [Mezzogiorno; Italian nationhood & national identity; cultural history of modern Italy], j.dickie@ucl.ac.uk

Simon M. Dixon, M.A. (Cantab.), Ph.D. (Lond.), Sir Bernard Pares Prof. of Russian Hist. [The Russian Orthodox church in imperial Russia; the Enlightenment in Russia; the reign of Catherine the Great], s.dixon@ucl.ac.uk

Nicholas Draper, B.A. (Cantab.), M.B.A., M.A., Ph.D. (Lond.), Res. Assoc. [Britain & the abolition of slavery], n.draper@ucl.ac.uk

Paulo Drinot, B.Sc.(Econ.) (Lond.), M.Phil., D.Phil. (Oxon.), Sen. Lect. in Latin Amer. Hist. [Modern Latin American history, esp. Peru in the 19th & 20th c.; labour & working class history; medicine & public health; state formation; travel writing; historiography], paulo.drinot@ucl.ac.uk

Natasha Eaton, Ph.D., Lect. in 18th & 19th c. Brit. Art [18th & 19th c. British art; postcoloniality & empire], n.eaton@ucl.ac.uk

Mechtild Fend, Ph.D., Lect. in the Hist. of Art. [18th & 19th c. French art], m.fend@ucl.ac.uk

Briony A. Fer, B.A., Ph.D., Prof. of the Hist. of Art [20th c. European & American art], b.fer@ucl.ac.uk

Margot Finn, B.S., M.A., Ph.D. (Columbia), Prof. of Mod. Brit. Hist. [18th–19th c. British social & cultural history; history of gender; consumption; law; empire], m.finn@ucl.ac.uk

John Foot, B.A. (Oxon.), Ph.D. (Cantab.), Prof. of Mod. Italian Hist. (Mod. Italian Hist.), j.foot@ucl.ac.uk

Charles W. Ford, B.A., Lect. in the Hist. of Art [17th c. Dutch painting], charles.ford@ucl.ac.uk

David Forgacs, M.A., M.Phil., Dott. di Ricerca, Prof. of Italian [Cultural history of Italy since 1870; history of mass media], d.forgacs@ucl.ac.uk

J. Adrian Forty, B.A. (Oxon.), M.A., Ph.D. (Lond.), Prof. of Architectural Hist., Bartlett Sch. of Architecture [Architectural thought], a.forty@ucl.ac.uk

Mary J.A. Fulbrook, M.A. (Cantab.), M.A., Ph.D. (Harv.), Prof. of German Hist., Dept. of German [Social history of G.D.R.; German national identity], m.fulbrook@ucl.ac.uk

Matthew Gandy, B.A. (Cantab.), Ph.D. (Lond.), Prof. of Geog. [Cultural & historical geography; representation; New York; environmental resources], m.gandy@geog.ucl.ac.uk

Tamar Garb, M.A., Ph.D. (Lond.), Prof. of the Hist. of Art [19th c. French art], t.garb@ucl.ac.uk

Mark J. Geller, B.A. (Princeton), M.A., Ph.D. (Brandeis), *Jewish Chronicle* Prof. of Jewish Stud., m.geller@ucl.ac.uk

Angus Gowland, B.A., M.Phil., Ph.D. (Cantab.), Reader in Intellectual Hist. [Intellectual history of early modern Europe], a.gowland@ucl.ac.uk

Andrew Gregory, B.Sc., M.Sc., Ph.D., Sen. Lect. in Hist. of Sc. [History of science in the ancient world, esp. history of cosmology & the relations between magic & science], andrew.gregory@ucl.ac.uk

Jane Gregory, Ph.D., Sen. Lect. in Sc. & Tech. Stud. [Science communication theory & scientists' use of the media], jane.gregory@ucl.ac.uk

*Thomas H. Gretton, B.A. (East Anglia), Ph.D. (Lond.), Sen. Lect. in Hist. of Art [British, French & Mexican 18th & 19th c. culture], t.gretton@ucl.ac.uk

Dina Gusejnova, B.A., M.Phil., Ph.D. (Cantab.), Leverhulme Early Career Fellow [Modern German intellectual, social & political history; political theory & modern Russian thought], d.gusejnova@ucl.ac.uk

Catherine M. Hall, B.A. (Birm.), M.A. (Essex), Prof. of Mod. Brit. Soc. & Cultural Hist. [The place of Jamaica in 19th c. English imagination], c.hall@ucl.ac.uk

Rebecca Haynes, M.A. (Oxon.), M.A., Ph.D. (Lond.), Sen. Lect. in Romanian Hist. [History of central & eastern Europe, with special reference to Romania], r.haynes@ucl.ac.uk

Andrew F. Hemingway, B.A. (Hull), M.A. (East Anglia), Ph.D., Prof. of Hist. of Art [19th & 20th c. American art & culture], a.hemingway@ucl.ac.uk

Mark Hewitson, B.A., D.Phil. (Oxon.), Sen. Lect. in German Pol., Dept. of German [German history, politics & social thought in the 19th & 20th c.], m.hewitson@ucl.ac.uk

Mary Hilson, B.A., Ph.D. (Exeter), Sen. Lect. in Contemp. Scandinavian Hist. [19th & 20th c. social history], m.hilson@ucl.ac.uk

Julian Hoppit, B.A., Ph.D. (Cantab.), Astor Prof. of Brit. Hist. (17th–19th c. Brit.) [Parliamentary legislation in Britain, 1660–1800], j.hoppit@ucl.ac.uk

L. Stephen Jacyna, B.A. (Cantab.), Ph.D. (Edin.), Reader in Hist. of Medicine [History of neurology in the late 19th & early 20th c.; history of medical microscopy; history of Scottish medicine], s.jacyna@ucl.ac.uk

Benjamin J. Kaplan, Ph.D. (Harv.), Prof. of Dutch Hist. & Institutions [The Low Countries; early modern religious, cultural & social history], b.kaplan@ucl.ac.uk

Egbert Klautke, M.A., Dr.phil. (Heid.), Lect. in the Cultural Hist. of Central Eur. [Modern central European history, esp. 19th & 20th c. political, cultural & intellectual history], e.klautke@ucl.ac.uk

Dilwyn Knox, B.A., Ph.D., Reader in Renaissance Stud. [Late medieval & Renaissance literature, history & philosophy], d.knox@ucl.ac.uk

Axel Körner, B.A. (Berlin), Ph.D. (E.U.I.), Prof. of Mod. Eur. Hist. (Mod. Eur.) [19th c. culture in French & German workers' movement; bourgeoisie in Italy from unity to fascism], a.korner@ucl.ac.uk

Andrew D.E. Lewis, M.A., LL.B. (Cantab.), Prof. of Comparative Legal Hist., Fac. of Laws [Montesquieu's *Collectio Juris* (for an edition); history of tithes], a.d.e.lewis@ucl.ac.uk

Avi S. Lifschitz, M.A. (Tel Aviv), D.Phil. (Oxon.), Sen. Lect. in Eur. Hist [Intellectual history of Europe, 17th–19th c.], avi.lifschitz@ucl.ac.uk

Vivienne Lo, B.A., M.A., Ph.D. (Lond.), Lect. in the Hist. of Medicine [History of Chinese medical theory & practice], v.lo@ucl.ac.uk

Neill Lochery, M.A., Ph.D. (Dunelm.), Sen. Lect. in Israeli Stud. (Mid. E. Pol.) [History of the State of Israel; Middle East peace process], n.lochery@ucl.ac.uk

London

Kris Lockyear, B.A., M.Sc., Ph.D., Lect. [Iron age & Roman archaeology & numismatics; nationalism; ethnicity & cultural identity], k.lockyear@ucl.ac.uk

Maria Loh, Ph.D., Lect. in Early Mod. Italian Art [Early modern Italian art & theory; Venice; theories of authorship & desire; repetition & the double in art & film], m.loh@ucl.ac.uk

Robert Lumley, B.A., M.A., Ph.D., Prof. of Italian Cultural Stud. [Modern Italian history & cultural studies; social movements; cinema & heritage], r.lumley@ucl.ac.uk

William MacLehose, B.A. (Vassar), M.A., Ph.D. (Johns Hopkins), Lect. in the Hist. of Medicine [Medical, natural philosophical & religious thought in western Europe in the 12th & 13th c.], w.maclehose@ucl.ac.uk

Keith McClelland, B.A. (Lancaster), Res. Assoc. [Class, gender, race & citizenship, 1848–1914; imperial history; socialism & empire, 1880–1914], k.mcclelland@ucl.ac.uk

Tony McCulloch, B.A. (Lond.), Ph.D. (Oxon.), Sen. Fellow in Canadian Stud. [U.S. foreign policy in the 20th c., esp. the F.D. Roosevelt era; U.S.-Canada relations], t.mcculloch@ucl.ac.uk

Kevin J. Middlebrook, A.B., Ph.D. (Harv.), Prof. of Latin Amer. Pol. [Comparative Latin American politics; comparative & international political economy; U.S.-Latin American relations], k.middlebrook@ucl.ac.uk

*Nicola A. Miller, B.A. (Cantab.), D.Phil. (Oxon.), Prof. of Latin Amer. Hist. (19th–20th c.) [Intellectuals & national identity in Spanish America], nicola.miller@ucl.ac.uk

*Maxine Molyneux, B.A., Ph.D. (Essex), Prof. of Sociology & Director of the Inst. of the Americas [Sociology, gender & development, human rights & social policy in Latin America, Ethiopia & South Yemen], m.molyneux@ucl.ac.uk

Iwan Morgan, B.A. (Wales), Ph.D. (Lond.), Prof. of U.S. Stud. [U.S. economic & fiscal policy in the late 20th & early 21st c.; presidents & the federal budget since 1945], i.morgan@ucl.ac.uk

Susan Morrissey, M.A., Ph.D. (Calif. at Berkeley), Prof. of Mod. Russian Hist. [Cultural, social & political history of Russia since the 18th c.], s.morrissey@ucl.ac.uk

Michael R. Neve, M.A., Ph.D. (Cantab.), Sen. Lect. in Hist. of Medicine [Concepts of degeneration from 1860s], m.neve@ucl.ac.uk

Marigold A. Norbye, M.A. (Cantab.), Ph.D. (Lond.), Teaching Fellow in Med. Manuscripts & Latin Palaeography, m.norbye@ucl.ac.uk

Vivian Nutton, M.A., Ph.D. (Cantab.), Prof. of the Hist. of Medicine [The classical tradition in medicine; Galen], v.nutton@ucl.ac.uk

Sophie L. Page, B.A. (Cantab.), M.A., Ph.D. (Lond.), Lect. in Later Med. Hist. [Later medieval history, esp. medieval magic & astrology], sophie.page@ucl.ac.uk

Jason Peacey, B.A. (Lancaster), M.A. (York), Ph.D. (Cantab.), Sen. Lect. in Brit. Hist. 1500–1700 [Politics & political culture in early modern Britain], j.peacey@ucl.ac.uk

Barbara Penner, B.A. (McGill), M.Sc., Ph.D. (Lond.), Lect. [Architectural history], b.penner@ucl.ac.uk

Kate Quinn, B.A. (Oxon.), M.A., Ph.D. (Lond.), Lect. in Mod. Hist. [Modern Caribbean history, esp. 1960s & 1970s; Black Power in the Caribbean & beyond; intellectual history of the Caribbean; Guyana in the Burnham period; the Cuban Revolution; culture & politics of the Caribbean left], katherine.quinn@ucl.ac.uk

Karen Radner, M.A., Ph.D. (Vienna), Prof. of the Hist. of the Anc. Near E. [Cuneiform cultures of the ancient Near East; Assyrian empire], k.radner@ucl.ac.uk

Martyn C. Rady, B.A., Ph.D. (Lond.), Prof. of Central Eur. Hist. [Habsburg monarchy; Hungarian history; central European legal history], m.rady@ucl.ac.uk

*Ada Rapoport-Albert, B.A., Ph.D. (Lond.), Reader in Jewish Hist., a.rapoport-albert@ucl.ac.uk

Thomas Rath, B.A. (Lond.), M.Phil. (Oxon.), Ph.D. (Columbia), Lect. in the Hist. of Latin Amer. [Political, social & cultural history of modern Latin America, esp. Mexico], t.rath@ucl.ac.uk

London

Jane Rendell, B.A., Dip. Arch., M.Sc., Ph.D., Reader in Architecture & Art [Interdisciplinarity, theory & history; gender & space; art & architecture; relationship between spatial theory & critical practice], j.rendell@ucl.ac.uk

Andrew Reynolds, B.A., Ph.D., Reader in Med. Archaeol. [Archaeology of early medieval societies in north-west Europe, esp. Britain, 700–1200], a.reynolds@ucl.ac.uk

Bernhard Rieger, M.A. (Erlangen), Ph.D. (Lond.), Sen. Lect. in Mod. Eur. Hist. [19th & 20th c. Europe; society, economics & culture in Britain & Germany], b.rieger@ucl.ac.uk

Kristin Roth-Ey, M.A., Ph.D. (Stanford), Lect. in Mod. Russian Hist. [History of the Soviet Union, esp. post-1945; historical dynamics of cultural production & consumption; mass media], k.roth-ey@ucl.ac.uk

Michael Rowlands, Ph.D. (Lond.), Prof. of Anthr. [Comparative interpretation of cultural rights legislation; role of cultural heritage & museums in imagining national cultures], m.rowlands@ucl.ac.uk

John Sabapathy, B.A. (Oxon.), M.A., Ph.D. (Lond.), Lect. in Med. Hist. [Medieval Europe c.1050–c.1350; accountability; dialogues], j.sabapathy@ucl.ac.uk

R.W. Benet Salway, M.A., D.Phil. (Oxon.), Sen. Lect. in Anc. Hist. [4th c. Roman legislation], r.salway@ucl.ac.uk

Rose Marie San Juan, Ph.D., Reader in Early Mod. Italian Art & Visual Culture [Early modern Italian visual culture (Rome & Naples); urban space & visual technologies (print/film)], r.sanjuan@ucl.ac.uk

Helga Satzinger, Dr.rer.nat (Braunschwieg), Reader in the Hist. of 20th c. Biomedicine [Genetics; brain research; science & gender studies], h.satzinger@ucl.ac.uk

Philip Schofield, B.A. (Manc.), Ph.D. (Lond.), Prof. of the Hist. of Legal & Political Thought [Bentham studies], p.schofield@ucl.ac.uk

Peter Schröder, M.A., Ph.D. (Marburg), Sen. Lect. in Eur. Hist. [17th & 18th c. European history; history of political ideas], p.schroder@ucl.ac.uk

Fredéric J. Schwartz, B.A., M.A., M.Phil., Ph.D. (Columbia), Lect. in the Hist. of Art [Modern German art & design], f.schwartz@ucl.ac.uk

Antonio Sennis, B.A. (Rome), Ph.D. (Turin), Sen. Lect. in Early Med. Hist. [Social, political, economic & religious history of late antique & early medieval western Europe, esp. Italy & Spain; early medieval papacy], a.sennis@ucl.ac.uk

Sonu Shamdasani, B.A. (Brist.), M.Sc., Ph.D. (Lond.), Reader in the Hist. of Medicine [History of psychiatry; psychology & the human sciences in the second half of the 19th c. & the first half of the 20th c.], s.shamdasani@ucl.ac.uk

David Siemens, M.A. (Freie Universität Berlin), Ph.D. (Humboldt), D.A.A.D. Lect. in German Hist. (German Hist.) [19th & 20th c. crime; law; culture; politics; historiography], d.siemens@ucl.ac.uk

David Sim, M.A., D.Phil. (Oxon.), Lect. in Hist. of the U.S. [U.S. history, esp. politics, diplomacy, imperialism & culture during the 19th c.], david.sim@ucl.ac.uk

Adam I.P. Smith, B.A. (Oxon.), M.A. (Sheff.), Ph.D. (Cantab.), Sen. Lect. in Amer. Hist. [U.S. history, esp. 19th c. political history & the Civil War period], a.i.p.smith@ucl.ac.uk

Sarah Snyder, B.A. (Brown), M.A. (Lond.), Ph.D. (Georgetown), Lect. in Int. Hist. [History of human rights; history of the Cold War; diplomatic history], s.snyder@ucl.ac.uk

Charles W. Stewart, B.A. (Brandeis), D.Phil. (Oxon.), Reader in Anthr. (Greece) [Dreams in Greece], c.stewart@ucl.ac.uk

Melvyn B. Stokes, M.A., D.Phil. (Oxon.), Sen. Lect. in Amer. Hist. (U.S.A.) [Film history; American Progressive thought], m.stokes@ucl.ac.uk

Frances Stracey, Ph.D., Lect. in Contemp. Art [Late 20th c. & contemporary European & American avant-gardes; the Situationist International, 1957–72], f.stracey@ucl.ac.uk

John Tait, M.A., D.Phil., Prof. of Egyptology [Ancient Egyptian social history; languages, texts & documents of ancient Egypt], w.tait@ucl.ac.uk

Charles Thorpe, B.A. (Oxon.), Ph.D. (Calif.), [Cultural & political role of scientists in the 20th c.; the relationship between science & the state; connections between the sociology of science & technology; sociology of intellectuals & social theory], c.thorpe@ucl.ac.uk
Ulrich Tiedau, Lect. in Mod. Low Countries Hist. & Soc. [Modern & contemporary Low Countries history & society from 1789; Dutch & Belgian cultural & intellectual relations to their neighbouring countries], u.tiedau@ucl.ac.uk
Henrietta C. (Riet) van Bremen, Dr.Litt. (Leiden), Sen. Lect. in Anc. Hist. (Greek World) [Hellenistic & Roman Asia Minor], r.vanbremen@ucl.ac.uk
Hans van Wees, Ph.D. (Leiden), Prof. of Anc. Hist. (Greece) [Early Greek society & economy; Homer; Greek warfare], h.wees@ucl.ac.uk
Andrew Wear, B.A., M.Sc., Ph.D. (Lond.), Reader in the Hist. of Medicine (Early Mod. Medicine), a.wear@ucl.ac.uk
Alison Wright, B.A., Ph.D. (Lond.), Reader in the Hist. of Art [Early Italian art], alison.wright@ucl.ac.uk
Dominik Wujastyk, B.Sc. (Lond.), D.Phil. (Oxon.), Sen. Res. Fellow [Medicine in pre-colonial India], d.wujastyk@ucl.ac.uk

Warburg Institute   Woburn Square, WC1H 0AB. 020 7862 8949.
                             Fax 020 7862 8955
                             http://warburg.sas.ac.uk

Charles S.F. Burnett, B.A., Ph.D. (Cantab.), F.B.A., Prof. of Hist. of Islamic Influences in Eur., charles.burnett@sas.ac.uk
Guido Giglioni, Laurea (Macerata), Ph.D. (Johns Hopkins), Cassamarca Lect. in Neo-Latin Cultural & Intellectual Hist., 1400–1700 [Early modern science, medicine & philosophy], guido.giglioni@sas.ac.uk
Alastair Hamilton, B.A., M.A., Ph.D. (Cantab.), Arcadian Visiting Res. Prof., Sch. of Advanced Study [Early modern intellectual & religious history], alastair.hamilton@sas.ac.uk
*Peter Mack, M.A. (Oxon.), M.Phil., Ph.D. (Lond.), D.Litt. (Warwick), Director, Prof. of the Hist. of the Classical Tradition [Renaissance literature, rhetoric & thought], peter.mack@sas.ac.uk
Raphaële Mouren, D.E.A. (Paris), archiviste paléographe (Paris), Ph.D. (Paris), Deputy Director & Librarian [Greek & Latin philology in the Renaissance; history of the book & libraries; management of documentary heritage in libraries], raphaele.mouren@sas.ac.uk
Alessandro Scafi, Laurea (Rome), Ph.D. (Lond.), Lect. in Med. & Renaissance Cultural Hist. [History of religion, literature & political thought, 1200–1600], alessandro.scafi@sas.ac.uk

LONDON METROPOLITAN UNIVERSITY

City Campus, 31 Jewry Street, London, EC3N 2EY. 020 7320 1000. Fax 020 7320 1163
North Campus, 166–220 Holloway Road, London, N7 8DB.
www.londonmet.ac.uk
Department of Business, Enterprise, Leisure & Arts Management
84 Moorgate, London, EC2M 7BU. 020 7320 1441. Fax 020 7320 1465
Department of Humanities, Arts & Languages
020 7320 1217/020 7753 5111. Fax 020 7320 1234/020 7753 3159
Department of Law, Governance & International Relations
Calcutta House, Old Castle Street, London, E1 7NT. 020 7320 1161. Fax 020 7320 1157
Department of Applied Social Sciences 020 7320 1040. Fax 020 7320 1034
Sir John Cass Department of Art, Media & Design
020 7320 1931. Fax 020 7320 1938

Kathryn A. Castle, B.A. (Cornell), M.A. (Lond.), Ph.D. (C.N.A.A), Princ. Lect., North Campus (U.S. Hist.) [Race & society in U.S. & Britain], k.castle@londonmet.ac.uk
Paul Cobley, B.A., Ph.D., Reader in Communication, City Campus (Amer. Cultural Hist.), p.cobley@londonmet.ac.uk
Mo Dodson, B.A., P.G.Dip. (Lond. & L.I.F.S.), Princ. Lect. in Communications, City Campus [Dance history & theory], m.dodson@londonmet.ac.uk
David H. Fletcher, M.A. (Oxon.), Ph.D. (Exeter), Sen. Lect. in Hist., City Campus (Cartographic Hist.) [History of cartography; estate maps; Ordnance Survey; the mapping of local government boundaries in England], d.fletcher@londonmet.ac.uk
John Gabriel, B.A., Ph.D. (Liv.), Prof. of Soc., City Campus [History of ethnic relations in U.K. & U.S.A.], j.gabriel@londonmet.ac.uk
Seán Glynn, B.Sc.(Econ.) (Lond.), M.Ec. (W. Aust.), M.Sc. (Wales), Ph.D. (Kent), University Reader, City Campus [History of London Guildhall University], s.glynn@londonmet.ac.uk
Nick Haeffner, B.A., Ph.D., Lect., City Campus (Cultural Hist.)
Jenny Harding, B.A., Ph.D., Lect., City Campus (Cultural Hist.), j.harding@londonmet.ac.uk
Jeffrey P. Haynes, B.A., Ph.D. (C.N.A.A), Prof. of Pol. (Afric. Hist.) [Third world in post-Cold War global system], j.haynes@londonmet.ac.uk
Steve Jones, B.A., Lect. in Language Stud., City Campus (Eng. Hist.), s.jones@londonmet.ac.uk
Katharine A. Lerman, B.A., D.Phil. (Sussex), Sen. Lect., North Campus (Mod. Eur.) [Bismarckian & Wilhelmine Germany], k.lerman@londonmet.ac.uk
Paul H.D. McGilchrist, B.A. (Middlesex), M.A. (Lond.), Sen. Lect., North Campus (The Black Diaspora) [Africans in 18th c. Britain], p.mcgilchrist@londonmet.ac.uk
Margaret R. May, B.A. (Wales), Ph.D. (Lond.), Princ. Lect. in Soc. Policy, City Campus, m.may@londonmet.ac.uk
Chris J. Rhodes, B.Sc., Ph.D. (Lond.), Sen. Lect. in Soc., City Campus [Trades union in 19th–20th c. U.K. & U.S.A.], c.rhodes@londonmet.ac.uk
Caroline Woodhead, B.A. (Liv.), Sen. Lect. in Econ. Hist., City Campus (19th–20th c. Brit & Int., Business) [19th–20th c. business], c.woodhead@londonmet.ac.uk

UNIVERSITY OF **MANCHESTER**

School of Arts, Languages & Cultures Samuel Alexander Building, Manchester, M13 9PL.
0161 275 8311.
www.alc.manchester.ac.uk
History Samuel Alexander Building, Manchester, M13 9PL. 0161 306 1240.
Fax 0161 306 1241
Centre for the History of Science, Technology & Medicine
Simon Building, Manchester, M13 9PL. 0161 275 5850. Fax 0161 275 5699
Archaeology Mansfield Cooper Building, Manchester, M13 9PL. 0161 306 1240.
Fax 0161 306 1241
Art History & Visual Studies Mansfield Cooper Building, Manchester, M13 9PL.
0161 306 1240. Fax 0161 306 1241
Classics & Ancient History Samuel Alexander Building, Manchester, M13 9PL.
0161 306 1240. Fax 0161 306 1241
English & American Studies Samuel Alexander Building, Manchester, M13 9PL.
0161 306 1240. Fax 0161 306 1241
Religions & Theology Samuel Alexander Building, Manchester, M13 9PL. 0161 306 1240.
Fax 0161 306 1241
Drama & Music Martin Harris Centre for Music & Drama, Manchester, M13 9PL.
0161 306 1240. Fax 0161 306 1241

Philip Alexander, B.A., D.Phil. (Oxon.), Prof. Emeritus of Post-Biblical Jewish Literature
[Jewish history in late antiquity], p.s.alexander@manchester.ac.uk
Thomas Tunstall Allcock, B.A., M.A., Ph.D. (Cantab.), Lect. in Amer. Hist. [20th c. U.S. foreign
relations; inter-American relations], thomas.tunstallallcock@manchester.ac.uk
Adelina Angusheva-Tihanov, M.A. (C.E.U. Budapest), Ph.D. (Sofia), L.M.S. (Toronto), Res.
Fellow [Medieval Slavic & Byzantine written cultures; prognostic texts; medieval medicine
in the Balkans], adelina.angusheva-tihanov@manchester.ac.uk
*Hannah J. Barker, B.A. (Sussex), D.Phil. (Oxon.), Prof. of Brit. Hist. (Late 18th
& early 19th c. Eng.) [Print culture; gender, work & family; northern towns],
hannah.barker@manchester.ac.uk
Mary Beagon, B.A., D.Phil. (Oxon.), Lect. in Anc. Hist. (Roman) [The elder Pliny; ancient
attitudes to nature], mary.a.beagon@manchester.ac.uk
Anke Bernau, B.A., M.A., Ph.D. (Cardiff), Sen. Lect. in Med. Literature & Culture [Late
medieval English literature; gender & sexuality; religious culture; memory; imagination;
periodisation; medievalism], anke.bernau@manchester.ac.uk
Francesca Billiani, B.A. (Trieste), Ph.D. (Read.), Sen. Lect. in Italian (19th & 20th c.
Italian Cultural & Intellectual Theory) [History of the book; fascism; periodical studies],
francesca.billiani@manchester.ac.uk
David Brown, B.A., M.A. (Lond.), Ph.D. (Hull), Sen. Lect. in Amer. Stud. (Amer. Hist.) [19th c.
U.S.; slavery; the South; American Civil War], brown.d@manchester.ac.uk
Laurence Brown, B.A., Ph.D. (York), Lect. in Migration Hist. [18th–20th c.
Caribbean; immigration in Britain & France; French & British empire],
laurence.brown@manchester.ac.uk
Ron P. Buckley, B.A., Ph.D. (Exeter), Sen. Lect. in Arabic Stud. [Classical Islamic history],
ronald.p.buckley@manchester.ac.uk
Ian A. Burney, B.A., M.A., Ph.D. (Calif. at Berkeley), Sen. Lect. in Medical Hist. [Victorian
science & culture; expertise; history of poisoning; stresses of war; history of forensics],
ian.a.burney@manchester.ac.uk

Ana Carden-Coyne, B.A., Ph.D. (Sydney), Sen. Lect. in the Cultural Hist. of Mod. War [Social, cultural & medical history of the First World War & its aftermath], a.cc@manchester.ac.uk

Jenny Carson, M.A. (Brist.), Ph.D. (Manc.), Lect. in Humanitarianism & Conflict Response [History of Quaker service; faith-based humanitarianism; history of humanitarianism], jennifer.carson@manchester.ac.uk

Youssef M. Choueiri, B.A. (A.U.B.), M.Sc. (Lond.), Ph.D. (Cantab.), Reader in Islamic Stud. [The formative period of Islam; modern Islam; Arab historiography; the Arab world & the West; Arab nationalism], youssef.choueiri@manchester.ac.uk

Georg Christ, Lic., Dr.phil. (Basel), Lect. in Med. & Early Mod. Hist. [Trade in the eastern Mediterranean, esp. Venice & Mamluk Empire; Hanseatic trade; cosmopolitanism; knowledge management], georg.christ@manchester.ac.uk

Kate Cooper, B.A. (Wesleyan), M.T.S. (Harv.), Ph.D. (Princeton), Prof. of Eccles. Hist. (Early Church) [Late antiquity: gender; rise of Christianity; pagans & Christians], kate.cooper@manchester.ac.uk

Mark W. Crinson, B.A. (Sussex), M.A. (Lond.), Ph.D. (Penn.), Prof. of Hist. of Art (19th–20th c. Brit. Architecture) [Colonial architecture; architectural education], mark.w.crinson@manchester.ac.uk

Andrew Crome, B.A. (Wales), Ph.D. (Manc.), Lect. in Hist. of Mod. Christianity [17th & 18th c. English religious history; apocalyptic thought; history of Christian Zionism; religion & media], andrew.crome@manchester.ac.uk

Laura Doan, Ph.D. (Chicago), Prof. of Cultural Hist. & Sexuality Stud. [Gender, sexuality & the First World War], laura.doan@manchester.ac.uk

Kathryn Dutton, M.A. (Glas.), M.A. (Lond.), Ph.D. (Glas.), Leverhulme Early Career Fellow [12th c. Anjou, Normandy & western France; political culture, esp. charters & diplomatic], kathryn.dutton@manchester.ac.uk

Andrew Fear, M.A., D.Phil. (Oxon.), Lect. in Anc. Hist. [Roman & Visigothic Spain; early Christianity], andrew.fear@manchester.ac.uk

Paul J. Fouracre, B.A. (Oxon.), Ph.D. (Lond.), Prof. of Med. Hist. (Early Med.) [European societies in the early middle ages], paul.j.fouracre@manchester.ac.uk

*Pierre E. Fuller, B.A. (Georgetown), Ph.D. (Calif.), Lect. in E. Asian Hist. [Disaster relief in modern China], pierre.fuller@manchester.ac.uk

Noelle Gallagher, B.A., M.A. (Brit. Col.), Ph.D. (Chicago), Lect. in 18th c. Brit. Literature & Culture [Rhetoric of health & illness; venereal disease; historical writing; satire & panegyric], noelle.gallagher@manchester.ac.uk

*Viv Gardner, B.A., Prof. Emeritus of Theatre Stud. [Theatre history & historiography; gender & performance, 1850–1914; provincial theatre, 1900–39], viv.gardner@manchester.ac.uk

Peter W. Gatrell, M.A., Ph.D. (Cantab.), Prof. of Econ. Hist. (Mod. Eur., esp. Russia) [Economy & social history of modern Russia; cultural history of war; refugees in modern world history], peter.gatrell@manchester.ac.uk

Till Geiger, Lic.oec.HSG (St. Gallen), M.Sc. (Lond.), Ph.D. (Aberd.), Lect. in Int. Hist. [The transatlantic relationship since 1945; American foreign assistance policy & the political economy of the Cold War; Irish foreign policy since 1919], till.geiger@manchester.ac.uk

Anindita Ghosh, B.A. (Calcutta), M.A. (New Delhi), Ph.D. (Cantab.), Lect. [Social & cultural history of the book; politics of language, culture & identity in colonial Bengal], anindita.ghosh@manchester.ac.uk

Hal Gladfelder, B.A. (Calif. at Berkeley), M.A., Ph.D. (Calif.), Sen. Lect. in 18th & 19th c. Eng. Literature & Culture [History of sexuality & gender; history of authorship], hal.gladfelder@manchester.ac.uk

Christopher Godden, B.A., M.A., Ph.D. (Manc.), Lect. in Econ. Hist. [Economic history of modern Britain; popular representations of the economy], christopher.godden@manchester.ac.uk

Christian Goeschel, B.A. (York), M.Phil., Ph.D. (Cantab.), Lect. in Mod. Eur. Hist. [Modern Germany & modern Italy], christian.goeschil@manchester.ac.uk

Esther Gómez-Sierra, B.A., M.A. (Madrid), Ph.D. (Manc.), Lect. [History of ideas in late medieval, Renaissance & golden age Spain; rhetoric & politics], esther.gomez@manchester.ac.uk

Jeremy Gregory, M.A., D.Phil. (Oxon.), Prof. of the Hist. of Christianity (18th c. Brit. Relig. Hist.), jeremy.gregory@manchester.ac.uk

Sasha Handley, M.A., Ph.D. (Warwick), Lect. in Early Mod. Hist. (Early Mod.) [17th & 18th c. British cultural history; supernatural beliefs; everyday life; material culture], sasha.handley@manchester.ac.uk

Liam Harte, B.A. (N.U.I.), Ph.D. (Dublin), Sen. Lect. in Irish & Mod. Literature [The literary & cultural history of the Irish in Britain since 1850], liam.harte@manchester.ac.uk

Jonathan H. Harwood, B.A. (Wesleyan), Ph.D. (Harv.), Emeritus Prof. of Hist. of Sc., Tech. & Medicine (19th–20th c. Biology, German Sc.) [Social history of agricultural sciences in Germany, 1880–1945], jonathan.harwood@manchester.ac.uk

Nicholas J. Higham, B.A., Ph.D. (Manc.), Emeritus Prof. of Early Med. & Landscape Hist. (Early Med. Brit., Landscape), nick.j.higham@manchester.ac.uk

Jeff A. Hughes, B.A. (Oxon.), M.Phil., Ph.D. (Cantab.), Sen. Lect., C.H.S.T.M. (19th–20th c. Physical Sc. & Tech.) [Nuclear history; science in 20th c. Britain], jeff.hughes@manchester.ac.uk

Charles L.G. Insley, M.A., D.Phil. (Oxon.), Sen. Lect. in Med. Hist. (Med.) [Early medieval Britain, 600–1100, esp. Anglo-Saxon England, 800–1066; medieval Wales, 1100–1300; early medieval documentary culture], charles.insley@manchester.ac.uk

Tim Insoll, B.A. (Sheff.), Ph.D. (Cantab.), Prof. of Archaeol. (Early Islamic Archaeol. of W. Central Afric.) [Theory & method of religions; African & Islamic archaeology], tim.insoll@manchester.ac.uk

Vladimir Jankovic, B.S. (Belgrade), Ph.D. (Notre Dame), Sen. Lect., C.H.S.T.M. [18th–20th c. environmental medicine; British weather; climate change; urban climatology], vladimir.jankovic@manchester.ac.uk

Matthew Jefferies, B.A. (Sussex), D.Phil. (Oxon.), Prof. of German Hist. [19th & 20th c. German culture, incl. architecture, painting, the environment, monuments & naturism], matt.jefferies@manchester.ac.uk

Leif W. Jerram, B.A. (Oxon.), Ph.D. (Manc.), Lect. in Eur. Hist. [Social & cultural history of cities; the built environment & the experience of city life, with a focus on Germany & Austria], l.jerram@manchester.ac.uk

H. Stuart Jones, M.A., D.Phil. (Oxon.), Prof. of Intellectual Hist. (Mod. France & Brit., Intellectual Hist.) [19th c. French & British political thought; French political culture], stuart.jones@manchester.ac.uk

Max H. Jones, B.A. (Oxon.), M.A., C.Phil. (Calif. at Berkeley), Ph.D. (Cantab.), Sen. Lect. (Mod. Brit.) [Heroes; exploration; cultural history of war], max.jones@manchester.ac.uk

Sian Jones, B.A., Ph.D. (Southampton), Prof. of Archaeol. (Archaeol. of Identity), sian.jones@manchester.ac.uk

Daniel Langton, B.A., Ph.D. (Southampton), Prof. of Hist. of Jewish-Christian Relations [Modern Jewish thought; Anglo-Jewish history; Jewish New Testament studies; Holocaust theology], daniel.langton@manchester.ac.uk

Peter Liddel, B.A. (Lond.), D.Phil. (Oxon.), Sen. Lect. in Anc. Hist. [Social & political history of classical & Hellenistic Greece], peter.liddel@manchester.ac.uk

David C. Lomas, MB.BS (Queensland), M.A. (Lond.), Ph.D. (Manc.), Prof. & Reader in Hist. of Art (Mod.) [Early Modernism; Cubism; Surrealist art]

Polly Low, M.A. (Oxon.), Ph.D. (Cantab.), Sen. Lect. in Anc. Hist. [Greek political history; war & the commemoration of war; epigraphy & monumentality], polly.low@manchester.ac.uk

Chris Manias, M.A., Ph.D. (Lond.), Lect. in Mod. Eur. Hist. [19th c. British, French & German history; history of human & biological sciences; history of nationalism & racial thought], chris.manias@manchester.ac.uk

Stephen J. Milner, B.A. (Cantab.), Ph.D. (Lond.), Prof. of Italian Stud. [Italian late medieval & Renaissance cultural history; history of the classical tradition], stephen.j.milner@manchester.ac.uk

Aaron W. Moore, B.A. (Oberlin), Ph.D. (Princeton), Lect. in Chinese Hist. (Mod. China), aaron.moore@manchester.ac.uk

Frank Mort, B.A. (York), M.A., Ph.D. (Birm.), Prof. of Cultural Hist. [Cultural history of metropolitan London, 1945–63; monarchy in the 20th century; modern history of sexuality], frank.mort@manchester.ac.uk

Stephen Mossman, M.A., M.St., D.Phil. (Oxon.), Lect. in Med. Hist. [Later medieval European history; intellectual encounters with Islam], stephen.mossman@manchester.ac.uk

Ewa Ochman, M.A. (Krakow), Ph.D. (Salford), Lect. [Cultural history of war; population displacement; borderlands & ethnic minorities; urban memory], ewa.ochman@manchester.ac.uk

David E. O'Connor, B.A. (Belf.), Lect. in Hist. of Art (Med. & 19th c. Stained Glass) [Late medieval & Victorian art & architecture, esp. stained glass]

Paul Oldfield, B.A., M.Res., Ph.D. (Leeds), Lect. in Med. Hist. [Medieval Mediterranean, 1000–1300; urban communities, sanctity & pilgrimage in Italy], paul.oldfield@manchester.ac.uk

Gale Redfern Owen-Crocker, B.A., Ph.D., Prof. of Anglo-Saxon Culture [Old English literature; Anglo-Saxon culture; medieval dress/textiles], groc@manchester.ac.uk

Mara Patessio, B.A. (Venice), Ph.D. (Cantab.), Lect. in Japanese Hist., mara.patessio@manchester.ac.uk

John V. Pickstone, B.A. (Cantab.), M.Sc., Ph.D. (Lond.), Emeritus Prof. of the Hist. of Knowledges, C.H.S.T.M. [19th–20th c. French science; medicine, science & technology, 1750–present; local history & heritage; contemporary history], john.pickstone@manchester.ac.uk

Steven Pierce, B.A. (Yale), Ph.D. (Michigan), Lect. in Mod. Afric. Hist. [Sub-Saharan Africa; northern Nigeria; historical anthropology; colonialism; law & politics; gender & sexuality], steven.pierce@manchester.ac.uk

Colin Richards, B.A., Ph.D. (Glas.), Prof. of World Pre-Hist. [World pre-history; archaeology], colin.richards@manchester.ac.uk

Susan Rutherford, Ph.D. (Manc.), Sen. Lect. in Music [19th c. Italian & French opera; history of vocal performance practice; critical reception], susan.rutherford@manchester.ac.uk

Philip C. Sadgrove, M.A., Ph.D. (Edin.), Sen. Lect. in Arabic Stud. (Mod. Arab Hist.) [Arab journalism; drama; the Namda], philip.sadgrove@manchester.ac.uk

Alexander Samely, M.A. (Frankfurt), M.St., D.Phil. (Oxon.), Prof. of Jewish Thought (Jewish Hist.) [Talmudic literature; Hebrew manuscripts], alexander.samely@manchester.ac.uk

Michael Sanders, B.A. (Kent), Ph.D. (Lond.), Sen. Lect. in 19th c. Writing [Chartist culture], michael.sanders@manchester.ac.uk

Dagmar Schäfer, M.A., Ph.D. (Würzburg), Prof. of Chinese Stud. [History of science & technology], dagmar.schaefer@manchester.ac.uk

Ian Scott, B.A. (Manc. Met.), M.A., Ph.D. (Keele), Lect. in Amer. Stud. (Amer. Hist., Pol. & Culture) [Hollywood screenwriting & film history; representations of politics & political institutions on film; social, cultural & historic links in football culture between the U.S. & Britain], ian.s.scott@manchester.ac.uk

Renate Smithuis, B.A., Ph.D., Lect. in Med. Jewish Stud. [Middle ages & early modern period], renate.smithuis@manchester.ac.uk

Jennifer Spinks, B.F.A., M.A. (Tasmania), Ph.D. (Melbourne), Lect. in Early Mod. Hist. [Print culture; gender; images as historical sources; intersection of religion & natural history in early modern northern Europe], jenny.spinks@manchester.ac.uk

Julie-Marie Strange, B.A., M.Phil. (Wales), Ph.D. (Liv.), Sen. Lect. in Mod.
Brit. Hist. [Victorian studies; history of emotion; history of humanitarianism], julie-marie.strange@manchester.ac.uk

A. Penny Summerfield, B.A., M.A., D.Phil. (Sussex), Prof. [Gender & home defence in Britain in the Second World War; the popular memory of the Second World War in post-war Britain], penny.summerfield@manchester.ac.uk

James B. Sumner, B.A. (Cantab.), M.A., Ph.D. (Leeds), Lect., C.H.S.T.M. [History of technology & computing; history of brewing], james.sumner@manchester.ac.uk

Daniel Szechi, B.A. (Sheff.), D.Phil. (Oxon.), Prof. of Early Mod. Hist. [Jacobitism; early modern Scottish Catholic church; society & politics in 18th c. Scotland; war & society in early modern Europe], daniel.szechi@manchester.ac.uk

Bertrand O. Taithe, L. ès L. (Montpellier), M.A. (Paris), Ph.D. (Manc.), Prof. of Cultural Hist. (Mod. Brit. & France) [Humanitarian medicine; war & medicine; Henry Mayhew; 1870 war; Contagious Diseases Act & regulation of prostitution; 19th c. French cultural history; history of the body; history of humanitarianism], bertrand.taithe@manchester.ac.uk

Carsten Timmermann, M.Sc. (Freie Univ., Berlin), M.A., Ph.D. (Manc.), Lect., C.H.S.T.M. [History of modern medicine & biomedical science], carsten.timmermann@manchester.ac.uk

Stephen Todd, M.A., Ph.D. (Cantab.), Prof. of Anc. Hist. [Greek social & legal history; Attic orators, esp. Lysias], stephen.todd@manchester.ac.uk

Simone Turchetti, M.Sc., Ph.D. (Manc.), Lect. (Hist. of Sc., Tech. & Medicine) [History of contemporary science & technology; science & secrecy; geosciences in the Cold War], simone.turchetti@manchester.ac.uk

Louise Tythacott, B.A. (Kent), M.A., Ph.D. (Manc.), Lect. in Museology [Collections & displays of non-Western objects in museums 17th–20th c., esp. Chinese], louise.tythacott@manchester.ac.uk

Aashish Velkar, B.Com., M.B.A. (Poona), M.Sc., Ph.D. (Lond.), Lect. in Econ. Hist. [Industrial transformation; standards & standardisation; metrology], aashish.velkar@manchester.ac.uk

Cordelia Warr, B.A. (Nott.), Ph.D. (Warwick), Sen. Lect. in Art Hist. [Italian art of the 13th–15th c., esp. patronage, clothing & the representation of stigmata], cordelia.warr@manchester.ac.uk

Charlotte Wildman, B.A., M.A., Ph.D. (Manc.), Lect. in Mod. Brit. Hist. [20th c. Britain; cities & urban culture; gender; religion; consumer culture], charlotte.wildman@manchester.ac.uk

*Michael Worboys, B.Sc., M.Sc., Ph.D. (Sussex), Prof. of Hist. of Sc., Tech. & Medicine, C.H.S.T.M. [Science, medicine & empire; history of infectious diseases; history of dog breeding], michael.worboys@manchester.ac.uk

Zheng Yangwen, B.A. (Oberlin), Ph.D. (Cantab.), Lect. in Chinese Hist. [Late imperial China], yangwen.zheng@manchester.ac.uk

Feroz A.K. Yasamee, B.A. (Cantab.), Ph.D. (Lond.), Sen. Lect. in Islamic Hist. (Mod. Mid. E. & S.E. Eur.) [19th–20th c. Balkans & Middle East]

Natalie A. Zacek, B.A. (Cornell), Ph.D. (Johns Hopkins), Lect. in Amer. Stud. (Colonial Amer. & W. Indies) [Colonial masculinities; race & gender], natalie.a.zacek@manchester.ac.uk

MANCHESTER METROPOLITAN UNIVERSITY

All Saints, Manchester, M15 6BH. 0161 247 2000. Fax 0161 247 6390
www.mmu.ac.uk
Department of History & Economic History
Geoffrey Manton Building, Rosamond Street West, off Oxford Road, Manchester, M15 6LL.
0161 247 1730

*Tony J. Adams, B.A., Ph.D. (Leicester), Princ. Lect. in Hist. (Late Mod. Brit. & Eur.) [British industrial relations & urban politics 1900–30], T.Adams@mmu.ac.uk

Patricia Ayers, B.A. (Liv.), Sen. Lect. in Hist. (20th c. Women's Hist.) [Family economy; labour markets; port economies], P.Ayers@mmu.ac.uk

Jason P. Crowley, B.A., M.A., Ph.D. (Manc.), Lect. in Anc. Hist. (Archaic & Classical Greece) [Ancient Greek warfare; Roman army; comparative military history; psychology of combat], J.Crowley@mmu.ac.uk

Catherine J. Danks, B.A., M.A. (Essex), Sen. Lect. in Hist. (Imp., Soviet & Mod. Russian Hist.) [Modern Russia], C.J.Danks@mmu.ac.uk

Ben Edwards, B.A., M.A., Ph.D. (Dunelm.), Lect. in Archaeol. & Heritage (Archaeol., Anc. Hist.) [Neolithic Britain; survey techniques; community archaeology; past in contemporary society], B.Edwards@mmu.ac.uk

Sam Edwards, B.A., M.A., Ph.D. (Lancaster), Lect. in Amer. Hist. (17th–20th c. Amer. Hist.) [Commemoration & war memory; Anglo-American relations; cultural history of modern war], S.Edwards@mmu.ac.uk

Mark Fenemore, B.A., M.A., Ph.D. (Lond.), Sen. Lect. in Hist. (Mod. Eur.) [Modern German history; history of youth; masculinities], M.Fenemore@mmu.ac.uk

Tilman Frasch, M.A., Ph.D. (Heid.), Sen. Lect. in Hist. (World Hist.) [S. & S.E. Asian history], T.Frasch@mmu.ac.uk

Craig Horner, B.A., Ph.D. (Manc. Met.), Lect. in Hist. (Community Hist.) [18th c. Manchester; early automobility; mass motoring], C.Horner@mmu.ac.uk

Kathryn Hurlock, B.A. (Lond.), Ph.D. (Wales), Lect. in Med. Hist. (Med. Eng. & Eur.) [Medieval Wales; the medieval frontier; crusading & the British Isles], K.Hurlock@mmu.ac.uk

Sam Johnson, B.A., Ph.D. (Keele), Sen. Lect. in Hist. (Mod. Eur.) [Eastern European Jewish history; history of European anti-Semitism]

*Brian McCook, B.A., M.A., Ph.D. (Calif. at Berkeley), Assoc. Dean/Head of Dept. (Mod. Eur./ World) [Migration; comparative history; Europe; U.S.], B.McCook@mmu.ac.uk

Marcus Morris, B.A, M.A., Ph.D. (Lancaster), Lect. in Mod. Eur. Hist. (Mod. Brit. & Eur.) [19th & 20th c. British & European socialism], Marcus.Morris@mmu.ac.uk

Rosamund B.M. Oates, B.A. (Oxon.), Ph.D. (York), Sen. Lect. in Early Mod. Hist. (16th & 17th c. Brit. & Eur.) [Elizabethan church & politics; Renaissance libraries], R.Oates@mmu.ac.uk

Gervase Phillips, B.A., M.Sc., M.Phil. (Wales), Princ. Lect. in Hist. (19th–20th c. U.S., the World Wars, Genocide & Persecution, Computing for Hist.) [Military history, 1450–1920; race; slavery & American Civil War], G.Phillips@mmu.ac.uk

Faye Simpson, B.A., M.A., Ph.D. (Exeter), Lect. in Archaeol. & Hist. (Community Archaeol., Hist. Environment, Public Hist.) [Value of community archaeology], F.Simpson@mmu.ac.uk

Joanne Smith, B.A., Ph.D. (Manc. Met.), Lect. in Hist. (Mod. Brit.) [20th c. women's & gender history; non-party political women's associations], J.N.Smith@mmu.ac.uk

Jonathan Spangler, B.A. (William & Mary), M.St., D.Phil. (Oxon.), Sen. Lect. in Early Mod. Hist. (17th & 18th c. France & Eur.) [Nobles; courts; families; frontiers; Lorraine], J.Spangler@mmu.ac.uk

Melanie J. Tebbutt, B.A. (York), Ph.D. (Leeds Met.), Sen. Lect. in Hist., Director of Manchester Centre for Regional Hist. (18th–20th c. Soc.) [History of youth; gender & maturity; working-class culture & communities in the late 19th & early 20th c.], M.Tebbutt@mmu.ac.uk

David Walsh, B.A., M.Sc., Ph.D. (Salford), Lect. in Hist. (19th & 20th c. Brit.) [Working-class conservatism; popular disorder]

Louise H. Willmot, B.A., D.Phil. (Oxon.), Princ. Lect. in Hist. (20th c. Eur.) [Nazi Germany], L.Willmot@mmu.ac.uk

Terry J. Wyke, B.A. (York), Princ. Lect. in Econ. Hist. (Regional Hist.) [Social history & bibliography of Manchester region], T.Wyke@mmu.ac.uk

NEWCASTLE UNIVERSITY

Newcastle upon Tyne, NE1 7RU. 0191 208 6000
www.ncl.ac.uk
School of History, Classics & Archaeology
Armstrong Building, Newcastle upon Tyne, NE1 7RU. 0191 208 7844. Fax 0191 222 6484
www.ncl.ac.uk/historical/about/history/

Joan Allen, B.A., Ph.D. (Northumbria), Sen. Lect. in Mod. Brit. Hist. [19th c. radicalism; Chartism; Irish immigration; the popular press; North-East history], joan.allen@ncl.ac.uk

Jonathan Andrews, B.A., Ph.D. (Lond.), Reader in the Hist. of Psychiatry [History of insanity; madness; the social & economic history of Britain], jonathan.andrews@ncl.ac.uk

Scott Ashley, B.A., D.Phil. (Oxon.), Lect. in Early Med. Hist. (Late Antiquity & Early Mod. Eur.) [Christianity; social memory; Carolingian Renaissance; Vikings; ethnicity], scott.ashley@ncl.ac.uk

Bruce E. Baker, B.A. (Clemson), M.A., Ph.D. (N. Carolina), Lect. in Amer. Hist. (19th & 20th c. Amer. South) [19th & 20th c. American South; labour; racial violence; reconstruction; business]

Claudia Baldoli, B.A., M.A. (Venice), Ph.D. (Lond.), Sen. Lect. in Mod. Eur. Hist. [Italian fascism; World War II; Italian communities in Britain & U.S.A.], claudia.baldoli@ncl.ac.uk

Helen M. Berry, B.A. (Dunelm.), Ph.D. (Cantab.), Prof. of Early Mod. Brit. Hist. (17th & 18th c. Brit.) [Print culture; national identity; gender], helen.berry@ncl.ac.uk

Jeremy P. Boulton, M.A. (St. And.), Ph.D. (Cantab.), Prof. (Early Mod. Soc.) [Poor & Poor Law in early modern England; London, 1500–1750], jeremy.boulton@ncl.ac.uk

Claire Brewster, B.A., M.A., Ph.D. (Warwick), Sen. Lect. in Amer. Hist. (Latin Amer.), claire.brewster@ncl.ac.uk

Keith Brewster, B.A., Ph.D. (Warwick), Sen. Lect. in Latin Amer. Hist. (20th c.) [Mexican Revolution; sporting cultures in Latin America], keith.brewster@ncl.ac.uk

Maria Brosius, D.Phil., Reader in Anc. Hist. [Ancient Persia], maria.brosius@ncl.ac.uk

Fergus Campbell, Reader in Soc. & Cultural Hist. [19th & 20th c. Irish social history; history of the British Isles; migration of populations], fergus.campbell@ncl.ac.uk

Sarah Campbell, B.A., M.A., Ph.D. (N.U.I.), Teaching Fellow in Irish/Brit. Hist. [19th & 20th c. Ireland; Northern Ireland; Anglo-Irish relations; public history; political violence], sarah.campbell@ncl.ac.uk

Livia Capponi, B.A. (Pavia), Ph.D. (Oxon. & San Marino), Lect. in Anc. Hist. [Roman history; the Jews in the Hellenistic & Roman periods; Egypt; papyrology], livia.capponi@ncl.ac.uk

Nicola Clarke, M.A. (St. And.), M.Phil., D.Phil. (Oxon.), Lect. in the Hist. of the Islamic World [Medieval Islamic social & religious history, esp. in Iberia & north Africa; medieval historiography; Muslim-Christian relations in the medieval period], nicola.clarke@ncl.ac.uk

Andrea Dolfini, Lect. in Later Prehist. [Prehistoric metallurgy; the house & the household], andrea.dolfini@ncl.ac.uk

Martin Dusinberre, B.A., M.A. (Lond.), D.Phil. (Oxon.), Lect. in Mod. Japanese Hist. [Social & cultural history of Japan, mid 19th–mid 20th c.], martin.dusinberre@ncl.ac.uk

Martin Farr, B.A. (Exeter), Ph.D. (Glas.), Sen. Lect. in Mod. Brit. Hist. (20th c.) [High politics; political economy; biography; elections], martin.farr@ncl.ac.uk

Susan-Mary C. Grant, M.A. (Edin. & Lond.), Ph.D. (Lond.), Prof. of Amer. Hist. (19th c. U.S.A.) [American Civil War; nationalism in 19th c.], susan.grant@ncl.ac.uk

*Rachel Hammersley, B.A. (Cantab.), M.A., D.Phil. (Sussex), Sen. Lect. in Intellectual Hist. (17th & 18th c. Anglo-French Hist.) [Intellectual history; democracy; republicanism; revolution], rachel.hammersley@ncl.ac.uk

Violetta Hionidou, B.Sc., M.Sc. (Athens), M.Sc. (Lond.), Ph.D. (Liv.), Sen. Lect. in Mod. Eur. Hist. [Demographic, social, economic & medical history of 19th & 20th c. Greece; famines; birth control; family history], violetta.hionidou@ncl.ac.uk

Benjamin Houston, B.A. (Rhodes Coll.), M.A., Ph.D. (Florida), Lect. in U.S. Hist. [Civil rights movement; southern U.S.; nonviolence; oral history], ben.houston@ncl.ac.uk

Timothy Kirk, B.A., Ph.D. (Manc.), Prof. of Eur. Hist. (Mod. Eur., esp. Central Eur.) [Nazi new order; urban culture in the Habsburg empire], tim.kirk@ncl.ac.uk

Mark Lawrence, Teaching Fellow in Hist. [19th & 20th c. European history; Spain; conflict], mark.lawrence@ncl.ac.uk

Joseph Lawson, B.A. (Otago), Ph.D. (Wellington), Lect. in Mod. Chinese Hist. (19th & 20th c.) [19th & 20th c. Chinese history; ethnic conflict; economic history; agricultural history; intellectual history], joseph.lawson@ncl.ac.uk

Don Miller, Teaching Fellow in Greek Hist., don.miller@ncl.ac.uk

Diana Paton, B.A. (Warwick), Ph.D. (Yale), Reader in Caribbean Hist. [Comparative slavery; slave emancipation; 18th–19th c. Anglophone Caribbean; gender], diana.paton@ncl.ac.uk

Matthew Perry, B.A., Ph.D. (Wolverhampton), Reader in Labour Hist. [Unemployment; political protest], matt.perry@ncl.ac.uk

Alejandro Quiroga, B.A. (Madrid), M.A. (Madrid & Florida International), Ph.D. (Lond.), Reader in Spanish Hist. [Modern European history; 20th c. Spain; nationalism], alejandro.quiroga@ncl.ac.uk

Luc Racaut, B.A., M.Phil, Ph.D., Lect. in Early Mod. Hist. [French Wars of Religion; Reformation Europe], luc.racaut@ncl.ac.uk

Anne E. Redgate, M.A. (Oxon.), Lect. in Hist. (Anglo-Saxon Eng., Early Med. Eur., Armenian Hist.) [Heresy; ethnicity; comparative history], anne.redgate@ncl.ac.uk

Thomas Rodgers, B.A., M.A. (Cantab.), Ph.D. (Warwick), Teaching Fellow in Hist. [18th & early 19th c. American history; British Atlantic world; history of the state, governance & political culture; American Revolution], tom.rodgers@ncl.ac.uk

Thomas Rütten, Ph.D. (Münster), Reader in Hist. of Medicine (Hist. of Medicine), thomas.rutten@ncl.ac.uk

Federico Santangelo, Lect. in Anc. Hist. [Roman Republic; ancient divination; Roman colonisation], federico.santangelo@ncl.ac.uk

David Saunders, M.A., D.Phil. (Oxon.), Prof. (19th–20th c. Eur., esp. Russia & Ukraine) [Russian & Ukrainian history, esp. society, politics, historiography & ethnic relations], d.b.saunders@ncl.ac.uk

Felix R. Schulz, B.A. (Kent), M.A., Ph.D. (York), Lect. in Mod. Eur. Hist. [Social & cultural history of 20th c. Germany & central Europe], felix.schulz@ncl.ac.uk

Samiksha Sehrawat, B.A., M.A. (Delhi), D.Phil. (Oxon.), Lect. in Indian Hist. (Hist. of Medicine), samiksha.sehrawat@ncl.ac.uk

Rowland Smith, Lect. in Anc. Hist. (Late Roman Antiquity, Early Christianity), rowland.smith@ncl.ac.uk

Anthony J.S. Spawforth, B.A., Ph.D. (Birm.), Prof. of Anc. Hist., tony.spawforth@ncl.ac.uk
Jane L. Webster, B.A. (Nott.), Ph.D. (Edin.), Sen. Lect. in Hist. Archaeol. (Archaeol.
 of Atlantic Slave Trade) [Historical archaeology, esp. the study of colonialism],
 jane.webster@ncl.ac.uk

UNIVERSITY OF **NORTHAMPTON**

Moulton Park, Northampton, NN2 7AL. 01604 735500. Fax 01604 720636
www.northampton.ac.uk
School of Social Sciences: Division of History

Jim Beach, B.A. (Plymouth), M.A. (Lond.), M.Sc. (Leicester), Ph.D. (Lond.), Sen. Lect. in Hist.
 (20th c.) [Military & intelligence history], Jim.Beach@northampton.ac.uk
William J. Berridge, B.A., M.A., Ph.D. (Dunelm.), Lect. in Hist. (Imp., Afric. & Mid. E., 19th &
 20th c.) [Colonial policing; civil protest], William.Berridge@northampton.ac.uk
Drew D. Gray, B.A. (Leicester), Ph.D. (Northampton), Sen. Lect. in Hist. (18th & 19th c. Brit.
 Soc. Hist.) [Crime & punishment], Drew.Gray@northampton.ac.uk
Paul N. Jackson, B.A. (Middlesex), M.A., Ph.D. (Oxf. Brookes), Lect. in Hist.
 (20th c. Brit. & Eur.) [Generic fascism & far right; cultures of modernism],
 Paul.Jackson@northampton.ac.uk
Matthew L. McCormack, B.A. (York), M.A., Ph.D. (Manc.), Sen. Lect. in Hist.
 (19th c. Brit. Soc. & Pol. Hist) [18th & 19th c. Britain; gender; cultural history],
 Matthew.McCormack@northampton.ac.uk
Ronald Mendel, B.A. (City Coll. of N.Y.), M.A. (N. Carolina), Ph.D. (City Univ.,
 N.Y.), Sen. Lect. in Hist. (U.S. Econ. & Soc.) [U.S. labour history c.1877–1919],
 Ron.Mendel@northampton.ac.uk
Tim Reinke-Williams, B.A., M.A., Ph.D. (Warwick), Lect. in Hist. (15th–18th c. Brit. & Eur.)
 [Social, economic & cultural history of early modern Britain; women & gender; London],
 Tim.Reinke-Williams@northampton.ac.uk
Mark Rothery, B.A., M.A., Ph.D. (Exeter), Sen. Lect. in Hist. (Mod. Brit.) [Landed elites;
 gender; pressure group politics], Mark.Rothery@northampton.ac.uk
*Catherine A. Smith, B.A. (Loughborough), Ph.D. (Nott.), Princ. Lect. in Hist., Head of Dept.
 (Early Mod.) [Social, economic & cultural development of urban society, 1680–1840; history
 of madness & asylums], Cathy.Smith@northampton.ac.uk
Sally I. Sokoloff, B.A., Ph.D. (Lond.), Lect. in Hist., p/t (Mod.) [Britain & the Second World
 War], Sally.Sokoloff@northampton.ac.uk
Jon V. Stobart, B.A., D.Phil. (Oxon.), Prof. of Hist. (18th & 19th c. Brit. Soc. & Econ.)
 [Early industrialisation & urban history; material culture; consumption & retailing],
 Jon.Stobart@northampton.ac.uk
David Waller, B.A. (Oxon.), M.A. (Lond.), Sen. Lect. in Pol. (U.S.) [Employment training &
 welfare reforms in U.S.], David.Waller@northampton.ac.uk

NORTHUMBRIA UNIVERSITY

Ellison Building, Ellison Place, Newcastle upon Tyne, NE1 8ST. 0191 232 6002.
Fax 0191 227 4017
www.northumbria.ac.uk
School of Arts & Social Sciences
Lipman Building, Sandyford Road, Newcastle upon Tyne, NE1 8ST. 0191 227 4995.
Fax 0191 227 4572

Charlotte Alston, B.A., M.Litt., Ph.D. (Newcastle), Sen. Lect. in Hist. (Int. Hist.) [History of
Russia & eastern Europe, c.1890–1940], charlotte.alston@northumbria.ac.uk
Tanja Bueltmann, M.A., Ph.D., Sen. Lect. in Hist. (Int. Hist.) [British world history; ethnic
associational culture; Scottish & English diaspora; Australasia; North America],
tanja.bueltmann@northumbria.ac.uk
Michael P. Cullinane, Ph.D. (N.U.I.), Sen. Lect. in Amer. Hist. [19th–20th c. diplomatic history],
michael.cullinane@northumbria.ac.uk
Sylvia Ellis, B.A., M.A., Ph.D. (Newcastle), Prof. [Anglo-American relations; Vietnam War;
post-war British & American history], sylvia.ellis@northumbria.ac.uk
Malcolm Gee, B.A. (Oxon.), M.A., Ph.D. (Lond.), Princ. Lect. in Art Hist. [20th c.
art movements; the art market; European urban cultures in the modern period],
malcolm.gee@northumbria.ac.uk
David T. Gleeson, Ph.D. (Mississippi State), Reader in Hist. (U.S.) [Irish & English immigrants;
ethnicity & race in the 19th c.], david.gleeson@northumbria.ac.uk
Anja-Silvia Goeing, M.St. (Oxon.), M.A., Dr.phil. (Würzburg), PD (Zurich), Anniversary Fellow
(Renaissance & Early Mod. Eur.) [Intellectual & cultural history; history of knowledge;
material cultures; history of the book]
Joseph Hardwick, Ph.D. (York), Lect. in Brit. Hist. (Brit.) [Political, imperial & religious history],
joseph.hardwick@northumbria.ac.uk
Alan L. Harvey, B.A., Ph.D. (Birm.), Sen. Lect. in Hist. (Med.) [Byzantine economic history,
10th–15th c.], alan.harvey@northumbria.ac.uk
Andrea E. Knox, B.A. (C.N.A.A.), M.Phil. (Northumbria), Sen. Lect. in Hist. (Early Mod.,
Gender) [Early modern Irish & English female criminality]
Elizabeth Kramer, Ph.D. (Manc.), Sen. Lect. in Design Hist. [Anglo-Japanese relations; 19th
c. textiles; material culture of manias], elizabeth.kramer@northumbria.ac.uk
Tom Lawson, B.A. (York), M.A. (Dunelm.), Ph.D. (Southampton), Prof. of Hist. (19th & 20th c.
Brit. & Eur.) [Holocaust; genocide; settler colonialism in Australia; history & memory]
Daniel Laqua, B.A., M.St. (Oxon.), Ph.D. (Lond.), Lect. in Eur. Hist. (Mod. Eur.) [Transnational
history; internationalism; western Europe, 19th & 20th c.], daniel.laqua@northumbria.ac.uk
James McConnel, Ph.D. (Dunelm.), Princ. Lect. in Hist. (Irish Hist.) [Irish politics, 1870–1918],
james.mcconnel@northumbria.ac.uk
Gaby Mahlberg, B.A., M.A., Ph.D. (East Anglia), Lect. in Hist. (Early Mod. Brit.) [Intellectual &
cultural history; republicanism; utopianism], gaby.mahlberg@northumbria.ac.uk
Matthew Potter, M.A., Ph.D. (Lond.), Sen. Lect. in Art & Design Hist. [British & world visual
culture; Anglo-German exchange, 1850–1939], matthew.potter@northumbria.ac.uk
Colin W. Reid, B.A., M.A., Ph.D. (Belf.), Sen. Lect. in Hist. (Mod. Irish) [19th &
20th c. Irish political, cultural & diaspora history; history of political thought],
colin.w.reid@northumbria.ac.uk
Nicole Robertson, B.A., M.A., Ph.D., Sen. Lect. in Hist. (Mod. Brit.) [Co-operative movement;
consumerism; labour history], nicole.robertson@northumbria.ac.uk

Joe Street, Ph.D. (Sheff.), Sen. Lect. in Amer. Hist. (Soc. & Cultural) [Post-1945
  African American politics & popular culture; post-1945 San Francisco Bay Area],
  joe.street@northumbria.ac.uk
Avram G. Taylor, B.A. (C.N.A.A.), Ph.D. (Dunelm.), Sen. Lect. in Hist. (Mod.)
  [History & theory; communities; credit, debt & poverty; Jews in 20th c. Britain],
  avram.taylor@northumbria.ac.uk
Anthony Webster, B.A., Ph.D. (Birm.), Prof. of Hist. (18th–20th c. Eur. Imp.) [History of the
  British empire & cooperative movement], tony.webster@northumbria.ac.uk
Howard J. Wickes, M.A. (Oxon.), Princ. Lect. in Hist. (Intellectual & Cultural) [Descartes; 17th
  c. natural philosophy], howard.wickes@northumbria.ac.uk

UNIVERSITY OF **NOTTINGHAM**

University Park, Nottingham, NG7 2RD. 0115 951 5151. Fax 0115 951 3666
www.nottingham.ac.uk
Department of History 0115 951 5928. Fax 0115 951 5948
www.nottingham.ac.uk/history/
Department of Archaeology 0115 951 4820. Fax 0115 951 4812
www.nottingham.ac.uk/archaeology/
Department of Art History 0115 951 3185. Fax 0115 846 7778
www.nottingham.ac.uk/arthistory/
Department of Classics 0115 951 4800. Fax 0115 951 4811
www.nottingham.ac.uk/classics/
Department of French, Department of Music
Department of Theology & Religious Studies 0115 951 5852. Fax 0115 951 5887
www.nottingham.ac.uk/theology/
School of American & Canadian Studies 0115 951 4261. Fax 0115 951 4270
www.nottingham.ac.uk/american/
School of English, School of Politics

Karen H. Adler, B.A., D.Phil. (Sussex), Lect. in Mod. Eur. [20th c. France; gender; Jewish
  history; France & Indochina], karen.adler@nottingham.ac.uk
Beverley Afton, B.A. (Open), Ph.D. (Read.), Special Lect. in Agrarian Hist.
Nicholas Alfrey, M.A. (Edin. & Lond.), Sen. Lect. in Art Hist. (17th–19th c. French Art)
David Appleby, B.A. (De Montfort), M.A. (Essex), Ph.D. (Keele), (17th c. Brit.),
  david.appleby@nottingham.ac.uk
Joerg Arnold, M.A., Ph.D. (Southampton), Lect. in Mod. Eur. Hist. [Modern German
  history; comparative history of de-industrialisation in Britain, Germany & the U.S.],
  joerg.arnold@nottingham.ac.uk
John Ashworth, B.A., M.Litt. (Lancaster), D.Phil. (Oxon.), Prof. of Amer. Hist. [Coming of U.S.
  Civil War; slavery debate]
Katie Attwood, B.A. (Lond.), D.Phil. (Oxon.), Lect. in Med. French (14th–15th c. French
  Literature), catherine.attwood@nottingham.ac.uk
Sarah Badcock, B.A. (Leeds), M.A., Ph.D. (Dunelm.), Sen. Lect. in Mod. Hist. [The Russian
  provinces, 1917–21], sarah.badcock@nottingham.ac.uk
John Baker, B.A., Ph.D. (Birm.), Res. Fellow, Institute for Name-Studies [Place-names; early
  medieval England; landscape history], john.baker@nottingham.ac.uk
Simon Baker, B.A., M.A., Ph.D. (Lond.), Lect. in Art Hist. [Surrealism & photography in France
  in 1920s & 1930s], simon.baker@nottingham.ac.uk

Rossano Balzaretti, B.A., Ph.D. (Lond.), Sen. Lect. in Med. Hist. (5th–15th c. Eur.), ross.balzaretti@nottingham.ac.uk

Stephen J. Bamforth, B.A., Ph.D. (Dunelm.), Prof. of Renaissance Stud. (16th c. French Literature & Hist.), stephen.bamforth@nottingham.ac.uk

Nicholas Baron, M.A., M.Phil. (Oxon.), Ph.D. (Birm.), Sen. Lect. in Mod. Hist. (Russian & E. Eur. Hist.), nick.baron@nottingham.ac.uk

John V. Beckett, B.A., Ph.D. (Lancaster), Prof. of Eng. Regional Hist. (16th–20th c. Brit. & Eur.) [Agricultural productivity in England, 1660–1914; British social history during World War I], john.beckett@nottingham.ac.uk

Richard Bell, B.Sc. (Lond.), M.A. (Oxon.), Ph.D. (Lond.), Dr.theol. (Tübingen), Reader in Theol. [New Testament; Paul], richard.bell@nottingham.ac.uk

William Bowden, B.A. (Lond.), Ph.D. (East Anglia), Lect. in Archaeol. [Roman empire; Roman & late antique Mediterranean; archaeology of urbanism], will.bowden@nottingham.ac.uk

Peter G. Boyle, M.A. (Glas.), Ph.D. (Calif.), Assoc. Prof. in Amer. Stud. (17th–20th c.)

Mark Bradley, M.A., Ph.D. (Cantab.), Lect. in Anc. Hist. [Visual & intellectual culture of Imperial Rome], mark.bradley@nottingham.ac.uk

Ken Brand, Special Lect. in Local Hist.

Sarah Browne, M.A. (Hons.), M.Litt., Ph.D. (Dundee), Teaching Assoc. in 20th c. Hist. (Contemp. World, Gender & Sexuality) [Late 19th & 20th c. Britain], sarah.browne@nottingham.ac.uk

Jayne Carroll, B.A., M.A. (Lond.), Ph.D. (Nott.), Director of Inst. for Name-Studies [Place- & personal names; Old English & Old Norse language & literature; history of English], jayne.carroll@nottingham.ac.uk

William G. Cavanagh, M.A. (Edin.), Ph.D. (Lond.), Emeritus Prof. of Archaeol. (2000–500 B.C. E. Mediterranean) [Greek bronze age; Bayesian statistics; Laconia; Sparta]

Paul Cavill, B.A., M.Phil. (Hull), Ph.D. (Nott.), Lect. in Early Eng. [Anglo-Saxon history & Old English literature; place-names; history of the language], paul.cavill@nottingham.ac.uk

Andrew J. Cobbing, B.A. (Brist.), M.A. (Kyushu), Ph.D. (Lond.), Sen. Lect. in Mod. Hist. [Cultural relations & modern Japan], andrew.cobbing@nottingham.ac.uk

Harry Cocks, B.A. (Birm.), M.A. (Sussex), Ph.D. (Manc.), Lect. [Modern Britain since 1750; history of gender, sexuality & the self], harry.cocks@nottingham.ac.uk

Helen Cooney, B.A., Ph.D. (Dublin), M.A. (Brist.), Lect. in Med. Eng.

David Crook, M.A., Ph.D. (Read.)

Fintan Cullen, B.A., M.A. (Dublin), Ph.D. (York), Prof. of Art Hist. (17th–19th c. Irish Art)

Roland Deines, Dip.dr.habil. (Tübingen), Assoc. Prof. & Reader in Theol. [New Testament], roland.deines@nottingham.ac.uk

Gwilym Dodd, B.A. (York), M.Phil. (Cantab.), D.Phil. (York), Sen. Lect. in Med. Hist., gwilym.dodd@nottingham.ac.uk

Eddy Faber, B.Sc., Ph.D. (Sheff.), Teaching Assoc. & Res. Technician [Archaeological materials, esp. ceramics], edward.faber@nottingham.ac.uk

Patrick Finglass, B.A., D.Phil. (Oxon.), Lect. in Classical Stud. [Greek poetry], patrick.finglass@nottingham.ac.uk

Alan Ford, B.A. (Dublin), Ph.D. (Cantab.), Prof. of Theol. (Reformation Hist.), alan.ford@nottingham.ac.uk

Rebecca Ford, B.A., Ph.D. (Exeter), [Enlightenment thought & literature; history of science in 18th c. France], rebecca.ford@nottingham.ac.uk

Lynn Fotheringham, M.A. (Edin.), D.Phil. (Oxon.), Lect. in Classics, lynn.fotheringham@nottingham.ac.uk

Chrysanthi Gallou, B.A. (Liv.), Ph.D. (Nott.), Lect. in Archaeol. [Greek bronze age], chrysanthi.gallou@nottingham.ac.uk

Richard Gaunt, B.A., Ph.D. (Nott.), Sen. Lect. in Mod. Hist. [Conservative party c.1806–52], richard.gaunt@nottingham.ac.uk

Richard J. Geary, M.A., Ph.D. (Cantab.), Emeritus Prof. (19th–20th c. Brit. & Eur.) [Unemployment in inter-war Europe; comparative history of slavery], dick.geary@nottingham.ac.uk

Hugh Goddard, M.A. (Oxon.), Ph.D. (Birm.), Prof. of Islamic Stud.

Richard Goddard, B.A., M.A. (Read.), Ph.D. (Birm.), Lect. in Med. Hist. (Eng. Urban Hist.), richard.goddard@nottingham.ac.uk

Philip Goodchild, B.A., M.A., Ph.D. (Lancaster), Prof. of Theol. [Philosophy of religion], philip.goodchild@nottingham.ac.uk

Christian Haase, M.A. (Berlin), D.Phil. (Oxon.), Lect. in Mod. Hist. [Modern German & West European history since 1860], christian.haase@nottingham.ac.uk

Sheryllynne Haggerty, B.A., Ph.D. (Liv.), Sen. Lect. in Early Mod. Brit. Hist. [18th c. British Atlantic trade & networks; slave trade; 18th c. towns], sheryllynne.haggerty@nottingham.ac.uk

*Elizabeth R. Harvey, B.A., D.Phil. (Oxon.), Prof. of Mod. Hist. (20th c. Eur.) [20th c. Germany; gender history], elizabeth.harvey@nottingham.ac.uk

James Helgeson, B.A. (Oberlin), Ph.D. (Princeton), [Early modern French history; literary historiography; history of first-person writing]

Jon C. Henderson, B.A., M.A. (Edin.), D.Phil. (Oxon.), Lect. in Archaeol. [Underwater archaeology; later prehistory of Europe], jon.henderson@nottingham.ac.uk

Julian Henderson, B.A. (Belf.), Ph.D. (Bradford), Prof. of Archaeol. (Med.) [Early medieval European & early Islamic technology]

Nicholas Hewitt, B.A., Ph.D. (Hull), Emeritus Prof. of French (20th c. France) [20th c. French cultural history], nicholas.hewitt@nottingham.ac.uk

Colin M. Heywood, B.A., Ph.D. (Read.), Emeritus Prof. of Econ. & Soc. Hist. (16th–20th c. Eur.) [History of Troyes (France); history of childhood], colin.heywood@nottingham.ac.uk

Stephen Hodkinson, B.A. (Manc.), Ph.D. (Cantab.), Prof. of Anc. Hist., stephen.hodkinson@nottingham.ac.uk

Richard Hornsey, B.A., Ph.D. (Sussex), Lect. in Mod. Brit. Hist. [Urban space; sexuality], richard.hornsey@nottingham.ac.uk

Daniel Hucker, B.Sc.(Econ.), M.Sc.(Econ.)., Ph.D. (Wales), Teaching Assoc. in 20th c. Hist. (British Foreign Policy, Mod. Hist.) [Role of public opinion in the foreign policy-making process], daniel.hucker@nottingham.ac.uk

Judith Jesch, B.A. (Dunelm.), Ph.D. (Lond.), Prof. of Viking Stud. (6th–11th c. Anglo-Saxons, Vikings) [Old English & Old Norse language & literature; Viking studies], judith.jesch@nottingham.ac.uk

Michael Jones, M.A., D.Phil., D.Litt. (Oxon.)

Mike Rodman Jones, B.A. (Oxon.), M.A., Ph.D. (York), Lect. in Med. Literature [Later medieval literature; religious cultures; Tudor literature]

Karen Kilby, B.A., Ph.D. (Yale), Assoc. Prof. in Theol. [Systematic & philosophical theology], karen.kilby@nottingham.ac.uk

Christopher King, B.A. (Reading), M.A. (York), Ph.D. (Reading), Lect. in Archaeol. [Medieval & post-medieval Britain; buildings archaeology], chris.king@nottingham.ac.uk

Richard H. King, B.A. (N. Carolina), M.A. (Yale), Ph.D. (Va.), Emeritus Prof. of Amer. Intellectual Hist. (20th c. Amer.) [Histories & theories of racism since 1945]

Frances Knight, B.D., M.Th. (Lond.) Ph.D. (Cantab.), Assoc. Prof. of Hist. Theol. [19th–20th c. religious history], frances.knight@nottingham.ac.uk

Alison Kraft, M.Sc., Ph.D. (Manc.)

Andreas Kropp, B.A. (Beirut), M.St. (Oxon.), Lect. in Classical Art, andreas.kropp@nottingham.ac.uk

Jonathan Kwan, B.A., LL.B. (Queensland), M.A. (Lond.), D.Phil. (Oxon.), Lect. in Mod. Hist. [Austro-Hungarian empire], jonathan.kwan@nottingham.ac.uk

Robert A. Lambert, M.A., Ph.D. (St. And.), Lect. in Environ. Hist. [British global & environmental history; tourism history; public history & heritage], robert.lambert@nottingham.ac.uk

David Laven, M.A., Ph.D. (Cantab.), Sen. Lect. in Mod. Eur. Hist. (Mod. Italian Hist.) [Modern Italy; modern France; formation of national identities; historical memory; Romantic literature & politics], david.laven@nottingham.ac.uk

Christina Lee, M.A., Ph.D. (Newcastle), Lect. in Viking Stud. & Anglo-Saxon Eng. [Viking studies; early medieval Britain; Old English & Old Norse language & literature], christina.lee@nottingham.ac.uk

Doug Lee, B.A. (Sydney), Ph.D. (Cantab.), Assoc. Prof. in Classical Stud., doug.lee@nottingham.ac.uk

Stephanie Lewthwaite, B.A., M.A., Ph.D. (Warwick), Lect. in Amer. Hist., stephanie.lewthwaite@nottingham.ac.uk

Peter J. Ling, B.A., M.A. (Lond.), Ph.D. (Keele), Prof. of Amer. Stud. (19th–20th c.) [Political education in civil rights movement; 20th c. African-American history]

Alexandra Livarda, B.Sc. (Coventry), M.Sc. (Sheff.), Ph.D. (Leicester), Lect. in Archaeol. [Archaeobotany], alexandra.livarda@nottingham.ac.uk

Katharina Lorenz, Ph.D. (Heid.), Assoc. Prof. in Classical Art [Graeco-Roman art & society], katharina.lorenz@nottingham.ac.uk

Anna Lovatt, B.A., M.A., Ph.D. (Lond.), Lect. in Art Hist. [Sculptural practices in New York in the 1960s & 1970s]

Christopher Loveluck, B.A., Ph.D., Lect. in Archaeol. [Societies in Europe A.D. 400–1500], christopher.loveluck@nottingham.ac.uk

Rob Lutton, B.A., Ph.D. (Kent), Lect. [Religious practices & beliefs of lay people in England in the 15th & 16th c.], rob.lutton@nottingham.ac.uk

Alison McHardy, M.A. (Edin.), D.Phil. (Oxon.)

Michael Mack, M.A., Ph.D. (Cantab.), Lect. in Relig. Stud., michael.mack@nottingham.ac.uk

David Marcombe, B.A. (York), Ph.D. (Dunelm.), Sen. Lect. in Hist., Adult Educ. (Brit. Local Hist.)

Richard Marsden, B.A. (York), Ph.D. (Cantab.), Emeritus Prof. of Med. Eng. [Old English language & literature; the earliest Biblical translations; the history of English; the Latin Bible], richard.marsden@nottingham.ac.uk

Joanna Martin, B.A., M.St., D.Phil. (Oxon.), Lect. [Late medieval English literature; older Scots literature; book history], joanna.martin@nottingham.ac.uk

Spencer W. Mawby, B.A. (Dunelm.), M.Sc. (Wales), Ph.D. (Lond.), Sen. Lect. in Mod. Hist. [International relations since 1945; the Middle East], spencer.mawby@nottingham.ac.uk

Helen E. Meller, B.A., Ph.D. (Brist.), Prof. Emerita (18th–20th c. Brit. & Eur.) [Social & cultural history of European cities, 1890–1990], helen.meller@nottingham.ac.uk

Julia F. Merritt, B.A., M.A. (Los Angeles), Ph.D. (Lond.), Sen. Lect. in Hist. [Social, religious & urban history of early modern England, esp. London]

Joe Merton, B.A. (Sheff.), M.St., D.Phil. (Oxon.), Teaching Assoc. in 20th c. Hist. (Mod. Hist., Vietnam War, Cold War) [Social & political history of the 20th c. U.S.], joe.merton@nottingham.ac.uk

A. John Milbank, Prof. of Theol. [Philosophical theology], john.milbank@nottingham.ac.uk

Alison Milbank, B.A. (Cantab.), Ph.D. (Lancaster), Assoc. Prof. in Theol. [Religion in post-Enlightenment thought], alison.milbank@nottingham.ac.uk

Vivien Miller, B.A. (Newcastle), M.A. (Florida State), Ph.D. (Open), Assoc. Prof. in Amer. Hist., vivien.miller@nottingham.ac.uk

Judith Mossman, M.A., D.Phil. (Oxon.), Prof. [Greek literature], judith.mossman@nottingham.ac.uk

Julie Mumby, [Early medieval English history]

Gabrielle Neher, M.A. (Aberd.), Ph.D. (Warwick), Lect. in Art Hist. (15th–16th Italian Art)

David Nicolle, M.A., Ph.D. (Edin.), Visiting Fellow in Med. Stud. (5th–16th c. Eur., Islam) [Medieval Muslim-Christian political & cultural relations]

Thomas O'Loughlin, B.A., B.D., M.Phil., Ph.D. (N.U.I.), Prof. of. Hist. Theol. (Early & Med. Church Hist., Hist. of Theol.) [History of medieval ideas; patristics; history of scriptural exegesis; insular Christianity in the medieval period; medieval cartography], tom.o'loughlin@nottingham.ac.uk

Hannah O'Regan, B.Sc. (Bradford), Ph.D. (L.J.M.U.), Lect. in Archaeol. (Archaeol.) [Pre-history; cave archaeology], hannah.o'regan@nottingham.ac.uk

David Parsons, B.A. (Lond.), M.A. (Nott.), Ph.D. (Cantab.), Reader in Name-Studies [Old English & Old Norse language; Anglo-Saxon inscriptions; English place-names; history of English dialects], david.parsons@nottingham.ac.uk

*Mark Pearce, M.A. (Cantab.), Ph.D. (Lancaster), Assoc. Prof. in Archaeol., mark.pearce@nottingham.ac.uk

Sara Pons-Sanz, B.A. (Valencia), M.Phil., Ph.D. (Cantab.), Lect. [Old & Middle English language & literature; history of the English language; Old Norse language & literature], sara.pons-sanz@nottingham.ac.uk

Andrew G. Poulter, B.A., M.A. (Birm.), Ph.D. (Lond.), Prof. of Archaeol. (500 B.C.–500 A.D. Roman), andrew.poulter@nottingham.ac.uk

Mark Rawlinson, B.A. (Nott. Trent), M.A., Ph.D. (Nott.), Lect. in Art Hist. [20th c. American art/ visual culture; critical & visual theory], mark.rawlinson@nottingham.ac.uk

John W. Rich, M.A., M.Phil. (Oxon.), Prof. of Classical Stud. (8th c. B.C.–5th c. A.D. Roman Hist.) [Roman history; ancient warfare & international relations]

Else Roesdahl, Cand. Art. (Copenhagen), Special Prof. in Viking Stud. (5th–12th c. Eur.) [Viking age; conversion; Scandinavia]

Alan Rogers, B.A., M.A., Ph.D. (Nott.)

Nicola Royan, M.A. (Glas.), D.Phil. (Oxon.), Lect. in Med. & Renaissance Literature [Late medieval & early modern literatures, English & Scottish; representations of kinship & national identity; devotional lyric & Arthurian romance], nicola.royan@nottingham.ac.uk

Maria Ryan, B.A. (Sheff.), M.Phil., Ph.D. (Birm.), Lect. in Amer. Hist., maria.ryan@nottingham.ac.uk

Bevan Sewell, B.A. (De Montfort), M.Phil. (Birm.), Ph.D. (De Montfort), Lect. in Amer. Foreign Relations, bevan.sewell@nottingham.ac.uk

Liudmyla Sharipova, Lect. [The European Reformations], liudmyla.sharipova@nottingham.ac.uk

Jackie Sheehan, B.A. (Cantab.), Ph.D. (Lond.), Lect. in Chinese Stud. [Workers' opposition in China]

Katherine Shingler, B.A., Ph.D. (Brist.), [Word & image studies; 19th & 20th c. visual culture], katherine.shingler@nottingham.ac.uk

Paul E.A. Smith, B.A. (Lond.), D.Phil. (Oxon.), Assoc. Prof. in French (20th c. France) [19th & 20th c. French politics, political institutions & political culture; Senate of French Third Republic], paul.smith@nottingham.ac.uk

Alan Sommerstein, M.A., Ph.D. (Cantab.), Prof. of Greek, alan.sommerstein@nottingham.ac.uk

Sarah Speight, B.A. (Manc.), Ph.D. (Nott.), Lect. in Hist., Cont. Educ. (Med.)

A.R. Sutcliffe, M.A. (Oxon.), D.U. (Paris), Special Prof. (Mod. Eur., Urban Hist.)

Naomi Sykes, B.Sc., M.Sc. (Lond.), Ph.D. (Southampton), Lect. in Archaeol. [Zooarchaeology; osteoarchaeology], naomi.sykes@nottingham.ac.uk

Claire Taylor, B.A., Ph.D. (Nott.), Sen. Lect. in Med. Hist., claire.k.taylor@nottingham.ac.uk

Anthony Thiselton, Ph.D., D.D., Prof. of Christian Theol.

Nicholas Thomas, B.A., Ph.D. (Warwick), Lect. in 20th c. Hist. (Brit. & Germany since 1945), nick.thomas@nottingham.ac.uk

Susan C. Townsend, B.A. (C.N.A.A.), Ph.D. (Sheff.), Sen. Lect. in Mod. Hist. (Japan), sue.townsend@nottingham.ac.uk

Thorlac S.F. Turville-Petre, M.A., B.Litt. (Oxon.), Emeritus Prof. of Med. Eng. Literature (13th–15th c. Brit.), thorlac.turville-petre@nottingham.ac.uk

Maiken Umbach, M.A., Ph.D. (Cantab.), Prof. of Mod. Hist. [Modern German & Spanish history; regionalism, federalism & urban history; culture & National Socialism; history of photography], maiken.umbach@nottingham.ac.uk

Betine van Zyl Smit, Assoc. Prof. in Classics, abzcv@nottingham.ac.uk

Robin Vandome, B.A., M.A., Ph.D. (Cantab.), Lect. in Amer. Culture & Intellectual Hist., robin.vandome@nottingham.ac.uk

Konstantinos Vlassopoulos, Lect. in Greek Hist., konstantinos.vlassopoulos@nottingham.ac.uk

Mathilde von Bülow, B.A. (Toronto), M.Phil. (Cantab.), Lect. in Mod. Hist. [20th c. international history; France; the Arab world], mathilde.vonbulow@nottingham.ac.uk

Margaret Walsh, M.A. (St. And. & Smith Coll., Mass.), Ph.D. (Wis.), Emerita Prof. of Amer. Econ. & Soc. Hist. (19th–20th c.) [Long-distance bus industry in U.S.; America's working women; the American West]

Lloyd Weeks, B.A., Ph.D. (Sydney), Lect. in Archaeol. [Western Asia, esp. Iran & Persian Gulf], lloyd.weeks@nottingham.ac.uk

Richard I. Winton, M.A., Ph.D. (Cantab.), Lect. in Classical Stud. (10th–3rd c. B.C. Greek) [Thucydides]

Jeremy Wood, B.A. (Read.), Assoc. Prof. in Art Hist. (17th c. Eng. Art)

Joanne Wright, M.A. (Edin.), (15th c. Italian Art)

Peter Wright, B.A., B.Mus. (Oxon.), M.A., Ph.D. (Nott.), Reader in Music (15th c. Italian Music)

Christopher J. Wrigley, B.A., Litt.D. (East Anglia), Ph.D. (Lond.), Emeritus Prof. of Mod. Brit. Hist. (19th–20th c. Brit. & Eur.) [20th c. British economic, social & political history; history of industrial relations], chris.wrigley@nottingham.ac.uk

Richard Wrigley, B.A. (Read.), D.Phil. (Oxon.), Prof. of Art Hist. [18th & 19th c. studies, esp. French material], richard.wrigley@nottingham.ac.uk

Kathrin Yacavone, B.A. (Freie Univ., Berlin), Ph.D. (Edin.), [Visual studies; history of photography], kathrin.yacavone@nottingham.ac.uk

John W. Young, B.A. (Nott.), Ph.D. (Cantab.), Prof. of Int. Hist. [Cold War & British foreign policy], john.young@nottingham.ac.uk

NOTTINGHAM TRENT UNIVERSITY
Burton Street, Nottingham, NG1 4BU. 0115 941 8418. Fax 0115 948 4766
www.ntu.ac.uk
School of Arts & Humanities
Department of History & Heritage
Clifton Lane, Nottingham, NG11 8NS. 0115 848 3175. Fax 0115 848 6385

Martyn Bennett, B.A., Ph.D., (Loughborough), Prof. of Early Mod. Hist. (Early Mod. Brit. & Ireland) [Formation & social, cultural & political development of the nations of the British Isles, c.1590–1689; Oliver Cromwell], martyn.bennett@ntu.ac.uk

Graham Black, B.A., A.M.A. (Leicester), Reader in Public Hist. & Heritage Management (Museum Learning & Interpretation, Public Hist.) [Informal learning & audience engagement in museums; city history museums; museums & civil engagement; history, memory & museums], graham.black@ntu.ac.uk

*Angela Brown, B.A. (Wales), M.A. (Open), Head of Hist. & Heritage [Early modern society & culture; teaching & learning of history in higher education], angela.brown@ntu.ac.uk

Stuart Burch, B.A. M.A. (Leeds), Ph.D. (Nott. Trent), Sen. Lect. in Public Hist. (19th & 20th c. Brit. & Scandinavian Hist.), stuart.burch@ntu.ac.uk

Mercedes Carbayo-Abengozar, B.A. (Alcalá), Ph.D. (Dunelm.), Lect. in Mod. Spanish Hist. (19th–20th c.) [Constructions of identity – gender, nation – through popular culture], mercedes.carbayo-abengozar@ntu.ac.uk

Amy Fuller, B.A., M.A., Ph.D. (Manc.), Lect. in the Hist. of the Americas (15th–18th c.) [Conquest; conversion; indigenous culture], amy.fuller@ntu.ac.uk

Kevin Gould, B.A., M.A., Ph.D. (Warwick), Lect. in Early Mod. Eur. Hist. (Med. Eur., Reformations) [Confessional violence in 16th c. France; urban conflict; death & remembrance; revelation], kevin.gould@ntu.ac.uk

Nick Hayes, B.A., Ph.D. (Open), Sen. Lect. in Mod. Hist. (19th & 20th c. Brit., Urban) [Urban history; World War II; post-war reconstruction; media history; quantitative & qualitative methods; civil society; voluntary & political associations; hospitals; class & status; post world war film; identity], nick.hayes@ntu.ac.uk

Natasha Hodgson, B.A., M.A. (Lond.), Ph.D. (Hull), Lect. in Med. Hist. (11th–14th c. Brit. & Eur.) [Crusade & settlement; gender], natasha.hodgson@ntu.ac.uk

Ian Inkster, B.A. (East Anglia), Ph.D. (Sheff.), Prof. of Int. Hist. (Global Hist., Asia, Hist. of Sc. & Tech.) [Science, technology & industrialisation; global dynamics; British & Japanese social & industrial history], ian.inkster@ntu.ac.uk

Sergio Lussana, B.A. (Aberystwyth), M.A., Ph.D. (Warwick), Lect. in Amer. Hist. (Mod. Amer. Hist.) [Masculinity; slavery; antebellum south], sergio.lussana@ntu.ac.uk

John McCallum, B.A. (York), M.Litt., Ph.D. (St. And.), Lect. in Early Mod. Hist. (Early Mod. Brit., Reformation) [Reformation; early modern Scotland; poor relief; climate], john.mccallum@ntu.ac.uk

Nicholas Morton, B.A., M.A., Ph.D. (Lond.), Lect. in Med. Hist. [Military orders & crusading], nicholas.morton@ntu.ac.uk

Gary W. Moses, B.A. (C.N.A.A.), M.A. (York), Ph.D. (Nott. Trent), Princ. Lect. in Mod. Hist. (English Soc. & Cultural Hist.) [Mid Victorian rural society; urban & rural popular culture], gary.moses@ntu.ac.uk

Bill Niven, M.A., Ph.D. (St. And.), Prof. of Contemp. German Hist. (19th–21st c. German Hist., Literature & Film) [Third Reich; G.D.R.; expulsion & genocide; Holocaust; memory of Nazism & G.D.R. socialism], william.niven@ntu.ac.uk

Lizbeth Powell, B.A. (Nott. Trent), Lect. in Hist. (Early Mod. Brit. & Ireland) [Gender; marriage; family relationships], lizbeth.powell@ntu.ac.uk

Deborah Skinner, B.A. (Manc. Met.), A.M.A. (Leicester/Museums Association), P.G.C.H.E. (Nott. Trent), Sen. Lect. in Museum & Heritage Management (Museums, Heritage Management) [British ceramics industry 18th–20th c.; national occupational standards for cultural heritage; review & development of the U.K. museums' accreditation scheme; museums & heritage resource management], deborah.skinner@ntu.ac.uk

Neville Stankley, B.A. (Liv.), P.G.Dip., P.G.C.H.E. (Nott. Trent), Sen. Lect. in Public Hist. (Museum & Heritage Management) [English country house; built environment; heritage sector professional entry training; museum & heritage management], neville.stankley@ntu.ac.uk

Jenny Woodley, B.A., M.Res., Ph.D. (Nott.), Lect. in Mod. Hist. (North Amer. Hist.) [Race; African American history; civil rights activism], jenny.woodley@ntu.ac.uk

THE OPEN UNIVERSITY

Walton Hall, Milton Keynes, Bucks., MK7 6AA. 01908 274066. Fax 01908 653750
www.open.ac.uk
Faculty of Arts 01908 653519. Fax 01908 653750
www.open.ac.uk/Arts/
Department of History 01908 65 3266. Fax 01908 653750
www.open.ac.uk/Arts/history/
Department of Art History 01908 652479. Fax: 01908 653750
www.open.ac.uk/Arts/arthistory/
Department of Classical Studies 01908 653247. Fax 01908 653750
www.open.ac.uk/Arts/classical-studies/
Department of Heritage Studies
www.open.ac.uk/Arts/heritage-studies/
Department of Religious Studies 01908 652032. Fax 01908 653750
www.open.ac.uk/Arts/religious-studies/

Gemma Allen, B.A., M.St., D.Phil. (Oxon.), Lect. in Hist. [16th c. women & gender; political & religious culture; correspondence], Gemma.Allen@open.ac.uk

Christian Bailey, Ph.D. (Yale), Lect. in Hist., Christian.Bailey@open.ac.uk

Deborah Brunton, B.Sc. (Edin.), Ph.D. (Penn.), Sen. Lect. in Hist. of Medicine, Deborah.Brunton@open.ac.uk

Rosalind Crone, B.A. (Queensland), M.Phil., Ph.D. (Cantab.), Lect. in Hist., Rosalind.Crone@open.ac.uk

Silvia de Renzi, Laurea, Ph.D. (Bologna), Lect. in Hist. of Medicine [Early modern medicine; cultural & social history of early modern Italy], S.De-Renzi@open.ac.uk

Clive Emsley, B.A. (York), M.Litt. (Cantab.), Emeritus Prof. of Hist. & Sen. Res. Assoc. (Mod. Brit., Eur. & U.S.) [Crime & policing in Europe c.1789–1914], C.Emsley@open.ac.uk

Amanda Goodrich, B.A. (Roehampton), Ph.D. (Lond.), Lect. in Hist. [18th & early 19th c. political ideas & cultural history], Amanda.Goodrich@open.ac.uk

Ole Grell, Ph.D., Reader in Hist., O.P.Grell@open.ac.uk

Karl A. Hack, B.A., M.A., D.Phil. (Oxon.), Sen. Lect. in Imp. & Mod. Brit. & Int. Hist. [British empire; military history; insurgency; Southeast Asia], K.A.Hack@open.ac.uk

Sandip Hazareesingh, B.A. (Kent), M.A. (Lond.), Ph.D. (Warwick), Lect. in Hist. [Modern India; colonial & global history], S.K.Hazareesingh@open.ac.uk

Janice Holmes, B.A. (Guelph), M.A. (Queen's, Ont.), Ph.D. (Belf.), Sen. Lect. in Hist. [19th & 20th c. Irish social & religious history], J.E.Holmes@open.ac.uk

Lotte Hughes, D.Phil. (Oxon.), Res. Fellow in Hist. [African history & heritage, esp. Kenya; environmental history; memory; identity politics], Lotte.Hughes@open.ac.uk

*Paula James, Ph.D. (Southampton), Sen. Lect. in Classical Stud. [Latin literature & Roman culture], P.James@open.ac.uk

E. Anne Laurence, B.A. (York), D.Phil. (Oxon.), Prof. of Hist. (Early Mod. Brit. & Eur.) [Women, patronage & finance in early modern England; Anglo-Irish relations], E.A.Laurence@open.ac.uk

Paul M. Lawrence, B.A. (Surrey), M.A., Ph.D. (Lond.), Sen. Lect. in Eur. Hist. (Mod. Brit. & Eur.) [Criminal justice history; nationalism studies], Paul.Lawrence@open.ac.uk

Donna Loftus, B.A. (Portsmouth), Ph.D. (Chichester), Sen. Lect. in Hist., Donna.Loftus@open.ac.uk

*Robin Mackie, M.A., Ph.D. (Edin.), Sen. Lect. in Hist. [19th & 20th c. Scottish business history], Robin.Mackie@open.ac.uk

John G. Maiden, Ph.D. (Stirling), Res. Assistant [Religion & national identity; 20th c. Church of England; anti-Catholicism; British evangelicalism; integrating historical research & contemporary religious institutions], J.Maiden@open.ac.uk

Annika Mombauer, Ph.D., Sen. Lect. in Hist. [First World War & its origins], Annika.Mombauer@open.ac.uk

James R. Moore, B.Sc. (Illinois), M.Div. (Trinity Sem., Ill.), Ph.D. (Manc.), Prof. of Hist. of Sc. & Tech. [Popular science in 20th c. Britain], J.R.Moore@open.ac.uk

Edwina Newman, B.A. (Birm.), Ph.D. (Kent), Lect. in Relig. Stud. [19th c. English rural society; history of Quakerism], E.S.L.Newman@open.ac.uk

Rosemary O'Day, B.A. (York), Ph.D. (Lond.), Emeritus Prof. of Hist. & Sen. Res. Assoc. (Early Mod. Brit. & Eur., U.S. & 19th c. Brit.) [British social, educational & religious history, 16th–18th c.; male & female roles; Charles Booth's London], Rosemary.Oday@open.ac.uk

Gillian M. Perry, B.A., M.Phil. (Sussex), Prof. of Art Hist.

Georgina Sinclair, B.A., Ph.D. (Reading), Res. Fellow in Hist. [20th c. police studies & international policing], Georgina.Sinclair@open.ac.uk

David Vincent, B.A. (York), Ph.D. (Cantab.), Prof. of Soc. Hist., David.Vincent@open.ac.uk

Daniel Weinbren, B.A., M.A., Ph.D., Res. Fellow [Friendly societies], D.Weinbren@open.ac.uk

Chris A. Williams, B.A. (Oxon.), M.A. (Leicester), Ph.D. (Sheff.), Sen. Lect. in Hist. (Mod. Brit. & Eur.) [History of crime & policing], Chris.Williams@open.ac.uk

John R. Wolffe, M.A., D.Phil. (Oxon.), Prof. of Relig. Hist. [National consciousness; responses to death; anti-Catholicism; religion in locality, esp. London & Yorkshire], J.R.Wolffe@open.ac.uk

Paul Wood, M.A. (Lond.), Sen. Lect. in Art Hist. [Theory of modern art]

UNIVERSITY OF **OXFORD**

Faculty of History Old Boys' High School, George Street, Oxford, OX1 2RL.
01865 61500. Fax 01865 615009
www.history.ox.ac.uk

Professors

James Belich, M.A. (Wellington), D.Phil. (Oxon.), Balliol College, Beit Prof. of Hist. of Brit. C'wealth [Racial identities in the Victorian empire], james.belich@history.ox.ac.uk

Paul Betts, M.A., Ph.D. (Chicago), St. Antony's College, Prof. of Mod. Eur. Hist. (19th–20th c. Eur.) [20th c. Germany], paul.betts@sant.ox.ac.uk

Richard Blackett, B.A. (Keele), M.A. (Manc.), Queen's College, Harmsworth Prof. of Amer. Hist., richard.blackett@queens.ox.ac.uk

W. John Blair, M.A., D.Phil. (Oxon.), Queen's College, Prof. (Med.) [Settlement, landscape & society of Anglo-Saxon England, esp. local church organisation & the parochial system, with an emphasis on archaeological evidence], john.blair@queens.ox.ac.uk

Laurence W.B. Brockliss, M.A. (Cantab. & Oxon.), D.Phil. (Oxon.), Ph.D. (Cantab.), Magdalen College, Prof. of Early Mod. French Hist. (Brit. & Eur. 1485–1800, Hist. of Sc.) [Early modern French education; science & medicine], laurence.brockliss@magdalen.ox.ac.uk

Michael Broers, M.A. (St. And.), D.Phil. (Oxon.), Lady Margaret Hall, Prof. of Western Eur. Hist. (18th & 19th c. Italy & France) [18th & 19th c. Italian & French social & political history; religious history; imperialism], michael.broers@lmh.ox.ac.uk

Patricia M. Clavin, B.A., Ph.D. (Lond.), Jesus College, Prof. of Int. Hist. (19th–20th c. Brit. & Eur.) [Great Depression, 1929–39; international economic diplomacy; the League of Nations], patricia.clavin@jesus.ox.ac.uk

Craig Clunas, B.A. (Cantab.), Ph.D. (Lond.), Trinity College, Prof. of the Hist. of Art [Art & cultural history of China from 1400 to the contemporary period, esp. that of the Ming period; methodology & historiography of art history], craig.clunas@trinity.ox.ac.uk

Pietro Corsi, D.Phil. (Oxon.), Linacre College, Prof. of Hist. of Sc. [History of earth & life sciences; science & religion], pietro.corsi@history.ox.ac.uk

Robert F. (Roy) Foster, M.A. (Dublin & Oxon.), D.Phil. (Oxon.), Ph.D. (Dublin), F.B.A., Hertford College, Carroll Prof. of Irish Hist. (Brit. & Eur. 1485 onwards) [Irish history, society & politics in the modern period; Victorian high politics & culture; authorised biography of W.B. Yeats], roy.foster@hertford.ox.ac.uk

Robert N. Gildea, M.A., D.Phil. (Oxon.), Worcester College, Prof. of Mod. French Hist. (19th–20th c. French & Eur. Hist.) [France, 1799–1914; Second World War; 1968 & society], robert.gildea@history.ox.ac.uk

Pekka Hämäläinen, M.A., Ph.D. (Helsinki), St. Catherine's College, Rhodes Prof. of Amer. Hist., pekka.hamalainen@stcatz.ox.ac.uk

Helena F. Hamerow, B.A. (Wis.), M.A., D.Phil. (Oxon.), St. Cross College, Prof. of Archaeol. (Eur. Archaeol., Early Med.) [Rural communities in north-west Europe, 400–900], helena.hamerow@stx.ox.ac.uk

Ruth Harris, M.A. (Penn.), M.A., D.Phil. (Oxon.), New College, Prof. of Mod. Hist. (Mod. Eur.) [Dreyfus Affair; French history; history of medicine; cultural history; women's history], ruth.harris@new.ox.ac.uk

Mark Harrison, B.Sc., M.A., D.Phil. (Oxon.), Wellcome Unit for the Hist. of Medicine, Prof. of the Hist. of Medicine [History of disease & medicine, especially in relation to the history of war & imperialism, 17th–20th c.; history of medicine & British imperial expansion, c.1700–1850], mark.harrison@wuhmo.ox.ac.uk

Angus B. Hawkins, B.A. (Read.), M.A. (Oxon.), Ph.D. (Lond.), Kellogg College, Prof. of Hist. (Victorian Pol. Hist.) [Biography of 14th earl of Derby, 1799–1869]

Dan Healey, B.A. (Toronto), M.A. (Lond.), M.A., Ph.D. (Toronto), Prof. of Mod. Russian Hist. (Mod. Russian Hist.) [Modern Russian & Soviet history], dan.healey@sant.ox.ac.uk

Howard Hotson, B.A., M.A. (Toronto), D.Phil. (Oxon.), St. Anne's College, Prof. of Early Mod. Intellectual Hist. (16th–17th c. Intellectual Hist., esp. Central Eur.) [Ramism; encyclopaedism; irenicism; millennarianism; universal reform; international systems of intellectual reform], howard.hotson@st-annes.ox.ac.uk

*K. Jane Humphries, M.A. (Cantab. & Cornell), Ph.D. (Cornell), All Souls College, Prof., Chair of Fac. Board (Econ., Soc., Brit. & Eur. 1800 onwards) [Relationship between the family & the economy; child labour in the British industrial revolution], jane.humphries@all-souls.ox.ac.uk

Alan S. Knight, M.A., D.Phil. (Oxon.), F.B.A., St. Antony's College, Prof. of Hist. of Latin Amer. (Hist. beyond Eur.) [Modern history & politics of Latin America, esp. Mexico; revolutions, state-building & peasant movements; British & U.S. relations with Latin America], alan.knight@lac.ox.ac.uk

Ian W.F. Maclean, M.A., D.Phil. (Oxon.), F.B.A., All Souls College, Prof. of Renaissance Stud. (Renaissance & Early Mod. Intellectual Hist.) [History of the book; Cardano, Montaigne], ian.maclean@all-souls.ox.ac.uk

Rana S.R. Mitter, B.A. (Cantab.), M.A. (Oxon.), M.Phil., Ph.D. (Cantab.), St. Cross College, Prof. of the Hist. & Pol. of Mod. China [Modern history & politics of China], rana.mitter@chinese.ox.ac.uk

Kevin Hjortshøj O'Rourke, B.A. (Dublin), M.A., Ph.D. (Harv.), All Souls College, Chichele Prof. of Econ. Hist., kevin.orourke@history.ox.ac.uk

Lyndal A. Roper, B.A. (Melb.), Ph.D. (Lond.), Balliol College, Prof. of Early Mod. Hist. (Early Mod. Eur.) [Social, cultural & religious history of 16th & 17th c. Germany; gender; witchcraft; Luther], lyndal.roper@balliol.ox.ac.uk

Robert J. Service, M.A. (Cantab., Essex & Oxon.), Ph.D. (Essex), F.B.A., St. Antony's College, Prof. of Russian Hist. (Mod. Russian Hist.) [History of 20th c. Russia], robert.service@sant.ox.ac.uk

Richard Sharpe, M.A. (Cantab. & Oxon.), Ph.D. (Cantab.), F.B.A., Wadham College, Prof. of Diplomatic (Med.) [Medieval documents; English royal diplomatic, 11th–12th c.; medieval Latin texts; books & libraries in medieval England], richard.sharpe@history.ox.ac.uk

Nicholas Stargardt, B.A., Ph.D. (Cantab.), M.A. (Oxon.), Magdalen College, Prof. of Mod. Eur. Hist. (19th–20th c. Eur. Hist.) [Social history of Nazi Germany; history of childhood], nick.stargardt@magd.ox.ac.uk

Hew F.A. Strachan, M.A., Ph.D. (Cantab.), All Souls College, Chichele Prof. of the Hist. of War [Military history from the 18th c. to the present, including contemporary strategic studies, esp. WW1 & the history of the British army], hew.strachan@all-souls.ox.ac.uk

Christopher J. Wickham, M.A., D.Phil. (Oxon.), F.B.A., All Souls College, Chichele Prof. of Med. Hist. [Early medieval Europe; 12th c. Italian society], chris.wickham@history.ox.ac.uk

Readers
There are fuller details for some staff under college lists:

Susan E. Brigden, Lincoln College, Reader in Mod. Hist.
Faisal F. Devji, St. Antony's College, Reader in Mod. S. Asian Hist.
Abigail F.F. Green, Brasenose College, Reader in Mod. Hist.

University Lecturers
There are fuller details for some staff under college lists:

Erica Charters, Wolfson College
John G. Darwin, Nuffield College
Nicholas S. Davidson, St. Edmund Hall
Gareth B. Davies, St. Anne's College
Jan-Georg Deutsch, St. Cross College
Hanneke Grootenboer, St Peter's College
Dan Healey, St. Antony's College
Geraldine A. Johnson, Christ Church
Sho Konishi, St. Antony's College
Miles Larmer, St. Antony's College
Sloan Mahone, St. Cross College
Deborah J. Oxley, All Souls College
Jay Sexton, Corpus Christi College
Peter J. Thompson, St. Cross College
Stephen G.N. Tuck, Pembroke College
Mark Whittow, Corpus Christi College
Alastair Wright, St. John's College

Oxford

University Lecturers (Inter-Collegiate)
There are fuller details for some staff under college lists:

Lesley J. Abrams, Balliol College
C. Catherine L. Andreyev, Christ Church
Ian W. Archer, Keble College
Martin H. Conway, Balliol College
Faramerz N. Dabhoiwala, Exeter College
John H. Davis, Queen's College
Christina de Bellaigue, Exeter College
Ian Forrest, Oriel College
Alexandra Gajda, Jesus College
E. Jane Garnett, Wadham College
George S. Garnett, St. Hugh's College
Perry Gauci, Lincoln College
John-Paul A. Ghobrial, Balliol College
Peter R. Ghosh, St. Anne's College
Kathryn J. Gleadle, Mansfield College
Lawrence N. Goldman, St. Peter's College
Adrian M. Gregory, Pembroke College
Matthew Grimley, Merton College
Steven J. Gunn, Merton College
Robert Harris, Worcester College
Catherine J. Holmes, University College
David Hopkin, Hertford College
Joanna M. Innes, Somerville College
Ben Jackson, University College
Georgy Kantor, St. John's College
Matthew S. Kempshall, Wadham College
Conrad C. Leyser, Worcester College
James R.C. McDougall, Trinity College
Julia Mannherz, Oriel College
Anna-Maria S. Misra, Keble College
Sarah C. Mortimer, Christ Church
Marc E. Mulholland, St. Catherine's College
John B.W. Nightingale, Magdalen College
Natalia Nowakowska, Somerville College
Jonathan Parkin, St. Hugh's College
David A. Parrott, New College
Senia Paseta, St. Hugh's College
David R. Priestland, St. Edmund Hall
A. Gervase Rosser, St. Catherine's College
Simon Skinner, Balliol College
Hannah Skoda, St. John's College
Hannah Smith, St. Hilda's College
Giora Sternberg, Hertford College
Alan L. Strathern, Brasenose College
Grant Tapsell, Lady Margaret Hall
Benjamin J. Thompson, Somerville College
Bryan R. Ward-Perkins, Trinity College

John L. Watts, Corpus Christi College
William H. Whyte, St. John's College
Brian W. Young, Christ Church
Oliver Zimmer, University College

Senior Instructor
Ida Toth, Wolfson College

Departmental Lecturers
There are fuller details for college staff under some lists:

Philip A. Booth, Trinity College
Igor Chabrowski, Merton College
Margret Frenz, St. Cross College
April Gallwey, Magdalen College
Jonathan A. Jarrett, Queen's College
Simon John, Balliol College
Tom Lambert, Exeter College
Jan Machielsen, New College
Julie E. Marfany, All Souls College
Oren J. Margolis, Somerville College
Rachel Moss, Corpus Christi College
Philipp Niewöhner, M.A., Ph.D. (Mainz), Institute of Archaeology, Departmental Lect. in Byz. Archaeol. & Material Culture, philipp.niewoehner@arch.ox.ac.uk
Tom Packer, St. Anne's College
Elina M. Screen, Trinity College
Hugo Service, Worcester College
Hannah Williams, St. Peter's College

Senior Research Fellow
W. Gregg Huff, Pembroke College

Teaching & Research Fellow
Elise Smith, Wolfson College

All Souls College OX1 4AL. 01865 279379. Fax 01865 279299
Paul Brand, M.A., D.Phil. (Oxon.), F.B.A., Fellow [English & Irish legal history, esp. later middle ages], paul.brand@all-souls.ox.ac.uk
Noel Malcolm, M.A., Ph.D. (Cantab.), F.B.A., Fellow (Early Mod. Intellectual) [17th c. philosophy, esp. Thomas Hobbes], noel.malcolm@all-souls.ox.ac.uk
Julie E. Marfany, M.Sc. (Oxon.), Ph.D. (Cantab.), julie.marfany@all-souls.ox.ac.uk
George Molyneaux, B.A. (Oxon.), Fellow [Early medieval history of the British Isles, esp. 10th & 11th c. England], george.molyneaux@all-souls.ox.ac.uk
Deborah J. Oxley, B.A. (N.S.W.), M.A. (Oxon.), Ph.D. (N.S.W.), (Soc. Hist.) [Height & health in history; micro-economics of the household; penal transportation to Australia; coercive labour systems; colonial Australian development; crime & punishment in Britain & Ireland], deborah.oxley@all-souls.ox.ac.uk
Nicholas Rodger, M.A., D.Phil. (Oxon.), F.B.A., Fellow [British & world naval history, 600–2000], nicholas.rodger@all-souls.ox.ac.uk

Oxford

Benjamin Wardhaugh, M.A. (Cantab.), D.Phil. (Oxon.), Fellow [History of mathematics, 1650–1750, esp. England], benjamin.wardhaugh@all-souls.ox.ac.uk
Thomas Welsford, M.A., D.Phil. (Oxon.), Fellow [History of central & inner Asia, 1200–1900; history of Iran & the Caucasus, 1500–1750; Islamicate historiography & genre; theories of power, legitimacy & loyalty; post-Soviet cinema], thomas.welsford@all-souls.ox.ac.uk

Balliol College OX1 3BJ. 01865 27777. Fax 01865 277803
Lesley J. Abrams, M.A. (Oxon.), M.A., Ph.D. (Toronto), Fellow & Tutor (Early Med. Brit. & Eur.) [Anglo-Saxon England; Viking Age Scandinavia & Scandinavian settlements overseas], lesley.abrams@balliol.ox.ac.uk
Martin H. Conway, M.A., D.Phil. (Oxon.), Fellow & Tutor (19th–20th c. Eur. & World) [European history c.1930–1960; history of Belgium], martin.conway@balliol.ox.ac.uk
John-Paul A. Ghobrial, B.A. (Tufts), M.Phil. (Oxon.), M.A., Ph.D. (Princeton), Res. Fellow (Early Mod. Eur. & Mid. E.) [History of communication; intellectual & cultural history; history of scholarship], jpg52@cam.ac.uk
Simon John, B.A., M.A., Ph.D. (Swansea), Departmental Lect. (Early Med. Hist) [Medieval Europe; noble mentalities & aristocratic culture], simon.john@balliol.ox.ac.uk
Simon Skinner, M.A., M.Phil., D.Phil. (Oxon.), Fellow & Tutor (Brit. Hist. since 1685) [High politics, paternalist & reactionary thought; religious & ecclesiastical dimensions], simon.skinner@balliol.ox.ac.uk

Brasenose College OX1 4AJ. 01865 277830. Fax 01865 277822
Rowena E. Archer, B.A. (Brist.), M.A., D.Phil. (Oxon.), Supernumerary Fellow in Med. Hist., & Lect. in Med. Hist., Christ Church (Med.) [Later medieval English history], rowena.archer@history.ox.ac.uk
Edward H. Bispham, M.A., D.Phil. (Oxon.), (Roman Hist.), ed.bispham@bnc.ox.ac.uk
Vernon B. Bogdanor, C.B.E., M.A. (Oxon.), F.B.A., Prof. of Pol. & Govt. [British & comparative government]
Abigail F.F. Green, M.A. (Oxon.), Ph.D. (Cantab.), Fellow & Tutor in Hist. (Eur. 1800 onwards) [19th c. German & international Jewish history], abigail.green@bnc.ox.ac.uk
George Southcombe, M.A., M.St., D.Phil. (Oxon.), British Academy Postdoctoral Fellow (15th–17th c. Brit. & Eur.) [The uses of history in the late 17th c.; 17th c. religion & literature]
Alan L. Strathern, M.A. (Lond.), D.Phil. (Oxon.), Tutorial Fellow (Early Mod.) [Portuguese imperialism; religious encounters], alan.strathern@bnc.ox.ac.uk
Abigail G. Wills, B.A., M.Phil., Ph.D. (Cantab.), Career Development Fellow (Mod. Brit.) [British social history since 1945], abigail.wills@bnc.ox.ac.uk

Christ Church OX1 1DP. 01865 276150. Fax 01865 794199
*C. Catherine L. Andreyev, M.A. (Oxon.), Ph.D. (Cantab.), Student (i.e., Fellow) & Tutor in Mod. Hist. (Mod. Hist.) [Russian history – esp. history of the Russian emigration], catherine.andreyev@chch.ox.ac.uk
Rowena E. Archer, B.A. (Brist.), M.A., D.Phil. (Oxon), Lect. in Hist. (Med. Hist.) [Later Medieval English History], rowena.archer@history.ox.ac.uk
David J. Hine, M.A., D.Phil. (Oxon.), Student & Tutor in Pol. (20th c. Eur. Pol.), david.hine@chch.ox.ac.uk
Geraldine A. Johnson, B.A. (Yale), M.A. (Cantab.), Ph.D. (Harv.), (Hist. of Art) [Visual culture of the Renaissance; women as art patrons], geraldine.johnson@hoa.ox.ac.uk
Edward Keene, B.A. (Oxon.), M.Sc., Ph.D. (Lond.), Student & Tutor in Pol. (20th c. Int. Hist.) [Late medieval & early modern international relations], edward.keene@chch.ox.ac.uk

Sarah C. Mortimer, M.St., D.Phil. (Oxon.), Student & Tutor in Hist. (16th & 17th c. Eur. & Brit.) [The intellectual, religious & political history of the early modern period; the relationship between political thought & religious ideas in the aftermath of the Reformation], sarah.mortimer@chch.ox.ac.uk

Brian W. Young, B.A. (Dunelm.), D.Phil. (Oxon.), (17th–18th c. Brit.) [British intellectual & religious history; the Victorians & the 18th c.; historiography], brian.young@chch.ox.ac.uk

Corpus Christi College OX1 4JF. 01865 276700. Fax 01865 276767

Judith D. Maltby, B.A., Ph.D. (Cantab.), Fellow & Tutor (16th–17th c. Eng. Relig., Pol. & Soc. Hist.)

Rachel Moss, M.A., Ph.D. (York), Tutor & Lect. (Late. Med. Brit.) [Gender, sexuality, family relationships, reading & culture in later medieval England], rachel.moss@ccc.ox.ac.uk

Jay Sexton, B.A. (Kansas), D.Phil. (Oxon.), Fellow & Tutor (Amer. Hist.) [International dimensions of the U.S. in the 19th c.], jay.sexton@history.ox.ac.uk

John L. Watts, M.A. (Cantab. & Oxon.), Ph.D. (Cantab.), Fellow & Tutor (Late Med. Brit. Pol. Hist.) [Later medieval England & Europe; the growth of government & the transition from 'medieval' to 'early modern' political forms], john.watts@history.ox.ac.uk

Mark Whittow, M.A., D.Phil. (Oxon.), Fellow in Byz. Stud. (Med. Hist.) [Mediterranean & Byzantine worlds c.500–1300, esp. landscape & settlement patterns & the social & political forces that shaped them], mark.whittow@ccc.ox.ac.uk

Exeter College OX1 3DP. 01865 279600. Fax 01865 279630

Faramerz N. Dabhoiwala, B.A. (York), M.A., D.Phil. (Oxon.), Fellow & Tutor (Brit. & Eur. 1485–1800) [History of the English-speaking world since the middle ages], faramerz.dabhoiwala@exeter.ox.ac.uk

Christina de Bellaigue, B.A. (Cantab.), D.E.A. (Paris), Ph.D. (Cantab.), Fellow & Tutor (Brit. & Eur. 19th–20th c.) [Social & cultural history of 19th c. Britain & France], christina.debellaigue@exeter.ox.ac.uk

Tom Lambert, B.A., M.A., Ph.D. (Dunelm.), Junior Res. Fellow & Lect. (Brit. & Eur. 300–1330) [Law, society & culture in early medieval England], thomas.lambert@exeter.ox.ac.uk

Hertford College OX1 3BW. 01865 279400. Fax 01865 279437

David Hopkin, M.A., Ph.D. (Cantab.), Fellow in Mod. Hist. (18th–20th c. Eur.) [Rural & coastal societies; oral & visual culture; folklore; military & maritime history], david.hopkin@hertford.ox.ac.uk

Giora Sternberg, M.A. (Tel Aviv), D.Phil. (Oxon.), Fellow & Tutor (Early Mod. Eur.) [Status interaction at the time of Louis XIV, esp court ceremonies & everyday correspondence; writing practices in the 17th & 18th c.], giora.sternberg@hertford.ox.ac.uk

Christopher J. Tyerman, M.A., D.Phil. (Oxon.), Fellow in Med. Hist. (Brit. & Eur.) [Crusades], christopher.tyerman@hertford.ox.ac.uk

Jesus College OX1 3DW. 01865 279700. Fax 01865 279687

Alexandra Gajda, B.A., D.Phil. (Oxon.), (Early Mod.) [Political & religious history of the late 16th & early 17th c.; literature & history; history of travel; Renaissance historiography], alexandra.gajda@jesus.ox.ac.uk

Keble College OX1 3PG. 01865 272727. Fax 01865 272705

Sarah Apetrei, M.A., Ph.D.(Oxon.), Acting Director of Stud. in Theol. (Eccles.) [Early modern religious history; women's history], sarah.apetrei@keble.ox.ac.uk

Ian W. Archer, M.A., D.Phil. (Oxon.), Fellow & Tutor (Mod. Hist.) [Social history of early modern London], ian.archer@keble.ox.ac.uk

Averil M. Cameron, M.A. (Oxon.), Ph.D. (Lond.), D.Litt. (Warwick), F.B.A., Hon. Fellow (Byz. Stud.), averil.cameron@keble.ox.ac.uk

Anna-Maria S. Misra, B.A., D.Phil. (Oxon.), Fellow & Tutor (Mod. Eur. & World) [Comparative impact of European colonial ideas & ideologies on the culture & politics of colonial & post-colonial states in Asia & Africa], anna-maria.misra@keble.ox.ac.uk

Mark Philpott, M.A., D.Phil. (Oxon.), Lect. in Mod. Hist. (Med. Hist. 900–1300), mark.philpott@keble.ox.ac.uk

Tracey A. Sowerby, M.A., D.Phil. (Oxon.), C.M.R.S. Career Development Fellow in Renaissance Hist. [Early modern politics & culture in Britain], tracey.sowerby@keble.ox.ac.uk

Kellogg College OX1 2JA. 01865 270360. Fax 01865 270309

Paul S. Barnwell, B.A., M.A., Ph.D. (Leeds), Fellow & Director of Stud. in the Historic Environment [Architectural history & the history of buildings; buildings & landscapes; medieval parish churches; vernacular architecture; late Roman administrative & legal history], paul.barnwell@kellogg.ox.ac.uk

Thomas C. Buchanan, M.A., D.Phil. (Oxon.), Fellow & Reader in Mod. Hist. (Mod. Hist. & Pol.) [China & the British Left; history of Amnesty International], tom.buchanan@kellogg.ox.ac.uk

Christopher J. Day, B.A. (Manc.), M.A. (Oxon.), Emeritus Fellow (Local Hist.) [Local history, esp. settlement history of the Oxford region], chris.day@kellogg.ox.ac.uk

Elizabeth A. Gemmill, B.A., M.A., Ph.D. (Manc.), Fellow [Medieval social, economic & ecclesiastical history]

Jonathan Healey, B.A. (Oxon.), M.A. (Reading), D.Phil. (Oxon.), Fellow [English rural & social history, 15th–19th c.], jonathan.healey@kellogg.ox.ac.uk

Christine A. Jackson, B.A. (Lond.), M.A. (Oxon.), Ph.D. (Read.), Fellow (16th–17th c. Brit. Econ., Soc. & Urban Hist.)

Yasmin Khan, M.A., D.Phil. (Oxon.), Fellow [British empire; India, 18th–20th c.], yasmin.khan@kellogg.ox.ac.uk

Catherine M. Oakes, B.A., Ph.D. (Brist.), M.A. (Oxon.), Fellow (Hist. of Art) [Medieval iconography in northern Europe; French & English art & architecture, 11th–12th c.], cathy.oakes@kellogg.ox.ac.uk

Claire I.R. O'Mahony, B.A. (Calif. at Berkeley), M.A., Ph.D. (Lond.), Fellow (Hist. of Art) [French art & design in 19th & 20th c.; *fin de siècle* Symbolist decoration], claire.omahony@conted.ox.ac.uk

Adrienne B. Rosen, M.A., D.Phil. (Oxon.), Emerita Fellow [Local history 16th–18th c.; English social & economic history]

Mark A. Smith, M.A., D.Phil. (Oxon.), Fellow [History of Christianity in England 18th–20th c.]

Kate Tiller, B.A., Ph.D. (Birm.), M.A. (Oxon.), Emerita Fellow [English social & local history, 18th–20th c.; rural change; religious history]

Lady Margaret Hall OX2 6QA. 01865 274300. Fax 01865 511069

Alex Middleton, M.A. M.Phil., Ph.D. (Cantab.), College Lect. (Brit. 1700–2000) [19th c. politics & intellectual life], alexander.middleton@lmh.ox.ac.uk

Grant Tapsell, B.A. (Oxon.), M.A., M.Phil., Ph.D. (Cantab.), Fellow & Tutor (Early Mod.) [Early modern Britain, Europe & colonial Americas], grant.tapsell@history.ox.ac.uk

Lincoln College OX1 3DR. 01865 279800. Fax 01865 279802

Susan E. Brigden, B.A. (Manc.), Ph.D. (Cantab.), Fellow & Tutor (Brit. & Eur. 1500–1600) [16th c. religion; court culture; diplomacy; friendship], susan.brigden@lincoln.ox.ac.uk

Perry Gauci, M.A., D.Phil. (Oxon.), Fellow & Tutor (Stuart & Hanoverian Britain) [Social, economic & political development of Britain, 1600–1800], perry.gauci@lincoln.ox.ac.uk
Alana Harris, B.A., LL.B. (Melb.), M.Div. (Melb. Coll. of Div.), M.A., D.Phil. (Oxon.), Darby Fellow (19th & 20th c. Brit. & Eur.) [Gender, religious & cultural history; transnational history], alana.harris@lincoln.ox.ac.uk
Paul Langford, M.A., D.Phil. (Oxon.), F.B.A., [Cultural & political history, 18th–19th c.]

Magdalen College OX1 4AU. 01865 276000. Fax 01865 276094
April Gallwey, B.A. (Lond.), M.St., M.Sc. (Oxon.), Ph.D. (Warwick), Departmental Lect. (20th c. Brit. Hist.) [20th c. British history], april.gallwey@magd.ox.ac.uk
John B.W. Nightingale, M.A., D.Phil. (Oxon.), Fellow & Tutor (Med. Hist.) [Carolingian Europe 800–1100, esp. monasteries, nobles, ritual & authority], john.nightingale@magd.ox.ac.uk

Mansfield College OX1 3TF. 01865 270999. Fax 01865 270970
Kathryn J. Gleadle, B.A., Ph.D. (Warwick), Tutorial Fellow in Mod. Hist. [Women's history; 18th & 19th c. British history; children & history of childhood], kathryn.gleadle@mansfield.ox.ac.uk
Helen Lacey, M.A., Ph.D. (York), (Late Med.), helen.lacey@mansfield.ox.ac.uk

Merton College OX1 4JD. 01865 276310. Fax 01865 276361
Igor Chabrowski, B.Ed., M.A. (Warsaw), M.R., D.Phil. (E.U.I.), Departmental Lect. (Mod. Chinese Hist.) [Modern Chinese history], igor.chabrowski@merton.ox.ac.uk
Matthew Grimley, M.A., D.Phil. (Oxon.), Fellow & Tutor (19th–20th c. Brit.) [Religion & political ideas in 20th c. Britain], matthew.grimley@merton.ox.ac.uk
Steven J. Gunn, M.A., D.Phil. (Oxon.), Fellow & Tutor (15th–17th c. Brit. & Eur.) [The councillors & courtiers of Henry VII; everyday life & accidental death in 16th c. England], steven.gunn@merton.ox.ac.uk
Patrick Lantschner, B.A., M.St. (Oxon.), Junior Res. Fellow (13th–15th c.) [Cities & political organisation in late medieval Europe & the middle east], patrick.lantschner@merton.ox.ac.uk

New College OX1 3BN. 01865 279555. Fax 01865 279590
Helen Jacobsen, M.A., D.Phil. (Oxon.), Lect. (Brit. & Eur. 1500–1700), helen.jacobsen@new.ox.ac.uk
Jan Machielsen, B.A. (Maastricht), M.A. (Leiden), M.St., D.Phil. (Oxon.), Stipendiary Lect. in Hist. (Early Mod. Brit. & Eur.) [Early modern demonology], jan.machielsen@history.ox.ac.uk
Robert C.T. Parker, M.A., D.Phil. (Oxon.), Wykeham Prof. of Anc. Hist., robert.parker@new.ox.ac.uk
David A. Parrott, M.A., D.Phil. (Oxon.), Fellow & Tutor (Brit. & Eur. 1485–1800) [French political & military history; Thirty Years' War; 17th c. Italy; aspects of political history, esp. relations between rulers, nobles, central & provincial power; early modern court studies & courtly culture], david.parrott@new.ox.ac.uk

Nuffield College OX1 1NF. 01865 278500. Fax 01865 278621
Robert C. Allen, B.A. (Carleton), M.A., Ph.D. (Harv.), Prof. of Econ. Hist. (Recent Soc. & Econ. Hist.), bob.allen@nuffield.ox.ac.uk
John G. Darwin, M.A., D.Phil. (Oxon.), Fellow (Hist. of Brit. C'wealth) [Theories of empire since c.1500; the British Empire as an international system 1830–1960; South African, Canadian & New Zealand history; decolonisation & the end of empire], john.darwin@nuffield.ox.ac.uk

Oriel College OX1 4EW. 01865 276555. Fax 01865 791823
Ian Forrest, M.A., M.Phil. (Glas.), M.A., D.Phil. (Oxon.), Fellow & Tutor (Med.) [Social &
religious history of Europe 1200–1500, esp. ecclesiastical institutions, popular politics,
heresy & inquisitions], ian.forrest@oriel.ox.ac.uk
Julia Mannherz, M.A. (Lond.), Ph.D. (Cantab.), (Mod.) [19th & early 20th c. cultural history of
the Russian empire], julia.mannherz@oriel.ox.ac.uk

Pembroke College OX1 1DW. 01865 276414/444/456/468. Fax 01865 276418
Adrian M. Gregory, M.A., Ph.D. (Cantab.), Fellow & Tutor in Mod. Hist. (Mod.
Brit. & Eur.) [Social & cultural history of early 20th c. Britain; World Wars I & II],
adrian.gregory@pmb.ox.ac.uk
W. Gregg Huff, B.Sc. (Penn.), Ph.D. (Lond.), [Southeast Asian economic history &
development; development economics; money & finance in developing countries;
economics of war], gregg.huff@pmb.ox.ac.uk
Stephen G.N. Tuck, B.A., M.A., Ph.D. (Cantab.), (Mod. Amer. Hist.) [Race relations, racial
protest & white supremacy from the Civil War to the present], stephen.tuck@history.ac.uk

Queen's College OX1 4AW. 01865 279120. Fax 01865 790819
John H. Davis, M.A., D.Phil. (Oxon.), Fellow, Tutor & Praelector in Hist. (19th–20th c. Brit.)
[Modern London], john.davis@history.ox.ac.uk

Regent's Park College OX1 2LB. 01865 288120. Fax 01865 288121
Leif Dixon, B.A. (Sussex), D.Phil. (Oxon.), (Early Mod. Hist.) [Religious history, 16th–17th c.],
leif.dixon@regents.ox.ac.uk
Katherine Low, B.A., M.St. (Oxon.), (Anc. Hist.) [Roman history], katie.low@regents.ox.ac.uk

Ruskin College OX3 9BZ. 01865 759600
Ruth Percy, B.A. (Sussex), Ph.D. (Toronto), Tutor [Modern Britain & U.S.; labour history;
women's/gender history], rpercy@ruskin.ac.uk
John G. Walker, B.A., M.Sc., Ph.D. (Lond.), Tutor [History of labour markets; 20th c. history of
western Europe]

St. Anne's College OX2 6HS. 01865 274800. Fax 01865 274899
Gareth B. Davies, B.A. (Lancaster), M.A., D.Phil. (Oxon.), Fellow (Amer. Hist.) [Social
policies & political crisis of the U.S. during the 1960s; the foundation of the New Deal
welfare state; American education policy; the growth of government in the U.S.],
gareth.davies@history.ox.ac.uk
Peter R. Ghosh, M.A. (Oxon.), Fellow & Tutor in Mod. Hist. (Hist. of Ideas, 1750 onwards)
[Max Weber's Protestant ethic in historical context; intellectual traditions underlying the
conduct of English politics 1850–1895; the evolution of European & British historiography
from the Enlightenment to the present], peter.ghosh@st-annes.ox.ac.uk
Tom Packer, B.Sc., M.A. (Lond.)., D.Phil. (Oxon.), (Mod. Amer. Hist) [American conservatism
in the second half of the 20th c.], thomas.packer@st-annes.ox.ac.uk

St. Antony's College OX2 6JF. 01865 274479. Fax 01865 310518
Timothy J. Garton Ash, C.M.G., M.A. (Oxon.), Professorial Fellow,
timothy.gartonash@sant.ox.ac.uk
Richard R.M. Clogg, M.A. (Edin. & Oxon.), Sen. Res. Fellow [History of Greece & the Greek
diaspora], richard.clogg@sant.ox.ac.uk
Malcolm D. Deas, O.B.E., M.A. (Oxon.), (Pol. & Govt. of Latin. Amer.) [Colombia],
malcolm.deas@sant.ox.ac.uk

Faisal F. Devji, B.A. (Brit. Col.), M.A., Ph.D. (Chicago), faisal.devji@sant.ox.ac.uk
Nandini Gooptu, B.A. (Calcutta), M.A. (Oxon.), Ph.D. (Cantab.), Fac. Fellow (S. Asian Stud.),
    nandini.gooptu@sant.ox.ac.uk
Charles Knickerbocker Harley, B.A. (Wooster), Ph.D. (Harv.), University Lect. in Econ. Hist.
Sho Konishi, B.A. (Georgetown), M.A. (Georgetown & Oxon.), Ph.D. (Chicago), (Mod.
    Japanese Hist.) [Cultural, intellectual & transnational history of Japan from 1700],
    sho.konishi@sant.ox.ac.uk
Miles Larmer, B.A. (C.N.A.A.), M.A. (Lond.), Ph.D. (Sheff.), Fellow (Afric. Hist.) [Political &
    military history of Africa], miles.larmer@sant.ox.ac.uk
Eugene L. Rogan, B.A. (Columbia), M.A. (Oxon.), M.A., Ph.D. (Harv.), University Lect. in the
    Mod. Hist. of the Mid. E. [Arab provinces of Ottoman empire], eugene.rogan@sant.ox.ac.uk
David A. Washbrook, M.A., Ph.D. (Cantab.), Professorial Fellow (Mod. S. Asian Hist.) [History
    of southern India], david.washbrook@sant.ox.ac.uk
Ann Waswo, M.A., Ph.D. (Stanford), Fac. Fellow (Mod. Japanese Hist.) [Housing & housing
    policy in post-war Japan], ann.waswo@nissan.ox.ac.uk

St. Catherine's College OX1 3UJ. 01865 271700. Fax 01865 271768
Marc E. Mulholland, M.A. (Oxon.), M.A., Ph.D. (Belf.), (Mod. Irish Hist.) [Ireland
    since the Famine; history of political thought since the French Revolution],
    marc.mulholland@stcatz.ox.ac.uk
A. Gervase Rosser, M.A. (Oxon.), Ph.D. (Lond.), Fellow & Tutor (Med. Hist.) [Medieval
    guilds in England; history of art in the Renaissance; miracle-working images in Italy],
    gervase.rosser@stcatz.ox.ac.uk

St. Cross College OX1 3LZ. 01865 278490. Fax 01865 278484
Jan-Georg Deutsch, M.A. (Hanover & Oxon.), Ph.D. (Lond.), (Afric. Hist.) [Social & economic
    history of Africa from the 19th c. to the present], jan-georg.deutsch@stx.ox.ac.uk
Margret Frenz, M.A., Ph.D. (Heidelberg), Departmental Lect. (Global & Imp. Hist.) [Social &
    cultural history of South India 18th–20th c.; medical history & global medical migration],
    margret.frenz@stx.ox.ac.uk
Diarmaid MacCulloch, M.A., Ph.D. (Cantab.), Dip. Theol. (Oxon.), Dip.Ar.Ad. (Liv.),
    Prof. of the Hist. of the Church, Fellow (Church Hist.) [English Reformation],
    diarmaid.macculloch@theology.ox.ac.uk
Peter J. Thompson, B.A. (Warwick), M.A. (Oxon.), Ph.D. (Penn.), Fellow (Amer.
    Hist.) [Social & cultural history of Britain's colonies in N. America, 1607–c.1800],
    peter.thompson@history.ox.ac.uk
Friedrich W. Zimmermann, M.A. (Erlangen), M.A., D.Phil. (Oxon.), Emeritus Fellow (Hist. of
    Islamic Thought) [Greek into Arabic; early Arabic thought], fritz.zim@orinst.ox.ac.uk

St. Edmund Hall OX1 4AR. 01865 279000. Fax 01865 279090
Nicholas S. Davidson, M.A. (Cantab. & Oxon.), (Hist. of the Renaissance & Reformation)
    [Early modern Italy, esp. social & religious history], nicholas.davidson@seh.ox.ac.uk
David R. Priestland, M.A., D.Phil. (Oxon.), (19th–20th c. Eur. Hist.) [History of the Soviet
    Union; history of communism], david.priestland@history.ox.ac.uk

St. Hilda's College OX4 1DY. 01865 276884. Fax 01865 276816
Katherine J. Clarke, M.A., D.Phil. (Oxon.), Fellow & Tutor in Anc. Hist. (Roman Hist.) [Ancient
    geography; historiography; perceptions of time], katherine.clarke@st-hildas.ox.ac.uk
Mark Hailwood, M.A., Ph.D. (Warwick), Stipendary Lect. In Hist. (16th & 17th c.
    Soc. & Cultural Hist. of Brit.) [Alehouses; sociability; work; collective identity],
    mark.hailwood@st-hildas.ox.ac.uk

Robert N. Portass, M.A., D.Phil. (Oxon.), Diploma de Estudios Avanzados (Santiago di Compostela), Leverhulme Early Career Fellow & Junior Res. Fellow in Hist. (Soc. & Econ. Hist. of Early Mod. Eur.) [Social relations; political structures; comparative history; Spain], robert.portass@st-hildas.ox.ac.uk

Hannah Smith, M.A., Ph.D. (Cantab.), Fellow & Tutor in Hist. (17th & 18th c. Pol. & Cultural Hist. of Brit.) [Monarchy; army; pro-woman writers], hannah.smith@history.ox.ac.uk

Selina Todd, B.A. (Warwick), M.A., D.Phil. (Sussex), Fellow & Tutor in Hist. (20th c. Soc. & Econ. Hist. of Brit.) [Class & gender relations; working-class life], selina.todd@st-hildas.ox.ac.uk

St. Hugh's College OX2 6LE. 01865 274900. Fax 01865 274912

George S. Garnett, M.A., Ph.D. (Cantab.), Fellow & Tutor, & College Lect., Lady Margaret Hall (Med.) [English history 10th–13th c., esp. Shifts in notions of kingship through the practice of royal succession; early modern political & legal thought], george.garnett@st-hughs.ox.ac.uk

Jonathan Parkin, M.A. (Oxon.), Ph.D. (Cantab.), Tutorial Fellow in Hist. [The interaction between ideas & practical politics in the early Enlightenment period; the reception of philosophical ideas & their impact upon political & cultural life], jon.parkin@st-hughs.ox.ac.uk

Senia Paseta, B.A. (Melbourne), M.A. (Oxon.), Ph.D. (A.N.U.), Fellow & Tutor (Mod. Brit. & Ireland) [Political & social history of 18th & 19th c. Ireland, esp. education, gender, political & social history], senia.paseta@st-hughs.ox.ac.uk

St. John's College OX1 3JP. 01865 277300. Fax 01865 277435

Richard Allen, Junior Res. Fellow [Ducal Normandy & the ecclesiastical history of northern France in the high middle ages]

Graham Barrett, Junior Res. Fellow [The socio-cultural history of the early medieval Iberian peninsula]

Sam Brewitt-Taylor, Non-Stipendiary Lect. [Christianity in 20th c. Britain]

Antonia Fitzpatrick, Junior Res. Fellow [Issues of individuality & identity in medieval philosophy]

Georgy Kantor, Tutorial Fellow in Anc. Hist. [The political, social & institutional history of the early Roman empire]

Hannah Skoda, D.E.A. (Paris), D.Phil. (Oxon.), Tutorial Fellow in Hist. [13th–15th c. Europe, with particular interest in Joan of Arc, medieval universities, conflict], hannah.skoda@sjc.ox.ac.uk

Catherine Whistler, Supernumerary Fellow in Art Hist. [Italian art of the 15th–18th c.]

William H. Whyte, B.A., M.St., D.Phil. (Oxon.), Tutorial Fellow in Hist. (Mod.) [How investigation of the built & natural environment affects existing narratives about modern British & European history, architecture, institutions such as schools, universities & churches], william.whyte@sjc.ox.ac.uk

Alastair Wright, B.A. (Cantab.), M.A. (Minn.), Ph.D. (Columbia), (Hist. of Art) [Modern art & visual culture; European modernisms], alastair.wright@sjc.ox.ac.uk

St. Peter's College OX1 2DL. 01865 278900. Fax 01865 278855

Daniel Gerrard, M.A., M.Litt., Ph.D. (Glas.), [Ecclesiastical & military history; British history 1000–1400; European history 900–1200]

Lawrence N. Goldman, M.A., Ph.D. (Cantab.), Fellow & Tutor in Mod. Hist., Editor, *Oxford Dictionary of National Biography* (Brit. 1800 onwards, Amer.) [British & American history since 1750; editor, *Oxford Dictionary of National Biography*], lawrence.goldman@spc.ox.ac.uk

Hanneke Grootenboer, M.A. (Rochester & Utrecht), M.A., Ph.D. (Rochester), (Hist. of Art) [Theories of vision in early modern paintings], hanneke.grootenboer@hoa.ox.ac.uk

Graciela Iglesias Rogers, M.A., D.Phil. (Oxon.), College Lect. in Med. Hist. [History of the Atlantic world since 1700]

Henrietta Leyser, M.A., B.Litt. (Oxon.), Emeritus Fellow in Med. Hist. [Social & cultural British history 500–1250]

Henry Mayr-Harting, M.A., D.Phil. (Oxon.), Emeritus Fellow in Med. Hist. [British & European history 400–1400]

Joshua Teplitsky, B.A. (Yeshiva), M.Phil., Ph.D. (N.Y.), Lehmann Junior Res. Fellow in Jewish Hist. [Jews in early modern Europe; Habsburg empire]

Hannah Williams, B.A. (Sydney), M.A., Ph.D. (Lond.), [17th & 18th c. French art], hannah.williams@spc.ox.ac.uk

Somerville College OX2 6HD. 01865 270600. Fax 01865 270620

Patrick Clibbens, M.A., M.Phil (Cantab.), Mary Somerville Junior Res. Fellow [20th c. South Asian & global history, esp. intellectual & political history of post-independence India; ideas of democracy; planning & social policy], patrick.clibbens@some.ox.ac.uk

Claire Copeland, M.A., D.Phil. (Oxon.), Mellon Postdoctoral Fellow (15th–17th c. Italian Hist.) [Early modern Catholicism], claire.copeland@history.ox.ac.uk

Beate Dignas, M.A., D.Phil. (Oxon.), Fellow & Tutor (Greek & Roman Hist.) [Greek religion & epigraphy; Asia Minor], beate.dignas@some.ox.ac.uk

Joanna M. Innes, M.A. (Cantab. & Oxon.), Fellow & Tutor (18th–20th c. Brit. & Eur.) [British social policy 1688–1840; re-imagining 'democracy' as a modern concept; Europe & Americas, 1750–1800], joanna.innes@some.ox.ac.uk

Oren J. Margolis, B.A. (U.S.C.), M.A. (Lond.), D.Phil. (Oxon.), Departmental Lect. (Early Mod. Hist.) [Politics & culture in Renaissance Europe; humanism & diplomacy; the Quattrocento], oren.margolis@some.ox.ac.uk

Natalia Nowakowska, M.A., D.Phil. (Oxon.), Fellow & Tutor (15th–17th c. Brit. & Eur.) [Late medieval & early modern Europe with a focus on the history of Poland in its European context], natalia.nowakowska@some.ox.ac.uk

Benjamin J. Thompson, M.A. (Cantab. & Oxon.), Ph.D. (Cantab.), D.Phil. (Oxon.), Fellow & Tutor (11th–16th c. Brit. & Eur.) [Church, society & politics, 1066–1540], benjamin.thompson@some.ox.ac.uk

Trinity College OX1 3BH. 01865 279900. Fax 01865 279911

Philip A. Booth, B.A., M.Phil., Ph.D. (Cantab.), philip.booth@trinity.ox.ac.uk

James R.C. McDougall, M.A. (St. And.), M.A., D.Phil. (Oxon.), Fellow & Tutor in Hist. (Mod. & Contemp. Hist.) [France, Mediterranean, Middle East & Africa; Islamic history since c.1700; global & imperial history], james.mcdougall@trinity.ox.ac.uk

Elina M. Screen, B.A., M.Phil., Ph.D. (Cantab.), (300–900 A.D.), elina.screen@trinity.ox.ac.uk

Bryan R. Ward-Perkins, M.A., D.Phil. (Oxon.), Fellow & Tutor in Hist. (Late Roman & Med. Hist.) [Mediterranean region in the period of transition from the Roman world to that of the middle ages c.300–700; urban & economic history], bryan.ward-perkins@trinity.ox.ac.uk

University College OX1 4BH. 01865 276602. Fax 01865 276790

Catherine J. Holmes, M.A. (Cantab.), D.Phil. (Oxon.), Tutor in Med. Hist. [Medieval Europe 900–1400; Byzantium], catherine.holmes@univ.ox.ac.uk

Ben Jackson, M.A. (Cantab. & Essex), D.Phil. (Oxon.), Tutor in Mod. Hist. (20th c. Brit.) [History of modern political thought; labour history], benjamin.jackson@univ.ox.ac.uk

Leslie Theibert, B.A. (Johns Hopkins), Ph.D. (Yale), Junior Res. Fellow [Early modern Britain & Atlantic world]

Oliver Zimmer, Lic.phil.l. (Zurich), M.A. (Oxon.), Ph.D. (Lond.), Tutor in Mod. Hist. (Mod.) [Social, cultural & political history of Europe 1760–1914; nationalism; identity], oliver.zimmer@history.ox.ac.uk

Wadham College OX1 3PN. 01865 277900. Fax 01865 277937
E. Jane Garnett, M.A., D.Phil. (Oxon.), Fellow & Sen. Tutor in Hist. (18th–20th c.) [19th & early 20th c. British & European intellectual, cultural & religious history; development of Victorian art criticism & visual culture; representation of women across the whole historical spectrum], jane.garnett@wadh.ox.ac.uk
Matthew S. Kempshall, M.A., D.Phil. (Oxon.), Fellow & Tutor in Hist. [Medieval & early Renaissance intellectual history & historiography; the influence of the classical tradition], matthew.kempshall@wadh.ox.ac.uk
Aribert J.H. Reimann, M.A., Dr.phil. (Tübingen), Thompson D.A.A.D. Fellow & Tutor in Mod. Hist. (19th–20th c.) [European social & cultural history of the First World War; social & cultural history of the Federal Republic of Germany; European avant-garde movements; protest culture & political radicalism since 1945; German exiles in Mexico, 1939–47], aribert.reimann@wadh.ox.ac.uk
Peter J. Thonemann, M.A., D.Phil. (Oxon.), Fellow & Tutor in Anc. Hist. (Archaic, Classical & Hellenic Greek Hist.) [History & archaeology of pre-Islamic Turkey; Greek epigraphy, particularly of Asia Minor; land tenure & village life in the Byzantine world], peter.thonemann@wadh.ox.ac.uk

Wellcome Unit for the History of Medicine   45–47 Banbury Road, OX2 6PE
01865 274600. Fax 01865 274605
Erica Charters, B.A. (Carleton), M.A. (Toronto), D.Phil. (Oxon.), (Hist. of Medicine) [Disease, state power, warfare & how these intersect in the 18th c., esp. in colonial contexts], erica.charters@wuhmo.ox.ac.uk
Sloan Mahone, B.A. (Hofstra), M.S. (Boston), M.Sc., D.Phil. (Oxon.), Deputy Director (Hist. of Medicine) [History of medicine & psychiatry in East Africa; prophetic & religious movements], sloan.mahone@wuhmo.ox.ac.uk
Saurabh Mishra, B.A., M.A., M.Phil., M.Sc., D.Phil. (Oxon.), [History of the Haj pilgrimage from South Asia during colonial times, with a focus on related medical & political developments; veterinary health & the peasant economy in colonial north India, 1860–1943], saurabh.mishra@wuhmo.ox.ac.uk

Wolfson College OX2 6UD. 01865 274100. Fax 01865 274125
Elise Smith, B.A. (McGill), M.Phil. (Cantab.), (Hist. of Medicine) [History of medicine & the life sciences in Britain & the British Empire since 1800; public health; anatomy; scientific racism & racial theory; eugenics; physical anthropology, esp. craniology; approaches to human differentiation in Britain & elsewhere], elise.smith@wolfson.ox.ac.uk
Ida Toth, B.A. (Oxon.), (Med. Latin & Greek), ida.toth@wolfson.ox.ac.uk

Worcester College OX1 2HB. 01865 278300. Fax 01865 278303
Robert Harris, B.A. (Dunelm.), D.Phil. (Oxon.), (Brit.) [18th c. British & Irish political, social & cultural history; early history of the press; urban history; history of gambling c.1650–1850], bob.harris@worc.ox.ac.uk
Conrad C. Leyser, B.A., D.Phil. (Oxon.), (Med.) [Religious & social history of the Latin West, 300–1100; asceticism; law, memory & social differentiation], conrad.leyser@worc.ox.ac.uk
Hugo Service, B.A., M.Phil., Ph.D. (Cantab.), hugo.service@worc.ox.ac.uk

OXFORD BROOKES UNIVERSITY

Faculty of Humanities & Social Sciences
Headington, Oxford, OX3 0BP. 01865 484095. Fax 01865 484082
www.brookes.ac.uk/about/faculties/hss/

Joanne Bailey, B.A. (Dunelm.), M.A. (Oxon.), Ph.D. (Dunelm.), Reader in Early Mod. Hist. (17th & 18th c. Soc. & Family Hist.) [Married life; marriage breakdown; women & the law; gender relations; family life; parenting], jbailey@brookes.ac.uk

James Cooper, B.A. (Wales), M.A. (Birm.), Ph.D. (Wales), Sen. Lect. in Amer. Hist. [Contemporary U.S. political history; connections with British politics], jamescooper@brookes.ac.uk

Matthew Craske, Ph.D. (Lond.), Reader in Hist. of Art [18th & 19th c. social history in art], mcraske@brookes.ac.uk

Tom Crook, B.A., M.A., Ph.D. (Manc.), Sen. Lect. in Mod. Brit. Hist. (19th c. Brit. Govt.) [Public health; bureaucracy; statistics], tcrook@brookes.ac.uk

Virginia Crossman, M.A., D.Phil. (Oxon.), Prof. (19th c. Ireland) [Local government, law & order; Poor Law], vcrossman@brookes.ac.uk

Elizabeth Darling, B.A., M.Sc., Ph.D. (Lond.), Reader in Architectural Hist. (19th & 20th c.) [Architectural modernism; social housing; gender & design], edarling@brookes.ac.uk

Anne Digby, M.A. (Cantab.), Ph.D. (East Anglia), Res. Prof. (18th–20th c. Soc. Hist.) [Doctors, patients & the state: a history of general practice 1850–1950; history of South African medicine], adigby@brookes.ac.uk

Johannes W. Dillinger, Staatsexamen (Tübingen), Ph.D., Habil. (Trier), Sen. Lect. (Early Mod. Hist.) [Political representation; peasant culture; magic], dillinger@brookes.ac.uk

Waltraud Ernst, M.A., Dipl.-Psych. (Konstanz), Ph.D. (Lond.), Prof. of Hist. of Medicine, Director of Centre for Health, Medicine & Soc.: Past & Present [History of psychiatry/mental health; history of colonial/indigenous medicine in S. Asia], wernst@brookes.ac.uk

Roger D. Griffin, M.A., D.Phil. (Oxon.), Prof. (Generic Fascism) [Theories of generic fascism], rdgriffin@brookes.ac.uk

Anne-Marie Kilday, M.A. (St. And.), Ph.D. (Strathclyde), Dean of Fac. of Humanities & Soc. Sc. (Crime & Gender in 18th c. Eur.) [Crime in Britain 1690–1800; Scottish history], akilday@brookes.ac.uk

Erik Landis, B.A. (Wesleyan), Ph.D. (Cantab.), Sen. Lect. (19th & 20th c. Russia) [Civil war; social movements; Russian history], elandis@brookes.ac.uk

Marika Leino, M.A., Ph.D. (Lond.), Sen. Lect. in Hist. of Art [Italian Renaissance art, esp. sculpture], mleino@brookes.ac.uk

Alysa Levene, M.A., M.Sc. (Oxon.), Ph.D. (Cantab.), Reader in Early Mod. Hist. [18th c. infant & child health & mortality; 20th c. municipal medicine], alevene@brookes.ac.uk

*Donal W. Lowry, B.A. (N.U.I.), Ph.D. (Rhodes), Reader (Brit. Imp., Pol. Thought, Ireland & Southern Africa) [Ulster loyalism/unionism; Irish nationalism & British empire; Rhodesia; white dominions/colonies of settlement], dlowry@brookes.ac.uk

Harry Mount, B.A. (Cantab.), M.A. (Chicago), Ph.D. (Cantab.), Princ. Lect. in Hist. of Art [British art & art theory 1660–1850, esp. reception of Dutch art, genre painting, minuteness], htmount@brookes.ac.uk

David S. Nash, B.A. (East Anglia), D.Phil. (York), Prof. (Law, Religion) [Blasphemy; republicanism; secularism], dsnash@brookes.ac.uk

Glen S. O'Hara, M.A., M.Sc. (Oxon.), Ph.D. (Lond.), Reader (19th & 20th c. Brit. Econ. & Soc. Hist.) [Government economic & social policy; public-governmental relations], go'hara@brookes.ac.uk

Christiane Payne, M.A., Ph.D. (Lond.), Prof. of Hist. of Art [19th c. British landscape & genre painting], cjepayne@brookes.ac.uk

Viviane Quirke, L. ès L., Maîtrise (Paris), D.Phil. (Oxon.), Lect. (20th c. Biomedicine) [Pharmaceutical research & development; drug discovery; biomedical disciplines; comparative history], vquirke@brookes.ac.uk

Thomas Robb, B.A., M.A., Ph.D. (Wales), Sen. Lect. in Amer. Hist. [U.S. & U.K. foreign policy; diplomatic & military history, 1775–present], trobb@brookes.ac.uk

Charles Robertson, B.A., Ph.D. (Lond.), Sen. Lect. in Hist. of Art [Painting & architecture in the Renaissance], cdrobertson@brookes.ac.uk

Andrew Spicer, B.A. (Southampton), M.A. (Leeds), Ph.D. (Southampton), Prof. (Early Mod. Eur.) [Socio-cultural impact of the Reformation], aspicer@brookes.ac.uk

Jane Stevens-Crawshaw, M.A. (Edin.), M.Phil., Ph.D. (Cantab.), Lect. (Early Mod. Eur.) [Early modern Venice], jane.stevens-crawshaw@brookes.ac.uk

Marius Turda, Ph.D., R.C.U.K. Academic Fellow in 20th c. Central & E. Eur. Bio-Medicine [History of eugenics, racism & bio-politics, 1800–1945], mturda@brookes.ac.uk

Katherine Watson, D.Phil. (Oxon.), Sen. Lect. in the Hist. of Medicine [History of crime & forensic medicine], kwatson@brookes.ac.uk

Paul J. Weindling, M.A. (Oxon.), M.Sc., Ph.D. (Lond.), Prof. (Soc. Hist. of Health, Welfare & Medical Sc.) [Medical war crimes trials; medical refugees in the 20th c.], pjweindling@brookes.ac.uk

UNIVERSITY OF PLYMOUTH

Drake Circus, Plymouth, Devon, PL4 8AA. 01752 600600. Fax 01752 232223
www.plymouth.ac.uk
Faculty of Arts: School of Humanities

Sandra Barkhof, M.Sc., Ph.D. (Plymouth), Lect. [Political history; German history; history of China & Japan; European integration; fashion history], sandra.barkhof@plymouth.ac.uk

G.H. Bennett, B.A., Ph.D. (Leicester), Assoc. Prof. (20th c. Brit. & Amer. Hist.) [20th c. American history; military history], h.bennett-1@plymouth.ac.uk

James Daybell, B.A. (Oxon.), M.A., Ph.D. (Read.), Assoc. Prof. (Early Mod. Brit. Hist.) [16th c. England; social & cultural history; gender & women; Renaissance literature], james.daybell@plymouth.ac.uk

Claire Fitzpatrick, B.A. (Monash), Ph.D. (Cantab.), Lect. (Mod. Irish Hist., Eng. Revolution & Reformation) [Modern Irish labour & the state; history of enlightenment & nationalism in the 18th–19th c.], c.fitzpatrick@plymouth.ac.uk

Richard Huzzey, B.A., D.Phil. (Oxon.), Lect. (19th & 20th c. Brit. & Imp. Hist.) [19th & 20th c. Britain; British empire; slavery & abolition; 19th c. U.S. history], richard.huzzey@plymouth.ac.uk

Kevin Jefferys, B.A., Ph.D. (Lond.), Prof. (Brit. Pol. Hist. since 1939) [British government & party politics, 1964–79], kjefferys@plymouth.ac.uk

Nick Smart, B.A. (Read.), Sen. Lect. (20th c. Brit. Pol. Hist.) [British politics between the wars], n.smart@plymouth.ac.uk

*Elizabeth Tingle, B.A. (Lond.), D.Phil. (Oxon.), Sen. Lect. (Early Mod. Eur. Hist.) [16th c. France; Counter & Catholic Reformations], elizabeth.tingle@plymouth.ac.uk

Simon Topping, B.A. (Ulster), M.A. (Sheff.), Ph.D. (Hull), Lect. [American history; African-American history; early civil rights history; American popular culture; the Republican party], simon.topping@plymouth.ac.uk

UNIVERSITY OF **PORTSMOUTH**

University House, Winston Churchill Avenue, Portsmouth, PO1 2UP. 023 9287 6543.
Fax 023 9284 3082
www.port.ac.uk
School of Social, Historical & Literary Studies
Milldam, Burnaby Road, Portsmouth, PO1 3AS. 023 9282 7681. Fax 023 9284 2174
Department of Economics, Portsmouth Business School
Richmond Building, Portland Street, Portsmouth, PO1 3DE. 023 9284 4600.
Fax 023 9284 4319
Department of Geography
Buckingham Building, Lion Terrace, Portsmouth, PO1 3HE. 023 9282 7681.
Fax 023 9284 2512
Portsmouth School of Art, Design & Media
Winston Churchill Avenue, Portsmouth, PO1 2DJ. 023 9284 3801. Fax 023 9284 3808
School of Language & Area Studies
Park Building, King Henry I Street, Portsmouth, PO1 2DZ. 023 9284 6060.
Fax 023 9284 6100

David R. Andress, B.A., D.Phil. (York), Prof. of Mod. Hist. [Popular political culture in the
French Revolution], david.andress@port.ac.uk
*Brad J. Beaven, B.A. (C.N.A.A), M.A. (Warwick), Ph.D. (De Montfort), Reader in Soc. &
Cultural Hist. [Working-class culture & leisure; popular culture & imperialism; 1860–1945
port towns], brad.beaven@port.ac.uk
Karl Bell, B.A. (C.N.A.A.), M.A. (Lond.), Ph.D. (East Anglia), Sen. Lect. [Magical mentalities &
the fantastical imagination in the modern period, 1780–1900], karl.bell@port.ac.uk
Susan Bruley, M.A., Ph.D. (Lond.), Reader in Mod. Hist. [Women in Britain since 1900, esp.
working-class women & factory work, 1930s–60], sue.bruley@port.ac.uk
Jodi Burkett, B.A. (Toronto), M.A. (McGill), Ph.D. (York, Canada), Sen. Lect. in Hist.
[Social movements, national identity, race & ethnicity in 20th c. Britain, esp. the 1960s],
jodi.burkett@port.ac.uk
Anthony D. Chafer, B.A. (Nott.), L. ès L. (Nantes), M.A. (Lond. & Read.), Ph.D. (Lond.), Prof.
in Contemp. French Area Stud., Sch. of Lang. [Decolonisation & post-colonialism in French
W. Africa], tony.chafer@port.ac.uk
Heather Coleman, B.A., M.A. (C.N.A.A.), Assoc. Sen. Lect. in Hist. & Theoretical Stud.,
Sch. of Art [Museums & exhibitions as sites of production of meaning around objects],
heather.coleman@port.ac.uk
Peter Collier, B.Sc., Ph.D. (Aston), Princ. Lect. in Geog. [History of cartography; social
networks; the development of geography], peter.collier@port.ac.uk
*Michele-Anne Dauppe, B.A., M.A. (Leeds), Head of Sch., Design & Media [Graphic design
history], michele-anne.dauppe@port.ac.uk
Laurie N. Ede, B.A., Ph.D. (Portsmouth), Princ. Lect. (Cultural & Film Hist.) [Film design],
laurie.ede@port.ac.uk
Mike Esbester, B.A. (Exeter), M.A., Ph.D. (York), Lect. in Hist. [Safety, accidents & risk in 20th
c. Britain; transport & mobility in 19th & 20th c. Britain], mike.esbester@port.ac.uk
Paul S. Flenley, M.A. (St. And.), Ph.D. (Birm.), Princ. Lect. in Russian & Soviet Hist. [Soviet
history 1917–29; Russian labour history; Russian nationalism], paul.flenley@port.ac.uk
Dominic Fontana, B.A., Ph.D. (Portsmouth), Sen. Lect. in Geog. [The use of
G.I.S. in historical studies; historical development of the Portsmouth region],
dominic.fontana@port.ac.uk

Portsmouth

Stuart Gard, B.A. (Portsmouth), Sen. Lect. in Hist. & Theoretical Stud., Sch. of Art, stuart.gard@port.ac.uk

Katy Gibbons, B.A., M.A., Ph.D. (York), Sen. Lect. in Early Mod. Hist. [England & France in the 16th c.; religious change; exile], katy.gibbons@port.ac.uk

Sue Harper, B.A., M.A., M.Phil., Ph.D., Emeritus Prof. of Film Hist. [British cinema, 1930–80], sue.harper@port.ac.uk

Richard G. Healey, M.A., Ph.D. (Cantab.), Prof. of Geog. [U.S. regional economic development, 1850–1900], richard.healey@port.ac.uk

Robert James, B.A., M.A., Ph.D. (Portsmouth), Sen. Lect. in Hist. [Working-class taste in film & literature], robert.james@port.ac.uk

Wolfram Kaiser, B.A., M.A., Ph.D. (Hamburg), Prof. of Eur. Stud. (Eur. Stud.) [Transnational European Union; museums & representations of Europe], wolfram.kaiser@port.ac.uk

Alastair Pearson, B.A. (Leeds), Ph.D. (Portsmouth), [Landscape evolution; application of G.I.S. to historical geography & archaeology], alastair.pearson@port.ac.uk

June Purvis, B.A. (Leeds), Ph.D. (Open), Prof. Emeritus of Women's Hist. [Suffragette movement; women's biography], june.purvis@port.ac.uk

Christopher Reid, B.A. (C.N.A.A.), Ph.D. (Portsmouth), Princ. Lect. in Econ., Dept. of Econ. [Modern British economic history], chris.reid@port.ac.uk

Timothy J.T. Rooth, B.Sc.(Econ.), Ph.D. (Hull), Prof. Emeritus in Econ. Hist., Dept. of Econ. [British 20th c. external economic policy], tim.rooth@port.ac.uk

Lee Sartain, B.A. (Kent), M.A. (Keele), Ph.D. (Lancaster), Sen. Lect. in Amer. Stud. [African American history/civil rights movement], lee.sartain@port.ac.uk

Mathias Seiter, M.A. (Augsburg), Ph.D. (Southampton), Lect. in Hist. [Modern German history, esp. nation-building during the long 19th c.; German-Jewish history], mathias.seiter@port.ac.uk

Humphrey Southall, M.A., Ph.D. (Cantab.), Reader in Geog. [Labour markets; regional differences in Britain; historical G.I.S.; gazetteers], humphrey.southall@port.ac.uk

James H. Thomas, B.A. (Lond.), Ph.D. (Southampton), Reader in Eng. Local Hist. [Maritime history; local history], james.thomas@port.ac.uk

Natalya Vince, B.A. (Oxon.), Ph.D. (Lond.), Lect. in French Stud. [Decolonisation & post-colonialism in France & Algeria], natalya.vince@port.ac.uk

Patrick L. Williams, B.A. (Nott.), Ph.D. (Lond.), Emeritus Prof. of Spanish Hist., Sch. of Lang. [Conciliar government in Habsburg Spain], patrick.williams@port.ac.uk

UNIVERSITY OF **READING**

Whiteknights, P.O. Box 217, Reading, RG6 2AH. 0118 9875123. Fax 0118 9314404
www.reading.ac.uk
Department of History 0118 378 8147. Fax 0118 378 6440
www.reading.ac.uk/history/
Department of Archaeology 0118 9318132
www.reading.ac.uk/archaeology/
Department of Art 0118 9318890. Fax 0118 9318918
www.reading.ac.uk/arthistory/
Department of Classics 0118 9318420
Department of Economics 0118 9318226. Fax 0118 9750236
Department of Modern Languages & European Studies 0118 378123

Grenville G. Astill, B.A., Ph.D. (Birm.), Prof. of Med. Archaeol. (Med.) [Archaeology of medieval monasticism; urbanism & economy], g.g.astill@reading.ac.uk

Emma Aston, B.A. (Oxon.), M.Phil. (Cantab.), Ph.D. (Exeter), Assoc. Prof. of Classics [Greek religion; classical & Hellenistic Thessaly], e.m.m.aston@reading.ac.uk

*Jonathan W. Bell, M.A. (Oxon.), M.Phil., Ph.D. (Cantab.), Sen. Lect. in Hist. (Amer.) [American politics & society in the 20th c.], j.w.bell@reading.ac.uk

*Martin Bell, B.Sc., Ph.D. (Lond.), Head of Dept. of Archaeol. [Geoarchaeology; prehistoric landscapes & wetlands], m.g.bell@reading.ac.uk

Stuart Black, Ph.D., Assoc. Prof. in Environmental Radioactivity [Forensic archaeology; archaeological dating techniques], s.black@reading.ac.uk

Richard J. Bradley, M.A. (Oxon.), F.B.A., Prof. of Archaeol. (Prehist.) [Prehistoric landscapes; rock art; ritual & social organisation; field archaeology], r.j.bradley@reading.ac.uk

Nicholas Branch, B.Sc., M.Sc., Ph.D. (Lond.), Sen. Lect. in Palaeoecology [Environmental archaeology], n.p.branch@reading.ac.uk

Roy D. Brigden, B.A. (Dunelm.), Ph.D. (Read.), Keeper of the Museum of Eng. Rural Life (Agricultural Hist.), r.d.brigden@reading.ac.uk

Jeremy F.S. Burchardt, B.A. (Oxon.), Ph.D. (Read.), Lect. in Rural Hist. [Allotment movement; attitudes to countryside], j.f.s.burchardt@reading.ac.uk

Robert W. Chapman, M.A., Ph.D. (Cantab.), Emeritus Prof. of Archaeol. (Prehist.) [W. Mediterranean prehistory; development of social, political & economic inequalities in human societies; archaeological theory], r.w.chapman@reading.ac.uk

Edward J.T. Collins, B.A. (Birm.), Ph.D. (Nott.), Emeritus Prof. of Rural Hist. [Agricultural output in Britain 1800–1939; world food grain consumption 18th–20th c.], e.j.t.collins@reading.ac.uk

John D. Creighton, B.A., Ph.D. (Dunelm.), Prof. of Archaeol. (Roman) [Roman & iron-age coinage; geophysical prospection techniques], j.d.creighton@reading.ac.uk

Antara Datta, B.A. (Delhi), B.A. (Oxon.), Ph.D. (Harv.), Lect. in Hist. [South Asia; migration history], a.datta@reading.ac.uk

J. Paul Davies, B.A. (Read.), M.A., Ph.D. (Lond.), Reader in Hist. of Art [Renaissance Italy], j.p.davies@reading.ac.uk

Timothy E. Duff, M.A., Ph.D. (Cantab.), Prof. of Classics [Plutarch's *Lives*; Greek & Roman historiography], t.e.duff@reading.ac.uk

Christopher J.H. Duggan, B.A., D.Phil. (Oxon.), Prof. of Italian Hist. [Nation building in 19th c. Italy], c.j.h.duggan@reading.ac.uk

Hella Eckardt, B.A. (Mainz), M.A. (Lond.), Ph.D. (Read.), Assoc. Prof. [Roman archaeology & artefacts with an emphasis on small finds], h.eckardt@reading.ac.uk

Reading

Joel Félix, D.Lett. (Paris), Prof. of French Stud. (Mod. France) [Finance in the ancien regime],
  j.m.felix@reading.ac.uk

Dominik Fleitmann, Ph.D., Prof. of Palaeoclimatology & Archaeol. [Paleoclimatology],
  d.fleitmann@reading.ac.uk

Rachel Foxley, M.A. (Oxon.), M.A. (York), Ph.D. (Cantab.), Lect. in Early Mod. Hist. (Pol.
  Thought, Levellers), r.h.foxley@reading.ac.uk

Michael G. Fulford, B.A., Ph.D. (Southampton), F.B.A., Prof. of Archaeol., Director of the
  Silchester Field Sch. (Roman) [Roman urban archaeology, economy & trade, material
  culture, landscape & technology], m.g.fulford@reading.ac.uk

Jane F. Gardner, M.A. (Glas. & Oxon.), Emeritus Prof. of Anc. Hist. [Roman family law],
  j.f.gardner@reading.ac.uk

Duncan Garrow, Ph.D., Lect. in Eur. Prehist. [British & European prehistory],
  d.j.garrow@reading.ac.uk

Roberta L. Gilchrist, B.A., D.Phil. (York), Prof. of Archaeol. (Med.) [Medieval gender &
  lifecourse; medieval burial & buildings archaeology], r.l.gilchrist@reading.ac.uk

Andrew Godley, B.Sc.(Econ.), Ph.D. (Lond.), Lect. in Econ. (Business Hist.),
  a.c.godley@reading.ac.uk

Lindy Grant, M.A. (St. And.), Ph.D. (Lond.), Prof. of Med. Hist. (Med.),
  l.m.grant@reading.ac.uk

Anna E. Gruetzner-Robins, B.A. (Toronto), M.A., Ph.D. (Lond.), Reader in Hist. of Art,
  a.e.gruetzner-robins@reading.ac.uk

Robert Hosfield, B.A., M.Sc., Ph.D. (Southampton), Assoc. Prof. in Palaeolithic Archaeol.
  [Palaeolithic archaeology], r.hosfield@reading.ac.uk

Richard W. Hoyle, B.A. (Birm.), D.Phil. (Oxon.), Prof. of Rural Hist. (Early Mod. Brit.)
  [Pilgrimage of Grace; 16th–17th c. economy & society], r.w.hoyle@reading.ac.uk

*Andrew F. Knapp, B.A., D.Phil. (Oxon.), Prof. of French Stud. (Mod. France) [20th c. French
  political parties; France in the Second World War; bombing], a.f.knapp@reading.ac.uk

Anne E. Lawrence, M.A. (Cantab.), M.A., Ph.D. (Lond.), Sen. Lect. in Hist. (Med.
  Culture) [Libraries & scriptoria in Anglo-Norman England; Cistercian scholarship],
  a.e.mathers-lawrence@reading.ac.uk

Jim Leary, B.A. (Cardiff), Ph.D. (Manc.), Lect. in Later Prehist. [British prehistory with an
  emphasis on the Neolithic], j.c.leary@reading.ac.uk

Simon Lee, B.A., Ph.D. (Read.), Sen. Lect. in Hist. of Art [Jacques-Louis David & his pupils],
  s.lee@reading.ac.uk

Mary Lewis, B.A. (Leicester), M.Sc., Ph.D. (Bradford), Assoc. Prof. in Biological Anthr.
  [Bioarchaeology with an emphasis on medieval children], m.e.lewis@reading.ac.uk

Rachel Mairs, B.A., M.A., M.Phil., Ph.D. (Cantab.), Lect. in Classics [Bactria; Hellenistic
  Egypt; epigraphy], r.mairs@reading.ac.uk

Patrick N. Major, B.A., D.Phil. (Oxon.), Prof. of Mod. Eur. Hist. (Mod. Eur.) [Modern Germany;
  Cold War culture], p.major@reading.ac.uk

Susan B. Malvern, B.A. (Read.), Sen. Lect. in Hist. of Art [Art & war; feminism & art],
  s.b.malvern@reading.ac.uk

*Annalisa Marzano, B.A., M.A. (Florence), M.Phil., Ph.D. (Columbia), Prof. of Anc. Hist.
  (Roman) [Roman social & economic history; villas & agriculture; marine resources],
  a.marzano@reading.ac.uk

Elizabeth Matthew, B.A., Ph.D. (Dunelm.), Lect. in Hist. [The English & the Irish in the middle
  ages], e.a.e.matthews@reading.ac.uk

Roger J. Matthews, Ph.D., Prof. of Near Eastern Archaeol. [Archaeology of the Middle East],
  r.j.matthews@reading.ac.uk

Wendy Matthews, M.A. (Edin.), Ph.D. (Cantab.), Lect. [Archaeology of the Middle East;
  micromorphology], w.matthews@reading.ac.uk

Esther Mijers, M.A. (Rijksuniversiteit Leiden), Ph.D. (St. And.), Lect. (Early Mod.) [The Dutch Republic; 17th c. imperialism], e.mijers@reading.ac.uk

Steven J. Mithen, B.A. (Sheff.), M.Sc. (York), Ph.D. (Cantab.), Prof. in Archaeol. (Prehist.) [Archaeology of early humans & early sedentism], s.j.mithen@reading.ac.uk

Gundula Müldner, M.A., M.Sc., Ph.D. (Bradford), Lect. in Palaeo-health & Diet [Human & animal isotopes & bioarchaeology; medieval food & nutrition], g.h.mueldner@reading.ac.uk

Lucy Newton, B.A., Ph.D. (Lond.), Lect. in Econ. (Business Hist.), lucy.lanewton@fsnet.co.uk

Matthew Nicholls, B.A., M.Phil., D.Phil. (Oxon.), Assoc. Prof. of Classics [Ancient libraries], m.c.nicholls@reading.ac.uk

Arietta Papaconstantinou, B.A., M.A., Ph.D. (Stras.), Reader in Anc. Hist. [Egypt & eastern Mediterranean 3rd–8th c. late antiquity], a.s.papaconstantinou@reading.ac.uk

Helen L. Parish, M.A. (St. And.), D.Phil. (Oxon.), Sen. Lect. in Hist. (Early Mod.) [English clergy in 16th c.; Protestant history writing; post-Reformation religious practice], h.l.parish@reading.ac.uk

Aleks Pluskowski, B.A., Ph.D. (Cantab.), Lect. in Med. Archaeol. (Archaeol. of Later Med. Eur. & Crusading) [Medieval archaeology; archaeology of crusading; medieval zooarchaeology], a.g.pluskowski@reading.ac.uk

Linda Risso, M.Phil, Ph.D. (Cantab.), Lect. (Mod. Eur.) [Modern Italian history; the Cold War], l.risso@reading.ac.uk

Rebecca Rist, B.A. (Oxon.), M.A., Ph.D. (Cantab.), Sen. Lect. (Med. Eur.) [The Crusades], r.a.c.rist@reading.ac.uk

E. Clare Robertson, M.A. (Oxon.), M.Phil., Ph.D. (Lond.), Prof. of Hist. of Art [Carracci], e.c.robertson@reading.ac.uk

Rhianedd Smith, M.Phil. (Oxon.), Ph.D. (Read.), Museum Stud. Programme Director, Museum of Eng. Rural Life [Museums & heritage], r.smith@reading.ac.uk

David Stack, B.A. (Lond.), Ph.D. (Cantab.), Reader in Hist. (Mod. Brit.) [Victorian social thought; Darwinism], d.a.stack@reading.ac.uk

Gabor Thomas, Ph.D., Assoc. Prof. in Early Med. Archaeol. [Early medieval archaeology; later Anglo-Saxon & Viking-age artefacts; the archaeology of early medieval conversion & monasticism], gabor.thomas@reading.ac.uk

Emily R. West, B.A., Ph.D. (Liv.), M.A. (Manc.), Sen. Lect. in Amer. Hist. [Slavery & the antebellum South], e.r.west@reading.ac.uk

Matthew Worley, B.A., Ph.D. (Nott.), Prof. of Hist. (Mod. Brit.) [Communist party; labour politics], m.worley@reading.ac.uk

Margaret Yates, B.A. (Read.), D.Phil. (Oxon.), Sen. Lect. in Hist. [Late medieval & early modern social & economic history], m.h.yates@reading.ac.uk

UNIVERSITY OF **ROEHAMPTON**

Department of Humanities
Digby Stuart College, Roehampton Lane, London, SW15 5PH. 020 8392 3000.
www.roehampton.ac.uk/humanities/

Margaret L. Arnot, B.A., M.A. (Melb.), Ph.D. (Essex), Princ. Lect. (19th c. Brit. Soc. & Cultural Hist., Women, Gender, Crime) [19th c. Britain: gender & crime; infanticide & child abuse], M.Arnot@roehampton.ac.uk

Charlotte Behr, Lic.phil. (Aix-en-Provence), Staatsexamen, Dr.phil. (Münster), Reader (Late Roman & Early Med. Eur.) [Migration period gold bracteates], C.Behr@roehampton.ac.uk

Michael Brown, B.A. (York), M.Sc. (Lond.), Ph.D. (York), Sen. Lect. (Hist. of Medicine, Mod. Brit.) [Social & cultural history of medicine in 19th c. Britain], Michael.Brown@roehampton.ac.uk
Susan J. Deacy, B.A., Ph.D. (Wales), Princ. Lect. (Anc. Greek Hist. & Literature) [Ancient Greek gender & sexuality; ancient Greek religion], S. Deacy@roehampton.ac.uk
*Trevor Dean, M.A., D.Phil. (Oxon.), Prof. (Late Med. Italian, Soc. & Pol.) [Renaissance Italy: crime; violence; weather], T.Dean@roehampton.ac.uk
Peter Edwards, B.A., M.A. (Leicester), D.Phil. (Oxon.), Emeritus Prof. (Early Mod. Eng. Local Hist.) [Logistics in British civil wars; royal stables 16th–17th c.; horses in society & economy of Tudor & Stuart England; rural society 16th–17th c.], P.Edwards@roehampton.ac.uk
Carrie Hamilton, B.A. (Toronto), M.A. (Concordia), Ph.D. (Lond.), Reader (Contemp. Spain & Latin Amer.) [Gender history; history of sexuality; oral history; histories of revolution & political violence]
Glyn Parry, M.A., Ph.D. (Cantab.), Prof. (Early Mod. Hist., esp. Historiography, Comparative Global Hist.) [Early modern magic & its wider culture; Shakespeare & his evironment; Tudor government in action; the decline of magic], Glyn.Parry@roehampton.ac.uk
Sara Pennell, M.A. (Cantab.), M.S. (Penn.), D.Phil. (Oxon.), Sen. Lect. (Early Mod. Brit. Soc. & Cultural Hist.) [17th & 18th c. food practices; health & domestic medicine; the non-elite interior], S.Pennell@roehampton.ac.uk
Krisztina Robert, B.A., M.A. (E.L.T.E., Hungary), Ph.D. (Houston), Sen. Lect. (19th & 20th c. Brit. & Eur. Soc. & Cultural Hist.) [Late Victorian & 20th c. Britain; gender & war; militarism; modernity], K.Robert@roehampton.ac.uk
Katharina Rowold, B.A., Ph.D. (Lond.), Sen. Lect. (Mod. Eur. Hist.) [Gender history; history of medicine & science; history of childhood], Katharina.Rowold@roehampton.ac.uk
H. Margaret Spufford, O.B.E., M.A., Ph.D. (Leicester), Litt.D. (Cantab.), F.B.A., Emerita Prof. [Early modern English society; local history]
John A. Tosh, B.A. (Oxon.), M.A. (Cantab.), Ph.D. (Lond.), Prof. (Gender & Soc. Hist. in Mod. Brit., Historiography) [Masculinities & manliness in 19th c. Britain; social rationale of historical study], J.Tosh@roehampton.ac.uk
Cornelie Usborne, B.A., Ph.D. (Open), Emerita Prof. (20th c. Germany, Soc. & Cultural Hist.) [Sexuality; reproductive health; medicine; women, gender & popular culture in Weimar & Nazi Germany], C.Usborne@roehampton.ac.uk
Edward Vallance, M.A., D.Phil. (Oxon.), Reader (Brit.) [17th c. British political & religious history, esp. the civil wars]
Andrew Wareham, B.A., M.A., (Lond.), Ph.D. (Birm.), Reader, Director, Hearth Tax Project [Early medieval & early modern English social & economic history]

UNIVERSITY OF ST. ANDREWS

St. Andrews, Fife, KY16 9AJ
www.st-andrews.ac.uk
School of History Office 01334 462900. Fax 01334 462914
Departments of Mediaeval History, Modern History, Scottish History
Department of Ancient History 01334 462600

David W. Allan, M.A. (Edin.), Ph.D. (Cantab.), Reader in Scot. Hist. [Early modern Scottish culture, intellectual life & politics], da2@st-andrews.ac.uk
Ralph Anderson, B.A., M.Phil., Ph.D. (Cantab.), Sen. Teaching Fellow in Anc. Hist. [Greek religion; anthropological theories of religion & ritual], rta1@st-andrews.ac.uk

Frances E. Andrews, B.A., Ph.D. (Lond.), Prof. of Med. Hist. [N. Italian social & religious history 12th–14th c.; Humiliati; Milan], fea@st-andrews.ac.uk

Ali M. Ansari, B.A., Ph.D. (Lond.), Prof. of Mod. Hist. (Pol. & Soc. Hist. of Mod. Mid. E.) [19th & 20th c. Middle East; ideologies of the modern Middle East; Britain & Iran], aa51@st-andrews.ac.uk

Robert J. Bartlett, M.A. (Cantab.), D.Phil. (Oxon.), F.B.A., Prof. of Med. Hist. (12th c.) [Frontiers & colonisation; cults of saints 12th c. England], rjb1@st-andrews.ac.uk

Riccardo Bavaj, M.A., Ph.D. (Bonn), Lect. in Mod. Hist. [19th & 20th c. Europe, esp. 20th c. Germany; intellectual-cultural history], rbflb@st-andrews.ac.uk

Ahab Bdaiwi, B.Sc. (Lond.), B.A., Teaching Fellow (Islamic & Iranian Hist.) [Late 15th & 16th c. Islamic intellectual history; Shiism; Islamic philosophy]

Michael H. Brown, M.A., Ph.D. (St. And.), Reader in Scot. Hist. [Medieval Welsh & late medieval British history], mhb@st-andrews.ac.uk

John F.M. Clark, B.A. (W. Ont.), M.A. (Toronto), D.Phil. (Oxon.), Lect. in Mod. Hist. (19th–20th c. Brit.) [Environment; science; medicine], jfc2@st-andrews.ac.uk

Jonathan C.N. Coulston, B.A. (Leicester), M.Phil., Ph.D. (Newcastle), Lect. in Anc. Hist. [History of city of Rome; Roman marble sculpture; military equipment], jcnc@st-andrews.ac.uk

Rory Cox, B.A., M.A. (Lond.), D.Phil. (Oxon.), Lect. (Late Med. Hist.) [13th–15th c. England & Europe; military history; political thought]

Gerard J. De Groot, B.A. (Whitman Coll.), Ph.D. (Edin.), Prof. of Mod. Hist. (20th c.) [Labour party; World Wars I & II; women soldiers & combat in World War II], gjdg@st-andrews.ac.uk

Sarah Easterby-Smith, B.A. (York), M.A., Ph.D. (Warwick), Lect. in Mod. Hist. [18th c. France & Britain; cultural & social history; history of science; global history], ses22@st-andrews.ac.uk

Kate Ferris, B.A. (Sussex), M.Sc., Ph.D. (Lond.), Lect. in Mod. Eur. Hist. [19th–20th c. Italian & Spanish political, social & cultural history; everyday life & the lived experience of mid 20th c. European dictatorships], kf50@st-andrews.ac.uk

Justine Firnhaber-Baker, M.A., Ph.D. (Harv.), Lect. in Late Med. Hist. [French political & legal history], jmfb@st-andrews.ac.uk

Aileen K. Fyfe, M.A., Ph.D. (Cantab.), Reader in Mod. Brit. Hist. (19th c. Brit.) [History of science, technology & communication], akf@st-andrews.ac.uk

Tim Greenwood, M.A., D.Phil. (Oxon.), Sen. Lect. in Med. Hist. (Eastern Christianity) [The Near East c.500–1200; Armenian & Byzantine political, social & cultural history; Armenian historiography & epigraphy], twg3@st-andrews.ac.uk

Jill D. Harries, M.A., D.Phil. (Oxon.), Prof. of Anc. Hist., p/t (Late Roman Empire) [Late Roman Gaul: law & society; rise of Christianity], jdh2@st-andrews.ac.uk

Emma F.K. Hart, B.A. (Oxon.), M.A., Ph.D. (Johns Hopkins), Lect. in Mod. Hist. (Amer.) [18th c. colonial America & Britain; economy; material culture], efh2@st-andrews.ac.uk

Bridget M. Heal, M.A. (Cantab.), M.A., Ph.D. (Lond.), Sen. Lect. in Mod. Hist. (16th–17th c.) [German religious & social history; visual culture of the Reformation], bmh6@st-andrews.ac.uk

Robert A. Houston, M.A. (St. And.), Ph.D. (Cantab.), Prof. of Mod. Hist. (Econ. & Soc.) [European education & literacy, 1500–1850; insanity in 18th c. Scotland], rah@st-andrews.ac.uk

*John G.H. Hudson, M.A. (Toronto), M.A., D.Phil. (Oxon.), Prof. in Med. Hist. (11th–13th c. Eng.) [Legal history 12th c. England], jghh@st-andrews.ac.uk

Tomasz Kamusella, M.A. (Katowice), M.A. (Potchefstroom), M.A. (Central European University), Ph.D. (Poznań), Lect. in Mod. Hist. (19th–20th c. Central Eur.) [Ethnicity & history of language & politics of modern central Europe], tdk2@st-andrews.ac.uk

St. Andrews

Dimitris Kastritsis, B.A. (Chicago), Ph.D. (Harv.), Lect. (Mid. E. Hist., 13th–16th c.) [Ottoman & Byzantine empires]

Chandrika Kaul, B.A. (Delhi), M.A., D.Phil. (Oxon.), Lect. in Mod. Hist. [Late 19th & 20th c. British empire in S. Asia; British press & politics; communications], ck24@st-andrews.ac.uk

Colin C. Kidd, M.A. (Cantab.), D.Phil. (Oxon.), Prof. of Mod. Hist. (Intellectual Hist. & Hist. of Pol. Thought) [Early modern intellectual history; 'British Question'; the Enlightenment; constitutional theory in the Atlantic world; history of anthropology], cck3@st-andrews.ac.uk

William W. Knox, M.A., Ph.D. (Edin.), Sen. Lect. in Scot. Hist. (18th–20th c.) [Work & politics in modern Scotland], wk@st-andrews.ac.uk

Myles P. Lavan, B.A. (Dublin), M.Phil., Ph.D. (Cantab.), Lect. in Anc. Hist. [Roman society & culture; imperialism; slavery; patronage; historiography], mpl2@st-andrews.ac.uk

Konrad M. Lawson, B.A. (Western Washington), M.I.A. (Columbia), M.A., Ph.D. (Harv.), Lect. (Mod. Hist.) [20th c. transnational; East Asia; aftermaths of modern war; Japanese empire], kml8@st-andrews.ac.uk

Sian Lewis, M.A., D.Phil. (Oxon.), Lect. in Anc. Hist. [Greek political & social history; Greek vase painting], sl50@st-andrews.ac.uk

Simon J. MacLean, M.A., M.Phil. (Glas.), Ph.D. (Lond.), Prof. in Med. Hist. (Early Med. Eur.), sm89@st-andrews.ac.uk

Roger A. Mason, M.A., Ph.D. (Edin.), Prof. of Scot. Hist. (15th–17th c.) [Scottish political thought; national identities in 15th–16th c. Britain], ram@st-andrews.ac.uk

Emily Michelson, Ph.D. (Yale), Lect. in Mod. Hist. (Early Mod. Relig.) [Italian Renaissance; Catholic reform; Italian preaching; intellectual & cultural history of early modern Europe], edm21@st-andrews.ac.uk

Gillian Mitchell, M.A., M.Phil. (Glas.), Ph.D. (Toronto), Lect. in Amer. Hist. [19th & 20th c. American social & cultural history; folk music], gamm2@st-andrews.ac.uk

Frank L. Müller, Staatsexamen (Berlin), D.Phil. (Oxon.), Prof. in Mod. Hist. [Political history of Germany, 1815–1914; Anglo-German relations], flm3@st-andrews.ac.uk

Steve Murdoch, M.A., Ph.D. (Aberd.), Prof. in Scot. Hist. [British relations with Scandinavia, 1560–1750; Scottish history in a British context; formation & retention of 'identities'], sm117@st-andrews.ac.uk

Frances Nethercott, B.A. (Dunelm.), M.Phil. (Oxon.), Ph.D. (Paris), Reader in Mod. Hist. (Russia) [19th & 20th c. intellectual & cultural history; modern historiography], fn4@st-andrews.ac.uk

James J. Nott, B.A., M.St., D.Phil. (Oxon.), Lect. in Mod. Hist. (Soc. & Cultural Hist.) [20th c. British popular culture & leisure, esp. popular music, dance halls, cinema, radio & gramophone; class & culture; inter-war Britain], jjn4@st-andrews.ac.uk

James Palmer, B.A. (Sheff.), M.Phil. (Cantab.), Ph.D. (Sheff.), Lect. in Med. Hist. (Eur.) [8th & 9th c. Frankish cultural history; time & apocalypticism; historiography], jtp21@st-andrews.ac.uk

Andrew Peacock, M.A. (Oxon.), M.Phil., Ph.D. (Cantab.), Lect. in Mid. E. Hist. (Islamic & Mid. E. Hist., 10th–17th c.), acsp@st-andrews.ac.uk

Andrew D.M. Pettegree, M.A., D.Phil. (Oxon.), Prof. in Mod. Hist. (Reformation) [Calvinism & its political impact; English & continental Reformation], admp@st-andrews.ac.uk

Jacqueline Rose, M.A., M.Phil., Ph.D. (Cantab.), Lect. in Mod. Hist. (16th–17th c. Brit.) [Early modern political, religious & intellectual history], jer9@st-andrews.ac.uk

Guy R. Rowlands, B.A., D.Phil. (Oxon.), Reader in Mod. Hist. (16th–18th c. W. Eur.) [17th & 18th c. France & Spain; war & international relations 1659–1763; Jacobitism], gr30@st-andrews.ac.uk

Katie Stevenson, B.A. Hons., Ph.D. (Edin.), Sen. Lect. in Scot. & Med. Hist. [15th c. Scotland; chivalry, knighthood & courtly culture], kcs7@st-andrews.ac.uk

Angus D. Stewart, M.A., M.Litt., Ph.D. (St. And.), Lect. in Med. Hist. [Middle East, 12th–14th c.; Mamluks; Mongols; Crusades], ads@st-andrews.ac.uk

Bernhard Struck, M.A. (Freie Univ., Berlin), Ph.D. (Paris), Reader in Mod. Hist. [18th & 19th c. Germany & France; travel & travel writing; history of sciences; translation history], bs50@st-andrews.ac.uk

Rebecca Sweetman, B.A. (Dublin), Ph.D. (Nott.), Sen. Lect. in Anc. Hist. [Archaeology of Roman & late antique Knossos; late antique Peloponnese, esp. Sparta], rs43@st-andrews.ac.uk

Stephen Tyre, M.A. (Edin.), M.Sc. (Lond.), Ph.D. (Edin.), Lect. in Mod. Hist. (Late 19th & 20th c. Eur. & Int. Hist.) [French history & decolonisation], st29@st-andrews.ac.uk

Richard Whatmore, Ph.D. (Cantab.), Prof. in Mod. Hist. (Early Mod. & Mod. Intellectual Hist.) [Theories of empire, democracy & war; enlightenment & revolution; republican diaspora; relations between Britain & Europe]

Alex Woolf, B.A., M.Phil. (Sheff.), Ph.D. (St. And.), Sen. Lect. in Med. Scot. Hist. [Early medieval Britain & Ireland; medieval Iceland; Anglo-Norman Scotland; transitions from tribalism to statehood], aw40@st-andrews.ac.uk

Greg D. Woolf, B.A. (Oxon.), Ph.D. (Cantab.), Prof. of Anc. Hist. [Cultural, social, religious & economic history of the Roman world], gdw2@st-andrews.ac.uk

ST. MARY'S UNIVERSITY, TWICKENHAM

Waldegrave Road, Strawberry Hill, Twickenham, TW1 4SX. 020 8240 4000.
Fax 020 8240 4255
www.smuc.ac.uk
School of Arts & Humanities

Mark Donnelly, B.A., Ph.D. (Surrey), Sen. Lect. (20th c. Brit. Hist.) [Historiography & theory; contemporary cultural history; revolutions; war memory; the 1960s], mark.donnelly@smuc.ac.uk

Fr. Robin Gibbons, B.A. (Kent), M.Th., Ph.D. (Lond.), Sen. Lect. (Late Med. Eccles. Hist.) [Church art & architecture]

Chris Keith, B.G., M.A., M.Div. (Cincinnati Christian Univ.), Ph.D. (Edin.), Prof. of New Testament & Early Christianity (1st–4th c. Christianity, Second Temple Judaism) [Ancient Jewish scribal culture; early Christian book culture; historical Jesus; canonical & non-canonical Gospels]

*Sinead McEneaney, B.A., Ph.D. (N.U.I.), Lect., Director of Hist. (19th & 20th c. U.S. Hist.; Post-War France) [Post-war protest movements, U.S.A. & France; gender], sinead.mceneaney@smuc.ac.uk

Nur Masalha, B.A., M.A. (Jerusalem), Ph.D. (Lond.), Prof. [Political history of the Middle East, esp. Israel & the Palestinians], nur.masalha@smuc.ac.uk

Daragh Minogue, B.A. (Portsmouth), Lect. (20th c. Irish Hist.) [Contemporary Irish history, esp. church-state relations], daragh.minogue@smuc.ac.uk

Claire Norton, B.A., M.A., Ph.D. (Birm.), Sen. Lect. in Hist. (Islamic Hist.) [Ottoman history, esp. identity formation in the Balkans & Ottoman history writing], claire.norton@smuc.ac.uk

Glenn J. Richardson, B.A. (Sydney), Ph.D. (Lond.), Reader in Early Mod. Hist. (16th–17th c. Brit. & Eur. Hist.) [16th c. Anglo-French political & cultural relations], glenn.richardson@smuc.ac.uk

Eugenia Russell, B.Mus. (Lond.), M.A. (Brist.), Ph.D. (Lond.), Lect. (Early Mod. Hist.) [Byzantium & the Renaissance], eugenia.russell@smuc.ac.uk

UNIVERSITY OF **SALFORD**

Salford, M5 4WT. 0161 295 5000. Fax 0161 295 5999
www.salford.ac.uk
School of English, Sociology, Politics & Contemporary History
0161 295 5540. Fax 0161 295 5077
www.espach.salford.ac.uk
School of Modern Languages 0161 295 5786
www.modlang.salford.ac.uk

Lars Berger, M.A., Ph.D. (Friedrich-Schiller), Lect. in Pol. & Contemp. Hist. of the Mid. E. [Islamism; terrorism; U.S. Middle East policy; Arab-Israeli conflict; international relations of the Arab world]
Martin Bull, B.A. (Nott.), Ph.D. (E.U.I.), Prof. of Pol. [Italian & comparative politics; party politics; democratisation], m.j.bull@salford.ac.uk
*John Callaghan, B.Sc. (Lond.), M.A. (Essex), Ph.D. (Manc.), Prof. of Pol. & Contemp. Hist. [Communism; social democracy; political ideologies; 20th c. European history], j.callaghan@salford.ac.uk
Jocelyn A. Evans, B.A. (Manc.), Ph.D. (E.U.I.), Sen. Lect. in Eur. Pol. [French politics; contemporary European extreme right], j.a.evans@salford.ac.uk
John Garrard, B.A. (Keele), M.A.(Econ.) (Manc.), Sen. Lect. in Pol. & Contemp. Hist. [Leadership & power in industrial towns, 1880–1914; the role of scandal in politics; history of democratisation; heads of the local state in past & present Europe], j.a.garrard@salford.ac.uk
John F.V. Keiger, Diplôme de l'Institut d'Etudes Politiques (I.E.P., Aix), Ph.D. (Cantab.), Prof. of Int. Hist., Head of French Section (Mod. French) [French international history 1870 to present], j.f.v.keiger@salford.ac.uk
Christopher J. Murphy, B.A. (Wales), M.A. (Sussex), Ph.D. (Read.), Lect. in Intelligence Stud. [British intelligence community in the 20th c.], c.j.murphy@salford.ac.uk
James L. Newell, B.A. (East Anglia), M.Sc. (Lond.), Ph.D. (E.U.I.), Prof. of Pol. [Italian politics; electoral & party politics; comparative politics; research methods in social sciences], j.l.newell@salford.ac.uk
Alaric Searle, M.A., M.Phil. (Edin.), Dr.phil. (Freie Univ., Berlin), Sen. Lect. in Milit. Hist. [European military history since 1815; history of military thought; German & British political, diplomatic & military history in the 20th c.; intelligence history], d.a.searle@salford.ac.uk

UNIVERSITY OF SHEFFIELD

Western Bank, Sheffield, S10 2TN. 0114 222 2000. Fax 0114 273 9826
www.sheffield.ac.uk
Department of History
Jessop West, 1 Upper Hanover Street, Sheffield, S3 7RA.
0114 222 2555. Fax 0114 222 2576
www.sheffield.ac.uk/history/
Department of Archaeology
Northgate House, West Street, Sheffield, S1 4ET. 0114 222 2900. Fax 0114 272 2563
www.sheffield.ac.uk/archaeology/

Umberto Albarella, M.Sc. (Naples), Ph.D. (Dunelm.), Sen. Lect. in Archaeol. [Archaeozoology; the archaeology of Britain, Italy & Greece; pig domestication]

Gianna Ayala, B.A. (Texas), M.A. (Rome), Ph.D. (Cantab.), Lect. in Archaeol. [Landscape formation processes; later prehistoric & early historic Italian society; field survey; land use systems]

John C. Barrett, B.Sc., D.Litt. (Wales), Prof. of Archaeol. [Landscape archaeology; archaeological theory; theory & practice; later prehistory]

Timothy P. Baycroft, B.A. (Mt. Allison), B.Phil. (Louvain), D.E.A. (Paris), Ph.D. (Cantab.), Sen. Lect. in Hist. (19th–20th c. France) [Modern French history; nationalism], t.baycroft@sheffield.ac.uk

John Bennet, Prof. of Aegean Archaeol. [Minoan & Mycenaean culture of late bronze age Aegean; archaeology & history of Crete; early writing & administrative systems; diachronic regional studies; Ottoman Greece], j.d.bennet@sheffield.ac.uk

Adrian C. Bingham, B.A., D.Phil. (Oxon.), Sen. Lect. in Mod. Brit. Hist. [20th c. British social & cultural history; popular press; gender; sexuality], adrian.bingham@sheffield.ac.uk

Michael J. Braddick, B.A., Ph.D. (Cantab.), Prof. of Hist. (Early Mod. Eng.) [State in early modern England, 1550–1700], m.braddick@sheffield.ac.uk

Keith Branigan, B.A., Ph.D. (Birm.), Emeritus Prof. [Aegean bronze age; Roman Britain; funerary behaviour; early metallurgy]

Maureen Carroll, B.A. (Brock), M.A., Ph.D. (Indiana), Prof. of Roman Archaeol. [Roman archaeology; Roman Europe; garden archaeology; funerary archaeology]

Esme R. Cleall, B.A., M.A. (Sheff.), Ph.D. (Lond.), Lect. in Hist. of the Brit. Empire [History of race, gender, disability; colonialism & postcolonialism], e.r.cleall@sheffield.ac.uk

John R. Collis, M.A., Ph.D. (Cantab.), Emeritus Prof. of Archaeol. [Iron age Britain & Europe; the Celts; excavation & methodology]

Peter M. Day, B.A. (Southampton), Ph.D. (Cantab.), Reader in Archaeol. [Ceramics; bronze age Crete; material science]

Miriam J. Dobson, M.A. (Cantab.), M.A., Ph.D. (Lond.), Sen. Lect. in Mod. Hist. (20th c. Russia), m.dobson@sheffield.ac.uk

Roger Doonan, Ph.D., Sen. Lect. in Archaeol. [Technological change; social change; metallurgy; experimental archaeology]

Catherine L. Fletcher, B.A. (Liv.), M.A., Ph.D. (Lond.), Lect. in Public Hist. [Renaissance Europe, esp. Italy; diplomacy; public history], catherine.fletcher@sheffield.ac.uk

Julie V. Gottlieb, B.A. (McGill), M.A., Ph.D. (Cantab.), Sen. Lect. in Hist. (20th c. Brit. Pol.) [Women's history; British fascism; history of race & ethnicity], julie.gottlieb@sheffield.ac.uk

Mark Greengrass, M.A., D.Phil. (Oxon.), Emeritus Prof. of Early Mod. Hist. (16th–17th c. France) [French Wars of Religion], m.greengrass@sheffield.ac.uk

Sheffield

Clare V.J. Griffiths, M.A., D.Phil. (Oxon.), Sen. Lect. in Mod. Hist. (19th & 20th c. Brit.) [20th c. British political & cultural history; agricultural & rural history; landscape; history of the British left], clare.griffiths@sheffield.ac.uk

Dawn M. Hadley, B.A. (Hull), Ph.D. (Birm.), Prof. of Med. Archaeol. [Medieval archaeology; society, economy & settlement in the Anglo-Saxon period; Vikings; gender]

Paul L.J. Halstead, M.A., Ph.D. (Cantab.), Prof. of Archaeol. [Neolithic & bronze age Greece; archaeozoology; ethnoarchaeology of Mediterranean farming]

Karen Harvey, B.A. (Manc.), M.A., Ph.D. (Lond.), Sen. Lect. in Cultural Hist. [Cultural history of the long 18th c.; gender, the body & the domestic interior], k.harvey@sheffield.ac.uk

Andrew Heath, B.A. (Lond.), Ph.D. (Penn.), Lect. in Amer. Hist. [19th c. U.S. history; urban history], a.d.heath@sheffield.ac.uk

Julia Hillner, M.A., Ph.D. (Bonn), Lect. in Med. Hist. [Late antiquity & the early middle ages, esp. city of Rome; family history; crime & punishment], j.hillner@sheffield.ac.uk

Caroline M. Jackson, B.A. (Lancaster), M.A., Ph.D. (Bradford), Reader in Archaeol. [Material science; glass & vitreous metals]

Robert Johnston, B.A., M.A., Ph.D. (Newcastle), Sen. Lect. in Archaeol. [Landscape; land enclosure; north European bronze age; field methodologies]

Glynis E.M. Jones, B.Sc. (Wales), M.Phil., Ph.D. (Cantab.), Prof. of Archaeol. [Archaeobotany; statistics; biomolecules]

Edmund King, M.A., Ph.D. (Cantab.), Emeritus Prof. of Med. Hist. (11th–15th c. Brit. Pol. & Econ.) [Anglo-Norman history], e.king@sheffield.ac.uk

Kevin Kuykendall, Ph.D. (Washington), Sen. Lect. in Archaeol. [Palaeoanthropology; South African Plio-pleistocene; early hominid life theory]

Tom Leng, B.A., Ph.D. (Sheff.), Lect. in Hist. [Intellectual history; commercial discourse & policy in 17th c. England], t.leng@sheffield.ac.uk

Simon T. Loseby, M.A. (Oxon. & York), D.Phil. (Oxon.), Sen. Lect. in Hist. (Early Med.) [Late antique & early medieval history & archaeology, esp. cities; exchange systems; Gaul/Francia; the Mediterranean; Gregory of Tours], s.t.loseby@sheffield.ac.uk

David Luscombe, M.A., Litt.D. (Cantab.), F.B.A., Emeritus Prof. of Med. Hist. [Thought & religion in the middle ages], d.luscombe@sheffield.ac.uk

Phil McCluskey, B.A., M.A., Ph.D. (St. And.), Lect. in the Hist. of Mod. Eur. [France & the Mediterranean world, c.1550–1750; Lorraine & Savoy], p.mccluskey@sheffield.ac.uk

Colin Merrony, B.A. (Sheff.), M.A. (Bradford), Teaching Fellow in Archaeol. [Geophysical survey; archaeological mapping; landscape archaeology; archaeology of the East Midlands & S. Yorkshire]

Simon Middleton, M.A. (Harv.), Ph.D. (City Univ., N.Y.), Sen. Lect. in Hist. [Colonial American social & cultural history], s.middleton@sheffield.ac.uk

Anthony Milton, B.A., Ph.D. (Cantab.), Prof. of Hist. (Early Mod. Eng.) [Early modern British political & religious history; Anglicanism; Anglo-Dutch relations; synod of Dordt (1618–19)], a.milton@sheffield.ac.uk

Bob Moore, B.A., Ph.D. (Manc.), Prof. of 20th c. Eur. Hist. [The Netherlands; prisoner of war history; Holocaust], r.moore@sheffield.ac.uk

*John F. Moreland, B.A. (Sheff.), Prof. of Hist. Archaeol. [Dark age Europe; archaeological theory]

Julia Moses, B.A. (Barnard/Columbia), M.Phil. (Oxon.), Ph.D. (Cantab.), Lect. in Mod. Hist. [19th & 20th c. Britain, Germany & Italy; political & social history; social policy; legal history], j.moses@sheffield.ac.uk

Pia Nystrom, B.A., M.A., Ph.D. (Washington), Lect. in Archaeol. [Biological anthropology; primate evolution; behavioural anthropology]

Caroline Dodds Pennock, B.A., M.St., D.Phil. (Oxon.), Lect. in Int. Hist. [Aztec, Spanish American & Atlantic history], c.pennock@sheffield.ac.uk

Ian R. Phimister, B.A. (Nott.), B.A., D.Phil. (Rhodesia), Prof. of Int. Hist. (C'wealth Hist.) [The City of London & British overseas investment, 1890–1940], i.phimister@sheffield.ac.uk

Amanda L. Power, B.A. (Sydney), Ph.D. (Cantab.), Sen. Lect. in Med. Hist. [Medieval religious, intellectual & cultural history, esp. 13th c .], a.power@sheffield.ac.uk

Abdel Razzaq Takriti, B.A. (Toronto), M.A. (York), D.Phil. (Oxon.), Lect. in Int. Hist. [Modern Middle Eastern history; modern Omani history; modern Palestine; 20th c. Arab revolutions & revolutionary movements]

Jane Rempel, B.A. (Ont.), M.A., Ph.D. (Michigan), Lect. in Classical Archaeol. [North coast of the Black Sea & ancient Greek colonisation; the Hellenistic east; funerary commemoration], j.rempel@sheffield.ac.uk

James Shaw, M.A. (Edin.), Ph.D. (E.U.I.), Sen. Lect. in Hist. [Early modern Italy; markets; law; ethics], j.e.shaw@sheffield.ac.uk

Susan Sherratt, M.A. (Cantab.), D.Phil. (Oxon.), Lect. in Archaeol. [Late bronze age & early iron age of the Aegean, Cyprus & wider eastern Mediterranean]

Robert B. Shoemaker, B.A. (Reed Coll.), Ph.D. (Stanford), Prof. of 18th c. Brit. Hist. (17th–19th c. Brit. Soc.) [Socio-cultural history of 18th c. London, esp. gender, crime & the law; digital history], r.shoemaker@sheffield.ac.uk

Martial J.M. Staub, L. ès L. (Paris I), M.ès L., D.Hist. (Paris X), Habil. (E.H.E.S.S./Paris), Prof. of Med. Hist. (Eur. 1200–1600), m.staub@sheffield.ac.uk

*M. Mary T. Vincent, B.A., D.Phil. (Oxon.), Prof. of Mod. Eur. Hist. (20th c. Spain) [Modern Spain; the history of Catholicism; gender & politics], m.t.vincent@sheffield.ac.uk

Charles West, M.A., M.Phil. (Birm.), Ph.D. (Cantab.), Lect. in Hist. [Medieval European & British history, esp. pre-1100], c.m.west@sheffield.ac.uk

Hugh Willmott, B.A., M.A., Ph.D. (Dunelm.), Sen. Lect. in Archaeol. [Later medieval & post-medieval Europe; production, use & deposition of material culture; archaeology of glass]

Philip J. Withington, M.A., Ph.D. (Cantab.), Prof. of Early Mod. Hist. [Early modern social, cultural & political history; urbanisation; popular politics; history of language; intoxication], p.withington@sheffield.ac.uk

Benjamin Ziemann, M.A. (Freie Univ., Berlin), Ph.D. (Bielefeld), Habil. (Bochum), Prof. of Mod. Hist. [19th & 20th c. German social, cultural & political history; peace research; concepts & theories for modern social history], b.ziemann@sheffield.ac.uk

SHEFFIELD HALLAM UNIVERSITY

Faculty of Development & Society
Owen Building, Howard Street, Sheffield, S1 1WB. 0114 225 3113. Fax 0114 225 5514
www.shu.ac.uk/prospectus/subject/history/

John D. Baxendale, M.A., D.Phil. (Oxon.), Princ. Lect. (19th–20th c. Brit. Soc. Hist.) [20th c. popular culture], j.d.baxendale@shu.ac.uk

Barbara J. Bush, B.A., M.Phil., Ph.D. (Sheff.), Prof. (Imp. Hist.) [History of the African diaspora; gender, race & empire in the 20th c.], b.bush@shu.ac.uk

Peter J. Cain, B.A., B.Litt. (Oxon.), Res. Prof. (Mod. Econ. & Imp. Hist.) [Economic history of British imperialism], p.j.cain@shu.ac.uk

*Bruce Collins, M.A., Ph.D. (Cantab.), Prof. (Mod. Hist.) [History of U.S.A., antebellum & post-1960s; British military & imperial history, 1775–1902], b.collins@shu.ac.uk

Myrddin J. Lewis, B.Sc.(Econ.), M.Sc.(Econ.) (Wales), Ph.D. (C.N.A.A.), Sen. Lect. (Business Hist., Hist. & Computing), m.j.lewis@shu.ac.uk

Roger Lloyd-Jones, B.A. (York), M.Sc. (Loughborough), Prof. (Econ. Hist.) [19th–20th c. British economic & business history], r.lloyd-jones@shu.ac.uk
Kevin F. McDermott, B.A., Ph.D. (Leeds), Sen. Lect. (Pol. Hist., Russian & E. Eur. Stud.) [Stalin & Stalinism; 20th c. Czechoslovakia], k.f.mcdermott@shu.ac.uk
David W. Mayall, B.A., M.A. (Warwick), Ph.D. (Sheff.), Princ. Lect. (19th–20th c. Soc. & Pol. Hist.) [Immigrant & minority history], d.w.mayall@shu.ac.uk
Clare Midgley, M.A. (Edin. & Essex), Ph.D. (Kent), Res. Prof. (Mod. Brit. Hist.) [Feminism & empire], c.midgley@shu.ac.uk
Matthew P. Stibbe, B.A. (Brist.) M.A., D.Phil. (Sussex), Sen. Lect. (Mod. Eur.) [Modern Germany; World War I; gender], m.stibbe@shu.ac.uk
Anthony D. Taylor, B.A. (York), M.A. (Birm.), Ph.D. (Manc.), Sen. Lect. (19th–20th c. Hist.) [Popular politics in 19th c. Britain; Red scares internationally]
Alison Twells, B.A. (Sussex), M.A. (Sheff. Hallam), D.Phil. (York), Sen. Lect. (19th–20th c. Brit. Soc.) [Race, gender & class formation; missionary practices & the 'civilising mission'], a.twells@shu.ac.uk

UNIVERSITY OF SOUTH WALES / PRIFYSGOL DE CYMRU

School of Humanities & Social Sciences
www.southwales.ac.uk/history/
Treforest Campus, Treforest, Wales, CF37 1DL. 08455 760101
Carleon Campus, Lodge Road, Newport, Wales, NP18 3QT. 08455 767778.

Richard C. Allen, B.A., P.G.C.E., Ph.D. (Wales), Reader in Early Mod. Cultural Hist. (Early Mod. Welsh, Brit. & Colonial Amer.) [16th–18th c. religious dissent; poor relief; emigration; folklore], richard.allen@southwales.ac.uk
Nick Carter, B.A., Ph.D. (Cardiff), Sen. Lect. (Mod. Eur. & Brit.) [19th & 20th c. Italy], nick.carter@southwales.ac.uk
Andrew J. Croll, B.A., Ph.D. (Wales), Princ. Lect. in Hist. (Brit. & Welsh Hist.) [19th & 20th c. popular culture; urban history; the poor law], andy.croll@southwales.ac.uk
Jonathan Durrant, B.A., M.A., Ph.D. (Lond.), Sen. Lect. in Early Mod. Hist. (16th–18th c. Eur.) [Witchcraft; deviance; gender; history on film], jonathan.durrant@southwales.ac.uk
Chris Evans, B.A., Ph.D. (Lond.), Prof. of Hist. [Steel as a material ingredient in the Enlightenment; Wales & Atlantic slavery; the design of goods consumed by slaves in the Atlantic world; Swansea copper as an agency of global change in the 19th c.], chris.evans3@southwales.ac.uk
Jane Finucane, B.A., M.Phil., Ph.D. (Dublin), Lect. in Early Mod. Hist. (16th–18th c. Eur.) [Reformation; war; intellectual history], jane.finucane@southwales.ac.uk
Sharif Gemie, B.A., Ph.D. (East Anglia), Prof. of Hist. (Eur., France) [Brittany; Galicia (Spain); refugees & the Second World War], sharif.gemie@southwales.ac.uk
Madeleine Gray, B.A., Ph.D. (Wales), Reader in Hist. (Welsh, Brit. & Eur. Hist.) [Visual & material culture; religion in late medieval & early modern society], madeleine.gray@southwales.ac.uk
David. R. Howell, B.A., M.A. (Leicester), Lect. in Heritage & Hist. [Heritage interpretation; museums; nationalism in heritage narratives, Wales, Iceland & Greenland], david.howell2@southwales.ac.uk

Raymond Howell, B.A., M.A., Ph.D. (Lond.), Prof. of Welsh Antiquity [Aspects of cultural continuity, esp. Iron Age/Roman & Romano British/early medieval interfaces], ray.howell@southwales.ac.uk

Brian Ireland, B.A., M.A. (Ulster), Ph.D. (Hawaii), Sen. Lect. in Amer. Hist. (Amer. Hist.) [American history & culture], brian.ireland@southwales.ac.uk

Jonathan A. Kissock, M.A. (Cantab.), Ph.D. (Leicester), Sen. Lect. in Hist. (Landscape Hist., esp. Med. Wales) [Landscape change, Roman to medieval; peasant land ownership patterns], jonathan.kissock@southwales.ac.uk

Norman La Porte, B.A. (C.N.A.A.), Ph.D. (Stirling), Sen. Lect. in Mod. Eur. Hist. [German labour history; G.D.R. history], norman.laport@southwales.ac.uk

Rachel Lock-Lewis, B.A. (Wales), P.G.C.E., M.A. (W. of Eng.), Sen. Lect. in Hist. (Brit. & Welsh Hist.) [20th c. gender, sex, marriage & the family; 19th & 20th c. women's activism], rachel.lock-lewis@southwales.ac.uk

*Fiona Reid, B.A. (W. of Eng.), M.A. (Wales), Ph.D. (W. of Eng.), Assoc. Head of Humanities [Social & cultural responses to war in 20th c. Europe], fiona.reid@southwales.ac.uk

UNIVERSITY OF **SOUTHAMPTON**

Highfield, Southampton, SO17 1BJ. 023 8059 5000. Fax 023 8059 3939
www.southampton.ac.uk
School of Humanities: Department of History 023 8059 2157. Fax 023 8059 3458
www.southampton.ac.uk/history

Rémy Ambühl, A.E.S.I. (Louvain-la-Neuve), Maîtrise, D.E.A. (Lille), M.Res., D.Phil. (St. And.), Lect. in Med. Hist. (Late Med. France & Eng.) [Laws of war; chivalry; combatants & non-combatants; treatment of the defeated; Hundred Years' War], r.ambuhl@soton.ac.uk

G.W. Bernard, M.A., D.Phil. (Oxon.), Prof. of Early Mod. Hist. (16th c. Eng.) [Politics & religion in the reign of Henry VIII, esp. break with Rome & religious policy in 1530s; Holbein; Anne Boleyn; vitality & vulnerability in the late medieval church], gwb@soton.ac.uk

David Brown, B.A. (East Anglia), M.A. (Wales), Ph.D. (Southampton), Prof. of Hist. [19th c. political history; British foreign policy; social reform & philanthropy; Victorian liberalism; Palmerston], d.s.brown@soton.ac.uk

Peter D. Clarke, B.A., Ph.D. (Manc.), Reader in Med. Hist. [Medieval ecclesiastical history, esp. the papacy & canon law; the papal penitentiary], p.d.clarke@soton.ac.uk

Eve Colpus, B.A., M.A., D.Phil. (Oxon.), Lect. in Hist. (Brit. & Eur. post-1850) [19th–20th c. British social & cultural history; citizenship; gender; the media], e.c.colpus@soton.ac.uk

Jonathan Conlin, B.A. (Oxon.), M.A. (Lond.), Ph.D. (Cantab.), Sen. Lect. in Mod. Hist. (18th–20th c. Brit.) [Museum history; 18th c. French history], j.conlin@soton.ac.uk

Mark Cornwall, B.A., Ph.D. (Leeds), Prof. of Mod. Eur. Hist. (19th–20th c. Eur.) [Collapse of Habsburg empire; Czech-German relations in the Bohemian lands; biography of Heinz Rutha; creation of Yugoslavia], j.m.cornwall@soton.ac.uk

Anne Curry, B.A. (Manc.), Ph.D. (C.N.A.A.), Prof. of Med. Hist. (Late Med. Eng. & France) [Hundred Years' War; Agincourt; late medieval women], a.e.curry@soton.ac.uk

Hormoz Ebrahimnejad, B.A. (Ferdowsi, Iran), D.E.A. (Paris IV), D.Phil. (Paris III), Lect. in Hist. [History of modern Iran, 1900–today; Iran & the West, 1850–today; rise of Islamism, 1980–present; history of medicine], h.ebrahimnejad@soton.ac.uk

Julie Gammon, B.A., M.A., Ph.D. (Essex), Lect. in Hist. (17th–19th c. Soc. Hist.) [Sexual violence in 18th c. England; crime & punishment; gender & childhood], j.gammon@soton.ac.uk

Shirli Gilbert, B.Mus. (Witwatersrand), M.St., D.Phil. (Oxon.), Assoc. Prof. of Jewish Hist. & Culture [Modern Jewish history; music in the Holocaust; history of Jews of South Africa; apartheid history], s.gilbert@soton.ac.uk

Neil Gregor, B.A., Ph.D. (Exeter), Prof. of Mod. Eur. Hist. (Mod. Germany) [Social & cultural history of Germany 1920s–60s; the legacy of the Third Reich], n.gregor@soton.ac.uk

Maria A. Hayward, B.A. (Kent), M.A., Ph.D. (Lond.), Prof. of Early Mod. Hist. (16th c. Brit.) [Material culture at the court of Henry VII; Tudor sumptuary legislation]

Rachel B. Herrmann, B.A. (N.Y.), M.A., Ph.D. (Texas), Lect. (Early Mod. Amer. Hist.) [Food history; Native American & Atlantic history; American Revolution; cannibalism], r.b.herrmann@soton.ac.uk

Nicholas Karn, M.St., M.A., D.Phil. (Oxon.), Lect. in Med. Hist. [Law & cultures of law in England, 900–1250; bishops & their acta, 1100–1300]

Matthew Kelly, B.A., M.St., D.Phil. (Oxon.), Sen. Lect. in Hist. (19th–20th c. Irish Hist.) [Nationalism; the Polish diaspora 1939–45], m.j.kelly@soton.ac.uk

A.R.J. (Tony) Kushner, B.A., Ph.D. (Sheff.), M.A. (Connecticut), Prof. of Jewish/Non-Jewish Relations (19th & 20th c. Brit. Hist.) [British Jewish history; 'race'; immigration & minority history; heritage of Holocaust studies], ark@soton.ac.uk

Craig L. Lambert, B.A., M.A., Ph.D. (Hull), Lect. in Hist. (Late Med. & Early Mod. Eng.) [Maritime history; social & economic history of coastal communities/seafarers; naval logistics; naval warfare; prosopography; demographics of port towns; urban history; restorative justice], c.lambert@soton.ac.uk

Claire Le Foll, M.A., Ph.D. (Paris), Lect. in E. Eur. Jewish Hist. & Culture [Russian Jewry; Jewish/non-Jewish relations; history of Belarus; Jewish art & culture]

Dan Levene, B.A. (Southampton), B.A., Ph.D. (Lond.), Reader in Hist. (Jewish Antiquity) [Magic bowls], d.levene@soton.ac.uk

Mark Levene, M.A. (Warwick), D.Phil. (Oxon.), Reader in Comparative Hist. (20th c. Eur. Hist.) [Genocide in the age of the nation state], m.levene@soton.ac.uk

John McAleer, M.A., Ph.D. (N.U.I.), Lect. in Hist. (17th–19th c. Brit. & Brit. Empire) [British imperial & maritime history; East India company; sub-Saharan Africa; museums, collecting & collections], j.mcaleer@soton.ac.uk

Jane H. McDermid, M.Ed. (Lond.), M.A., Ph.D. (Glas.), Reader in Hist. (Mod. Brit. & Russian Hist., Women, Educ.) [Women's history in late 19th & 20th c. Scotland & Russia], j.mcdermid@soton.ac.uk

Pritipuspa A. Mishra, B.A. (Mumbai), M.A. (Hyderabad), Ph.D. (Minnesota), Res. Fellow in S. Asian Hist. (19th & 20th c. India) [Language & territoriality in colonial & postcolonial India; social history of development], priti.mishra@soton.ac.uk

Kendrick J. Oliver, B.A. (Read.), Ph.D. (Lond.), Sen. Lect. in Hist. (U.S.A.) [Post-war U.S. foreign policy; Vietnam War; U.S. space programme]

*Sarah J.K. Pearce, B.D. (Lond.), D.Phil. (Oxon.), Prof. of Jewish/Non-Jewish Relations [Graeco-Roman period Jewish history & literature; Philo of Alexandria], s.j.pearce@soton.ac.uk

Christer Petley, M.A., Ph.D. (Warwick), Lect. in Hist. (Amer.) [Slavery & abolition; the Atlantic world; colonial societies], c.petley@soton.ac.uk

Christopher M. Prior, B.A., M.A., Ph.D. (Dunelm.), Lect. in Hist. (20th c. Brit.) [British imperial history; Africa, esp. north-east Africa; post-war British socio-cultural history], c.prior@soton.ac.uk

Andres H. Rodriguez, B.A. (Católica, Chile), M.Phil. (Oxon.), Lect. in Mod. Hist.
[Modern China; Republican period; nationalism & ethnicity; Christianity in China],
a.rodriguez@soton.ac.uk
Joachim Schlör, M.A., Dr.res.soc. (Tübingen), Dr.phil.habil. (Potsdam), Prof. of Mod.
Jewish/Non-Jewish Relations [Urban history; German-Jewish history; migration],
j.schloer@soton.ac.uk
Adrian Smith, B.A., M.A., Ph.D. (Kent), Prof. of Mod. Brit. & C'wealth Hist. [Labour history;
newspaper history; civil military relations, esp. Lord Mountbatten; post-war Coventry;
history of sport], adrian.smith@soton.ac.uk
François Soyer, M.A. (St. And.), M.Phil., Ph.D. (Cantab.), Lect. in Early Mod. Eur. Hist. [Spain
& Portugal; the Inquisition; Spanish & Portuguese empires], f.j.soyer@soton.ac.uk
Helen Spurling, B.A., M.Phil., Ph.D. (Cantab.), Lect. (Jewish Stud.) [Jewish history &
culture in late antiquity; Judaism, Christianity & Islam in late antiquity; apocalypticism],
h.spurling@soton.ac.uk
Mark J. Stoyle, B.A. (Southampton), D.Phil. (Oxon.), Prof. of Early Mod. Hist. (17th c. Brit.)
[English Civil War; Cornish & Welsh particularism; popular memory], mjs@soton.ac.uk
*Ian A. Talbot, B.A. (Lond.), M.A. (Oxon.), Ph.D. (Lond.), Prof. of Mod. Brit. Hist. [20th c.
Indian history; Pakistan since independence; South Asian diaspora], i.a.talbot@soton.ac.uk
Joan L. Tumblety, B.A. (W. Aust.), Ph.D. (Cantab.), Lect. in Hist. (Mod. France) [20th c.
French cultural history; sport; gender; the radical right; Vichy], j.tumblety@soton.ac.uk
Christopher M. Woolgar, B.A. (Southampton), Ph.D. (Dunelm.), Dip. Arch. Admin (Liv.),
Prof. of Hist & Archival Stud. (Late Med. Eng.) [Social & economic history; culture of food;
diplomatic & archives, medieval to modern], c.m.woolgar@soton.ac.uk

SOUTHAMPTON SOLENT UNIVERSITY

East Park Terrace, Southampton, SO14 0YN. 023 8031 9000. Fax 023 8022 2259
www.solent.ac.uk

Edward Chaney, B.A. (Read.), Laurea (Pisa), M.Phil., Ph.D. (Lond.), Prof. of Fine &
Decorative Arts, Founding Chair of the Hist. of Collecting Res. Centre [Anglo-Italian cultural
relations; the Grand Tour; history of collecting; Shakespeare, Inigo Jones & English/Italian
visual culture; receptions of ancient Egypt in early modern England/Europe; the idea of
ancient Egypt in early modern England/Europe], Edward.Chaney@solent.ac.uk

STAFFORDSHIRE UNIVERSITY

01782 294000.
www.staffs.ac.uk
Faculty of Arts, Media & Design: Department of History & Politics
College Road, Stoke-on-Trent, ST4 2DE. 01782 294415. Fax 01782 294760

Owen R. Ashton, B.A., M.A., Ph.D. (Birm.), Emeritus Prof. of Mod. Brit. Soc. Hist. (Brit. Hist.)
[Chartism], o.r.ashton@staffs.ac.uk
Sita Bali, B.A. (Bombay), M.A., Ph.D. (Kent), Sen. Lect. [S. Asia; migration; international
security], s.bali@staffs.ac.uk

Martin T. Brown, B.A. (Cantab.), Sen. Lect. (Soc. & Cultural Hist.) [19th c. Italy],
m.t.brown@staffs.ac.uk
Tony Craig, B.A. (Dublin), M.Phil., Ph.D. (Cantab.), Sen. Lect. (Mod. Brit. Hist.) [Political
history of Britain & Ireland; intelligence & security history], t.craig@staffs.ac.uk
Pauline Elkes, B.A. (Staffs.), Ph.D. (Sheff.), Sen. Lect. (Int. Hist.) [British Intelligence;
propaganda; the Third Reich], p.elkes@staffs.ac.uk
Peter Lamb, B.A. (Staffs.), M.Sc. (Keele), M.A., Ph.D. (Manc.), Sen. Lect. (Int. Rel.)
[International relations theory; political theory], p.h.lamb@staffs.ac.uk
Fiona Robertson-Snape, B.A., M.A., Ph.D. (Kent), Sen. Lect. in Int. Rel. [Diplomacy; security],
f.robertson-snape@staffs.ac.uk
Alan Russell, B.A. (Staffs.), Ph.D. (Kent), Princ. Lect. [History & international political
economy of technology], a.m.russell@staffs.ac.uk

UNIVERSITY OF **STIRLING**

Stirling, FK9 4LA. 01786 473171. Fax 01786 643000
www.stir.ac.uk
School of Arts & Humanities
Division of History & Politics 01786 467580. Fax 01786 467581
www.historyandpolitics.stir.ac.uk
Centre for Environmental History & Policy 01786 467861. Fax 01786 467581
www.cehp.stir.ac.uk
Centre for Scottish Studies

David W. Bebbington, M.A., Ph.D. (Cantab.), Prof. of Hist. (Brit., Pol. Thought, Historiography)
[International evangelicalism, 18th–21st c.; W.E. Gladstone], d.w.bebbington@stir.ac.uk
Jacqueline L.M. Jenkinson, M.A. (Glas.), M.Sc., Ph.D. (Edin.), Lect. in Hist. (Brit., Computing
& Hist.) [Scottish health policy, 1900–48; black British history in 19th–20th c.; immigration
to Britain in 19th & 20th c.], j.l.m.jenkinson@stir.ac.uk
Robin C.C. Law, B.A. (Oxon.), Ph.D. (Birm.), Emeritus Prof. of Afric. Hist. [Social history of
Ouidah (Benin); English Royal African Company; Atlantic slave trade], r.c.c.law@stir.ac.uk
Emma Vincent Macleod, M.A., Ph.D. (Edin.), Lect. in Hist. (Brit.) [British (incl. Scottish)
attitudes to the French revolutionary wars; British attitudes to America c.1783–c.1832],
e.v.macleod@stir.ac.uk
Alastair J. Mann, B.A., Ph.D. (Stirling), Dip. Pub. (Napier), Lect. in Hist. (Scot.) [16th–18th c.
Scotland; political history; the Scottish parliament; book trade in Scotland & Europe],
a.j.mann@stir.ac.uk
Benjamin J. Marsh, M.A., Ph.D. (Cantab.), Lect. in Hist. (U.S. Hist.) [17th & 18th c. British
America; colonial women's history; Georgia], ben.marsh@stir.ac.uk
Catherine J. Mills, B.A. (Birm.), Ph.D. (Exeter), Lect. in Hist. (Brit.) [19th–20th c. Britain;
health & safety regulation of the mining industries; regulatory politics of clean air; polluted &
derelict landscapes]
Holger Nehring, M.A. (Tübingen), D.Phil. (Oxon.), Prof. in Contemp. Eur. Hist. [Post-1945
British & German political, cultural & social history; history of social movements; historical
peace research], holger.nehring@stir.ac.uk
Colin C. Nicolson, M.A., Ph.D. (Edin.), Lect. in Hist. (U.S.) [American Revolution: loyalist
ideology, royal government, prosopography & political behaviour, counter-revolution,
loyalism & imperial administration; Gov. Francis Bernard, friendship: John Adams,
Jonathan Sewell; historical documentary editing], colin.nicolson@stir.ac.uk

Richard D. Oram, M.A., Ph.D. (St. And.), Prof. of Hist. (Scot. Med. & Environmental Hist.) [Scottish history c.800–1300; the medieval environment; institutional history of the medieval church; castles & castle landscapes; elite culture & society], r.d.oram@stir.ac.uk

Diego Palacios Cerezales, M.A. (Lisbon), Ph.D. (Madrid), Lect. in Hist. (Eur. Hist.) [19th–20th c. Iberia; social movements; popular protest; policing; political history], dp16@stir.ac.uk

Michael A. Penman, M.A., Ph.D. (St. And.), Sen. Lect. in Hist. (Scot.) [13th–15th c. Scotland; Wars of Independence; Bruce dynasty; kingship & government; chivalry & piety], m.a.penman@stir.ac.uk

Alasdair Ross, M.A., Ph.D. (Aberd.), Sen. Lect. in Hist. [Environmental & medieval history, esp. landscape history]

James J. Smyth, M.A. (Glas.), Ph.D. (Edin.), Sen. Lect. in Hist. (Brit. & Scot.) [Labour politics; urban poor in the 19th & 20th c.; housing; record linkage; crime & punishment; historical reputations & national identity], jjs1@stir.ac.uk

Phia Steyn, B.A., M.A., Ph.D. (Free State, Bloemfontein), Lect. in Hist. (Afric. & Latin Amer. Environmental Hist.) [South African environmentalism; apartheid & environment; popular environmental struggles; resource & oil politics; big business in developing countries], m.s.steyn@stir.ac.uk

UNIVERSITY OF **STRATHCLYDE**

McCance Building, 16 Richmond Street, Glasgow, G1 1XQ. 0141 552 4400.
Fax 0141 552 8509
www.strath.ac.uk
Department of History 0141 552 4400 x2236. Fax 0141 552 8509

Angela Bartie, B.A. (Strathclyde), Ph.D. (Dundee), Lect. in Hist. (20th c. Brit.) [20th c. British history; oral history], angela.bartie@strath.ac.uk

Patricia S. Barton, M.A., Ph.D. (Glas.), Lect. in Hist. (India, Japan, Hist. of Medicine) p.barton@strath.ac.uk

Alison Cathcart, M.A., Ph.D. (Aberd.), Sen. Lect. in Early Mod. Hist. (Brit., Scot. & Ireland) [Kinship & clientage within clan society; Scotland & Ireland within an archipelagic context, c.1450–1625; maritime communities of the Irish Sea], a.cathcart@strath.ac.uk

C. Mark D. Ellis, M.A., Ph.D. (Aberd.), Sen. Lect. in Hist. (Mod. Amer.) [African-Americans in the first quarter of the 20th c.], m.ellis@strath.ac.uk

Richard J. Finlay, B.A. (Stirling), Ph.D. (Edin.), Prof. in Hist. (Mod. Scot.), richard.finlay@strath.ac.uk

Mary E. Heimann, B.A. (Vassar), D.Phil. (Oxon.), Reader in Hist. (20th c. Czech Hist., 19th c. Relig. Hist.) [Modern European intellectual, political & religious history; English Catholic/ European Christian thought & practice], mary.heimann@strath.ac.uk

Erin Jessee, B.A. (Simon Fraser), M.A., Ph.D. (Concordia), Lect. in Hist. (Hist. of Genocide, Oral Hist.) [Cultural anthropology; transitional communities, esp. post-genocide Rwanda & Uganda; victims of war], erin.jessee@strath.ac.uk

Allan I. MacInnes, M.A. (St. And.), Ph.D. (Glas.), Prof. of Hist. (Early Mod.), allan.macinnes@strath.ac.uk

Arthur J. McIvor, B.A. (Nott.), Ph.D. (Manc.), Prof. of Soc. Hist. (Brit. Econ., Labour) [Employers; occupational health; labour history; oral history], a.mcivor@strath.ac.uk

James H. Mills, M.A., Ph.D. (Edin.), Prof. of Hist. of Medicine & Sport [History of drugs & intoxicants; history of sports & physical culture in South Asia], jim.mills@strath.ac.uk

Martin Mitchell, M.A., Ph.D. (Strathclyde), Teaching Fellow (Mod. Scot. & Irish), m.mitchell136@msn.com

Emma Newlands, B.A. (Stirling), M.A. (Glas. & Strathclyde), Ph.D. (Strathclyde), Lect. in Hist. (Hist. of Medicine & Warfare) [History of health & healthcare, 1939–45], e.newlands@strath.ac.uk

Rogelia Pastor-Castro, B.Sc. (Surrey), Ph.D. (Central Lancs.), Lect. in Hist. (20th c. Brit. & France), rogelia.pastor-castro@strath.ac.uk

Matthew Smith, B.A., B.Ed., M.A. (Alberta), Ph.D. (Exeter), Lect. in Hist. [Medical history], m.smith@strath.ac.uk

Karine Varley, B.A. (Cantab.), M.A. (Leeds), Ph.D. (Lond.), Lect. in Hist. & French (France; Eur.) [Memory & commemoration of war; constructions of national identity; visual arts in late 19th c. France; French-Italian relations in the Second World War; Corsican history & politics], karine.varley@strath.ac.uk

Manuela Williams, B.A. (Lecce), M.A., Ph.D. (Nott.), Lect. in Hist. (20th c. Int. Hist.) [20th c. international history; the Middle East], manuela.williams@strath.ac.uk

John R. Young, M.A., Ph.D. (Glas.), Sen. Lect. in Hist. (Scot., Early Mod. Brit.) [The Scottish Parliament; early modern Scotland & the British archipelago], john.r.young@strath.ac.uk

UNIVERSITY OF **SUNDERLAND**

Priestman Building, Green Terrace, Sunderland, SR1 3PZ.
0191 515 2000. Fax 0191 515 2044
www.sunderland.ac.uk
School of Arts, Design, Media & Culture
Department of History 0191 515 3430. Fax 0191 515 2415

Gillian Cookson, B.A. (Leeds), D.Phil. (York), County Editor, *V.C.H. Durham* [18th–19th c. economic & social history, esp. north of England], Gill.Cookson@sunderland.ac.uk

Jack Dawson, B.A. (C.N.A.A.), M.Litt. (Glas.), Sen. Lect. in Art & Design Hist. (19th c. Local Art, Ruralism, Arts & Crafts), Jack.Dawson@sunderland.ac.uk

Peter J. Durrans, B.A. (Hull), M.A. (Carleton), D.Phil. (Oxon.), Princ. Lect. in Hist. (Imp., 19th c. Brit.), Peter.Durrans@sunderland.ac.uk

Anthony C. Hepburn, M.A. (Cantab.), Ph.D. (Kent), Prof. (Mod. Irish Hist.), Tony.Hepburn@sunderland.ac.uk

W. Stuart Howard, B.A., Ph.D. (C.N.A.A.), Sen. Lect. in Hist. (Labour) [Literature of labour; history of coalmining], Stuart.Howard@sunderland.ac.uk

Gwenda Morgan, B.A., M.Phil. (Southampton), M.A. (William & Mary), Ph.D. (Johns Hopkins), Reader in Hist. (Amer.) [Law & society in 18th c.], Gwenda.Morgan@sunderland.ac.uk

Graham R. Potts, B.A. (Dunelm.), M.A. (Leicester), Hon. Fellow in Hist. (19th c. Pol.) [Nonconformist architecture in N.E. England], Graham.Potts@sunderland.ac.uk

Peter Rushton, M.A. (Cantab.), Ph.D. (Manc.), Reader (Hist. Sociology), Peter.Rushton@sunderland.ac.uk

Colin B. Trodd, B.A., M.A., D.Phil. (Sussex), Sen. Lect. in Art Hist. (19th–20th c.), Colin.Trodd@sunderland.ac.uk

Michael J. Turner, B.A., D.Phil. (Oxon.), M.A. (Rochester, N.Y.), Prof. of Hist. (Mod. Brit.) [19th c. reform movements], Michael.Turner@sunderland.ac.uk

Kevin Yuill, B.A. (East Lond.), M.Phil. (Cantab.), Lect. in Amer. Stud. (Amer.) [Civil rights in 20th c. America], Kevin.Yuill@sunderland.ac.uk

UNIVERSITY OF **SUSSEX**

Falmer, Brighton, BN1 9QX. 01273 678899. Fax 01273 623246
www.sussex.ac.uk

Anne-Marie Angelo, Ph.D. (Duke), Lect. in Amer. Hist. (Amer. Hist.) [20th c. U.S.; U.S. civil rights], a.angelo@sussex.ac.uk

Hester Barron, D.Phil. (Oxon.), Lect. in Hist. (20th c. Brit.) [20th c. British history; labour history & the history of the working classes], h.barron@sussex.ac.uk

Robert Cook, B.A. (Warwick), D.Phil. (Oxon.), Prof. of Amer. Hist. (Amer. Hist.) [American history esp. race, politics & society in the 19th & 20th c.; American civil war], r.cook@sussex.ac.uk

Matthew F. Cragoe, B.A. (Lond.), M.A. (Wales), D.Phil. (Oxon.), Prof. (18th–20th c. Brit. Soc. & Pol.) [Conservative party; politics & electioneering; religion; rural history], m.cragoe@sussex.ac.uk

Vinita Damodaran, B.A. (Delhi), M.A., M.Phil. (J. Nehru), Ph.D. (Cantab.), Sen. Lect. in Hist. (20th c. S. Asia) [Constructions of tribe in colonial India; resistance in Chotanagpur], v.damodaran@sussex.ac.uk

Tom Davies, B.A., M.A., Ph.D. (Leeds), Lect. in Amer. Hist. (Amer. Hist.) [20th c. U.S.; Black Power], t.a.davies@sussex.ac.uk

Jim Endersby, B.A. (New S. Wales), M.Phil., Ph.D. (Cantab.), Lect. in Hist. [British history; history of science], j.j.endersby@sussex.ac.uk

Martin Evans, Prof. of Mod. Eur. Hist. (French Colonial Hist., Algeria), m.j.evans@sussex.ac.uk

Richard Follett, B.A. (Wales), M.A. (Lond.), Ph.D. (Louisiana), Prof. of Amer. Hist. (19th c. U.S.) [Slavery & emancipation; sugar], r.follett@sussex.ac.uk

Ian S. Gazeley, B.A. (Warwick), D.Phil. (Oxon.), Sen. Lect. in Econ. Hist. (20th c. Brit. Soc. & Econ.) [Wages rates in British manufacturing, 1914–46], i.s.gazeley@sussex.ac.uk

Tim Hitchcock, B.A. (Calif. at Berkeley), D.Phil. (Oxon.), Prof. of Digital Hist. [18th c. poverty, gender, sexuality & religion; humanities computing], t.hitchcock@sussex.ac.uk

Alun J. Howkins, B.A. (Oxon.), Ph.D. (Essex), Emeritus Prof. of Soc. Hist. (19th–20th c. Brit. Soc.) [History of the rural areas esp. the rural poor], a.j.howkins@sussex.ac.uk

Rob Iliffe, Prof. of Intellectual Hist. & Hist. of Sc. [History of science, 1550–1800; science & technology in the West; science & religion; Newton], r.iliffe@sussex.ac.uk

Hilary Kalmbach, M.A., Ph.D. (Oxon.), Lect. in Mid. E. Asian Hist. (Mid. E. Asian Hist.) [Modern Islamic history; women in Islam], h.kalmbach@sussex.ac.uk

*Claire Langhamer, B.A. (Manc.), Ph.D. (Central Lancs.), Prof. of Mod. Brit. Hist. (20th c. Brit.) [Social & cultural history; history of emotions], c.l.langhamer@sussex.ac.uk

Iain McDaniel, Ph.D. (Cantab.), Lect. in Intellectual Hist. (Intellectual Hist., Hist. of Pol. Thought) [European political thought; Scottish englightenment; republicanism; empire; democracy], i.r.mcdaniel@sussex.ac.uk

Maurizio Marinelli, Sen. Lect. in E. Asian Hist. (E. Asian Hist.) [China; colonial & post-colonial history], m.marinelli@sussex.ac.uk

Jacob Norris, Ph.D. (Cantab.), Lect. in Mid. E. Hist. [19th–20th c. Palestine], j.norris@sussex.ac.uk

Gideon Reuveni, Reader in Hist., Director of the Centre for German Jewish Stud. [20th c. Germany; history of consumption], g.reuveni@sussex.ac.uk

Lucy Robinson, B.A. (Oxf. Brookes), M.A., D.Phil. (Sussex), Sen. Lect. in Contemp. Hist. [Britain since 1945; youth culture], l.robinson@sussex.ac.uk

Darrow Schecter, Reader in Italian [Critical theory & sociological theory; political integration in late modernity], d.schecter@sussex.ac.uk

Eric Schneider, B.A. (Puget Sound), M.Phil., D.Phil. (Oxon.), Lect. in Econ. Hist. (Mod. Hist.) [Health; family size; wages], e.b.schneider@sussex.ac.uk

Claudia Siebrecht, Ph.D. (Dublin), Lect. in Mod. Eur. Hist. [Cultural history of war & violence in 20th c. Germany & Europe; World War I history; visual history], c.siebrecht@sussex.ac.uk

Bjorn Siegel, Daad Fachlektorat, b.siegel@sussex.ac.uk

David Tal, Yossi Harel Prof. in Mod. Israel Stud. [20th c. diplomatic history], d.tal@sussex.ac.uk

J.K. James Thomson, B.A. (Cantab.), Ph.D. (Read.), Prof. of Econ. Hist. (18th–19th c. France & Spain), j.thomson@sussex.ac.uk

Christopher Warne, Ph.D. (Birm.), Lect. in French [France since 1945; popular culture], c.m.warne@sussex.ac.uk

Clive Webb, B.A. (Warwick), M.A. (Sheff.), Ph.D. (Cantab.), Prof. of Mod. Amer. Hist. (19th–20th c. Amer.) [Race & ethnicity; 20th c. U.S.], c.j.webb@sussex.ac.uk

Gerhard Wolf, M.A. (Sussex), Ph.D. (Humboldt), Lect. in Hist. [20th c. Germany; Holocaust; genocide; National Socialism], g.wolf@sussex.ac.uk

SWANSEA UNIVERSITY

Singleton Park, Swansea, SA2 8PP. 01792 205678
www.swansea.ac.uk
Department of History & Classics 01792 295227. Fax 01792 295746
www.swansea.ac.uk/history/
Department of Political & Cultural Studies 01792 295302. Fax 01792 295716
www.swansea.ac.uk/politics/

David Anderson, M.A., Ph.D. (Dundee), Lect. [19th c. America], d.j.anderson@swansea.ac.uk

Robert J. Bideleux, M.A. (Edin. & Sussex), Sen. Lect. in Russian Econ. Hist., Centre of E. Eur. Stud., r.j.bideleux@swansea.ac.uk

Anne Borsay, B.A., M.A., D.Phil. (Wales), M.Litt. (Oxon.), Prof. [History of medicine], a.borsay@swansea.ac.uk

Huw V. Bowen, B.A., Ph.D. (Wales), Prof. of Mod. Hist. [Asian & British history, 1700–1900], h.v.bowen@swansea.ac.uk

Helen Brocklehurst, B.Sc.(Econ.), Ph.D. (Wales), Lect. in Pol. (Gender Hist.), h.brocklehurst@swansea.ac.uk

Rebecca A. Clifford, B.A. (Queen's, Ont.), M.A. (Toronto), D.Phil. (Oxon.), Lect. in Hist. [20th c. Europe; World War II; memory; oral history], r.a.clifford@swansea.ac.uk

Jonathan Dunnage, B.A., M.A., Ph.D. (Hull), Lect. [Modern Italian history; policing], j.dunnage@swansea.ac.uk

Stefan Halikowski-Smith, M.A. (Cantab.), Ph.D. (E.U.I.), Sen. Lect. [History of Portuguese in Asia], s.halikowski-smith@swansea.ac.uk

Mark Humphries, B.A., M.Litt. (Dublin), Ph.D. (St. And.), Prof. of Anc. Hist. [Late antiquity; early Christianity in the Roman world], m.humphries@swansea.ac.uk

Leighton S. James, B.Sc., M.Sc. (Wales), Ph.D. (Glamorgan), [Social & economic history; war & society since 1700]

Martin Johnes, B.A., Ph.D. (Wales), Sen. Lect. (Mod. Hist.) [History of sport & modern Wales], m.johnes@swansea.ac.uk

Christoph Laucht, Staatsexamen (Kiel), M.A. (New Mexico), Ph.D. (Liv.), Lect. in Mod. Hist. [20th c. Britain, Europe & the U.S.; the Cold War; the nuclear age; transnational history; film & history; the history of science, technology & medicine], c.laucht@swansea.ac.uk

John E. Law, M.A. (St. And.), D.Phil. (Oxon.), Reader in Hist. (Italian) [Late medieval & early Renaissance Italian history; the discovery of the Renaissance in the 19th c.], j.e.law@swansea.ac.uk

Jill J. Lewis, B.A., Ph.D. (Lancaster), Reader in Soc. Hist. [20th c. Austrian & central European history], jill.lewis@swansea.ac.uk

Chris Millington, Ph.D. (Cardiff), Lect. in Hist. [20th c. France]

Martina Minas-Nenpal, M.A. (Trier), M.Phil. (Oxon.), D.Phil. (Trier), Sen. Lect. in Egyptology [Religious history of Egypt; Egyptian languages; religious history of Graeco-Roman Egypt], m.minas-nenpal@swansea.ac.uk

Louise Miskell, B.A., Ph.D. (Wales), Sen. Lect. in Hist. [19th c. British urban & industrial history], l.miskell@swansea.ac.uk

John R. Morgan, M.A., D.Phil. (Oxon.), Prof. of Classics [Ancient fiction & narrative literature], john.morgan@swansea.ac.uk

Adam Mosley, B.A., Ph.D. (Cantab.), Sen. Lect. [History of astronomy & cosomology; scientific instruments; museums & collecting; early modern correspondence networks; history of reading & of the book; early modern universities], a.j.mosley@swansea.ac.uk

Eddie J. Owens, M.A., Ph.D. (Sheff.), Sen. Lect. in Anc. Hist. [Town planning & urban life in antiquity; Roman republican history; Roman Britain]

Nigel Pollard, M.A. (Cantab.), M.A., Ph.D. (Michigan), Lect. [Roman history], n.d.pollard@swansea.ac.uk

Regina Pörtner, M.A. (Bochum), D.Phil. (Oxon.), Lect. (Early Mod.), r.poertner@swansea.ac.uk

Daniel Power, M.A., Ph.D. (Cantab.), Prof. of Med. Hist. [Anglo-Norman world], d.j.power@swansea.ac.uk

Maria Pretzler, Mag.phil. (Graz), D.Phil. (Oxon.), Lect. in Anc. Hist. [Greek history; travel & travel literature in the ancient world; landscape; archaeology], m.pretzler@swansea.ac.uk

Ian Repath, B.A. (Oxon.), Ph.D. (Warwick), Lect. in Classics [Ancient prose fiction], i.repath@swansea.ac.uk

Tracey Rihll, B.A. (Kent), Ph.D. (Leeds), Lect. in Anc. Hist. [Greek history; ancient science & technology], t.e.rihll@swansea.ac.uk

Troy L. Sagrillo, M.A. (Arizona), Ph.D. (Louvain), [Egypt in the 1st millennium B.C.]

Steven J. Sarson, B.A. (East Anglia), M.A., Ph.D. (Johns Hopkins), Lect. in Hist. (Amer.) [American colonies & revolution], s.j.sarson@swansea.ac.uk

John Spurr, M.A., D.Phil. (Oxon.), Prof. of Hist. (Early Mod.) [Oaths; religion; English politics, 1660–1690], j.spurr@swansea.ac.uk

Matthew F. Stevens, Ph.D. (Wales), Lect. in Med. Hist. [Medieval towns], m.f.stevens@swansea.ac.uk

Kasia Szpakowska, B.A. (San Francisco), Ph.D. (Calif.), [Egyptology], k.szpakowska@swansea.ac.uk

Noel Thompson, M.A. (St. And.), M.Sc. (Belf.), Ph.D. (Cantab.), Prof. of Hist. [History of economic thought], n.thompson@swansea.ac.uk

David M. Turner, M.A., D.Phil. (Oxon.), Sen. Lect. in Gender Hist. [The history of sexuality & culture in the 17th & 18th c.], d.m.turner@swansea.ac.uk

Maurice Whitehead, B.A. (Dunelm.), Ph.D. (Hull), Prof. [History of education & religion], m.whitehead@swansea.ac.uk

Deborah Youngs, B.A. (Warwick), Ph.D. (Keele), Sen. Lect. in Hist. [Lifecycle in the medieval world; late medieval British history], d.youngs@swansea.ac.uk

UNIVERSITY OF **TEESSIDE**

Borough Road, Middlesbrough, Cleveland, TS1 3BA. 01642 218121. Fax 01642 342067
www.tees.ac.uk

School of Arts & Media: History Subject Group

Neil Armstrong, B.A. (Huddersfield), M.A., Ph.D. (York), Sen. Lect. in Hist. [Christian priests in 20th c. England], N.Armstrong@tees.ac.uk

Nigel Copsey, B.A. (C.N.A.A.), M.A. (Lancaster), Ph.D. (Portsmouth), Prof. of Hist. (Mod. Eur.) [Fascism & the extreme right; anti-fascism], N.Copsey@tees.ac.uk

Paul Denison, B.A. (Southampton), M.A. (Lond.), Lect. in Design Hist. (19th–20th c.) [French design history after 1945], P.Denison@tees.ac.uk

Matthew A. Feldman, B.A., M.A., Ph.D. (Oxf. Brookes), Reader in Contemp. Hist. [Nazism; Holocaust; fascism; right-wing terrorism; modernism], M.Feldman@tees.ac.uk

Graham Ford, B.A., Ph.D. (East Anglia), Sen. Lect. in Hist. (19th–20th c. German) [Trade unions & industrial relations, 1871–1914], G.Ford@tees.ac.uk

Ulán Gillen, B.A. (Belf.), D.Phil. (Oxon.), Sen. Lect. in Hist. [French Revolution & Ireland], U.Gillen@tees.ac.uk

*Margaret T. Hems, B.A., M.A. (C.N.A.A.), Princ. Lect. (17th–18th c. Brit.) [Reign of James II; the Turner family: local politics after the Glorious Revolution], M.Hems@tees.ac.uk

Roisin Higgins, M.A., Ph.D. (St. And.), Sen. Lect. in Hist. [19th & 20th c. Britain & Ireland; commemoration; historical memory; heritage; social history], R.Higgins@tees.ac.uk

Charlie McGuire, B.A. (Belf.), Ph.D. (N.U.I.), Sen. Lect. in Hist. [20th c. Irish & British labour history], C.Mcguire@tees.ac.uk

Kenneth Moore, B.A., Ph.D. (St. And.), Sen. Lect. in Hist. [Ancient Greek cities]

Diana Newton, B.A., Ph.D. (Liv.), Reader in Hist. [Reformation & the north-east of England]

Anthony J. Pollard, B.A., Ph.D. (Brist.), Emeritus Prof. of Hist. (Late Med., Econ., Soc. & Pol.) [N. England, esp. 1450–1500], A.Pollard@tees.ac.uk

Ben Schiller, B.A., Ph.D. (Edin.), Sen. Lect. [Slavery & the American tropics]

Richard G. Sober, B.A. (Staffs.), Lect. in Architectural Hist. [Participatory design; recent urban development], R.Sober@tees.ac.uk

Natasha Vall, B.A. (Sheff.), Ph.D. (Northumbria), Reader in Hist. [The north-east of England & regeneration; public history]

UNIVERSITY OF WALES, **TRINITY SAINT DAVID**

Lampeter, Ceredigion, SA48 7ED. 01570 422351. Fax 01570 423423
www.trinitysaintdavid.ac.uk
School of Archaeology, History & Anthropology 01570 424872. Fax 01570 432885
www.trinitysaintdavid.ac.uk/en/schoolofarchaeologyhistoryandanthropology/
School of Classics 01570 424723. Fax 01570 423877
www.trinitysaintdavid.ac.uk/en/schoolofclassics/
School of Theology, Religious Studies & Islamic Studies
01570 424708. Fax 01570 423641
www.trinitysaintdavid.ac.uk/en/facultyofhumanities/
schooloftheologyreligiousstudiesandislamicstudies/
School of Welsh & Bilingual Studies 01570 424754. Fax 01570 423874
www.trinitysaintdavid.ac.uk/en/schoolofwelshandbilingualstudies/

Andrew Abram, B.A., Ph.D. (Wales), Lect. in Med. Hist. [Monastic orders, esp. the Augustinian canons], andrew.abram@tsd.ac.uk

David Austin, B.A. (Southampton), Dip.Arch. (Dunelm.), Emeritus Prof. of Archaeol. [Medieval & later landscapes; archaeological theory; settlements; castles; later monasticism], d.austin@tsd.ac.uk

Barry C. Burnham, M.A., Ph.D. (Cantab.), Emeritus Prof. of Archaeol., Pro Vice-Chancellor [Urbanism in Roman Britain, esp. the 'small towns'], b.burnham@tsd.ac.uk

Janet E. Burton, B.A. (Lond.), D. Phil. (York), Prof. of Hist. (Med.) [Medieval monastic & religious orders], j.burton@tsd.ac.uk

Jane Cartwright, B.A., Ph.D. (Wales), Sen. Lect. in Welsh & Welsh Stud. [Medieval Church history; female monasticism; middle Welsh literature], j.cartwright@tsd.ac.uk

Kathy Ehrensperger, Lic.theol. (Basel), Ph.D. (Wales), Sen. Lect. [Inter-testamental Judaisms; early Christianity; women in the ancient world], k.ehrensperger@tsd.ac.uk

Colin C. Eldridge, B.A., Ph.D. (Nott.), Emeritus Prof. of Hist., p/t (Imp.) [British empire & Commonwealth history; literature of imperialism], c.eldridge@tsd.ac.uk

Johannes Hoff, M.A. (Bonn), Dipl.theol., Ph.D., Dr.habil., P.D. (Tübingen), Lect. [History of late medieval thought; history of ideas; Nicholas of Cusa], j.hoff@tsd.ac.uk

Amjad M. Hussain, B.A., Ph.D. (Wales), Sen. Lect. (Islamic Stud. & Relig. Stud.) [Islamic theology; Islamic civilisation], a.hussain@tsd.ac.uk

Mawil Izzi Dien, B.A. (Baghdad), Ph.D. (Manc.), Reader (Islamic Stud.) [History of Islam; Islamic law; Islam & ecology], izzidien@tsd.ac.uk

Karen Jankulak, B.A., M.A. (Toronto), Lect. [Medieval Celtic history; Church history, esp. cult of saints; Arthurian studies], k.jankulak@tsd.ac.uk

Lester Mason, B.A. (Open), Ph.D. (Wales), Lect. in Hist., p/t [Social, political & cultural impact of the Great War, with particular attention given to the rural communities of west Wales]

D. Densil Morgan, B.A., B.D., D.D. (Wales), D.Phil. (Oxon.), Prof. [Christianity in 19th & 20th c. Wales; Protestant nonconformity; 20th c. Protestant theology, esp. Karl Barth], d.d.morgan@tsd.ac.uk

David Noy, B.A., Ph.D. (Read.), Lect. in Classics, p/t [Jews & other minorities in the Roman world; Roman social history; death in the ancient world; medieval Latin documents for local history]

Martin O'Kane, B.A., M.A., L.S.S., Ph.D. (Edin.), Sen. Lect. (Biblical Stud.) [Old Testament; Biblical interpretation; Bible & the arts], m.okane@tsd.ac.uk

Mirjam Plantinga, B.A. (Amsterdam), Ph.D. (St. And.), Lect. in Classics [Hellenistic poetry; epic poetry; Augustan poetry]

Robert Pope, B.A., Ph.D. (Wales), Reader [Contemporary theology; religion & film; Protestant nonconformity], r.pope@tsd.ac.uk

James Richardson, M.A. (Auckland), Lect. in Classics [The history & historiographical tradition of early Rome; Roman myths & legends]

Keith G. Robbins, M.A., D.Phil. (Oxon.), D.Litt. (Glas.), Hon. Prof. of Hist. & Theol. [British relations with 'Europe' since 1789; world history since 1945; 20th c. British Christianity], k.robbins@tsd.ac.uk

Francisca Rumsey, M.A., Ph.D. (Wales), [Early medieval theology; history of monasticism; history of women in religion; history of liturgy], p.rumsey@tsd.ac.uk

Bettina E. Schmidt, M.A., Ph.D, Dr.habil (Marburg), Sen. Lect. [Afro-America, including trans-Atlantic slave trade; Latin America & Caribbean history, culture & religions], b.schmidt@tsd.ac.uk

*Jeremy W. Smith, B.A. (Exeter), M.A., Ph.D. (Lond.), Sen. Lect. in Hist. (19th & 20th c. Brit. Pol.) [Modern British history; Anglo-Irish relations in the 20th c.; the Ulster crisis, 1910–14; British Conservative party & politics], jeremy.smith@tsd.ac.uk

Bryn Willcock, B.A., M.A., Ph.D. (Wales), Lect. in Hist., p/t (World Pol. Affairs) [Cold War; war & peace; nuclear history; European integration & international security; 19th & 20th c. American history; American politics & popular culture], b.willcock@tsd.ac.uk

Catrin Williams, B.A. (Wales), Ph.D. (Cantab.), Sen. Lect. (New Testament Stud.) [Late Second Temple Judaism & Christian origins; Johannine literature], c.williams@tsd.ac.uk

Jonathan M. Wooding, B.A., Ph.D. (Sydney), Sen. Lect. (Eccles. Hist.) [Monasticism; Celtic Christianity; Catholic Church in 19th c. Australia], j.wooding@tsd.ac.uk

UNIVERSITY OF ULSTER

Cromore Road, Coleraine, County Londonderry, BT52 1SA.
028 7012 3456. Fax 028 7012 4927
www.ulster.ac.uk
School of English, History & Politics
Coleraine campus, BT52 1SA. 028 7012 4474. Fax 028 7012 4952
Magee campus, Londonderry, BT48 7JL. 028 716 75597
School of Creative Arts & Technologies
Magee campus, Londonderry, BT48 7JL. 028 716 75597

Allan Blackstock, B.A., Ph.D. (Belf.), Reader in Soc. & Econ. Hist., Coleraine [Irish social & military history; Irish loyalism 1789–1870], a.blackstock@ulster.ac.uk

Elizabeth Crooke, B.A. (Dublin), M.Phil., Ph.D. (Cantab.), Prof. of Heritage & Museum Studies (Museum Practice & Management) [Political, social & archaeological context of museums], em.crooke@ulster.ac.uk

Aglaia De Angeli, B.A. (Venice), Ph.D. (Lyon), Lect. in E. Asian Hist, Coleraine (E. Asian Hist.) [Chinese social & political history; Western & Japanese colonialism; gender history in East Asia], a.deangeli@ulster.ac.uk

Gabriel Guarino, B.A., M.A. (Haifa), Ph.D. (Cantab.), Lect. in Early Mod. Hist., Coleraine [Early modern European cultural history], g.guardino@ulster.ac.uk

Kyle Hughes, B.A., Ph.D. (Northumbria), Lect., Coleraine (Brit. Hist.) [British & Irish social & political history, 19th & 20th c.], k.hughes1@ulster.ac.uk

William Kelly, B.A. (Dublin), Ph.D. (Cantab.), Lect. in Ulster Scots Stud., Magee [Early modern Irish history; Ulster Scots history], bp.kelly@ulster.ac.uk

Liam Kennedy, B.Sc., M.Sc. (N.U.I.), D.Phil. (York), Prof. of Econ. & Soc. Hist of Ulster, Coleraine [Irish economic & demographic history; Ulster economy & society; marriage & inheritance in rural society], l.kennedy@ulster.ac.uk

Dianne Kirby, B.A., Ph.D. (Hull), Reader in Amer. Stud., Magee [Religion & the Cold War], d.kirby@ulster.ac.uk

James P. Loughlin, B.A. (Ulster), Ph.D. (Dublin), Reader, Magee (Irish Hist.) [Ulster unionism; British identity], jp.loughlin@ulster.ac.uk

Leanne McCormick, M.A. (Cantab.), Ph.D. (Ulster), Lect. in Mod. Irish Soc. Hist., Coleraine [Women's history; history of medicine; history of sexuality; Northern Irish social history], lv.mccormick@ulster.ac.uk

Robert McNamara, B.A., Ph.D. (N.U.I. Cork), Sen. Lect. in Int. Hist., Coleraine [Britain & the Middle East since 1945; British decolonisation & the Republic of Ireland since independence], rm.mcnamara@ulster.ac.uk

Donald M. MacRaild, B.A. (C.N.A.A.), Ph.D. (Sheff.), Prof. in Brit. & Irish Hist., Coleraine [Irish & British social & labour history, 1750–1914; British & Irish diasporas; theory & methods], dm.macraild@ulster.ac.uk

Ian Miller, B.A., Ph.D. (Manc.), Wellcome Trust Res. Fellow in Medical Hist. [British & Irish medical history, 1790–1981], i.miller@ulster.ac.uk

Leonie Murray, B.A., Ph.D. (Ulster), Lect. in Int. Pol., Magee [U.S. foreign policy; the U.N. system; the peacemaking pantheon; intervention issues; African policy; development issues; post-September 11th international relations & security issues], lg.murray@ulster.ac.uk

Éamonn Ó Ciardha, B.A., M.A. (N.U.I.), Ph.D. (Cantab.), Sen. Lect. in Irish/Eng. Literature/ Hist. Stud. (Irish Hist. & Literature) [Irish literary, cultural, military, environmental & landscape history; Irish book history; Irish political ballads], e.ociardha@ulster.ac.uk

P. Emmet J. O'Connor, M.A. (N.U.I.), Ph.D. (Cantab.), Sen. Lect. in Hist., Magee (Labour Hist.), pej.oconnor@ulster.ac.uk

Andrew Sneddon, B.A. (Herts.), M.Litt. (St. And.), Ph.D. (Leicester), Lect. in Int. Hist., Coleraine [Early modern European witchcraft; Irish parliamentary legislation; state intervention & institutional medicine in Britain & Ireland; Church of England/Ireland & Roman Catholicism], a.sneddon@ulster.ac.uk

Ian D. Thatcher, B.A., M.Sc. (C.N.A.A.), M.Litt., Ph.D. (Glas.), Prof. of Hist., Coleraine (Mod. Russian Hist.), i.thatcher@ulster.ac.uk

Owain Wright, B.A., Ph.D. (Lancaster), Lect., Coleraine (Int. Hist.) [Modern European, incl. British, history], oj.wright@ulster.ac.uk

Nerys Young, B.A., Ph.D. (Ulster), Lect. in Amer. Hist., Coleraine [Organised crime in America; the gangster film genre; 20th c. American history; film & politics], nl.young@ulster.ac.uk

UNIVERSITY OF **WARWICK**

Coventry, Warwicks., CV4 7AL. 024 7652 3523
www.warwick.ac.uk
Department of History 024 7652 2080. Fax 024 7652 3437
www.warwick.ac.uk/fac/arts/history/
Department of History of Art
www.warwick.ac.uk/fac/arts/arthistory/
Department of Classics & Ancient History 024 7652 3023. Fax 024 7652 4973
www.warwick.ac.uk/fac/arts/classics/
Department of Economics 024 7652 3055. Fax 024 7652 3032
Institute of Education 024 7657 2880. Fax 024 7652 4177

David Anderson, B.A., M.A. (Oxon.), Ph.D. (Cantab.), Prof. of Afric. Hist. [African history
& politics, esp. eastern Africa & the Horn; political violence; civil conflict; security; war],
D.M.Anderson@warwick.ac.uk
Victoria Avery, B.A., Ph.D. (Cantab.), Lect. in Art Hist. (15th & 16th c. Italian Art) [Venice
& sculpture; bronze as an artistic medium in Renaissance Italy: its production, uses &
reception], Victoria.Avery@warwick.ac.uk
James Baldwin, B.A. (Oxon.), Ph.D. (N.Y.), Assistant Prof. of Hist. [The legal, social & political
history of Ottoman Egypt during the 17th & 18th c.], J.E.Baldwin@warwick.ac.uk
Maxine L. Berg, B.A. (Simon Fraser), M.A. (Sussex), D.Phil. (Oxon.), F.B.A., Prof. of Hist.
(17th–20th c. Econ., Soc. & Cultural) [Global history; consumer culture in Europe & Asia],
Maxine.Berg@warwick.ac.uk
Roberta E. Bivins, B.A. (Columbia), Ph.D. (M.I.T.), Assoc. Prof. of Hist. (Technology &
Medicine), R.Bivins@warwick.ac.uk
Daniel Branch, B.A., M.A., D.Phil. (Oxon.), Prof. of Afric. Hist. (Afric. Hist.) [Political & social
history of postcolonial Kenya, esp. the Mau Mau rebellion], D.P.Branch@warwick.ac.uk
Louise Campbell, B.A. (Sussex), M.A., Ph.D. (Lond.), Sen. Lect. in Art Hist. (20th c.
Architecture) [The design of cities; artists' studios], L.E.M.Campbell@warwick.ac.uk
Howard Chiang, B.A., M.A. (S. Calif.), Ph.D. (Princeton), Assistant Prof. of Mod. Chinese Hist.
[Modern Chinese history & cultural studies; history of science & medicine; gender, sexuality
& the body; sinophone postcolonial studies; critical theory & quantitative methodology in
the social sciences], H.H.Chiang@warwick.ac.uk
Alison Cooley, M.A., D.Phil. (Oxon.), Sen. Lect. in Classics [All aspects of the Roman world
– social, cultural, economic & political; Roman Italy; use of inscriptions in both ancient &
modern times], A.Cooley@warwick.ac.uk
Donal Cooper, B.A. (Oxon.), M.A., Ph.D. (Lond.), Lect. in Art Hist. (Eccles. Art & Architecture
in Late Med. & Renaissance Italy) [Patronage of the Franciscan & other mendicant
orders; art & culture in Renaissance Umbria; the decorative arts in Italy to 1600],
D.A.Cooper@warwick.ac.uk
Camillia Cowling, B.A. (Oxon.), M.A. (Lond.), Ph.D. (Nott.), Assistant Prof. of Hist.
[Slavery & abolition in the Americas & Atlantic world, specifically Brazil & Cuba],
C.Cowling@warwick.ac.uk
Nicholas Crafts, B.A. (Cantab.), Prof. of Econ. Hist. [Comparative history of long-run
economic growth; British Industrial Revolution; British relative economic decline],
N.Crafts@warwick.ac.uk
James Davidson, M.A. (Oxon.), M.A., M.Phil. (Columbia), D.Phil. (Oxon.), Reader in Classics
[Greek social & cultural history & historiography]

Jonathan Davies, B.A., Ph.D. (Liv.), Assoc. Prof. of Hist. [Elites; ritual; violence; the history of the Italian states, 1300–1600; European universities, 1150–1800], J.D.Davies@warwick.ac.uk

Angela Davis, B.A. (Lond.), M.St., D.Phil. (Oxon.), Assistant Prof. of Hist. [The history of motherhood in post-war Britain; Jewish maternity in England & Israel with an emphasis on oral history], Angela.Davis@warwick.ac.uk

Rosie Dias, B.A., M.A., Ph.D. (York), Lect. in Art Hist. (Brit. Art & Culture in the 18th & Early 19th c.) [History of exhibitions & art institutions], Rosemarie.Dias@warwick.ac.uk

Rebecca A. Earle, B.A. (Bryn Mawr), M.Sc., M.A., Ph.D. (Warwick), Assoc. Prof. of Hist. (Late Colonial & 19th c. Spanish Amer.) [Race, history & national identity in 19th c. Spanish America; clothing industry; history of food], R.Earle@warwick.ac.uk

Roger J. Fagge, B.A. (Lond.), Ph.D. (Cantab.), Assoc. Prof. of Hist. (19th–20th c. Amer.) [Society, politics & culture in 20th c. U.S.; 1950s America; popular music & culture in the U.S.], Roger.Fagge@warwick.ac.uk

Julian Gardner, M.A. (Oxon.), Ph.D. (Lond.), Prof. of Hist. of Art [Artistic patronage; Rome; tomb structure; Giotto], Julian.Gardner@warwick.ac.uk

Anne Gerritsen, M.A. (Leiden), Ph.D. (Harv.), Assoc. Prof. of Hist. (China) [Social & cultural history of early modern China], A.T.Gerritsen@warwick.ac.uk

Gabriel Glickman, B.A., M.Phil, Ph.D. (Cantab.), Assistant Prof. of Hist. [British politics & religion c.1660–1750, concentrating on the significance of the international context], G.Glickman@warwick.ac.uk

Abigail Graham, B.A. (Colgate), D.Phil. (Oxon.), Lect. in Anc. Hist. [Greek & Roman epigraphy; urbanism], Abigail.Graham@warwick.ac.uk

Bishnupriva Gupta, B.A. (Calcutta), D.Phil. (Oxon.), [Comparative economic history; economic history of colonial India], B.Gupta@warwick.ac.uk

Joachim Häberlen, M.A., Ph.D. (Chicago), Assistant Prof. of Hist. [Modern European history; Germany & France in the 20th c.; comparative, transnational & global history; cultural history of the political; micro-history; history of emotions; political & social movements, revolts & revolutions], J.Haeberlen@warwick.ac.uk

Anna Hájková, M.A. (Humboldt), Ph.D. (Toronto), Assistant Prof. of Hist. [History of the Holocaust; Nazi Germany & modern central & eastern Europe; history of genocide; gender; nationalities; history of everyday life], Anna.Hajkova@warwick.ac.uk

Mark Harrison, M.A. (Cantab.), D.Phil. (Oxon.), Prof. of Econ. [Russian, Soviet & international economic history], Mark.Harrison@warwick.ac.uk

Sarah Hodges, B.A. (Brown), M.A., Ph.D. (Chicago), Assoc. Prof. of Hist. [Modern S. Asia; social history of science, technology & medicine], S.Hodges@warwick.ac.uk

Stanley Ireland, B.A. (Hull), Ph.D. (Cantab.), Sen. Lect. in Classics [Roman Britain; Roman comedy; Greek new comedy; numismatics], S.Ireland@warwick.ac.uk

John P. King, M.A. (Edin.), B.Phil., D.Phil. (Oxon.), Prof. in Latin Amer. Literature [Latin American cultural history; Latin American film], J.P.King@warwick.ac.uk

Mark Knights, D.Phil. (Oxon.), Prof. of Hist. [Early modern British political culture c.1500–1800], M.J.Knights@warwick.ac.uk

Beat Kümin, Lic.phil. (Bern), Ph.D. (Cantab.), P.D. (Bern), Prof. of Hist. (Late Med. & Early Mod. Soc. & Cultural Hist.) [Public houses in early modern Europe; parishes in the age of the Reformation; food history; spatial approaches to the past], B.Kumin@warwick.ac.uk

David Lambert, B.A., Ph.D. (Cantab.), Reader of Caribbean Hist. [Caribbean & Atlantic histories; British imperialism, exploration & cartography in the 'long' 19th c.; counterfactual histories; histories of Whiteness; historical geography], D.Lambert@warwick.ac.uk

Tim Lockley, M.A. (Edin.), Ph.D. (Cantab.), Reader in Hist. (18th–19th c. Amer.) [Slavery, race, gender & reform in the colonial & antebellum South], T.J.Lockley@warwick.ac.uk

*Maria Luddy, M.A., Ph.D. (N.U.I.), Prof. of Hist., Head of Hist. [Women in Irish society; 19th & 20th c. social & political Irish history], M.Luddy@warwick.ac.uk

Hilary Marland, B.A., Ph.D. (Warwick), Prof. of Hist. (Soc. Hist. of Medicine) [Childbirth; insanity; adolescent health], Hilary.Marland@warwick.ac.uk

Peter Marshall, M.A., D.Phil. (Oxon.), Prof. of Hist. (Early Mod. Eng. Relig. & Cultural Hist.) [Reformation & its impact], P.Marshall@warwick.ac.uk

Christoph Mick, M.A., Ph.D., Dr.habil (Tübingen), Assoc. Prof. of E. Eur. Hist. (Mod. German & E. Eur. Hist.) [Poland, Russia, Ukraine; history of science & technology; memorial culture & nation building], C.Mick@warwick.ac.uk

Zahra Newby, M.A. (Oxon.), Ph.D. (Lond.), Sen. Lect. in Classics [Classical art; Greek athletics; Roman art & the interplay between art & literature], Z.L.Newby@warwick.ac.uk

Daniel Orrells, M.A., Ph.D. (Cantab.), Lect. in Classics (Greek & Latin Literature & Reception Stud.), D.Orrells@warwick.ac.uk

Mark Philp, B.A. (Bradford), M.Sc. (Leeds), M.Phil., Ph.D. (Oxon.), Prof. of Hist. [Political theory & sociology; political corruption & issues relating to standards in public life; history of political thought & British history at the time of the French Revolution], Mark.Philp@warwick.ac.uk

Pierre Purseigle, B.A. (Sciences Po, Lyon), D.E.A., Eur.Doct. (Toulouse), Assoc. Prof. of Hist. [Comparative history of the First World War], P.Purseigle@warwick.ac.uk

Christopher J. Read, B.A. (Keele), M.Phil. (Glas.), Ph.D. (Lond.), Prof. of Hist. (20th c. Eur. Hist.) [Russian revolution], C.J.Read@warwick.ac.uk

Sarah Richardson, B.A. (Manc.), M.A. (Hull), Assoc. Prof. of Hist. (18th–19th c. Brit. Pol.) [Political culture; electoral politics; history & computing], Sarah.Richardson@warwick.ac.uk

Harriet Riches, B.A., M.A., Ph.D. (Lond.), Lect. in Art Hist. (20th c. Contemp. Art) [Issues of self-representation & the performance of identity in photographic practices], H.Riches@warwick.ac.uk

Giorgio Riello, Ph.D. (Lond.), Prof. of Cultural Hist. [Global history; history of fashion & textiles; material culture], G.Riello@warwick.ac.uk

Penny Roberts, B.A., Ph.D. (Birm.), M.A. (Warwick), Reader in Hist. (16th–17th c. French) [Wars of religion], Penny.Roberts@warwick.ac.uk

Wendy Robinson, B.Ed., Ph.D. (Cantab.), M.A. (Lond.), Lect. in Educ. [History of education; teacher training; women's education], Wendy.Robinson@warwick.ac.uk

Michael Rosenthal, B.A., Ph.D. (Lond.), M.A. (Cantab.), Prof. of Art Hist. (18th & Early 19th c. Eng. Art & Culture) [Art & exploration; the culture of colonialism; Australian art], M.J.Rosenthal@warwick.ac.uk

Rosa Salzberg, B.A., Ph.D (Lond.), Assistant Prof. of Renaissance Hist. [Renaissance history], R.Salzberg@warwick.ac.uk

Aditya Sarkar, M.A., M.Phil. (J. Nehru), Ph.D. (Lond.), Assistant Prof. of Hist. [History of modern S. Asia, esp. social histories of labour & capitalism], Aditya.Sarkar@warwick.ac.uk

Laura Schwartz, B.A., Ph.D. (East Lond.), Assistant Prof. of Mod. Brit. Hist. [Modern British history, esp. feminism & domestic workers], L.Schwartz@warwick.ac.uk

Robert J.A. Skidelsky, M.A., D.Phil. (Oxon.), F.B.A., Prof. of Pol. Econ.

Benjamin Smith, B.A., Ph.D. (Cantab.), Assoc. Prof. of Latin Amer. Hist. [Modern Mexican history, esp. post-revolutionary state formation & religion & popular conservatism], B.Smith.1@warwick.ac.uk

*Paul G. Smith, B.A., Ph.D. (Lond.), Prof. of Hist. of Art (Later 19th c. French Painting) [Art theory, criticism & literature more generally; theory & philosophy of art], Paul.G.Smith@warwick.ac.uk

Jennifer Smyth, B.A. (Wellesley), Ph.D. (Yale), Assoc. Prof. in Hist. (Late 19th & 20th c. Amer. Cultural Hist.) [Historiography; cinema], J.E.Smyth@warwick.ac.uk

G. Charles Walton, B.A. (Calif. at Berkeley), M.A., Ph.D. (Princeton), Assoc. Prof. of Hist. [Ancien Régime, Enlightenment & revolutionary France with emphases on democratisation, human rights, liberalism & economic justice], Charles.Walton@warwick.ac.uk

UNIVERSITY OF THE **WEST OF ENGLAND, BRISTOL**

Coldharbour Lane, Bristol, BS16 1QY. 0117 965 6261
www.uwe.ac.uk
Department of History
St. Matthias Campus, Oldbury Court Road, Fishponds, Bristol, BS16 2JP.
0117 328 4416. Fax 0117 328 4417

Madge J. Dresser, B.A. (Calif.), M.Sc. (Lond. & Brist.), D.Phil. (W. of Eng.), Assoc. Prof. (18th–20th c. Brit. Soc. Hist., Women) [British Atlantic slavery; history of religious & ethnic minorities in Britain since 1700], madge.dresser@uwe.ac.uk

E. Kent Fedorowich, B.A., M.A. (Saskatchewan), Ph.D. (Lond.), Assoc. Prof. (Brit. Imp. & C'wealth Hist.) [Empire migration 1919–39; PoWs in World War II; Anglo-dominion relations], kent.fedorowich@uwe.ac.uk

*John Fisher, M.A. (Glas.), Ph.D. (Leeds), Joint Head of Hist., Lect. (Int. & Imp. Hist.) [Middle East; central Asia; North Africa], john.fisher@uwe.ac.uk

Peter W. Fleming, B.A., Ph.D. (Wales), Prof. of Hist. (Med. & Early Mod. Brit. Hist.) [15th–16th c. English cultural & urban history], peter.fleming@uwe.ac.uk

June B. Hannam, B.A., M.A. (Warwick), Ph.D. (Sheff.), Emeritus Prof. (Labour & Women's Hist.) [Women & socialist politics in Britain, 1880–1930s], june.hannam@uwe.ac.uk

James Lee, B.A., Ph.D. (W. of Eng.), Lect. (Early Med. Brit. & Eur.) [Early modern British & European history c.1450–1750], james5.lee@uwe.ac.uk

Philip G. Ollerenshaw, B.A. (Leeds), M.Sc. (Lond.), Ph.D. (Sheff.), Assoc. Prof. (Irish Hist., Business Hist.) [British employers' associations, 1916–65], philip.ollerenshaw@uwe.ac.uk

Steve W. Poole, B.A. (W. of Eng.), Ph.D. (Brist.), Prof. (Brit. Soc. & Cultural Hist., Historiography) [Crowds & popular sovereignty in the 18th c.], steve.poole@uwe.ac.uk

Michael R. Richards, B.A., Ph.D. (Lond.), Assoc. Prof. (Eur. Hist.) [20th c. Spain; comparative fascism; public history; memory of war], michael.richards@uwe.ac.uk

*Martin Simpson, B.A. (Oxon.), M.A. (Manc.), Ph.D. (Lond.), Joint Head of Hist., Lect. (Mod. Eur. Hist.) [National identity & the right in 19th–20th c. France], martin.simpson@uwe.ac.uk

Glyn A. Stone, B.A. (Lancaster), M.A. (Sussex), Ph.D. (Lond.), Emeritus Prof. (Int. Hist.) [British arms sales diplomacy, 1934–40; Britain & Portuguese Africa 1961–75; Iberian foreign relations 1931–41; Anglo-French relations 1930s], glyn.stone@uwe.ac.uk

Peter Wardley, B.Sc.(Econ.), Ph.D. (Wales), Prof. (Econ. & Business Hist.) [Business history; economic history; labour history], peter.wardley@uwe.ac.uk

Elizabeth White, B.A. (Leeds), M.St. (Oxon.), Ph.D. (Birm.), Lect. in Russian Hist. (Mod. Russian Hist.) [Russian emigration; refugees & international organisations; history of childhoold], elizabeth.white@uwe.ac.uk

Michael Woodiwiss, B.A. (Essex), M.Phil (Sheff.), D.Phil. (W. of Eng.), Lect. (Amer. Hist.) [Organised & corporate crime in the U.S.; transnational organised crime], michael.woodiwiss@uwe.ac.uk

UNIVERSITY OF **WESTMINSTER**

School of Social Sciences, Humanities & Languages
309 Regent Street, London, W1B 2UW. 020 7911 5000.
Fax 020 7911 5106
www.westminster.ac.uk/history/

Peter Catterall, M.A. (Cantab.), Ph.D. (Lond.), Reader [Relationship between identities; ideas & political culture], p.catterall@westminster.ac.uk

Mark Clapson, B.A., M.A. (Lancaster), Ph.D. (Warwick), Reader (Soc. Hist.) [Social & urban history], m.clapson@westminster.ac.uk

Martin A. Doherty, B.Sc.(Econ.) (Lond.), M.Soc.Sc. (Belf.), M.A. (Westminster), Ph.D. (Kent), Princ. Lect. [Political propaganda; Northern Ireland], m.a.doherty@westminster.ac.uk

Helen Glew, B.A., M.A. (Lancaster), Ph.D. (Lond.), Lect. [Gender history, late 19th/early 20th c.; modern British history], h.glew@westminster.ac.uk

Anthony Gorst, B.A. (Lancaster), M.A. (Lond.), Princ. Lect. [British foreign & defence policy in 20th c.], a.gorst@westminster.ac.uk

Richard H. Harding, B.A. (Leicester), Ph.D. (Lond.), Prof. of Organisational Hist. [Naval & maritime history], hardinr@westminster.ac.uk

Frances M.B. Lynch, B.Sc., Ph.D. (Manc.), Reader in French Stud. (Mod. Eur., esp. France & E.U.) [Franco-British economic co-operation], lynchf@westminster.ac.uk

*Charles J. Sandeman-Allen, B.A. (Sussex), Ph.D. (Lond.), Lect. [19th c. British religious history], c.sandemanallen@westminster.ac.uk

Katja Seidel, M.A. (Tübingen/Aix-en-Provence), Ph.D. (Portsmouth), [European integration history; German history], k.seidel@westminster.ac.uk

Patrick Smylie, B.A. (Westminster), Ph.D. (Belf.), Lect. [20th c. trade unionism], p.smylie@westminster.ac.uk

Peter Speiser, B.A. (Westminster), M.A. (Lond.), Lect. [20th c. Anglo-German relations], p.speiser1@westminster.ac.uk

UNIVERSITY OF **WINCHESTER**

www.winchester.ac.uk
West Hill, Winchester, SO22 4NR. 01962 841515. Fax 01962 842280
Faculty of Humanities & Social Sciences: History & Archaeology Departments

Mark A. Allen, B.A. (Hull), Ph.D. (Southampton), Sen. Lect. in Hist. [19th c. British social & economic history; history & computing], mark.allen@winchester.ac.uk

Natalya Chernyshova, B.A. (Amer. Univ. in Bulgaria & Minsk), M.A., Ph.D. (Lond.), Lect. in Mod. Hist. (Russia) [Soviet social & cultural history; consumption; Russian cinema], natalya.chernyshova@winchester.ac.uk

Neil S.J. Curtin, B.A. (Lancaster), M.A. (Lond.), Sen. Lect. (Amer. Hist.) [American democracy; the American South; European fascism; the Cold War], neil.curtin@winchester.ac.uk

Paul Everill, B.A. (Wales), M.A., Ph.D. (Southampton), Lect. in Applied Archaeol. Techniques [History of archaeology; contemporary commercial archaeology; theory & practice of teaching archaeological fieldwork; Georgia], paul.everill@winchester.ac.uk

Niall P. Finneran, B.A. (Lond.), Ph.D. (Cantab.), Reader in Archaeol., p/t (Med.) [Late antique/
early medieval Ethiopia, Egypt, western Asia; post-Roman western Britain; archaeology of
early Christianity; historical archaeology in the Caribbean], niall.finneran@winchester.ac.uk
Carey Fleiner, B.A. (Delaware), M.A., Ph.D. (Virginia), Sen. Lect. in Hist. (Classical)
[Roman empire & Roman culture; Greek world & culture; Carolingian medieval history;
ancient & medieval popular culture; 20th c. popular music in culture & society],
carey.fleiner@winchester.ac.uk
Joyce F. Goodman, B.Ed. (C.N.A.A.), M.Ed., Ph.D. (Manc.), Dean & Prof. of Hist. of Educ.
[Women's history; gender, colonialism & education; women's international organisations;
comparative & transnational histories of education], joyce.goodman@winchester.ac.uk
Christina M. Grande, B.A., M.A. (Birm.), Lect. in Archaeol., p/t (Classical) [Roman Italy &
Roman culture; Greek world & culture; classical art & architecture; classical tradition],
christina.grande@winchester.ac.uk
Xavier Guégan, Ph.D. (Northumbria), Lect. (Colonial & Post-colonial Hist.) [Cultural
implications of British colonialism in S. Asia & French colonialism in Maghred; British &
French encounters with Ottoman Empire; post-colonial history & theory; comparative
history; anti-colonial history, 19th & 20th c.], xavier.guegan@winchester.ac.uk
Colin M. Haydon, M.A., D.Phil. (Oxon.), Reader in Early Mod. Hist. (18th c. Relig.,
Pol. & Soc. Hist.) [Religion, society & politics in England c.1660–c.1830],
colin.haydon@winchester.ac.uk
*Michael A. Hicks, B.A. (Brist.), M.A. (Southampton), D.Phil. (Oxon.), Prof. (Late Med. Hist.)
[Richard III; political culture; bastard feudalism; inquisitions post mortem; overland trade],
michael.hicks@winchester.ac.uk
Louise Hill Curth, B.Sc. (Illinois), M.A., Ph.D. (Lond.), Reader in Medical Hist. [Early
modern medical & veterinary history; early modern almanacs; history of books; history of
advertising; history of astrology], louise.curth@winchester.ac.uk
Matthew L. Holford, B.A. (Cantab.), M.A., Ph.D. (York), Lect. (Med.) [Late medieval England;
inqusitions post mortem; middling sort; liberties], matthew.holford@winchester.ac.uk
Tom Beaumont James, M.A., Ph.D. (St. And.), Prof. Emeritus (Med. & Early Mod.) [English
urban history; elite architecture; archaeology & landscape; demography & death],
tom.james@winchester.ac.uk
Anthony C. King, B.A., Ph.D. (Lond.), Director of Res., Prof. (Roman Hist.) [Ancient diet;
Romano-Celtic religion], tony.king@winchester.ac.uk
Ryan L. Lavelle, B.A. (Lond.), M.A. (York), Ph.D. (Southampton), Sen. Lect. in Hist. [Late
Anglo-Saxon political history, esp. Wessex; Norman conquest; early medieval landholding
& warfare], ryan.lavelle@winchester.ac.uk
Camilla Leach, B.A., Ph.D. (Southampton), Res. Fellow [Women's & Quaker history; religion
& history], camilla.leach@winchester.ac.uk
Phil C. Marter, B.A., P.G.Dip. (Oxon.), Ph.D. (Southampton), Lect. in Applied Archaeol.
Techniques [Medieval archaeology; medieval pottery industry; archaeology of World War II;
archaeological techniques], phil.marter@winchester.ac.uk
Jean Morrin, B.A. (Read.), Ph.D. (Dunelm.), Res. Fellow, p/t (Early Mod. & Mod. Brit.) [Church
estates; local history; new V.C.H. Hampshire], jean.morrin@winchester.ac.uk
Emiliano Perra, B.A. (Bologna), M.A., Ph.D. (Brist.), Lect. in Hist. (Mod. Eur.)
[Holocaust & genocide; political & cultural history of Italy; history & film],
emiliano.perra@winchester.ac.uk
Roger C. Richardson, B.A. (Leicester), Ph.D. (Manc.), Prof. Emeritus (17th c., Historiography)
[Historiography of English Revolution; social & cultural history of domestic servants; English
social & local history; 17th c. religious biography], roger.richardson@winchester.ac.uk

Simon Roffey, B.A., M.Res. (Lond.), Ph.D. (Southampton), Sen. Lect. in Archaeol. (Med.) [Medieval hospitals; medieval archaeology; historical archaeology; archaeology of religion & belief], simon.roffey@winchester.ac.uk

James A. Ross, B.A., M.St., D.Phil. (Oxon.), Sen. Lect. in Hist. (Late Med.) [English political culture; nobility; royal government], james.ross@winchester.ac.uk

Simon R. Sandall, B.A., M.A., Ph.D. (E. Anglia), Lect. in Hist. (Early Mod. Brit.) [Custom & popular politics, social, economic & cultural history of Britain; English civil wars; English local history], simon.sandall@winchester.ac.uk

William Sheward, B.A. (East Anglia), M.A., M.Sc. (Lond.), Ph.D. (Southampton), Sen. Lect. in Amer. Stud., Pol. & Global Stud. [American politics & political ideologies; American foreign policy; American South], william.sheward@winchester.ac.uk

Alasdair Spark, B.A., Head of Internationalisation (Amer. Stud.) [20th c. America; film], alasdair.spark@winchester.ac.uk

Stephanie Spencer, B.A. (Open), M.A. (Lond.), Ph.D. (Southampton), Reader in Hist. of Women's Educ. (20th c. Brit.) [Women's & gender history; history of education; oral history], stephanie.spencer@winchester.ac.uk

*I. Nicholas Thorpe, B.A., Ph.D. (Read.), Princ. Lect. (Prehist.) [Meso-Neolithic north-west Europe; warfare; old age; prehistoric Britain], nick.thorpe@winchester.ac.uk

Keith N. Wilkinson, B.Sc., Ph.D. (Lond.), Reader in Environmental Archaeol. [Geoarchaeology; geographic information systems; Palaeolithic archaeology; Quaternary environments], keith.wilkinson@winchester.ac.uk

Elena C. Woodacre, B.A. (Open), M.A. (Reading), Ph.D. (Bath Spa), Lect. in Hist. (Early Mod. Eur.) [Female rule; political & cultural history of France, Spain & Italy; Renaissance; royal & court studies], ellie.woodacre@winchester.ac.uk

Barbara A.E. Yorke, B.A., Ph.D. (Exeter), Emerita Prof. (Early Med.) [Anglo-Saxon kingdoms & politics; church/secular relations in early middle ages; Anglo-Saxon women], barbara.yorke@winchester.ac.uk

UNIVERSITY OF **WOLVERHAMPTON**

Wulfruna Street, Wolverhampton, WV1 1LY. 01902 321000
www.wlv.ac.uk
School of Law, Social Sciences & Communications
Millennium City Building, Wulfruna Street, WV1 1LY. 01902 323484.
Fax 01902 323379/322739

Stephen Badsey, M.A., Ph.D. (Cantab.), Prof. of Conflict Stud. [Military history; media & propaganda history], Badsey@wlv.ac.uk

John D. Buckley, B.A., Ph.D. (Lancaster), Prof. of Milit. Hist. (20th c. Milit.) [20th c. military history; air power; technology in World War II], J.Buckley@wlv.ac.uk

Simon Constantine, B.A., M.A. (Manc.), Ph.D. (Nott.), Sen. Lect. [19th & 20th c. German history], smconstantine@wlv.ac.uk

Martin Durham, B.A., Ph.D. (Birm.), Sen. Lect. (Pol.) [Right-wing politics in Britain & the U.S.], M.Durham@wlv.ac.uk

Howard J. Fuller, B.A. (Ohio), M.A., Ph.D. (Lond.), [Naval history; 19th c. Anglo-American history], H.Fuller@wlv.ac.uk

Keith Gildart, B.A. (Manc.), Ph.D. (York), Reader [19th & 20th c. British & U.S. labour history], Keith.Gildart@wlv.ac.uk

Richard A. Hawkins, B.A. (Portsmouth), M.Sc., Ph.D. (Lond.), Sen. Lect. [American economic & social history], R.A.Hawkins@wlv.ac.uk

*Paul Henderson, B.A., Ph.D. (East Anglia), Princ. Lect. (19th–20th c. S. Amer., Spain), P.Henderson@wlv.ac.uk

David P. Hussey, B.A., M.A. (Leeds), Ph.D. (Wolverhampton), Sen. Lect. (16th–18th c. Eng.) [Internal trade & consumption in England, 1660–1880], D.P.Hussey@wlv.ac.uk

Christopher Norton, B.A., M.A., Ph.D. (Ulster), Sen. Lect. (Pol.) [20th c. Irish history & politics], C.Norton@wlv.ac.uk

Margaret Ponsonby, B.A. (Brighton), M.A. (R.C.A.), Ph.D. (Wolverhampton), Sen. Lect. (Design Hist.) [18th–19th c. domestic interiors & material culture], M.Ponsonby@wlv.ac.uk

Gary Sheffield, B.A., M.A. (Leeds), Ph.D. (Lond.), Prof. of War Stud. [Military history; Britain in the age of total war, 1914–45], G.Sheffield@wlv.ac.uk

Laura Ugolini, B.A., M.A. (Cardiff), Ph.D. (Greenwich), Reader in Hist. [Gender history; consumption; World War I], L.Ugolini@wlv.ac.uk

UNIVERSITY OF WORCESTER

Henwick Grove, Worcester, WR2 6AJ. 01905 855000. Fax 01905 855132
www.worcester.ac.uk
Department of Arts, Humanities & Social Sciences

Maggie Andrews, B.A., M.A., D.Phil. (Sussex), Prof. of Cultural Hist. (Mod. Brit.) [Women, culture & media], maggie.andrews@worc.ac.uk

Jeff Bowersox, B.A., M.A., Ph.D. (Toronto), Sen. Lect. (Mod. German) [Colonial culture; race], j.bowersox@worc.ac.uk

*Patrick McNally, B.A., Ph.D. (Belf.), Head of Hist., Princ. Lect. (Ireland) [Irish politics, 1690–1848], p.mcnally@worc.ac.uk

Darren Oldridge, B.A. (Nott.), Ph.D. (Warwick), Sen. Lect. (Early Mod. England) [Religion & popular belief], d.oldridge@worc.ac.uk

Suzanne Schwarz, B.A., Ph.D. (Liv.), Prof. of Hist. [Transatlantic slave trade; Sierra Leone], s.schwarz@worc.ac.uk

Wendy Toon, B.A., Ph.D. (Keele), Sen. Lect. (Mod. U.S.A.) [Foreign relations; propaganda], w.toon@worc.ac.uk

UNIVERSITY OF YORK

Heslington, York, YO10 5DD. 01904 430000.
www.york.ac.uk
Department of History 01904 322981.
www.york.ac.uk/history/
Borthwick Institute of Historical Research University of York, Heslington, York YO10 5DD.
01904 321166 (Archive Enquiries)
01904 321160 (Publications)
Department of Archaeology The King's Manor, York, YO1 2EP. 01904 433901.
www.york.ac.uk/archaeology/
Department of Economics & Related Studies 01904 323788/9. Fax 01904 323759
Department of History of Art 01904 322978. Fax 01904 323427

Tara Alberts, M.A., M.Phil., Ph.D. (Cantab.), Lect. in Hist. [16th–17th c. Catholicism in Southeast Asia; cultural encounters between Europe & Asia; medicine & spiritual history], tara.alberts@york.ac.uk

Henrice Altink, B.A. (Zwolle), M.A. (Nijmegen & Lancaster), Ph.D. (Hull), Sen. Lect. in Mod. Hist. [Slavery & emancipation; race relations in the Americas; Caribbean social & gender history, 1865–1980], henrice.altink@york.ac.uk

Jo Applin, B.A. (Lond.), M.A. (Essex), Ph.D. (Lond.), Lect. in Hist. of Art [Modern & contemporary art & theory], jo.applin@york.ac.uk

Steve Ashby, B.Sc. (Birm.), M.Sc., Ph.D. (York), Lect. in Archaeol. [Early medieval; bone & antler; portable antiquities], steve.ashby@york.ac.uk

Tim Ayers, B.A. (Oxon.), M.A., Ph.D. (Lond.), Sen. Lect. in Hist. of Art [Medieval art, including stained glass], tim.ayers@york.ac.uk

Oleg Benesch, B.A. (Alaska), M.A. (Reitaku), Ph.D. (Brit. Col.), Lect. in Hist. [Early modern & modern East Asia, esp. Japan], oleg.benesch@york.ac.uk

Richard J. Bessel, B.A. (Antioch), D.Phil. (Oxon.), Prof. of 20th c. Hist. (Mod. German) [19th & 20th c. German social & political history; aftermath of World Wars; history of G.D.R.; history of policing], richard.bessel@york.ac.uk

Sanjoy Bhattacharya, B.A. (Delhi), M.A. (J. Nehru), Ph.D. (Lond.), Prof. of Hist. of Medicine [19th & 20th c. South Asia; international & global health], sanjoy.bhattacharya@york.ac.uk

Peter P.A. Biller, M.A., D.Phil. (Oxon.), F.B.A., Prof. of Hist. (Med. Eur.) [Medieval heresy & inquisitions; medieval proto-racial themes], pete.biller@york.ac.uk

Lawrence Black, B.A. (Exeter), M.A. (Warwick), Ph.D. (Lond. Guildhall), Prof. of Mod. Brit. Hist. [20th c. Britain; political culture; consumerism], lawrence.black@york.ac.uk

James Boaden, B.A., M.A., Ph.D. (Lond.), Lect. in Hist. of Art [American art from mid 20th c.], james.boaden@york.ac.uk

Sue Bowden, B.A., Ph.D. (Lond.), Prof. of Mod. & Econ. Hist., Director of Centre for Hist., Econ. & Related Stud. [Historical roots of poverty, esp. disease; historical demography; business history], sue.bowden@york.ac.uk

Don R. Brothwell, M.A. (Cantab.), Ph.D. (Stockholm), Prof. Emeritus in Palaeoecology [Human palaeoecology; Europe & New World; archaeology of food], archaeology@york.ac.uk

Sarah Brown, B.A. (Lond.), M.A. (York), Lect. in Hist. of Art [Stained glass & the history of its restoration & reception], sarah.brown@york.ac.uk

Elizabeth A. Buettner, B.A. (Barnard), M.A., Ph.D. (Michigan), Sen. Lect. in Hist. (19th–20th c. Soc. & Cultural, Brit. & Brit. Empire) [Migration; European decolonisation in comparative perspective; ethnicity; families; childhood & memory], elizabeth.buettner@york.ac.uk

*Stuart M. Carroll, B.A. (Brist.), Ph.D. (Lond.), Prof. of Hist. (Early Mod. Eur.) [Early modern France; neighbourliness in the early modern West; violence], stuart.carroll@york.ac.uk

Martin O.H. Carver, B.Sc. (Lond.), Emeritus Prof. of Archaeol. [Archaeology of medieval Europe], martin.carver@york.ac.uk

Sabine Clarke, B.Sc., M.Sc., Ph.D. (Lond.), Lect. in Hist. [20th c. British empire, science, technology & medicine], sabine.clarke@york.ac.uk

David W. Clayton, B.A., Ph.D. (Manc.), Sen. Lect. in Econ. & Soc. Hist. (Mod. Int.) [The British empire, China & Hong Kong], david.clayton@york.ac.uk

John P.D. Cooper, M.A., D.Phil. (Oxon.), Sen. Lect. in Hist. [Political, religious & literary history of 16th c. Britain], j.p.d.cooper@york.ac.uk

Helen Cowie, B.A., Ph.D. (Warwick), Lect. in Hist. [18th–19th c. cultural history; history of animals; history of science in the Hispanic world], helen.cowie@york.ac.uk

Laura Crombie, M.A., M.Litt., Ph.D. (Glas.), Lect. in Med. Hist. [Towns of the late medieval Low Countries], laura.crombie@york.ac.uk

Catherine R.E. Cubitt, M.A. (Cantab. & Lond.), Ph.D. (Cantab.), Prof. of Med. Hist. (Early Med.) [Anglo-Saxon history; early medieval religious & cultural history], katy.cubitt@york.ac.uk

Geoffrey T. Cubitt, M.A., Ph.D. (Cantab.), Sen. Lect. in Hist. [Memory, commemoration & the uses of the past; heroes & reputations; political, cultural & religious history of modern France], geoff.cubitt@york.ac.uk

Joanna C. de Groot, B.A., D.Phil. (Oxon.), Sen. Lect. in Hist. [Social & cultural history of Europe & the Middle East, esp. Iran, since 1750; gender & women's history; imperial history, esp. Indian], joanna.degroot@york.ac.uk

Simon R. Ditchfield, B.A. (York), M.Phil., Ph.D. (Lond.), Reader in Hist. (Early Mod. Relig., Italy) [The making of Roman Catholicism as a world religion; uses of the past in early modern Europe], simon.ditchfield@york.ac.uk

Colin Divall, B.Sc. (Brist.), M.Sc., Ph.D. (Manc.), Prof. of Railway Stud. (Transport Hist., Soc. Hist. of Tech., Public Hist.), colin.divall@york.ac.uk

Mark Edmonds, B.A., Ph.D. (Read.), Prof. of Archaeol. [Prehistory, landscape & memory; the social dimensions of technology], mark.edmonds@york.ac.uk

Jason Edwards, B.A., M.A., Ph.D. (Cantab.), Prof. of Hist. of Art [British sculpture, 1760–1940; queer & animal theory; world & other complex systems], jason.edwards@york.ac.uk

Jonathan Finch, M.A., Ph.D. (East Anglia), Sen. Lect. in Archaeol. [Late medieval & early modern landscapes], jonathan.finch@york.ac.uk

Mary D. Garrison, B.A. (Harv.), M.A., Ph.D. (Cantab.), Lect. in Hist. (Early Med.) [Medieval Latin; Anglo-Saxon; Carolingian literacy; literary & cultural history], mary.garrison@york.ac.uk

Anthony Geraghty, B.A. (Birm.), M.A. (Lond.), Ph.D. (Cantab.), Lect. in Hist. of Art [Early modern English architecture; Wren], anthony.geraghty@york.ac.uk

Kate F. Giles, B.A., M.A., Ph.D. (York), Sen. Lect. in Archaeol. [Archaeology of public buildings; interdisciplinary study (history & archaeology)], kate.giles@york.ac.uk

Natasha A.F. Glaisyer, B.A. (Canterbury, N.Z.), Ph.D. (Cantab.), Lect. in Hist. [Cultural, social & economic history of 17th & 18th c. England], natasha.glaisyer@york.ac.uk

P. Jeremy P. Goldberg, M.A. (Cantab. & York), Ph.D. (Cantab.), Reader in Hist. [Later medieval social & cultural history; gender, household & family], jeremy.goldberg@york.ac.uk

Alex Goodall, M.A., M.Phil., Ph.D. (Cantab.), Lect. in Mod. Hist. [20th c. U.S. history; U.S. foreign relations, esp. Latin America], alex.goodall@york.ac.uk

Hannah Greig, B.A., M.A. (Lond. & Oxon.), Ph.D. (Lond.), Lect. in Hist. [Social & cultural history of 18th c. Britain], hannah.greig@york.ac.uk

Nicholas Guyatt, B.A., M.Phil. (Cantab.), Ph.D. (Princeton), Lect. in Hist. [18th & 19th c. North America; Atlantic world], nicholas.guyatt@york.ac.uk

Guy R.W. Halsall, B.A., D.Phil. (York), Prof. of Med. Hist. [Barbarian migrations; Merovingian Gaul; history & archaeology of 6th & 7th c. Europe], guy.halsall@york.ac.uk

Jane Hawkes, B.A., Ph.D. (Newcastle), Reader in Hist. of Art [Late antique & early medieval art & iconography], jane.hawkes@york.ac.uk

Helen Hills, B.A. (Oxon.), M.A., Ph.D. (Lond.), Prof. of Art Hist. [Italian Baroque art & architecture; gender; architectural theory], helen.hills@york.ac.uk

Jonathan J. Howlett, B.A., M.A. (Brist.), M.Phil. (Oxon.), Ph.D. (Brist.), Lect. in Mod. Asian Hist. [Modern China; Chinese communism; Shanghai], jon.howlett@york.ac.uk

Mark S.R. Jenner, M.A., D.Phil. (Oxon.), Reader in Hist. (Early Mod. Brit., Soc. Hist. of Medicine), mark.jenner@york.ac.uk

Amanda C. Jones, B.A., M.A., Ph.D. (Warwick), Archivist, Borthwick Inst. [Riot & rebellion in mid Tudor England; early modern & modern archives], amanda.jones@york.ac.uk

Catriona Kennedy, B.A. (Dublin), Ph.D. (York), Lect. in Mod. Hist. [18th & 19th c. British & Irish history], catriona.kennedy@york.ac.uk

Amanda Lillie, B.A. (Auckland), M.A., Ph.D. (Lond.), Sen. Reader in Hist. of Art [Italian art & architecture, 1400–1600], amanda.lillie@york.ac.uk

Emanuele Lugli, B.A. (Bologna), M.A. (Lond.), Ph.D. (N.Y.), Lect. in Hist. of Art [Medieval & early modern art & architecture], emanuele.lugli@york.ac.uk

Gerard McCann, M.A., M.Phil., Ph.D. (Cantab.), Lect. in Mod. Hist. [African & South Asian history, esp. Asia-Africa relations; transnational history], gerard.mccann@york.ac.uk

Aleks McClain, B.A. (Yale), M.A., Ph.D. (York), Lect. in Archaeol. [Medieval; churches; commemoration], aleksandra.mcclain@york.ac.uk

Richard Marks, M.A., Ph.D. (Lond.), Emeritus Prof. of Hist. of Art [Stained glass production & reception of images in the later middle ages], richard.marks@york.ac.uk

David Moon, B.A. (Newcastle), Ph.D. (Birm.), Anniversary Prof. of Hist. [Russian history, 17th–20th c.; environmental history], david.moon@york.ac.uk

Matthias Morys, M.A. (Humboldt), Diplom. (O.U., Germany), M.Sc., Ph.D. (Lond.), Lect. (19th–20th c. Econ. Hist.) [Monetary & financial history, 19th & 20th c., esp. exchange rate regimes], matthias.morys@york.ac.uk

Christopher Norton, M.A., Ph.D. (Cantab.), Prof. of Hist. of Art [Ecclesiastical art & architecture in England & France, 600–1600], christopher.norton@york.ac.uk

Jeanne Nuechterlein, B.A. (Rice), M.A., Ph.D. (Calif. at Berkeley), Sen. Lect. in Hist. of Art [Visual arts in northern Europe, 1400–1600], jeanne.nuechterlein@york.ac.uk

W. Mark Ormrod, B.A. (Lond.), D.Phil. (Oxon.), Prof. of Med. Hist. (Later Med. Eng.) [Reign of Edward III; constitutional, political & administrative history, 1200–1500], mark.ormrod@york.ac.uk

Shane P. O'Rourke, B.A., M.A. (East Anglia), D.Phil. (Oxon.), Sen. Lect. in Hist., shane.orourke@york.ac.uk

Sarah R. Rees Jones, B.A. (Oxon.), D.Phil. (York), Sen. Lect. in Hist. (Med., Regional) [Medieval urban history], sarah.reesjones@york.ac.uk

Chris Renwick, B.A. (Lancaster), M.A., Ph.D. (Leeds), Lect. in Mod. Brit. Hist. [19th & 20th c. British intellectual history, esp. history of biological & social sciences], chris.renwick@york.ac.uk

Julian D. Richards, M.A. (Cantab.), Ph.D. (C.N.A.A.), Prof. of Archaeol. [Anglo-Saxon & Viking settlement & burial], julian.richards@york.ac.uk

Mark Roodhouse, B.A. (Cantab.), M.Sc. (Oxon.), Ph.D. (Cantab.), Lect. in Mod. Hist. (20th c. Brit.) [Economic & social history], mark.roodhouse@york.ac.uk

Stephen P. Roskams, B.A. (Cantab.), Sen. Lect. in Archaeol. [Roman & medieval urbanism; Roman-medieval transitions; Marxism], steve.roskams@york.ac.uk

Lucy Sackville, B.A. (Newcastle), M.A., Ph.D. (York), Lect. in Med. Hist. [History of heresy & its repression, including inquisition, 13th c.], lucy.sackville@york.ac.uk

James A. Sharpe, B.A., D.Phil. (Oxon.), Prof. of Hist. [Crime in early modern England; witchcraft], jim.sharpe@york.ac.uk

Nitin Sinha, M.A. (J. Nehru), Ph.D. (Lond.), Lect. in Mod. Hist. [Colonial South Asian history; transport & urban history; agrarian-ecological history; labour history], nitin.sinha@york.ac.uk

Judith Spicksley, B.A., M.A., Ph.D. (Hull), Lect. (Econ., Soc. & Cultural Hist.) [Debt & credit relations], judith.spicksley@york.ac.uk

Craig Taylor, M.A., D.Phil. (Oxon.), Sen. Lect. in Med. Hist. [Late medieval France; Hundred Years' War; chivalry], craig.taylor@york.ac.uk

Cordula van Wyhe, M.A., Ph.D. (Lond.), Lect. in Hist. of Art [17th c. northern European Baroque art], cordula.vanwhye@york.ac.uk

Hanna Vorholt, M.A. (Lond.), Ph.D. (Berlin), Anniversary Res. Lect. in Hist. of Art [Medieval art; early history of the book; Jerusalem studies], hanna.vorholt@york.ac.uk

Kevin J. Walsh, B.A., Ph.D. (Leicester), Sen. Lect. in Archaeol. [Early medieval landscapes; Mediterranean prehistory], kevin.walsh@york.ac.uk

Sethina C. Watson, B.A. (Carleton), M.St., D.Phil. (Oxon.), Sen. Lect. in Med. Hist. [Ecclesiastical history, charity & hospitals, esp. in England, 1100–1300], sethina.watson@york.ac.uk

*Christopher C. Webb, B.A. (Dunelm.), M.A. (York), Keeper of Archives, Borthwick Inst. [Early modern churchwardens; urban estates & clergy], chris.webb@york.ac.uk

Michael White, B.A. (Lond.), M.A., Ph.D. (Essex), Reader in Hist. of Art [Constructivism; Dada; surrealism], michael.white@york.ac.uk

David Wootton, M.A., Ph.D. (Cantab.), Anniversary Prof. of Hist. [Early modern intellectual history; the scientific revolution], david.wootton@york.ac.uk

YORK ST. JOHN UNIVERSITY

Faculty of Arts
Lord Mayor's Walk, York, YO31 7EX. 01904 624624. Fax 01904 876316
www.yorksj.ac.uk

Peter Bell, B.A., Ph.D. (Leeds), Sen. Lect. in Hist. (Hist.) [Anglo-American relations in the 1930s; newsreels], p.bell2@yorksj.ac.uk

Ian A. Horwood, B.A. (Manc.), M.A. (Missouri), Ph.D. (Leeds), Sen. Lect. (Mod. Hist., Amer. Hist.) [Vietnam War; airpower history], i.horwood@yorksj.ac.uk

*Wayne Johnson, B.A., M.A., Ph.D. (Keele), Sen. Lect., Head of Programme, Hist. (U.S. Hist.) [Antebellum South], w.johnson@yorksj.ac.uk

David Powell, B.A. (Wales), D.Phil. (Oxon.), (Hist.) [Modern British political history], d.powell@yorksj.ac.uk

Robert Whiting, M.A. (Cantab.), Ph.D. (Exeter), Princ. Lect. (Early Mod. Hist.) [English Reformation], b.whiting@yorksj.ac.uk

UNIVERSITIES IN THE REPUBLIC OF IRELAND

UNIVERSITY COLLEGE CORK
(NATIONAL UNIVERSITY OF IRELAND)

Western Road, Cork
Department of History +353 21 4902551. Fax +353 21 4270191
www.ucc.ie/en/history/
Department of History of Art +353 21 4902124. Fax +353 21 4903254
http://historyofart.ucc.ie/

Andy Bielenberg, M.Litt. (Dublin), Ph.D. (Lond.), Statutory Lect. in Hist. (Mod. Ireland) [War & revolution in Cork 1914–23; Irish economic & social history since 1800]
Flavio Boggi, M.A., Ph.D. (Glas.), Sen. Lect. in Art Hist. (Med. & Renaissance Italian Art & Architecture) [14th & 15th c. painting in Tuscany]
Damian Bracken, Ph.D., Sen. Lect. in Hist. (Med. Ireland & Eur.) [Insular inheritance of late antique culture; early Ireland & Europe – culture contact; St. Columbanus]
Bozena Cierlik, M.A. (K.U.L.), Ph.D. (N.U.I.), Lect. in Hist. (Mod. Eur.) [Irish-Polish relationships; Irish & Polish constitutions, 1918 –39; the Balkans]
Mike Cosgrave, B.A., M.A., Ph.D. (N.U.I.), Lect. in Hist. (Mod. Hist.) [Digital history; digital humanities; military history; peacekeeping; scholarship of teaching & learning in history]
Gabriel Doherty, B.A. (Oxon.), M.A. (N.U.I.), Lect. in Hist. (Mod. Ireland) [Modern Ireland; Northern Ireland; criminal justice history; history of sport]
Finola Doyle-O'Neill, Ph.D., Lect. in Hist. (Mod. Ireland) [Irish media & broadcasting history]
David Edwards, Ph.D. (Dublin), Sen. Lect. in Hist. (Early Mod. Ireland) [Power & society in Ireland, c.1400–1650; early modern colonialism; Renaissance & Reformation Europe], d.edwards@ucc.ie
David Fitzgerald, B.A., M.A., Ph.D. (N.U.I.), Lect. in Int. Pol. (Mod. Amer.) [History of U.S. foreign relations; military history; history of counterinsurgency], d.fitzgerald@ucc.ie
Laurence M. Geary, B.A., M.A., Ph.D. (N.U.I.), Sen. Lect. in Hist. (Mod. Ireland) [Great Famine; social history of medicine in 19th c. Ireland]
Jason Harris, Ph.D. (Dublin), Lect. in Hist. (Early Mod., Hist. of Sc.) [Low Countries & Germany during the Reformation; Irish Renaissance Latin]
Detmar Klein, B.A., Ph.D. (Lond.), Lect. in Hist. (Mod. Eur.) [History of anti-Semitism; 19th & 20th c. Germany & Alsace; German nationalism]
Simon Knowles, B.A., M.A. (Birm.), Ph.D. (N.U.I.), Lect. in Art Hist. (Early Mod. & Mod. Art Hist. & Theory) [Victorian painting]
Małgorzata Krasnodebska-D'Aughton, M.A., Ph.D. (N.U.I.), Lect. in Hist. (Med.) [Cultural & religious history of the Irish mendicant orders; art & piety in the middle ages; Irish liturgical silver in the late medieval & early modern periods; illuminated manuscripts; Polish medieval art]
Edward Krčma, B.A. (Nott.), M.A., Ph.D. (Lond.), Lect. in Art Hist. (Mod. & Contemp. Art & Theory) [European & American art after 1945; history & theory of drawing]
Sabine Kriebel, B.A. (Calif. at Berkeley), M.A. (Williams), Ph.D. (Calif. at Berkeley), Lect. in Art Hist. (Mod. & Contemp. Art & Theory) [20th c. German art & theory]
Andrew McCarthy, Ph.D., Lect. in Hist. (Mod. Ireland) [20th c. Irish financial & administrative history; post-war Irish public health; economic modernisation of Ireland in the 1960s]
Hiram Morgan, M.A., Ph.D. (Cantab.), Sen. Lect. in Hist. (Early Mod. Ireland) [Art history; intellectual, diplomatic & military history; imperialism & historiography; Hugh O'Neill, earl of Tyrone; Stanihurst's *De Rebus in Hibernia Gestis* (1584)]

Donal Ó Drisceoil, B.A., Ph.D. (N.U.I.), Lect. in Hist. (Mod. Ireland, Local Hist.) [Irish media history; the Irish revolution; history of Irish brewing]
Mervyn O'Driscoll, B.A., M.A. (N.U.I.), Ph.D. (Cantab.), Sen. Lect. in Hist. (Mod. Ireland, Int. Rel.) [Ireland & European integration; Irish foreign policy/diplomacy; Anglo-American nuclear diplomacy/strategy; Anglo-French diplomacy since 1939]
Rory O'Dwyer, M.A. (N.U.I.), Lect. in Hist. (Mod. Ireland) [Career of Frank Aiken; Eucharistic Congress in 1932; contested identities in the Irish monumental landscape]
Clare O'Halloran, B.A., M.A. (N.U.I.), Ph.D. (Cantab.), Lect. in Hist. (Early Mod. & Mod. Ireland, Early Mod. Eur.) [Irish cultural history, 17th–19th c.], c.ohalloran@ucc.ie
*Geoffrey Roberts, Ph.D. (Lond.), Prof. of Hist. (Mod. Eur.) [Soviet & international history; World War II & the Cold War; international relations theory; philosophy of history; Ireland & World War II]
David Ryan, B.A. (Toronto), Ph.D. (N.U.I.), Prof. (Chair in Mod. Hist.) (Mod. Amer.) [History of U.S. foreign policy/relations]
Diarmuid Scully, B.A., M.A., Ph.D. (N.U.I.), Lect. in Hist. (Med. Hist.) [Bede; representations of Irish identity in text & image from antiquity to the early modern era, with a current focus on Gerald of Wales; medieval maps], d.scully@ucc.ie

UNIVERSITY COLLEGE DUBLIN
(NATIONAL UNIVERSITY OF IRELAND)

Belfield, Dublin 4
School of History and Archives +353 1 716 8371. Fax +353 1 716 8602
www.ucd.ie/history/

Maurice Bric, Ph.D. (Johns Hopkins), Assoc. Prof. of Hist. (18th c. Ireland, Amer.) [The history & culture of the 18th & early 19th c. Atlantic world, esp. Ireland & America; Irish-American interactions since 1970.], Maurice.Bric@ucd.ie
Edward Coleman, D.Phil. (Oxon.), Lect. in Hist. (Med. Eur., 1000–1300, Crusades) [Early medieval European history; Italian city states in the 12th & 13th c.; the Crusades], Edward.Coleman@ucd.ie
Catherine Cox, Ph.D. (N.U.I.), Lect. in Hist. (Mod. Irish Soc. & Medical Hist., late 18th & 19th c.) [History of mental illness, development of medical provision, orthodox & heterodox, & the dissemination of 'medical knowledge' in the Irish & European contexts; history of the Great Famine; social & cultural history, women's history & the history of urban development in 18th & 19th c. Ireland], Catherine.Cox@ucd.ie
Mary Daly, D.Phil. (Oxon.), Prof. of Hist. (20th c. Ireland) [The state, economy & society & historical commemoration; social history of medicine in 19th & 20th c., including history of family planning & reform of health services; the Irish diaspora; Irish women's history], Mary.E.Daly@ucd.ie
Judith Devlin, D.Phil. (Oxon.), Sen. Lect. in Hist. (Mod. Eur.) [Cultural & political history of Russia & the Soviet Union in the 19th & 20th c.; cultural history of France in the 19th & 20th c.], Judith.Devlin@ucd.ie
Charles Doherty, M.A. (N.U.I.), Sen. Lect. in Hist. (Early & Med. Ireland, 400–1600) [Early & medieval Irish history, 400–1600; Irish hagiography; settlement history; anthropology & the urban form], Charlie.Doherty@ucd.ie

Declan Downey, Ph.D. (Cantab.), Lect. in Hist. (Early Mod. Eur.) [Habsburg Spain, the
Netherlands, Austria & Germany, 1500–1870; Japan, Korea & China, 1700–1960; Irish-
European relations, 1500–1800; 'the wild geese'; contemporary European Union-Asian
relations], Declan.Downey@ucd.ie

Lindsey Earner-Byrne, Ph.D. (N.U.I.), Lect. in Hist. (Mod. Irish Soc. Hist.) [Modern Irish
social history; gender, health & welfare in 19th & 20th c. Ireland & Europe; Irish emigration
history], Lindsey.Earner@ucd.ie

Diarmaid Ferriter, Ph.D. (N.U.I.), Prof. of Mod. Irish Hist. (Mod. Ireland) [Social, cultural
& political history of 20th c. Ireland; Irish women's history; history of sexuality],
Diarmaid.Ferriter@ucd.ie

Roy Flechner, D.Phil. (Oxon.), Ph.D. (Cantab.), Lect. in Hist. (Early Med. Eur., 500–1000)
[Early medieval Irish & Anglo-Saxon law; conversion to Christianity], Roy.Flechner@ucd.ie

Robert Gerwarth, D.Phil. (Oxon.), Prof. of Hist. (19th & 20th c. Eur.) [History of modern
Germany; history of violence], Robert.Gerwarth@ucd.ie

Ailsa C. Holland, M.A. (N.U.I.), Head of Subject (Archivistics) [Irish estates maps of the 18th &
19th c.; record keeping and accountability in Ireland], Ailsa.Holland@ucd.ie

*Edward James, M.A., D.Phil. (Oxon.), Prof. of Med. Hist., Head of Sch. (Early Med. Eur.,
esp. France & Brit.) [The barbarians & the invasion of the Roman empire; medievalism
in science fiction & fantasy; history of science fiction; the writings of Gregory of Tours],
Edward.James@ucd.ie

Elva Johnston, D.Phil. (Oxon.), Lect. in Hist. (Early Med. Ireland) [Literacy & the creation of
identity in early medieval Ireland; late antique Christianity & Christian controversy; history
of sexuality; medieval travel literature], Elva.Johnston@ucd.ie

David Kerr, D.Phil. (Oxon.), Lect. in Hist. (Mod. Eur.) [Political, social & cultural history of
France 1789–1945; history of Paris; 19th c. popular theatre & political caricature; social &
cultural history of Italy, 1860–1960; 20th c. Italian popular culture; fascist welfare policy;
history of the Italian beach; memory of fascism in post-war Italian film], David.Kerr@ucd.ie

John McCafferty, Ph.D. (Cantab.), Sen. Lect. in Hist. (Med. & Early Mod. Ireland)
[Late medieval & early modern church in Ireland; Church of Ireland in the 16th &
17th c.; early modern hagiography; history of religious orders, esp. mendicants],
John.McCafferty@ucd.ie

Charles Ivar McGrath, Ph.D. (Lond.), Lect. in Hist. (Early Mod. Ireland & Brit., 16th–18th c.)
[The British empire; politics, parliament, legislation & government; religion; public finance,
taxation, national debt & credit; early modern chartered trading companies & monopolies;
the Hudson's Bay Company], Ivar.McGrath@ucd.ie

William Mulligan, Ph.D. (Cantab.), Lect. in Hist. (Mod. Brit. & Germany) [History of
international relations & warfare in 19th–20th c.], William.Mulligan@ucd.ie

Elizabeth Mullins, Ph.D. (N.U.I.), H.Dip.A.S. (N.U.I.), Lect. in Archives [Archival arrangement,
description & advocacy; the interface between archives & history; archives, diplomatic &
palaeography], Elizabeth.Mullins@ucd.ie

Eamon O'Flaherty, Ph.D. (Cantab.), Sen. Lect. in Hist. (Early Mod. Eur.) [17th–18th c. French
intellectual history; social history of ideas; 18th c. Irish history], Eamon.Oflaherty@ucd.ie

Tadhg Ó hAnnracháin, Ph.D. (E.U.I.), Sen. Lect. in Hist. (Early Mod. Ireland) [European
Counter-Reformation; Middle Eastern history], Tadhg.Ohannrachain@ucd.ie

Susannah Riordan, Ph.D. (Cantab.), Lect. in Hist. (Mod. Brit. & Ireland) [Social, intellectual &
religious history of 19th & 20th c. Britain & Ireland, particularly the development of social
policy; intellectual movements & sexuality in 20th c. Ireland], Susannah.Riordan@ucd.ie

Paul Rouse, Ph.D. (N.U.I.), Lect. in Hist. (Mod. Ireland) [History of the Gaelic Athletic
Association (G.A.A.); Irish agriculture], P.Rouse@ucd.ie

Sandra Scanlon, Ph.D. (Cantab.), [United States foreign policy & the Vietnam War; American
political development during the 20th c.; American conservatism; transatlantic relations],
Sandra.Scanlon@ucd.ie

Michael Staunton, Ph.D. (Cantab.), Lect. in Hist. (Ireland & Brit. in the Central & Later Middle Ages) [12th c. religious & intellectual life; historical & hagiographical writing in the central middle ages], Michael.Staunton@ucd.ie

Sandy Wilkinson, Ph.D. (St. And.), Lect. in Hist. (Early Mod. Eur.) [European print culture at the beginning of the modern age, 1450–1650; the social & cultural history of early modern Europe, esp. France, Scotland & Spain; the history of crime & punishment in early modern Europe], Alexander.Wilkinson@ucd.ie

NATIONAL UNIVERSITY OF IRELAND, GALWAY

University Road, Galway
Department of History +353 91 492537. Fax +353 91 494556
www.nuigalway.ie/history/

Gearóid Barry, B.A., Ph.D. (Dublin), Lect. in Hist. (Mod. Eur.) [Modern & contemporary France; cultural & political history of World War I in Europe; European pacifism between the World Wars; religion in modern & contemporary Europe (incl. popular religiosity); French Catholicism since the French Revolution; the origins of Christian democracy in Europe; 20th c. Franco-Irish links], Gearoid.Barry@nuigalway.ie

Sarah-Anne Buckley, B.A., Ph.D. (N.U.I.), Lect. in Hist. (Mod. Ireland) [History of child welfare; history of family; history of women; social history of Ireland & Britain in the 19th & 20th c.], Sarahanne.Buckley@nuigalway.ie

Caitríona Clear, M.A., Ph.D. (N.U.I.), Sen. Lect. in Hist. (Mod. Ireland) [History of women; social history of Ireland & Europe in the 18th & 19th c.], Caitriona.Clear@nuigalway.ie

John Cunningham, B.A., Ph.D. (N.U.I.), Lect. in Hist. (Mod. Ireland) [Labour history; local history; urban history; dynamics of social protest], John.Cunningham@nuigalway.ie

Enrico Dal Lago, Laurea (Rome), M.A. (Kansas), M.A., Ph.D. (Lond.), Lect. in Hist. (Mod. Amer.) [U.S. social & political history, esp. 19th c.; American slavery in comparative perspective; native North Americans, esp. the plains' tribes], Enrico.Dallago@nuigalway.ie

*Steven Ellis, B.A., M.A. (Manc.), Ph.D. (Belf.), D.Litt. (N.U.I.), Prof. of Hist. (Early Mod. Brit. & Ireland) [British & Irish history, 15th–17th c.; historiography; early modern Europe], Steven.Ellis@nuigalway.ie

Tomás Finn, B.A., M.A., Ph.D. (N.U.I.), Lect. in Hist. (Mod. Ireland) [20th c. Irish history; intellectuals & ideas; Church-state relations; the Irish diaspora; Northern Ireland], Tomas.Finn@nuigalway.ie

Alison Forrestal, M.A. (N.U.I.), Ph.D. (Manc.), Lect. in Hist. (Early Mod. Eur.) [17th c. France; history of religion, particularly early modern Catholic culture & society; 17th c. Ireland], Alison.Forrestal@nuigalway.ie

Mary N. Harris, B.A., M.A., H.Dip.Ed. (N.U.I.), Ph.D. (Cantab.), Sen. Lect. in Hist. (Mod. Ireland) [Ireland in the 19th & 20th c., with particular reference to church-state relations & Northern Ireland; colonial Spanish America], Mary.Harris@nuigalway.ie

Róisín Healy, M.A. (N.U.I.), M.A.G.E.S., Ph.D. (Georgetown), Lect. in Hist. (Mod. Eur.) [Modern German history; history of religion; 19th & 20th c. European social history], Roisin.Healy@nuigalway.ie

Pádraig Lenihan, Ph.D. (N.U.I.), Lect. in Hist. (Early Mod. Ireland & Eur.) [Historiography of Stuart Ireland; military history; history of technology & social change; the Irish long 18th c., 1691–1800], Padraig.Lenihan@nuigalway.ie

Kimberly LoPrete, B.A. (Duke), M.A. (Notre Dame), Ph.D. (Chicago), Lect. in Hist. (Med. Eur.) [Social, political & cultural history of medieval Europe, in particular 11th–12th c. & France; women in medieval society, notably aristocratic women; gender & lordship; the first crusade & the history of crusading; Europeans' encounters with non-Europeans], Kimberly.LoPrete@nuigalway.ie

Lawrence Marley, M.A., Ph.D. (N.U.I.), Lect. in Hist. (Mod. Ireland) [Land & society in modern Ireland; Davitt, ideas & radical social movements in modern Ireland], Lawrence.Marley@nuigalway.ie

Ged Martin, Ph.D. (Cantab.), Adjunct Prof. of Hist. (Brit. Empire) [Australian, British, British imperial, Canadian, Irish & New Zealand history from the late 18th to the 20th c.; career of Sir John A. Macdonald (1815–91), first prime minister of Canada; British-Canadian relations & the intellectual origins of Canadian Confederation (1867)], Ged.Martin@nuigalway.ie

Niall Ó Ciosáin, B.A. (Dublin), Ph.D. (E.U.I.), Sen. Lect. in Hist. (Mod. Ireland & Eur.) [Social history of Ireland & Europe, 17th–19th c.], Niall.Ociosain@nuigalway.ie

Dáibhí Ó Cróinín, B.A., M.Phil., Ph.D. (N.U.I.), Prof. of Med. Hist. [Ireland, Britain & Europe during the early middle ages; computistics; medieval Latin palaeography; Irish traditional music and song], Daibhi.Ocroinin@nuigalway.ie

Kevin O'Sullivan, B.A., Ph.D. (Dublin), Lect. in Hist. (Mod. Ireland & Empire) [History of decolonisation; social & political legacies of imperialism; humanitarianism; non-governmental organisations; globalisation; international relations], Kevin.K.Osullivan@nuigalway.ie

UNIVERSITY OF LIMERICK

Limerick. +353 61 202700. Fax +353 61 330316
Department of History
www.history.ul.ie

Ciara Breathnach, B.A., M.A., Ph.D. (N.U.I.), [Social history of medicine; history of family; Ireland under the Union]

Odette Clarke, B.Sc. (Manc. Met.), M.A., Ph.D. (Limerick), [History of the family; gender history; 19th c. British & Irish history; history of emotions]

David Fleming, B.A. (Limerick), M.St., D.Phil. (Oxon.), [Early modern Ireland; history of localities; political, social & cultural aspects of 18th c. Ireland]

Richard Kirwan, B.A., Ph.D. (Dublin), [Social & cultural history of universities in the early modern period with a focus on Germany, esp. scholarly social status & social functions of academic representational culture],

Anthony McElligott, B.A. (Essex), Ph.D. (Manc.), [Germany in the 20th c., including urban politics, cultural history & the Holocaust]

Alistair Malcolm, M.A. (St. And.), D.Phil. (Oxon.), [Spain in the golden age; diplomatic & court politics; cultural history; politics & artistic patronage.]

Ruán O'Donnell, B.A., M.A. (N.U.I.), Ph.D. (A.N.U.), [Modern Irish, European & Australian history; the United Irishmen; imperialism; Irish revolutionary movements]

Conor Reidy, B.A. (N.U.I.), M.A., Ph.D. (Limerick), [The borstal system in Ireland, 1906–21; Irish juvenile penal history, 1775–1922; gender & criminality; modern Irish social history]

*Bernadette Whelan, B.A., M.A., Ph.D. (N.U.I.), [Irish foreign policy, 1900–60; 19th & 20th c. American-Irish relations; recovery & reconstruction after WWII; women in Ireland, 1900–60]

MARY IMMACULATE COLLEGE

South Circular Road, Limerick. +353 61 204300. Fax +353 61 313632
Department of History
www.mic.ul.ie/academicdepts/history/

*Liam Chambers, B.A., M.A., Ph.D. (N.U.I.), Sen. Lect. in Hist. (18th & 19th c. Irish & Eur.
Hist.) [Irish migration to continental Europe, esp. France, in the 17th & 18th c.; the history
of the Irish Colleges in Paris, 1578–2000; 18th c. Ireland; history of ideas in the 17th & 18th
c.], liam.chambers@mic.ul.ie
Maura Cronin, B.A., M.A. (N.U.I.), Ph.D. (Leicester), Sen. Lect. in Hist. (Mod. Ireland, Oral
Hist.) [Social & urban history; oral history; 19th c. Ireland], maura.cronin@mic.ul.ie
Deirdre McMahon, B.A., M.A. (N.U.I.), Ph.D. (Cantab.), Lect. in Hist. (Contemp. Irish & World
Hist.) [20th c. Ireland; British empire and Commonwealth (incl. India); 20th c. Irish church
history, particularly mission history], deirdre.mcmahon@mic.ul.ie
Úna Ní Bhroiméil, B.A., M.A., H.D.E. (N.U.I.), Ph.D. (Lehigh), Lect. in Hist. (Amer. & Irish-
Amer. Hist.) [The Irish-American press and the invention of ethnicity during World War I; the
formation of female teachers in the late 19th and early 20th c. in Ireland; the use of images
as political, sociological & historical artefacts], una.bromell@mic.ul.ie
Catherine Swift, B.A. (N.U.I.), M.Phil. (Dunelm.), D.Phil. (Oxon.), Lect. in Irish Stud. (Early
Med. Ireland & Eur. Hist.) [Celts; ogam stones; Irish saints; Hiberno-Scandinavian culture;
Old/Middle Irish culture], catherine.swift@mic.ul.ie
Clodagh Tait, B.A., Ph.D. (N.U.I.), Lect. in Hist. (Early Mod. Irish & Eur. Hist.) [British
Isles social & religious history; death & commemoration; violence & martyrdom],
clodagh.tait@mic.ul.ie

NATIONAL UNIVERSITY OF IRELAND, MAYNOOTH

Maynooth, Co. Kildare
Department of History +353 1 708 3729. Fax +353 1 708 3314
www.nuim.ie/academic/history/

John Bradley, M.A. (N.U.I.), Sen. Lect. in Hist. (Med. Ireland, Historiography) [Archaeology of
Ireland; urban archaeology; crannogs; the medieval Irish town; death & burial in the middle
ages]
Terence A. Dooley, M.A., Ph.D. (N.U.I.), Prof. of Hist. (Mod. Ireland) [Irish & political history of
the 19th & 20th c., esp. the land question; the fortunes of great houses & estates; the work
of the Irish Land Commission; the local politics of the revolutionary period]
M. Denise Dunne, M.A., Ph.D. (N.U.I.), Lect. in Hist. (Mod. Eur., Int. Rel.) [History of
European integration, esp. British policy; U.S.-European transatlantic relations; the
institutional development of the E.U. from inception to date]
Colmán Etchingham, Ph.D. (Dublin), Lect. in Hist. (Early Med. & Viking-Age Ireland) [Pre-
Norman Ireland 5th–12th c., esp. the church and its role in society, early Irish law, Irish
kingship, the annals, Vikings as raiders & settlers & Viking-Age relations between Britain &
Ireland]
Alison FitzGerald, Ph.D. (R.C.A.), Lect. in Hist. (Art Hist. of Mod. Eur. & Ireland) [Irish design
history & material culture, esp. the study of Irish goldsmiths, jewellers & allied traders]

Raymond Gillespie, Ph.D. (Dublin), Prof. of Hist. (Early Mod. Ireland, Local Hist.) [Social & cultural change in early modern Ireland; the diffusion of print & the changing experience of reading in Ireland 1580–1700]

Jacqueline R. Hill, Ph.D. (Leeds), Prof. of Hist. (Early Mod. Ireland, Four Nations) [Protestant anniversary tradition in Ireland; 18th c. Irish loyalism; Irish attitudes to monarchy; early 19th c. Dublin trades]

David Lederer, Ph.D. (N.Y.), Sen. Lect. in Hist. (Early Mod. Eur., Renaissance, Reformation) [Renaissance & reformation; early modern Germany; history of psychiatry; gender studies]

*Marian Lyons, M.A., M.ès L., Ph.D. (N.U.I.), Prof of Hist. [Early modern migration to Europe; witchcraft in early modern Europe; history through film]

Brian McKenzie, Ph.D. (S.U.N.Y., Stony Brook), Lect. [Cold war; Americanisation; U.S. public diplomacy & the Marshall plan; Ireland's Cold War; Americanisation of anti-communism]

Dympna McLoughlin, M.A., Ph.D. (Syracuse), Lect. in Hist. (Mod. Irish Soc. Hist. & Emigration, Hist. of Medicine) [Irish social history; gender in 19th c. Ireland; history of medicine; poverty & subsistence in 19th c. Ireland; emigration & the poor law; children; 19th c. Ireland]

JoAnne Marie Mancini, Ph.D. (Johns Hopkins), Lect. in Hist. (U.S. & World Hist.) [History of the U.S. & its colonial antecedents; intersections of American & world history]

David Murphy, Ph.D. (Dublin), Lect. in Hist. (Mod. Ireland, Milit. Hist.) [Military history esp., Irish regiments in British & continental service; the Crimean War & French military archives]

John P. Newman, Ph.D. (Southampton), Lect. [Balkan & Yugoslav cultural history, esp., World War I & its legacy in the region]

Thomas O'Connor, Ph.D. (Paris IV), Sen. Lect. in Hist. (Early Mod. Eur.) [Irish in Europe 1550–1800; Jansenism in 17th c.; Spanish Inquisition 17th c.; political thought 1550–1700]

Jacinta Prunty, Ph.D. (N.U.I.), Sen. Lect. in Hist. (Maps in Hist., Hist. Archives) [Urban, social & cartographic history, esp. the history of town mapping & archival studies]

Jennifer Redmond, Ph.D. (Dublin), Lect. [20th c. Irish female emigration to England; gender & sexual politics; women & education; Irish women in the labour force; digital humanities; 20th c. Irish history]

Filipe Ribeiro de Meneses, Ph.D. (Dublin), Sen. Lect. in Hist. (Contemp. Eur.) [Spanish & Portugeuese 20th c. history; World War I & the development of fascism; Europe's colonial empires in the 19th & 20th c.]

Ian A. Speller, M.Sc. (Wales), Ph.D. (Lond.), Lect. in Hist. (Milit. Hist., War Stud., Strategic Stud.) [20th c. British foreign & defence policy; military history & defence studies; naval history & maritime strategy; the Irish War of Independence & the Irish Civil War]

ST. PATRICK'S COLLEGE
(a college of Dublin City University)

Drumcondra, Dublin 9
Department of History +353 1 884 2101. Fax +353 1 837 6191
www.spd.dcu.ie/main/academic/history/

Juliana Adelman, B.Sc. (Stanford), M.Sc. (D.C.U.), Ph.D. (N.U.I.), Assistant Lect. In Hist. (Early Mod. Eur., Hist. of Sc., Hist. of Disease) [Social & economic history of 19th c. Ireland; history of Disease; environmental history], juliana.adelman@spd.dcu.ie
Marnie Hay, B.A. (Winnipeg), M.A. (Dalhousie), M.A. (Belf.), Ph.D. (N.U.I.), Teaching Fellow in Hist. (Mod. Ireland) [Irish nationalism in the late 19th–early 20th c.; youth culture in early 20th c. Ireland], marnie.hay@spd.dcu.ie
*James Kelly, M.A., Ph.D. (N.U.I.), Cregan Prof. of Hist. (Late Early Mod. Ireland, Mod. Amer., Historiography) [Politics & society in late early modern Ireland; history of medicine; associational culture; history of sport], James.Kelly@spd.ucd.ie
Daire Keogh, B.A. (N.U.I.), B.Phil. (Gregorian), M.Th. (Glas.), Ph.D. (Dublin), Sen. Lect. in Hist. (Early Mod. Ireland & Eur.) [Religious history of modern Ireland], Daire.Keogh@spd.ucd.ie
Carla R. King, B.A. (N.U.I.), M.A. (Lond.), Ph.D. (N.U.I.), Lect. in Hist. (Mod. Eur., Amer. before 1861, Mod. Russia, Irish Women's Hist.) [Late 19th c. Ireland; Michael Davitt; Horace Plunkett], Carla.King@spd.ucd.ie
Daithí Ó Corráin, B.A., Ph.D. (Dublin), Assistant Lect. in Hist. (19th & 20th c. Ireland, Int. Rel. since 1945) [National Volunteers; 20th c. Irish political violence; Irish ecclesiastical history & church-state relations; cultural history], Daithi.Ocorrain@spd.ucd.ie
Matthew Stout, B.A., Ph.D. (Dublin), Lect. in Hist. (Landscape Hist., Early Med. Hist. & Archaeol., Historiography) [Irish landscape; early medieval history; agricultural history; Cistercian archaeology], Matthew.Stout@spd.ucd.ie

TRINITY COLLEGE DUBLIN
(UNIVERSITY OF DUBLIN)

College Green, Dublin 2
School of Histories and Humanities
www.histories-humanities.tcd.ie
Department of History
+353 1 896 1020/1791. Fax +353 1 896 3995
Centre for Gender & Women's Studies
+353 1 896 2225. Fax +353 1 896 3997
Department of Classics
+353 1 896 1208. Fax +353 1 671 0862
Department of the History of Art & Architecture
+353 1 896 1995. Fax +353 1 896 1438
School of Languages, Literatures & Cultural Studies
www.tcd.ie/langs-lits-cultures
Department of Russian & Slavonic Studies
+353 1 896 1896. Fax +353 1 896 2655
School of Natural Sciences
www.naturalscience.tcd.ie

Balazs Apor, M.A. (Debrecen), Ph.D. (E.U.I.), Lect. in Eur. Stud. (Mod.) [19th & 20th c. eastern Europe, esp. culture, communism & Hungary]
Robert Armstrong, B.A. (Lond.), Ph.D. (Dublin), Sen. Lect. in Mod. Hist. (Brit. since 1603) [17th–18th c. Ireland, esp. politics, religion & Anglo-Irish relations]
Terence B. Barry, B.A. (Birm.), M.A. (Dublin & Fordham), Ph.D., Dip.Ed. (Belf.), Assoc. Prof. of Med. Hist. (Med. Ireland & Brit.) [Castles; settlement; archaeology of medieval Ireland]
*Ciaran F. Brady, B.A., Ph.D. (Dublin), Assoc. Prof. of Mod. Hist. (Early Mod. Ireland, Amer.) [16th–17th c. Irish political & intellectual history; Irish historiography]
Christine Casey, B.A., M.A. (N.U.I.), Ph.D. (Dublin), Sen. Lect. in Hist. of Art (Hist. of Architecture) [18th c. Irish architecture; migrant craftsmen in Ireland & Europe]
Anna Chahoud, Laurea (Bologna), M.A., Ph.D. (Pisa), Prof. of Latin (Anc.) [Historical classical scholarship; early Latin; textual criticism]
*Peter G. Cherry, B.A. (Essex), M.A., Ph.D. (Lond.), Lect. in Hist. of Art (16th–18th c. Eur.) [17th & 18th c. Spanish painting & sculpture]
Joseph M. Clarke, B.A., M.A. (N.U.I.), Ph.D. (E.U.I.), Lect. in Mod. Hist. (18th–19th c. Eur.) [Napoleonic France]
Ashley Clements, B.A. (Lond.), M.Phil., Ph.D. (Cantab.), Lect. in Greek (Anc. Hist.) [Greek literature, philosophy & politics, 5th–4th c. B.C.]
Martine Cuypers, B.A., M.A., Ph.D. (Leiden), Lect. in Greek (Anc. Hist.) [Hellenistic history & poetry; Second Sophistic; gender & sexuality]
David J. Dickson, B.A., Ph.D. (Dublin), Assoc. Prof. of Mod. Hist. (18th–19th c. Ireland, 20th c. Afric.) [Ireland, 1650–1850, esp. towns, economy & health; Ireland & empire]
David Ditchburn, M.A., Ph.D. (Edin.), Sen. Lect. in Med. Hist. (Med. Eur., Brit. & Scot. Hist.) [Medieval Scottish contacts with foreign countries]
Hazel Dodge, B.A., Ph.D. (Newcastle), L.C. Purser Sen. Lect. in Classical Archaeol. (Anc. Hist.) [Construction, urbanisation & technology in ancient Rome & the Roman world]
Anne Dolan, B.A., M.A. (N.U.I.), Ph.D. (Cantab.), (20th c. Ireland) [Ireland in the 1920s]
Seán Duffy, B.A., M.Litt., Ph.D., H.Dip.Ed. (Dublin), Assoc. Prof. of Med. Hist. (Med. Ireland) [Medieval Dublin; 11th–14th c. Ireland]

David P.B. Fitzpatrick, B.A. (Melb.), Ph.D. (Cantab.), Prof. of Mod. Hist. (19th–20th c. Ireland) [Irish nationalism, republicanism, loyalism, demography & emigration since 1795]

Monica Gale, B.A., Ph.D. (Cantab.), Assoc. Prof. of Latin (Anc. Hist.) [Roman poetry of the late Republic & Augustinian period]

Daniel Geary, B.A. (Virginia), M.A., Ph.D. (Calif. at Berkeley), Mark Pigott Lect. in Amer. Hist. (Amer.) [American radicalism in the 20th c.]

Patrick Geoghegan, B.A., Ph.D. (N.U.I.), Lect. in Mod. Hist. (Amer.) [Ireland; Anglo-Irish & Irish American relations, 18th–19th c.]

Crawford Gribben, B.A., Ph.D. (Strathclyde), Sen. Lect. in Early Mod. Print Culture (Early Mod. Brit.) [Early moden apocalypticism & eschatology]

Mark Hennessy, B.A. (N.U.I.), M.A. (Dublin), Ph.D. (N.U.I.), Lect. in Geog. (Hist. Geog.) [Historical geography of medieval Ireland]

John N. Horne, B.A. (Oxon.), D.Phil. (Sussex), Prof. of Mod. Eur. Hist. (19th–20th c. Eur.) [France & the Great War; cultural demobilisation; war crimes & trials]

Alan R. Kramer, B.A., M.A. (Newcastle), Ph.D. (Hamburg), Prof. of Eur. Hist. (19th–20th c. Eur.) [World War I, esp. Germany, Italy & Belgium]

Philip D. McEvansoneya, B.A. (C.N.A.A.), M.A. (Dublin & Lond.), Ph.D. (Leicester), Lect. in Hist. of Art (17th–19th c. Art) [Painting in Ireland, Britain & France, 17th–19th c.]

Brian McGing, B.A., M.A. (Dublin & Toronto), Ph.D. (Toronto), Regius Prof. of Greek (Anc. Hist.) [Asia Minor; Judaism in Hellenistic period; Greco-Roman Egypt]

Christine Morris, B.A. (Cantab.), Ph.D. (Lond.), A.G. Leventis Sen. Lect. in Greek Archaeol. & Hist. (Anc. Hist.) [Aegean & Cypriot archaeology; goddesses in the Mediterranean world]

Rachel Moss, B.A., Ph.D. (Dublin), Lect. in Hist. of Art (Med.) [Medieval Irish art, architecture & sculpture; architectural conservation]

Graeme Murdock, B.A., D.Phil. (Oxon.), Lect. in Hist. (16th–17th c. Eur.) [Hungary & Transylvania, 16th–17th c.; reformed religion in eastern Europe & France]

Eunan J. O'Halpin, B.A., M.A. (N.U.I.), Ph.D. (Cantab.), Bank of Ireland Prof. of Contemp. Irish Hist. (20th c. Ireland & Brit.) [Intelligence & terrorism in Britain, Ireland & Afghanistan in the 20th c.]

Micheál Ó Siochrú, B.A., Ph.D. (Dublin), Sen. Lect. in Hist. (17th–20th c. Ireland) [17th c. Ireland; Oliver Cromwell; digital humanities]

Jane H. Ohlmeyer, M.A. (St. And., Illinois & Dublin), Ph.D. (Dublin), Erasmus Smith's Prof. of Mod. Hist. (17th c. Ireland) [17th c. Irish aristocracy]

Ian S. Robinson, B.A. (Manc.), D.Phil. (Oxon.), Lecky Prof. of Hist. (Med. Eur.) [Empire, papacy, crusades & chronicles, 11th–13th c.]

Yvonne Scott, B.B.S., M.A. (N.U.I.), Ph.D., Dip.H.E.P. (Dublin), Sen. Lect. in Hist. of Art (Mod. & Contemp. Irish Art) [Modern & contemporary Irish art; international art]

M. Katharine Simms, B.A., Ph.D. (Dublin), Sen. Lect. in Med. Hist. (Med. Ireland, 5th–11th c. Eur.) [Gaelic Ireland]

Roger A. Stalley, B.A. (Oxon.), M.A. (Dublin & Lond.), Prof. of the Hist. of Art (Med.) [Medieval art, architecture & sculpture in Ireland & Brit.]

Claire Taylor, B.A. (Nott.), M.A. (Lond.), Ph.D. (Cantab.), Welsh Family Lect. in Greek Hist. (Anc. Hist.) [Greek social & economic history]

INDEX OF PERSONS

Index of Persons

Asbridge, Thomas S., 97
Ash, Timothy J. Garton, 137
Ashby, Steve, 179
Ashley, Scott, 116
Ashton, Nigel J., 93
Ashton, Owen R., 160
Ashworth, John, 120
Ashworth, William J., 81
Astill, Grenville G., 146
Aston, Emma, 146
Aston, Nigel R., 76
Atherton, Ian J., 66
Atherton, Louise, 40
Atkins, Gareth, 25
Atkinson, Paul, 63
Attard, Bernard P., 76
Attewell, Guy, 103
Attwood, Katie, 120
Austin, David, 168
Austin, Kenneth, 17
Avery, Victoria, 171
Aveyard, Stuart, 7
Awan, Akil N., 99
Ayala, Gianna, 154
Ayers, Patricia, 115
Ayers, Tim, 179
Ayton, Andrew C., 64
Azad, Arezou, 9
Azzolini, Monica, 44

BABAIE, Sussan, 86
Baccini, Leonardo, 93
Badcock, Sarah, 120
Badger, Anthony J., 19
Badsey, Stephen, 177
Baer, Marc D., 93
Bagchi, David V.N., 64
Bailey, Christian, 127
Bailey, Joanne, 142
Bailey, Mark, 40
Bailey, Paul, 38
Baines, Dudley E., 93
Baird, Jennifer, 84
Baker, Bruce E., 116
Baker, Catherine, 64
Baker, John, 120
Baker, John H., 20
Baker, Simon, 120
Baker-Brian, Nicholas J., 29
Bakker, Gerben, 93

Baldoli, Claudia, 116
Baldwin, James, 171
Bali, Sita, 160
Ball, Simon J., 72
Ball, Stuart R., 76
Balmer, Brian, 103
Balshaw, June, 61
Balzaretti, Rossano, 121
Bamforth, Stephen J., 121
Bamji, Alexandra E., 72
Bankoff, Greg, 64
Barber, Alex, 38
Barber, Sarah E., 70
Barefoot, Guy, 76
Barker, Hannah J., 110
Barker, Rodney S., 94
Barker, Sara, 53
Barkhof, Sandra, 143
Barnard, Michaela, 64
Barnes, A. John L., 94
Barnwell, Paul S., 135
Baron, Nicholas, 121
Barr, Colin, 1
Barrau, Julie, 21, 23
Barrett, Graham, 139
Barrett, John C., 154
Barringer, Judith M., 44
Barron, Caroline M., 100
Barron, Hester, 164
Barrow, Julia S., 72
Barry, Gearóid, 186
Barry, Jonathan, 53
Barry, Terence B., 191
Bartie, Angela, 162
Bartlett, Robert J., 150
Bartlett, Thomas, 1
Barton, Huw J., 76
Barton, Patricia S., 162
Bartosiewicz, Laszlo, 44
Bashford, Alison, 20
Bassett, Steven R., 9
Bastow, Sarah, 63
Bates, Crispin P., 45
Bates, David, 40
Bates, Victoria, 17
Batey, Colleen, 57
Bátonyi, Gábor, 16
Bavaj, Riccardo, 150
Baxendale, John D., 156
Baxter, Stephen D., 89

Index of Persons

Index of Persons

Index of Persons

Index of Persons

Index of Persons

Index of Persons

Index of Persons

Index of Persons

Index of Persons

Index of Persons

Index of Persons

Index of Persons

Index of Persons

Index of Persons

Smith, Graham, 101
Smith, Hannah, 131, 139
Smith, H. Camilla, 14
Smith, Jeremy W., 169
Smith, Joanne, 115
Smith, Julia M.H., 60
Smith, Karen E., 96
Smith, Leonard D., 14
Smith, Mark A., 135
Smith, Mark B, 74
Smith, Matthew, 163
Smith, Paul E.A., 124
Smith, Paul G., 173
Smith, Rhianedd, 148
Smith, Richard M., 21
Smith, Rowland, 117
Smith, Simon C., 65
Smithuis, Renate, 114
Smylie, Patrick, 175
Smyth, James J., 162
Smyth, Jennifer, 173
Smythe, Dion, 9
Snape, Michael F., 14
Sneddon, Andrew, 170
Snell, Keith D.M., 79
Snyder, Sarah, 107
Sober, Richard G., 167
Sokoloff, Sally I., 118
Solkin, David H., 87
Solomou, Solomos, 21
Sommerstein, Alan, 124
Sonenscher, Michael, 25
Sood, Gagan D.S., 96
Southall, Humphrey, 145
Southcombe, George, 133
Sowden, Colin, 32
Sowerby, Tracey A., 135
Soyer, François, 160
Spaeth, Donald A., 60
Spalding, Roger H., 43
Spangler, Jonathan, 115
Spark, Alasdair, 177
Spary, Emma, 22, 23
Spawforth, Anthony J.S., 118
Speight, Sarah, 124
Speiser, Peter, 175
Speller, Ian A., 189
Spencer, Catherine, 49
Spencer, Diana, 14
Spencer, Stephanie, 177

Spencer-Longhurst, Paul S., 14
Spicer, Andrew, 143
Spicksley, Judith, 182
Spiers, Edward M., 74
Spinks, Jennifer, 114
Spohr, A.R. Kristina, 96
Spooner, Sarah, 42
Spufford, H. Margaret, 149
Spurling, Helen, 160
Spurr, John, 166
Stack, David, 148
Stafford, David A.T., 49
Stallabrass, Julian P., 87
Stalley, Roger A., 192
Stammers, Tom, 39
Standen, Naomi, 14
Stankley, Neville, 126
Stanonis, Anthony, 9
Stapleton, Julia, 39
Stargardt, Nicholas, 130
Starkey, David J., 65
Stathakopoulos, Dionysios, 92
Staub, Martial J.M., 156
Staunton, Michael, 186
Stedman Jones, Gareth, 99
Stephenson, Jill R., 50
Sternberg, Giora, 131, 134
Stevens, Matthew F., 166
Stevens-Crawshaw, Jane, 143
Stevenson, Christine, 87
Stevenson, David, 96
Stevenson, Jane B., 2
Stevenson, Katie, 151
Stewart, Angus D., 152
Stewart, Charles W., 107
Stewart, Dan, 79
Stewart, David, 33
Stewart, Iain, 99
Stewart, John, 61
Stewart, Laura, 85
Steyn, Phia, 162
Stibbe, Matthew P., 157
Stobart, Jon V., 118
Stock, Paul, 96
Stockwell, Sarah E., 92
Stokes, Melvyn B., 107
Stokes, Raymond G., 60
Stone, Dan, 101
Stone, Glyn A., 174
Storrs, Christopher D., 37

Index of Persons

Index of Persons

Index of Persons

Lightning Source UK Ltd.
Milton Keynes UK
UKOW05f1808140414

229958UK00005B/50/P